Mental Health Social Work

Jennifer Martin is an accredited mental health social worker and Associate Professor of Social Work at RMIT University in Melbourne Australia. Her practice, advocacy, policy, research and teaching centres on human rights, social justice and access and equity in relation to mental health and well-being. Recent research and publications are on the topics of stigma, youth mental health, education and employment, safety and carers in the LGBTI community. Jennifer challenges the harm done through discriminatory and inhumane policies and practices that social workers can be complicit with. She is a keen advocate for mental health literacy locally and internationally and has a close association with the Sarawak Mental Health Association. As a social work practitioner, Jennifer has worked in both the old stand-alone psychiatric hospitals and the integrated psychiatric units and emergency departments in the general hospitals and in community settings. She was a founding member of one of the first 24-hour Community Assessment and Treatment Teams in the state of Victoria and also has experience as a social worker in community mental health, intellectual disability services and child, youth and family services. She is currently a community visitor in the mental health stream with the Office of the Public Advocate.

Jennifer Martin

Mental Health Social Work

GP

Acknowledgements

Sincere thanks to the people who have helped to develop my thinking and understandings of social and emotional well-being. Particular thanks to everyone I have had the privilege to work with over the years as a social worker in mental health. Thanks to Stephen Matthews of Ginninderra Press for his ongoing support, guidance and patience in preparing this book for publication. To my family, I am very grateful for your unconditional love, care and support.

Thank you to the educators who use this book to prepare students for practice in mental health and to those who read this book for reflecting on how to work and interact more effectively with people experiencing mental health difficulties in ways that are respectful and promote social justice, helping people to lead fulfilling lives, achieving their hopes and dreams in spite of mental health issues.

Mental Health Social Work
ISBN 978 1 76041 285 2
Copyright © Jennifer Martin 2017

This edition published 2017 by
GINNINDERRA PRESS
PO Box 3461 Port Adelaide 5015
www.ginninderrapress.com.au

Contents

In loving memory of my mother, who cared so much.

Introduction

Mental Health Social Work (2017) is the third iteration of *Mental Health Social Work* (2012) and *Mental Health Practice* (2008). This new edition includes changes to contemporary practices such as co-design, peer support, mindfulness and an increased focus on trauma-informed care and practice. The focus is on creative and innovative responses to complex problems in accordance with principles of social justice and human rights. This extends beyond the acquisition of knowledge and skills to a way of being with others that affords utmost respect and supports collaborative processes. It is only in collaboration with consumers and carers and those from other disciplines, within and beyond health and human services, and in particular architecture and design, that significant change for the better will occur.

Recovery is included as a separate chapter so as to locate mental health practice within this dominant paradigm, clearly highlighting policy and practice implications that arise for consumers, carers and human services workers. I find the term recovery problematic due to misunderstandings about what recovery means in relation to mental health as opposed to physical health problems, use of alcohol and other drugs and disaster management. However, its dominance in the funding and design and delivery of mental health services, and the significant impact it has on people's lives, has led me to focus more on how to work ethically from a recovery-oriented approach upholding principles of social justice and human rights.

Social and emotional well-being has been adopted in this edition as this term is preferred rather than mental health for Aboriginal and Torres Strait Islanders. The term has application to all cultures and communities due to the holistic approach to well-being from a physical, psychological, social, cultural, environmental and spiritual perspective that extends beyond the traditional bio-psycho-social approach used in contemporary mental health services. It recognises the connectedness of people to their environments and the importance of community. This is crucial to recovery, particularly given the prevalence of the detrimental effects of loneliness and isolation for many people who experience ongoing mental health issues. This approach has arisen from collectivist cultures. However, it is increasingly relevant for people across all cultures and it is argued in this new edition that this is the preferred approach to contemporary mental health practice.

A danger with changes in terminology is the risk of losing sight of who we are actually talking about and this is a particular danger in mental health. For this reason, the term mental health will still be used as well as social and emotional well-being, as this is the dominant language of mental health services and includes the spectrum of mental health conditions. This is important as, alongside changes in terminology, we must ensure that those in greatest need of mental health services are not lost or left behind. Persistent contradictions and confusion with language occurs within mental health services and this is reflected in this book. I will endeavour to note where this lack of clarity exists and do my best not to get caught up in this confusion while at the same time using a strengths approach that focuses on affirming and respectful language. If you are wondering when is it best to use the term mental health, mental health problem, mental health condition, mental health issue, mental illness or mental disorder, you are not alone. Previous conventions were to use mental illness to denote a more persistent and enduring mental health issue, while mental disorder was used for what was seen as less serious. Consumers have been critical of the term serious mental health issues as it is argued that all mental health issues are serious and that everyone can recover. The preferred terms today are mental health or well-being. This can cause confusion, as this term is used to indicate both positive and problematic mental health states.

Throughout this text, I have used the dominant terminology according to the relevant historical context. In the contemporary context, I use the term mental health issues, rather than the neutral or positive term mental health, to denote when assistance may be required. Mental illness and mental disorder have been removed from any contemporary discussion unless necessary due to the more narrow medical response that may be evoked. This use of language is consistent with a strengths approach focused on social and emotional well-being. It is important to never adopt the dehumanising approach of calling a person by their diagnosis. Rather, they are a person who is perhaps experiencing mental health issues.

Social work has a long-established history of improving outcomes for people with mental health issues; social workers were first employed in mental health services in Victoria in 1944.[1] Much has happened since these early days when mental health social work services in Western countries around the world were hospital-based, working within a dominant bio-medical model. It was not until three decades later that Engel (1977) coined the term 'bio-psycho-social approach', advocating for the formal recognition of the psychological and social aspects of mental health care.[2] This now extends to social and emotional well-being that also considers the influence of cultural, environmental and spiritual aspects on a person's well-being. In social work, the notion of environment includes connectedness to land and the environment but also to the broader political and economic factors that shape our lives.

Much of my learning in mental health has been from the people I have worked with, consumers, carers and colleagues. The consumers of mental health services I have worked with have taught me the importance of humility. I have learnt the centrality of genuine working relationships with people and the risks and benefits involved in forming such relationships. As social workers, we come and go from people's lives often uninvited. We expect them to tell us their most intimate secrets as part of our 'assessment'. We stay for a while and then we move on. While we endeavour to help, we sometimes inadvertently cause pain and suffering under the guise of caring. Others often see what we are doing as more controlling than caring.

I have learnt from consumers and carers the importance of maintaining a sense of humour, courage and hope in the face of adversity. I have learnt the importance of working with people rather than for or against them. However, it is not enough to show genuine care and concern. Social workers need to be knowledgeable and skilful in social work assessments and interventions in mental health.

The benchmark of successful social work interventions is how consumers of mental health services and their families and carers regard social workers. Unfortunately, people's experience of social workers is often not as positive as we would like it to be. In mental health this is particularly due to the involuntary nature of much of social work practice. Some social workers choose not to work in mental health because of such practices and the dominance of medical models of intervention. However, since the deinstitutionalisation of mental health services and the advent of community care, social workers no longer have a choice whether to work in mental health or not. It is no longer just social workers who choose to specialise in mental health that need the knowledge and skills to work in mental health. It is workers in health and community services generally. People with mental health issues are no longer locked away in institutions hidden away from society. They are living in the community and using mainstream community services. Regardless of agency location or context, most social workers will work with people who have mental health concerns and with their families and friends. Therefore, all social workers and human service workers need to be aware of the legal, ethical, policy and practice issues for effective practice in mental health.

As a beginning social worker in mental health, the staff I found most generous with their time were psychiatric nurses and a psychiatrist. Part of my difficulty, and one faced by many social workers employed in mental health settings, is that initially I was a lone social worker in teams comprised of medical and other allied health staff, predominantly psychiatric nurses. I remember a psychiatrist teaching me how to conduct a mental status examination and a nurse explaining the effects of the different neuroleptic medications and medical terminology used. One psychiatrist asked me early on if I believed schizophrenia existed. I did not tell him I had no idea what schizophrenia was even meant to be, apart from what I knew in the popular media. I recall taking the *Diagnostic and Statistical Manual of Mental Disorders* home that evening for bedtime reading.

Fortunately, social work education today prepares social work students for beginning practice in mental health. Those with mental health issues, their families and the community expect social workers to have knowledge and skills that will help improve the quality of people's lives in ways that are respectful drawing upon the latest developments in professional knowledge and skills. This does not mean that social workers do not maintain a healthy critique and scepticism of mental health systems and services. At the same time, however, they need to be able to recognise when mental health issues are causing problems and how to best intervene. This knowledge extends beyond personal and family experience that is valuable but does not always translate into professional practice. Mental health education is essential.

While I learnt from staff in other disciplines, I still needed to develop my own identity as a social worker in mental health and learn how a social work contribution differed particularly from that of colleagues in psychiatry, nursing and psychology. The nurses told me that many of the textbooks they used in their training were also used in social work education. They told me they knew how to conduct psycho-social assessments and case management as well as being able to do biological observations, assessments and interventions. They also seemed to do this fairly quickly and manage higher caseloads than the social workers did. Likewise the psychologists told me that really they were community psychologists and had expertise in both the psychological and social aspects of assessment as well as being able to conduct psychological testing.

I saw the temptations as well as the dangers of being subsumed into the dominant medical model culture of the organisation even though we were providing a community service. I had to learn the distinctiveness of social work practice in mental health and how this fitted with the contribution from other disciplines. Much of this developed from reflective and empowering practices even when people were denied basic civil liberties. As social workers, we can easily become part of a system that supposedly does things for a person's own good and for that of society. Unfortunately often, social work 'best practice' is what social workers think is best. This makes it easy to legitimise involuntary practices and the removal of people's liberties as we deemed it was necessary at the time, usually for issues of personal safety. We can turn a blind eye to the use of medication as a form of restraint and follow policy guidelines that restrict services. Or we can work creatively with consumers and carers and colleagues to develop recovery-focused policies and practices that are respectful and relevant and instil a sense of hope and dignity.

Mental health is an area that social workers must be well prepared to practise in. Consumers, carers, allied health professionals and those who work in community services have an increasingly important role to play in the design and delivery of mental health services today. It is widely recognised that the greatest benefits are gained from interventions that are responsive to the individual's social as well as biological and psychological needs. The social and emotional well-being approach extends this approach to include cultural, spiritual and environmental needs also. The bio-psycho-social assessment is commonplace in mental health settings. As the name implies, this assessment relies upon information concerning the biological, psychological and social factors affecting the individual. Unfortunately, however, in practice in mental heath settings, social factors have often tended to be neglected; medical and psychological responses have dominated. This situation is gradually changing, however, with the focus on recovery since the late 1990s putting a far greater emphasis on the social aspects of a person's life. Issues related to appropriate and affordable housing and income security are now seen as just as important as compliance with medication. Regardless of what you think of 'recovery' as a concept, it has shifted policy directions and service planning to take far greater account of the social aspects of people's lives. It has also given increased voice to consumer participation, now referred to as 'consumer leadership' in the recovery literature.

I hope that this book provides you with useful ideas to inform your thinking and practice in mental health as well as practical suggestions for social work assessment and intervention.

In Chapter 1, different reality states are explored, including those that are socially sanctioned and those that are not. Reality states discussed are sleep states and dreams as well as daydreaming and imaginary childhood companions. Altered mind states experienced as a result of stress and trauma and death and bereavement are also discussed. The effects of mind altering substances are also considered, as well as changed mental states achieved through mystical experiences and spiritualism. The focus of the discussion of reality states and mental health is on the phenomenon of hearing voices.

Changing paradigms in mental health are explored in Chapter 2 by providing an historical overview of the development of different views on mental health and changing models of service design and delivery. Dominant values and beliefs and issues of power are explored in determining how mental health is defined and subsequently managed. This is according to whether it is defined as having supernatural, biological, psychological, social or environmental causes. This in turn influences decisions as to who is best equipped to intervene and in what manner.

Recovery and social and emotional well-being are discussed in Chapter 3. The meaning of recovery is explored and consideration is given to living well in the presence or absence of symptoms of mental health issues. The discussion of well-being focuses on quality of life, housing, income, education and employment and the negative impacts of stigma associated with mental health issues. The design and delivery of mental health services is considered in ways that support recovery-focused practice with social workers supporting consumer-led recovery movements.

Chapter 4 examines the context of social work practice in mental health according to legislation, policies, practice standards and professional ethics. The dominant medical model of assessment, diagnosis and treatment is explored and the power of psychiatrists in mental health. Consideration is given to the challenge of working in ways that are cognisant of professional social work values and ethics and respect for human rights, particularly in situations where involuntary interventions are deemed necessary.

The main theoretical frameworks relevant for social workers in mental health settings are discussed in Chapter 5. These include biological, psychological, emotional and social theories. While the focus of social work is on the application of social theories it is important to take a holistic approach. Theories discussed include Erikson's stages of psycho-social development, Maslow's hierarchy of human needs and systems and ecological perspectives. Critical social work theories are helpful due to the focus on broader structural factors and include Marxist, structural, feminist, anti-discriminatory, anti-oppressive and postmodern approaches.

Chapter 6 focuses on the social work assessment, including interview skills. A holistic approach is taken to assessment that is informed by the theories discussed in Chapter 5. This includes a bio-psycho-social assessment that is sensitive to issues of gender, age and culture. Areas of assessment include presenting situation, physical health, personal and social history, family history and spirituality. An initial assessment interview pro forma is presented, including the Mental Status Examination, as well as useful interview questions.

In Chapter 7, The main diagnoses used to determine eligibility for mental health services are also presented. These include trauma, psychotic disorders, mood disorders, personality disorders, anxiety disorders, eating disorders and organic brain disorders. Diagnosis is an area that social workers have often felt uncomfortable with and have tended to associate only with the psychiatric diagnoses in the *Diagnostic and Statistical Manual of Mental Disorders* (DSM) and the *International Classification of Diseases* (ICD). These diagnostic categories are not presented in this chapter as readers are advised to go the source to be sure they have accurate information from the most recent editions of both manuals. However, the focus of a social work diagnosis is on the social contextual factors that impact upon a person's mental health. Diagnosis is discussed in relation to recovery and social work practice.

The story of Luisa is presented in Chapter 8 to illustrate an assessment and the integration of theory and practice.

Chapter 9 is devoted to consumer leadership, peer support and co-design. Issues of power are explored particularly in relation to crisis intervention. The concept of 'cooperative power' is discussed and the promotion of meaningful and reciprocal relationships with consumers of mental health service providers. Issues for families and carers are considered and the importance of listening to carers and respecting their decisions about their willingness and ability to provide care. Support for carers is also discussed and social work involvement with consumer and carer-led groups and advocacy campaigns.

In Chapter 10, the main interventions used in mental health are presented within the context of recovery and community care from a strengths perspective focusing on well-being, prevention and health promotion. Work with individuals is considered from a family-centred perspective alongside community development models for working with families. Solution-focused therapy, crisis intervention and task-centred models are presented with attention to issues of violence and abuse, and loss, trauma and grief. Group work and interdisciplinary teamwork are also included.

Chapter 11 is devoted to focused psychological strategies, the evidence-based interventions approved for use by accredited mental health social workers under programs of managed care. These strategies include motivational interviewing, cognitive behaviour therapy, relaxation strategies, skills training, interpersonal and narrative therapy.

In Chapter 12, the incidence of suicide in the general population is discussed, followed by consideration of suicide and mental health issues. Areas of assessment are protective and precipitating factors and warning signs; useful skills for assessing suicide and self-harm are provided. Recovery-focused social work interventions presented include involvement of families and carers, continuity of care and suicide prevention and health promotion.

Due to the high incidence of substance misuse and abuse by people with mental health issues, Chapter 13 is devoted to alcohol and other drugs. Reasons for use and abuse are explored, particularly in relation to mental health. The focus is on cannabis and alcohol as they are the main mind-altering drugs used in the community generally and by those with a severe mental health issues. Issues for assessment and intervention are discussed with a focus on integrated dual diagnosis services and early psychosis prevention and intervention.

Mental health issues for women prisoners are explored in Chapter 14, with consideration of social contextual factors. The impact of the prison environment on a woman's mental health is discussed and implications for program development and service delivery.

Chapter 15 is on social work and disaster recovery, due to people with mental health issues being worst affected in disaster situations, alongside members of other vulnerable groups in the community. Disasters also see an increase in mental health issues during the disaster relief, recovery and reconstruction stages. Social workers perform important traditional, and new and emerging roles in disaster planning and recovery.

The information in this book is located in the Australian context but also draws heavily on recovery-focused practices in New Zealand. It is relevant to social work practice in Asia and the Pacific, Europe, Canada and the United States of America. This book is designed for students in social work, welfare studies and the human services generally. It is also intended for social workers and health professionals working in the community and human services sector as well as for students and workers in other disciplines and members of the general public who are in contact with people with mental health issues. Every effort has been made to make this book both educational and useful. Stories are included in an endeavour to make it more interesting and relevant. These are based on my experiences with the people I have had the privilege of working with as a mental health social worker.[3]

1

Reality States

The success of J.R. Tolkien's *The Lord of the Rings* is attributed to his ability to enter the 'secondary world' of the imagination with the freedom to deviate from reality replacing it with 'strangeness and wonder'. However, this secondary world needed to be credible creating 'secondary belief'. Tolkien achieved this by carefully combining fantasy with reality. Middle-earth is a place of many marvels. But they are all carefully fitted into a framework of climate and geography, familiar skies by night, familiar shrubs and trees, beasts and birds on earth by day... Familiar but not too familiar, strange but not too strange...[1] Tolkien was aware of people's desire to engage with different reality states of fantasy and the imagination while also acutely aware of the limits he could go to in terms of social acceptability. In this chapter, different reality states are explored. Socially sanctioned reality states discussed include sleep states and dreams, daydreaming and childhood imaginary friends. Altered mind states from death and bereavement and stress and trauma are also considered. The effects of mind-altering substances are discussed, as well as mystical experiences and spiritualism. When thinking and behaviour becomes unfamiliar and too strange, the person affected is often considered to be experiencing mental health issues. Mental health issues are discussed with a focus on reality states and hearing voices.

Reality states and voice experiences

The way people experience and understand their environment, or make sense of reality, is determined by 'sensory' and 'cognitive' processes. 'Perception' is related to the five senses of sound, sight, touch, smell and taste. The information gained by the senses is processed by the mind and its defence mechanisms. Sometimes this information is processed in ways that seem strange or unusual, with this considered a distorted sense of reality or 'illusion'. 'Depersonalisation' is a term used when a person appears to be detached from her or his environment with 'derealisation' used to describe a loss of sense of reality. 'Hallucinations' are regarded as false sensory perceptions that do not exist in reality. Auditory hallucinations are the most common for those experiencing mental health issues.[2] As discussed later, care needs to be taken not to assume that hearing voices on its own necessarily equates with mental health issues. A guide to reading this book, and for effective practice in mental health settings, is to keep an open, observant mind and compassionate approach. Assume nothing.

Voice experiences are influenced by individual physical and psychological endowment combined with social, environmental, cultural and spiritual aspects influencing thoughts and behaviour. Voice experiences on their own cannot be considered 'abnormal' due to their prevalence amongst the general population. Voices can occur in a variety of different forms and circumstances.

For some people, voices occur at random, while for others they are closely associated with the context the person is in when they are heard. These can range from voices that are caring and supportive to those that are distressing and tormenting. The definition of hallucination used by mental health workers is 'A sensory perception that has the compelling sense of reality of a true perception but that occurs without external stimulation of the relevant sensory organ.'[3] Hearing voices is a far more common human experience than previously thought. Due to the negative connotations associated with hearing voices, and the connection between hearing voices and mental health issues, people are often reluctant to share their experiences. It is interesting, however, that once hearing voices is presented as an ordinary human experience how willing people are to share their stories. I asked a class of 30 tertiary students studying mental health to share their experiences of hearing voices. Two-thirds of the group described hearing voices, or another phenomenon such as music, when there was no physical presence to explain this.

In my own experience, when I first started working in mental health, I began hearing music when there was no external source. At first I thought it was coming from my neighbour's house. They had just had a baby and I thought it must be music to help the baby sleep. I found this distressing and it disturbed my sleep. I also thought it was inconsiderate of my neighbour. I was to discover that the music was not only when I was at home and began to wonder if I was becoming mentally unwell. Remember, I had little to no knowledge of mental health from my social work degree and was quite ignorant when compared with workers from other disciplines. With great trepidation, I approached our consultant psychiatrist following a home visit together and told him of my concern. To my great surprise and relief, he told me that he had the same experience and how annoying it was for him especially when he was trying to enjoy the peace and quiet of nature. He explained it was an ear problem and I was overjoyed to hear this. I went to my doctor, who diagnosed it as such, and I now accept that this music will come and go.

A number of famous people throughout history have described hearing voices or visions. These include the founder of psychoanalysis, the Viennese psychiatrist Sigmund Freud; the Swiss psychiatrist Carl Jung; the Greek philosopher Socrates; the poet William Blake; India's spiritual and political leader Mahatma Gandhi; and musical composer Robert Schumann. Freud has described often hearing his name called out aloud by someone dear to him, particularly when he was alone in a foreign country, describing it as a hallucinatory experience.[4] Jung held conversations with voices that he heard and even gave them names. He saw these imaginary figures as lifelike teachers and providers of spiritual guidance.

Sleep states and dreams

Dreams are hallucinations that occur in the general population during sleep. Different stages of sleep and dreams are associated with vivid imagery and hearing voices. The main times for this are when a person is starting to go to sleep and just before they wake up. The former are called 'hypnagogic' and the latter 'hypnopompic'. Hypnagogic experiences, those occurring when the person is going to sleep, are more prevalent than hypnopompic types. As a person gradually falls asleep, thoughts become less focused and take the form of images. These images generally change quickly; however, there is often a connection between these images and a person's experiences immediately prior to falling asleep.[5] Hypnagogic experiences are usually related to the person's thoughts or lived experiences. There are numerous stories of people who have received significant information when close to sleep. This may be the voice of someone close to them who is later found to have died around the same time as the voice experience occurred.

People generally think of visual images associated with dreams; however, the auditory aspects of dreams can be quite marked, and some people describe dreams that are characterised by auditory rather than visual experiences. It is believed in many cultures that significant visual and spoken messages are conveyed in dreams. There are also accounts of people finding things or solving problems in their dreams, including scientific discoveries.[6] German chemist Friedrich Kekule, who attributes his scientific discovery of the benzene ring to a dream, comments, 'Let us learn to dream and then perhaps we shall learn the truth.'[7]

Dreams have been a source of creativity in music, literature and arts. A number of composers, writers and artists who have produced highly acclaimed works have attributed these to inner or outer voice experiences. Socrates spoke of a deep inner voice that provided guidance that he believed was of a divine origin. The poet William Blake described long conversations with the deceased poet John Milton. Mahatma Gandhi spoke of an inner voice that provided both guidance and assurance. Many have claimed that their work was the result of dictation from an invisible presence. Robert Louis Stevenson attributed much of his writing, including his famous work *Dr Jekyll and Mr Hyde*, to an ability to create entire stories within his dreams. He claimed an ability to pause dreams and continue them over successive nights to complete his works. There are also accounts of composers attributing entire musical compositions to dreams.[8] Robert Schumann claimed to hear inner voices that provided inspiration and guidance in his work. He gave names to two of these voices that he claimed dictated some of his most famous compositions.[9]

Given that dreams are related to everyday life experience, coupled with the problem-solving and creative capacity of dream states, it is possible that they can provide insights or even solutions to everyday problems.[10] They can provide us with increased self-knowledge and self-awareness, as in the case of Freud's analysis of his dreams to gain increased understanding and reconciliation of significant events in his early childhood.[11]

Dreams can also be very disturbing and distressing. Survivors of torture and trauma often have frightening dreams where they continually return to the place where the trauma was experienced.[12] There are many similarities between dreams and hallucinations associated with mental health issues. This was recognised by Eugene Bleuler in his classic work on schizophrenia. He wrote, 'The human dream life is identical with the sphere of the voices of the insane [sic].'[13]

Dream states also occur while people are awake – in daydreams and childhood imaginary companions.

Daydreaming and imaginary childhood friends

Daydreaming occurs in young children, adolescents, adults and older people. However, it is seen to be more common during adolescence.[14] The degree to which people are able to partake in daydreaming depends upon the demands upon them. Daydreaming can provide temporary relief from routine tasks and boredom. It can also provide a means of creativity and enrichment, or relief through fantasy. By altering a person's mood, stress is lowered and frustration and irritability are reduced. The result can be a more positive attitude with increased flexibility and responsiveness. Daydreams can act as a stimulus for change to achieve goals.[15]

> Claire had her first child at 18 and had four children by the time she was 24. She cleaned houses to supplement the family income. While cleaning, she daydreamed of how things might have been if she had gone to university and studied before having a family. This helped to pass the time and reduce the monotony of the cleaning while also planning in her mind how she might achieve the dream. Years later she fulfilled this dream and returned to study.

Young children between the ages of one and three often create imaginary friends. These generally last a year or two but in some instances these friends last much longer, into adolescence and even adulthood. The friend and playmate is often larger than life providing not only companionship but also protection and assistance. An imaginary friend might keep monsters away at night in the dark or help children assert themselves against rules and authority figures, usually parents.[16] In this way, the child can explore new skills and behaviours in play while not being held accountable for things their friend may have said or done, or told them to do. Imaginary friends and play provide children with scope to explore different roles often copied from adult models. They can also act out stressful or painful experiences in play.

> Jessica, a three-year-old girl, had an imaginary friend Brian who was a great source of comfort when the family was moving house. Brian had been saying he did not want to move and that he was not going to. In fact he might even run away so that he did not have to move. As the move got closer, Brian featured more, but in the end he reluctantly agreed to go under certain conditions. Jessica was able to convey her distress about moving while not actually opposing her parents or appearing difficult, as it was Brian saying these things and not her. Secretly, her parents were hoping that in fact Brian did run away and not move with them. However, this was not to be.

Death and bereavement

Many people vividly describe near-death experiences where they have experienced another world.[17] A number of people who are close to death, or who have had near-death experiences undergo 'out-of-body' experiences and heightened spiritual awareness. This frequently involves travelling very fast through a dark tunnel towards a bright light at the end. This is often an encounter with deceased relatives and friends, or a supernatural being. A review of the person's life occurs and the voice of a spirit is heard. Heightened spiritual awareness is characterised by a feeling of greater insight and moving into another world. This can be calming and reassuring or deeply disturbing.[18]

It is very common for people to hear, see or feel the presence of someone close to them who has died.[19] This is particularly so for older people in the period immediately following a bereavement. Sometimes these experiences continue over several years, with the deceased included in daily activities. A widow is reported to have returned home from a visit to her sisters so that her husband who was deceased would not be lonely.[20] People with such experiences have generally had long and happy relationships, but spouses in unhappy marriages are not likely to have them. These voice experiences are generally found to be comforting. Often, only a few words are said, though in some cases people hold lengthy conversations with the deceased person. These voices are not associated with a psychiatric diagnosis of depression or any physical complaint but rather are directly related to bereavement as experienced in the general population.

Children and adolescents who are grieving the loss of a parent often report hearing the deceased parent's voice shortly after the death. Themes of these voices are usually the parent giving advice or disciplining them.[21] They may also experience recurrent nightmares related to the loss. Such experiences are considered a normal part of the grief process, and are expected to occur in those who are recently bereaved. Most people in Western cultures, however, who have these experiences do not share them with others for fear of being judged and labelled as 'mad'. In other societies, such as China and Japan, where there is no stigma attached to hallucinatory experiences following bereavement, these experiences are openly shared and viewed as a normal part of grieving.[22]

Stress, trauma and sensory deprivation

Hearing voices, as well as other hallucinatory experiences, are often found in association with situations of extreme physical and emotional stress, trauma or deprivation. A high incidence of auditory hallucinations has been found in survivors of childhood sexual assault, particularly incest.[23]

Amanda was admitted to a psychiatric unit due to persistent and disturbing thoughts and auditory hallucinations. She was continually preoccupied with thoughts about trying to remove stains from her underwear and tormenting voices telling her how bad and dirty she was. This was disregarded by the psychiatrist who was treating her for 'psychotic' symptoms that would disappear 'once they got the medication right'. It was later discovered Jane had a traumatic history of sexual abuse.

People who have been deprived of sleep, food or water over extended periods of time have been found to experience auditory and other forms of hallucinations. Likewise, those who have experienced extreme sensory deprivation due to isolation and immobilisation have been found to experience hallucinations. These may occur in hospital settings among people being treated for severe burns, those in post-operative rooms and in intensive care units. Hallucinations are also associated with migraine, temporal lobe epilepsy and viral encephalitis.

When auditory hallucinations occur in physical disorders, they are usually sounds such as ringing or buzzing rather than voices. The increase in brain temperature caused by fever can induce hallucinations.[24]

It has been estimated that approximately 35 per cent of refugees worldwide have been subjected to severe physical and psychological torture. High numbers of refugees are diagnosed with post-traumatic stress disorder and depression.[25] The impacts of trauma include high anxiety, difficulty with concentration and flashbacks. Interestingly, however, those in war torn countries who witness and are regularly subjected to atrocities report lower levels of trauma than those in Western developed countries. The reasons for this are unclear and may relate to removal from the traumatic situation and further trauma related to the migration process, atrocities, hardship and uncertainty. It could emanate from a loss of hope, boredom due to lack of purposeful engagement or activity and concerns for friends and relatives lost along the way or left behind. There is also possibly an increased propensity for people to be given a psychiatric diagnosis in Western developed countries, particularly in recent years.

After migrating to Australia from Vietnam, Trang experienced what he referred to as 'feelings of depression' and wishing he was dead. He felt particularly distressed when experiencing flashbacks of his memories of Vietnam and felt even worse for not succeeding in Australia. He spoke of persistent nightmares of bombings and seeing dead people lying on the roads in his village, years after these events. He commenced self-mutilation when he was feeling particularly distressed. He did this by cutting his arms with a knife and burning his arms with cigarettes. He had also taken drug overdoses on four or five occasions.

For those with pre-existing mental health issues, the stress and trauma of refugee migration and resettlement is likely to trigger psychosis. Extreme social isolation can cause hallucinatory experiences for those alone or in small groups. This includes lone aviators and prisoners in solitary confinement. Studies of people with hearing loss indicate an increase in auditory hallucinations characterised by hearing music, singing and voices.[26] Likewise people with autism and other forms of intellectual disability may experience hallucinations.[27]

Substance use and altered mind states[28]

Prescribed medications, alcohol intoxication and illicit drugs can all produce altered mind states.[29] Certain drugs are seen as more likely to induce hallucinatory experiences and are also referred to as 'psychedelic' or 'hallucinatory'.[30] The effect is one of increased sensory perception and cognitive changes with different experiences according to the substance used, the environment and individual differences including gender. The environment in which the drug use occurs will influence the experience with 'bad' experiences bearing similarity to the confusion and paranoia often associated with mental health issues. Cocaine and other drugs have been found to produce different responses, according to the stage of a woman's menstrual cycle.[31] Hallucinatory experiences from substance use are predominantly visual although auditory hallucinations of voices, sounds or music can also occur.

> Kerry had been drinking heavily for several days. As we spoke in her lounge room she kept looking over my shoulder putting her hand over her mouth and giggling. When I asked her what was happening, she pointed over my shoulder and said, 'Look. How embarrassing, Can't you see them?' I asked, 'What are they doing?' She giggled again and said in surprise, 'What do you think they're doing? They're having sex of course.' These images were very real to Kerry and it had not occurred to her that I might not be able to see them.

The sensory and perceptual effects of hallucinatory drugs are similar to those that occur during mystical experiences. Aldous Huxley observed, 'Alcoholism and other forms of drug addiction are as much a consequence of self-transcendent yearnings as are mystical theology, spiritual exercises and yoga.'[33] The main difference is the lifestyle associated with each. This is influenced by social sanctions that determine legal status, personal and financial costs and addiction qualities of alcohol and some drugs. While the mystic may reach heightened awareness in a relaxed and supportive environment, a person addicted to drugs will frequently have poor physical health and engage in criminal activity to support the habit. Recent years have seen an increased presentation of people at emergency departments in a highly agitated state following methamphetamine, commonly known as ice, usage. This altered reality state is often one of high agitation that may include paranoia and impaired cognition. Depending upon usage, the person may not have slept for days. This may appear similar to mania. However, the level of agitation, and often aggression, associated with ice use is not generally seen in mania.

Minor tranquillisers, frequently prescribed by male physicians to their female clients, also produce altered states of consciousness. These changes produce a numbing effect to daily stresses and may make life more bearable in the short term. However, the avoidance of problems and reliance or dependence upon minor tranquillisers can create further problems in the long term.[32] The side effects, or toxic effects, of some prescribed medications can also cause hallucinatory experiences. These can be from medications used to treat physical conditions as well as those used to treat psychosis. These include local anaesthetics, analgesics such as aspirin, sedatives and hypnotics used for sleep disturbance, cardiovascular drugs used to treat heart disease and anti-infection and anti-inflammatory drugs such as antibiotics.

Mystical experiences and spirituality

Changed reality states occur in mystical experiences. In contemplative meditation, this occurs by focusing concentration on an object, idea, physical movement or breathing and excluding all other stimuli. Prolonged focus can bring about changes in perception and heightened sensory awareness including visions similar to a hypnotic state.[34] Hypnotic states can arouse vivid visual images.[35] Mystical experiences can be deliberately brought about or may be spontaneous. Spontaneous mystical experiences can occur in everyday activities such as listening to music, during sexual arousal and childbirth.[36]

Spirituality remains one of the few areas within Western society where people can legitimately claim to hear voices and not be seen to be mentally ill. Spiritual voice experiences have been attributed to calling a person to a vocation or for conversion to particular religious beliefs. Many Bible stories contain accounts of inspiration, guidance and direction from voices, particularly the voice of God. One of the most well known and influential is Moses being told the Ten Commandments by God on Mount Sinai. There are also stories of voices being heard by more than one person at a time, one of the most significant being when Jesus spoke to Saul (Saint Paul) on the road to Damascus, with Saul and those travelling with him reporting hearing a voice but not seeing anyone present.

The founder of the Religious Society of Friends (commonly known as the Quakers) George Fox, claimed to hear voices as did Joseph Smith, the founder of the Mormons, and Mohammed, the founder of Islam. George Fox was guided by a voice from which he received the commands of God. The Mormon Church was founded on a mystical experience of its founder, Joseph Smith. This was a vision and voices guiding and instructing him to form a new religion. Followers believe that similar happenings occur in the Mormon Church today. Muslims believe that the holy book of Islam, the Koran, is a record of a message delivered to Mohammed by the archangel Gabriel. The mystical Sufi tradition of Islam continues the practice of pursuing direct contact with the spiritual world.[37]

Spiritualism is based upon the philosophical belief that it is possible to communicate with spirits of the dead. Mediums claim an ability to communicate with the spirits of the dead on behalf of a third party. It is not uncommon in many Eastern societies for techniques to be used to induce a mind-altered state so as to facilitate communication with spirits. This is sometimes done in a trance in which visions of higher beings appear. Messages are usually conveyed through thoughts, and external voices are occasionally heard.

The term shaman generally refers to traditional healers in Indigenous populations. Colloquial terms sometimes used for shamans are witch doctor and medicine man. The healing powers of the shaman are derived from the ability to communicate with the spirits. These spirits are often in the form of an animal or inanimate natural object or phenomenon such as a rock or the sky.

The state of altered consciousness of mystical experiences, characterised by heightened sensory perception and cognitive change, is similar to that associated with the onset of schizophrenia.[38] Positive mystical experiences often produce a sense of closeness to others and increased self-awareness. Some people with schizophrenia describe similar experiences. This is not always the case however; the changes associated with mental health issues often result in alienation from self and others.[39] The main differences are choice and the impact of the experience. People may choose mystical and spiritual experiences for enlightenment but nobody chooses mental health issues. With mental health issues the journey is generally characterised by pain and suffering not usually associated with mystical experiences.

Lily presented to the hospital for a psychiatric admission after a mystical journey that had not gone well. She was highly agitated and extremely frightened that the people from the group that she was member of would hunt her down and kill her for leaving the group. She was prescribed a large dose of sleeping medication and major tranquillisers and sent home in the care of her husband. In the words of the psychiatric registrar who saw her, 'the medication would bomb her out for the night.' After she went to sleep, her husband went to sleep himself, only to discover she had got up in the night and cut her throat. She had decided that she would kill herself rather than let her persecutors get her. Fortunately her husband discovered her in time to save her life. Her high level of agitation had meant that the medications did not have the desired effect and in this instance it was unrealistic to expect her husband to watch over her for the entire night.

Mental health issues and voice experiences

The voice experiences of people with mentally illness vary. Sigmund Freud believed that auditory hallucinations were a manifestation of unconscious attempts to grapple with complex, and distressing realities in the external world.[40] This view has been shared by many other psychologists and social workers who argue that inner emotional conflicts can be transformed into hallucinations as a coping mechanism. As such, they are a vital part of an individual's defence mechanisms. In all situations, the voice experiences must be distinguished according to their origin.

Unfortunately, a tendency has developed within psychiatry for hearing voices to be automatically associated with schizophrenia.[42] This tendency is exemplified in the well known experiment by psychologist, David Rosenham conducted in the early 1970s.[43] The study involved a number of people considered to be 'normal' presenting at the admissions offices of a number of psychiatric hospitals complaining of hearing voices. All of the study participants were admitted to hospital, all but one with schizophrenia. This one person was diagnosed as having manic depression (now known as bipolar affective disorder). All of the study participants were prescribed neuroleptic medications with the length of stay in hospital between seven and 52 days, with an average stay of 19 days. It is not so easy to be admitted to hospital today for psychiatric treatment, but it is possible that people continue to be misdiagnosed with schizophrenia on the basis of hearing voices alone.

Apart from voices, other auditory hallucinations that might be experienced include crying, laughter, whispering and music, as in my own experience mentioned earlier in the chapter.

My experience bears marked similarities to that of Remi, Fortunately however, I did not end up being taken involuntarily to hospital by the police.

Remi was 27 years of age and staying in his sister's flat while she was on holidays. He was living there alone and doing some renovations to surprise her when she returned. He played music while he worked and watched television in the evenings. He was getting increasingly frustrated by interference when listening to his music and watching television. He found that when he turned these off the interference remained. This interference sounded like music used to settle a baby with. He couldn't understand why it was being played so loudly all day and all night. He was at his wits' end and decided to try and locate the source of the music. He knocked on the doors of all of the neighbours one evening demanding to know who had a baby so he could locate the source of the music. The police were called and they told him they wanted him to go with them to the local hospital emergency department for a chat and then he could go home again. On arrival at the hospital emergency department, he was restrained and transferred to the psychiatric unit. He had not had any prior experience with mental health services and was very shocked and confused about what had happened to him.

Interestingly, in Western cultures the most common type of hallucination is auditory whereas in non-Western societies visual hallucinations are often more prevalent than auditory ones. It seems that auditory hallucinations have become more prevalent within Western cultures during the past century.[44] The hearing of voices is a personal experience that will differ between individuals. The voices may begin gradually with the person needing to focus on what the voices are actually saying, or they may begin quite suddenly. The voices tend to first appear following a stressful event, or series of events, in the person's life and to increase in intensity during periods of high stress.

Following the death of her sister, writer and literary critic Virginia Woolf is described as experiencing headaches and irritability. Later she heard birds singing to her in Greek and according to her nephew she believed that King Edward VII was hiding in her garden and verbally abusing her.[45] Often due to the convincing sound and content of the voices, people believe they are coming from an external source and that others nearby can also hear the voices. They may believe that those caring for them are colluding with the voices that are trying to harm them. There is the very real danger that they may act in accordance with the voices or harm themselves in an attempt to escape them. Virginia Woolf is reported to have rejected the care of the three nurses employed to look after her, believing they were evil, and refused to eat the food they prepared for her, fearing it was poisoned. She attempted suicide by throwing herself out of a window.[46]

At times the voices occur concurrently with an external stimulus. It has generally been thought that voices associated with schizophrenia seem as if they are coming from an external source but Romme has found that the mode of hearing voices varies between individuals and it is not possible to link them to a particular diagnosis.[47] Voice experiences can change with the individual's mental and emotional state. During times of significant stress, voice experiences may be louder and appear to be located externally, while in times of relative calm the voices might be seem to be internal and softer and quieter, seemingly like loud thoughts.

People will often develop complex beliefs in an endeavour to understand and explain their thinking and behaviour. They may believe that the voices are coming from the television, radio or other electrical items in the house: Tony believed he was receiving special messages via his toaster. Alternatively they may believe that the voices are located internally, like Susan who believed she had a special detector implanted in her brain. Due to the voices seeming to know so much about the person and their thoughts, they are often attributed to spirits or other supernatural phenomena.

The form and organisation of the voices will vary, from one or two simple words to complex sentences and lengthy conversations, with this changeable over time. The voices may be slow or rhythmic, speak with a different accent or in an unfamiliar language. They may have a distinctive way of addressing and talking to the person, sometimes calling her or him by name. There may be two or more voices engaged in conversation about the person who is listening in to what they are saying. Instances such as this, where the individual is being referred to in the third person, are seen as characteristic of schizophrenia by many psychiatrists.[48]

The voices of schizophrenia frequently take the form of criticisms, curses, threats, commands, running commentary and thought echo.[49] People describe feelings of having their privacy invaded by such thoughts. They can also be seen to be taunting and abusing the person by taking away their thoughts or by making terrible things happen to them. The language of the voices often has sexual themes and in some cases can be considered so offensive to the person that they are too embarrassed or disgusted to repeat the content of the voices. 'Running commentary' is when a person's thoughts, feelings and behaviours are described and commented upon as they happen. This is often in a critical tone with snide remarks added. With 'thought echo', people hear their thoughts being spoken out loud. This may occur internally with the thoughts repeated in the person's mind or from outside causing the person to believe that others can also hear these thoughts. Sometimes, people mistakenly think that others are speaking their thoughts to them and can therefore read their mind. It is not uncommon for people with schizophrenia to hear voices commanding them to behave in a particular manner – these behaviours are generally idiosyncratic, such as walking in a particular manner – and the voices can then criticise the person for obeying.

Often, voices can give different and contradictory messages, leaving the person confused and bewildered. Voice experiences can be extremely distressing, but at times they can be very positive, providing companionship, support and guidance.[50] Even when voices are predominantly harsh and critical, they can also be supportive. Voices are sometimes divided in the person's mind between those that are supportive and helpful and those that are hostile. Voices can provide guidance and advice and assist the person in making decisions. Some people have described pleasurable conversations with their voices. In many instances, these voices are attributed a spiritual or religious significance. This positive aspect of hearing voices is often overlooked or not acknowledged by mental health professionals.

Unfortunately in recent times, the psychological and social aspects of hallucinations have been treated as less significant than biological features. However, with the focus now on recovery, there is renewed interest in the psychological, social and cultural aspects of hearing voices or sounds. This is not to deny that in some instances there clearly are biological causes that can be treated. It is essential that biological causes are investigated initially and that mental health issues are only considered when biological causes have been eliminated by a qualified medical practitioner. In the stand-alone psychiatric hospitals of the past, all people who presented for admission were given a physical examination in the first instance to rule out possible biological causes. This does not always happen today, given the location of treatment is in the community. A person you are seeing may not even have a general practitioner. An important part of your role is to assist with linking the person with an appropriate general practitioner who is knowledgeable in mental health issues. It is essential to obtain a physical examination early on with caution and care exercised due to cultural considerations and the possibility of past or current abuse.

Conclusion

Reality states are socially and culturally determined. Everybody experiences altered reality states at different times of the day and night. This is due to 'sensory' and 'cognitive' processes considered within the realm of 'normality'. These most commonly occur in different sleep states and in our dreams. However, for both children and adults, they also occur during waking hours. Hearing voices is a common phenomenon that is often not discussed due to the association with mental health issues. Children may have imaginary friends that only they can see and communicate with. In circumstances of loss and grief, people have described seeing the person who has passed away; this is a common feature of some cultures. In situations of stress and trauma and extreme deprivation, people have spoken of experiencing hallucinations and distorted thinking. The use of alcohol and other drugs can also trigger sensory changes. Hypnotic states and near-death experiences can result in out-of-body experiences and heightened spiritual awareness. Creativity has at times been attributed to perceptual experiences rather than logic. Spiritual experiences and calls to a religious vocation have been attributed to visions and voice-hearing experiences. Some physical illnesses and medications can also cause changes to the senses and thinking. However, it is when changed reality states, without a biological cause, go beyond the limits of social acceptability and become 'too unfamiliar and too strange' that people are considered to have mental health issues.

Reflection

What different reality states have you experienced?

When is an altered reality state considered to be a mental health issue?

What contact have you had with someone with a mental health issue? What was the context of this contact and was it of your own choosing? Who initiated this? What is/was the nature of this relationship?

In relation to Remi, was the explanation given to him by the police appropriate?

2

Changing Paradigms in Mental Health:
An Historical Overview

Definitions of 'mental health' and 'mental health issues' have changed over time; an analysis of power is central to understanding these developments. The following historical account of mental health service development illustrates how the socially powerful define and treat those deemed to be of inferior status. This is in accordance with dominant values and beliefs that determine whether mental health issues are viewed predominantly as a supernatural, biological, psychological, social or environmental concern. These values and beliefs determine the types of services and methods of intervention adopted as well as the terminology used.[1] Competing ideologies raise the question of service delivery and who is best equipped to deal with such issues. Questions such as these have been debated since ancient times and services have been developed and planned according to the prevailing dominant ideological, moral, social, political and economic influences.

This chapter begins with a discussion of the biological and supernatural views of ancient times. This is followed by examination of how definitions of mental health issues and witchcraft became entwined in Europe during the Middle Ages. Initiatives leading to the development of 'mental asylums' for the 'insane' in the nineteenth and twentieth centuries are explored, as well as the development of psychological and social perspectives. The deinstitutionalisation of mental health services and programs of community mental health that began in the twentieth century and continue today are discussed. This includes the human rights movements of the mid-1900s and the 'anti-psychiatry movement'.

Ancient times

In ancient times, mental health issues was associated with the biological and the supernatural. The ancient Greeks and Romans assumed that mental health issues had a biological cause. In approximately 700 BC, the physician-priest Alcaeon argued that mental health issues was caused by an illness of the brain.[2] Hippocrates (460–367 BC) propounded a biological view of mental health issues with it arising from an imbalance of the humours of the body. Treatment techniques included purgatives, emetics and bleeding.[3] Hippocrates also claimed that 'hysteria', commonly known as 'the mother', was a uniquely female disorder arising from a uterus that wandered about the body.[4]

By the sixteenth century, hysteria was seen as a medical condition, originating from a uterine condition arising out of a disorder of the womb. A feature of the condition was a swollen abdomen. Unmarried women in their late teens to early 20s were seen to be most at risk of developing hysteria; it was considered unusual for hysteria to develop before 18 years of age. The cause of hysteria was seen to be an excess of menstrual blood that could be remedied by sexual activity that would unblock the womb.[5]

Plato (429–347 BC) developed a supernatural view delineating four different kinds of madness. Interestingly, two of these implied possession by good spirits. These were prophetic and poetic madness. The other two were erotic and ritual madness. Aristotle (384–320 BC) supported Hippocrates' biological view, yet he claimed that it was the heart that caused mental health issues. Asclepidus (100 BC) rejected this biological view, emphasising the importance of environmental factors. Over 150 years later, Anetaeus (AD 30–90) argued that mental health was an extension of the normal personality.

Mental health issues and witchcraft

During the Middle Ages, hysteria and melancholy, or other forms of mental confusion, were sometimes taken for witchcraft. There was an overlap in ideas about witchcraft and possession. Unexplained behaviours were sometimes attributed to witchcraft if no natural causes or remedies were available; the person was seen as 'possessed' or 'bewitched'. Witchcraft was entwined in the major social institutions of the law, medicine and religion. Increased mobility created a new class of urban and rural poor that were seen as a threat to the establishment. Instances of begging were becoming more prevalent due to marked population growth that was not matched with sustained economic development and prosperity. The increase in beggars was not well tolerated by the middle and upper classes, who were caught between the emerging notions of individualistic capitalism and those of a more collective communal society of the past. The recasting of the starving beggar woman as a witch, as in the fairy tale 'Beauty and the Beast', made the victim the aggressor to be feared and scorned, rather than personal guilt by those of wealth due to the emergence of an under-class of poor. Frequently, accusations of bewitchment came from young mothers who accused older women of bewitching their children. These older women were usually poor, single and elderly. They were generally viewed as troublemakers and of 'bad' moral character. The accusers, on the other hand, were generally wealthy and had the protection of a patriarchal household.

A patriarchal society used accusations of witchcraft to further dominate and oppress women. Male-dominated medical opinion during this period regarded the female body as unstable and irregular. Patriarchal views and practices in religion, science and medicine were borne on the premise of the physical, moral and intellectual inferiority of the female gender. Society demanded obedience, respect and repressive or 'puritanical godliness' from females. Those who rebelled ran the risk of being accused as witches and treated accordingly; defiance was seen to be the work of demons or the devil. However, for those who were seen to be bewitched, defiance was accepted, and they were not held responsible for their behaviour. It may have been preferable to be viewed as a witch rather than suffering from a mental health issue. Mental health issues during this time was attributed to weakness or infirmity, and the mentally ill were imprisoned.

There were both good and bad witches. 'Good' witches were called 'cunning folk'; knowledge of their powers and whereabouts was widespread. Some of the remedies used by cunning folk were magical practices involving the use of charms and drinking potions. Their remedies were sought by those from all levels of society; including peasants, gentry, medical practitioners and clergy.[6] The majority of cunning folk were male. This is in contrast to 'bad' or 'malefic' witches, who were predominantly female. Officially, however, all witches were regarded with suspicion and hostility. Witches were generally seen to have inherited their powers from a female relative, usually the witch's mother. However, the clergy were of the view that the powers of a witch derived from a pact with the devil, and this view became more dominant during the seventeenth century. The Reformation was characterised by theologians stressing the importance of overcoming temptations of the devil and hence was not tolerant of witchcraft, which was seen as superstitious and intrinsically evil. Witchcraft was regarded as a threat to Christianity and civilised society by both Protestants and Catholics. In England and on the Continent during this period, witchcraft was a crime that could be tried at secular courts and carried the death penalty.

The first statute against witchcraft instituted in English Law was in 1542 under the late reign of Henry VIII. This was superseded by the somewhat harsher Witchcraft Act of 1604, under James I. Many people, mostly women, accused of being witches were arrested and tortured and/or killed. Torture included flogging, 'the production of fright', seclusion in darkness, fetters and other means of mechanical restraints. It has been estimated that from 1450 to 1750 approximately 40,000 people, mostly women, were accused of witchcraft and executed, with many of this number burnt at the stake. In some parts of Europe the sabbat, or gathering of witches, sometimes resulted in mass executions. Dutchman Johan Weyer (1516–1588) insisted that witches were mentally ill and advocated for humane treatment. The last conviction of a witch in England occurred in 1685.[7]

While it was possible to instigate legal proceedings against a suspected witch, many people tried other remedies rather than the costly recourse to the legal system. Often, people were put through arduous tests in an endeavour to establish the validity of their own, or others', claims of bewitchment. Those who made such decisions were males from the upper social classes. False claims and accusations were seen frequently to emanate from long-standing local disputes. A number of cures were tried to rid the person of the bewitching demon. It was generally believed that, if some thatch from the roof of a suspected witch's house was burned, the person who had been bewitched would be released from the witch's curse. A traditional remedy was to scratch the face of the witch until the blood flowed out. The burning of the witch's hair was seen as another cure.

People who were bewitched were supposed to lack normal feelings and sensitivity to physical pain or bleeding. Thus the person would be subjected to pain, such as sticking pins into a woman's breasts so as to see the response.[8] Protestant clergymen used prayer and fasting, while the Catholics performed exorcisms in an endeavour to rid a person of an evil spirit.

Regardless of whether they were viewed as mentally ill, as witches or as bewitched, people with mental health issues were subjected to extremely cruel and harsh treatment during this period.

Mental asylums for the insane

In Europe in the eighteenth century, the mentally ill were chained and incarcerated in jails. It is uncertain whether or not this practice ended due to the efforts of social reformers or by other prisoners outraged at having to live with the mentally ill, or a combination of both.[9]

It was through the efforts of the Frenchman Phillippe Pinel (1745–1826) in the social context of the French Revolution, that a humanitarian approach towards the mentally ill was introduced. He advocated against the inhumane treatment of the mentally will and, in particular, against the use of restraints. Instead, Pinel emphasised the importance of occupational activities and a 'limited degree of freedom'.

Psychiatrist Emil Kraeplin (1855–1926) made the first attempt at organising mental health issues. There was increasing pressure for governments to take responsibility for the care of the mentally ill. In the 1840s in the United States, Dorothea Dix (1802–1887) advocated for the building of state-supported 'psychiatric hospitals' also known as 'mental hospitals' or 'asylums'. The biological view of mental health gained increased support during the nineteenth century and treatment was in the hands of physicians. The mentally ill were now to be segregated from society and placed in public asylums for the 'insane' alongside people with intellectual disabilities. In Australia, Victoria's first mental hospital was opened in 1848 at Yarra Bend in Fairfield. In 1952, Victoria's Mental Hygiene Authority described the design of the hospital at Fairfield as being similar to that of a jail.[10] More mental hospitals were built in remote locations away from residential areas in grand buildings with beautiful architecture and expansive grounds and facilities. These hospitals were self-contained communities with a range of occupational therapy activities such as art and drama with expansive sports and recreational facilities including tennis courts, football ovals, dance halls and chapels.[11] The ongoing inhumane treatment of the mentally ill within the walls of the asylums was in stark contrast to the beautiful peaceful surroundings with straightjackets and other methods of physical or mechanical restraint used to control behaviours and ensure compliance with treatment. Psychiatric hospitals became the main place of treatment for people deemed 'mentally ill' for the next 100 years. For many people, the asylum was their 'home'. This was particularly so for those who were assessed as 'treatment resistant'. These were the 'forgotten people'.

In the late nineteenth century, the linkage between psychological processes and mental health issues was first described by Sigmund Freud (1856–1939). Assisted by Joseph Breuer, Freud studied the unconscious state of the human mind. His work led to the development of psychoanalysis as a theory of personality development as well as a means of treating mental disorders.[12]

At the beginning of the twentieth century, psychological, social, environmental and cultural processes were included in debates surrounding mental health issues. The twentieth century heralded a radical shift in the views and attitudes towards mental health issues, resulting in major changes in service development and delivery.

The late nineteenth and early twentieth centuries witnessed a period of rapid industrial and technical change as well as increased urbanisation and immigration in Western countries. These changes have been associated with a decreased tolerance and ability of society to contain deviant behaviour.[13] Mental health issues was viewed as becoming a more serious problem, occurring more frequently, of greater variety, more chronic and less curable.[14] Reform movements began to develop in the United States and Britain, advocating improvements in the care and treatment of the mentally ill and for an increase in the number of mental hospitals provided by the state. The emphasis was still very much focused on the institutional care of the mentally ill.[15]

In Australia, the Depressions of the 1890s and the 1930s, with World War I (1914–18) in between, resulted in scarce allocation of funds to mental hospitals. However, the overcrowding of existing mental hospitals led the Victorian government to build two new mental hospitals in the early 1940s. The demands of World War II (1939–1945) resulted in both of these hospitals being used for housing. This continued until 1951 for one of these hospitals and 1955 for the other, even though mental hospital overcrowding and staff shortages were most acute at this time.[16]

Increased public concern about the inadequacies of the mental hospital system during the 1940s led to the establishment of the Mental Hospital Enquiry Committee. In 1948 this committee reported on its findings and recommended legislative changes, the separation of people with intellectual disabilities from those suffering with a mental health issue, regular independent inspections of hospitals, a review of mechanical restraints, improved care for the mentally insane and a review of the treatment of the mentally ill in observation units in prisons. They also called for improved facilities and were critical of the difficulties and delays with the mental hospital building program. Staff training and a new system of administration were also deemed necessary.

In 1949, following the Mental Hospital Enquiry Committee's report, the Victorian government invited Professor Alexander Kennedy to conduct further investigations into the condition of the state's psychiatric hospitals. Kennedy's report further highlighted the deficiencies in the system at that time and included a number of recommendations for reform. Like the Mental Hospital Enquiry Committee's report, Kennedy also called upon the government to instigate legislative changes. This led to the passing of the *Mental Hygiene Act 1950* and the establishment of the Mental Hygiene Authority.

In 1952, however, the Mental Hygiene Authority was still confronted with overcrowding and extremely poor facilities and practices. Dr Cunningham Dax, the chairperson of Victoria's Mental Hygiene Authority, poignantly described these conditions:

The wards were mostly dirty... Chamber pots were used nearly everywhere and frequently stored in the same place as the food was prepared... The smell was abominable... There was a considerable amount of mechanical restraint and solitary seclusion used... The serving of the food and its presentation was revolting.[17]

This was the beginning of a period of major reforms, involving both government and voluntary authorities, aimed at improving the quality of care in mental hospitals. Alongside these reforms came the medical discovery and introduction of psychoactive drugs in the mid-1950s. The introduction of psychoactive medication, combined with growing disenchantment with the costly psychiatric hospital system and the increased prevalence of more humanistic ideologies, led to the development of community mental health programs and less extreme forms of institutional care.[18]

Civil rights: anti-psychiatry movement

During the 1960s, civil rights movements focused on the rights of full community participation for people who were subject to oppression and discrimination as well as protection of those deemed vulnerable. This saw the rise of a range of activist groups and movements including black activists, gay activists and the women's movement. In the intellectual disability field, a focus was on 'normalisation' for people with disabilities to be able to participate in the community and enjoy the basic rights and civil liberties afforded members of the general population.[19] In mental health the 'anti-psychiatry' movement radicalised the debate on the treatment of the mentally ill. Three key individuals in the anti-psychiatry movement were Erving Goffman and Thomas Szasz in the United States and R.D. Laing in Britain.

Goffman developed the concept of the 'total institution', which he described as

A place of residence and work where a large number of like-situated individuals, cut off from the wider society for an appreciable period of time, together lead an enclosed, formally administered round of life.[20]

Writing of his experiences working in mental hospitals between 1954 and 1957, Goffman claimed mental hospitals were total institutions. He highlighted what he saw as many of the negative effects, including demoralisation, loss of purpose and culture, personal defacement, regimentation, loss of self determination and stigmatisation.

Szasz criticised psychiatric institutions from a 'labelling perspective'.[21] Like Goffman, he saw the labels attached to psychiatric patients as stigmatising. He argued that these labels fostered the view that psychiatric patients were not only sick but also to be feared and scorned. According to Szasz, people became psychiatric patients as a result of behaviour arising from 'problems in living'. He believed that people who engaged in behaviour that was regarded as 'socially offensive' were labelled mentally ill by 'socially powerful others'. The central proposition of Szasz and other labelling theorists was that in a clinical sense mental health issues did not exist. Laing also criticised psychiatric institutions as dehumanising and a means of social control. He studied individual experience and the process of alienation questioning the concept of 'normality' from a psychological perspective.[22]

While members of the anti-psychiatry movement were vehemently critical of the treatment methods in mental hospitals, psychiatrists continued to insist that the profession was scientific, emphasising somatic factors within the dominant medical model. Nonetheless, the social reforms introduced in the field of mental health might not have been so dramatic in the absence of this anti-psychiatry movement.

Deinstitutionalisation and community mental health

Community health programs developed within a policy framework of 'deinstitutionalisation' and 'normalisation' similar to the intellectual disability field.[23] From a rights perspective, deinstitutionalisation gave people rights and opportunities to full participation in the community. Historically, normalisation has two meanings. The first is within a rights discourse and sees deinstitutionalisation as a process whereby people live in the community with the same rights and opportunities as afforded to so-called 'normal' members of society. The second focuses on change within the person to be able to 'fit in' and pass as 'normal'. This first meaning requires major shifts in community attitudes whereas the second requires individual change and adaptation.[24] The reality is that both are required. Community living is a process that requires adaptation to social norms and values alongside community education and development activities that influence these. Regardless of the intent, the successful application of deinstitutionalisation is dependent upon the transfer of resources from the closure of the institutions to the community to support people in community living. It also requires major shifts in community attitudes towards mental health issues. Unfortunately, neither of these has happened to the extent required.

In the United States in the early 1960s, federal government assistance, under President John Kennedy, was directed toward the development of community mental health centres. This development endorsed the view that mental health issues was one of many psychological problems common in the community. Community mental health centres were introduced in the United States at a time of economic prosperity with adequate financial assistance available to support these developments.[25] Social welfare was a major concern of the Australian federal Labor government led by Gough Whitlam between 1972 and 1975. Under the Australian Assistance Plan 1973, there was increased expansion and expenditure in the welfare sector, with local community participation and control. Universal programs of government-funded community health under Medicare, legal aid and education were introduced during this period. There was an associated growth in the number of social work positions and career opportunities.

In 1973 community mental health was incorporated into the Australian community health program that was being developed at the time.[26] The aim of community health was to provide comprehensive, accessible, non-stigmatising services to people in their own locality.

The focus was on the individual and family in the context of their environment. Individuals were viewed as members of families and communities subject to the pressures of everyday life.[27] Community health was considered to be more economically viable than costly hospital care. In the latter half of the 1970s, Australia experienced an economic recession with severe unemployment and cutbacks in welfare expenditure. It also witnessed the dismissal of Whitlam and the termination of the mandate of the Labor government late in 1975, to be replaced by the federal Liberal government of Malcolm Fraser. The focus of community mental health was on policies of 'economic rationalism', with community care seen as far more cost-effective than hospital care. Psychiatric hospitals were seen as providing costly 'hotel type' services for people who did not actually require the medical facilities of a hospital.

The growth of community mental health programs led to a decrease in the number of people resident in psychiatric hospitals.[28] This was accompanied, however, by an increase in re-admissions resulting in an overall increase in admission rates and came to be known as 'the revolving door syndrome'.[29] It was suggested that as many as half to three-quarters of readmissions could be avoided if comprehensive programs of continuous care existed in the community.[30] There was also concern about the increased poverty and homelessness of many people with mental health issues who were not receiving adequate treatment in the community.[31]

An extension of the community mental health program was seen as necessary for comprehensive care for the mentally ill in the community. This led to the development of community psychiatric crisis services in the USA in the early 1970s and in Australia in the late 1970s. In 1979 a number of community crisis services were introduced in New South Wales. These services were a component of the Richmond Implementation Program. A main feature of this program was the establishment of a 24-hour crisis team as a research project in the Sydney regions of Lower North Shore and Manly Warringah under the leadership of psychiatrist John Hoult. This evidence-based research project is of significant value in that a large sample was used, with people presenting for psychiatric hospital admission randomly allocated into either the 'project' (community treatment) or 'control' (hospital treatment group).

Hoult found that the majority of people with a mental health issue could be effectively treated in the community as an alternative to hospital. He argued that community treatment was preferred by service users and their families, it was not detrimental to the community and a better clinical outcome was achievable at less cost. Hoult's findings indicated that community treatment was appropriate for people with either acute or chronic psychiatric problems. The findings showed that hospital admissions were helpful for acutely psychotic and disorganised people without any family support, people with chronic psychiatric problems determined to be admitted as well as those who may need asylum or require the specialist services available as an in-patient. This included people suffering from severe psychotic depression, who were actively suicidal or homicidal and intent on carrying out these actions, and those who needed acute psycho-organic assessments. Hoult noted, however, that it was only those who needed acute psycho-organic assessments who actually required the facilities of a hospital.

On the basis of Hoult's findings, the program was further expanded with a number of extended hours crisis teams established in both urban and rural areas of NSW.[32] These initiatives were later adopted by the Victorian Office of Psychiatric Services with three 24-hour crisis services starting operations in varying stages in 1988. Since then the program has been expanded with further 24-hour crisis teams established and the introduction of extended hours mobile treatment teams. The Office of the Public Advocate was established in Victoria in 1986 to protect the rights of people with mental health issues, disabilities and older people. Initiatives included the appointment of guardians and administrators and community visitors. Community visitors conducted on-the-spot visits of psychiatric hospitals and were critical of the gross denial of human rights and advocated for further development of community mental health services.[33]

Contemporary models of mental health services are based in the community, using a well-being, or wellness, model focused on biological, psychological and social approaches (bio-psycho-social). This approach is informed by the recovery paradigm discussed in the next chapter. General practitioners are the main point of referral for mental health services. Services are limited in number for a range of focused psychological strategies, discussed in Chapter 11. To access these services, a person is assessed as having an approved mental health diagnosis and put on a mental health care plan. Increasingly, mental health social workers employed in private practice are delivering these services that are predominantly provided for people with anxiety and depression. These services can also be suitable for people with schizophrenia and other mental health issues. However, social workers are tending not to work with these people on mental health care plans. Reasons for this vary and include the greater demands of working with people who experience psychosis and problems associated with perception, thought processes and cognition. Those who demonstrate difficult and disruptive behaviours are also considered less desirable for private practitioners. Anecdotally, social workers have commented that for their private practices to succeed they need clients who are reliable in attending appointments and not troublesome in their waiting rooms. These concerns have also been expressed by general practitioners, who do not want people with mental health issues upsetting other patient in their clinics.

These are not views generally expressed and, rather than dismiss them as harsh or unsympathetic, it is important to engage with them, as increasingly mental health services are being provided by private practitioners under neo-liberal service frameworks. It can be daunting for a lone social worker to deal with difficult and complex behaviours when they might not have other colleagues or security present. My own experience in community health highlights the complexities of waiting areas.

Patricia was very lonely and socially isolated. She often threatened members of the community and workers and had regular police involvement. Threats of harm were also directed towards me and my family. So it is not surprising that the waiting room became a nightmare for the reception staff and those waiting alongside Patricia even when plans were put in place to see her as soon as she arrived and not keep her waiting, even if she arrived early early. On a couple of occasions, Patricia's behaviour was so disruptive in the waiting room that she was forcibly removed. I am ashamed to say that I was an active, yet reluctant, participant in this forced removal. The manager of the service, who was a nurse, came into my office and said, 'We need to evict Patricia and you need to assist because she is your client.' In my mind, the fact that she was my client was very good reason for me not to assist. My pleas of not wanting to do so, and lack of training in restraint, fell on deaf ears and I was ordered to participate. The manager had Patricia by one arm forced up her back and myself the other. We marched her towards the lift and took her down to the street level. All the time she swore and cursed at us as we simply pushed her out onto the street. Rather than any debriefing, my manager told me that it was a disgrace that social workers were not trained in restraint and walked off.

On the second occasion, Patricia was found going through staff offices and it was considered she was intent on theft. She was directed back to the waiting area and then went into the toilets, where she climbed over the wall of an adjoining cubicle and pounced upon a worker who was sitting on the toilet. The staff involved were furious, not only with Patricia but also with me as I was somehow held responsible for Patricia's behaviours as I was her case manager and primary worker. I was once again ordered to forcibly remove her from the building and to 'manage' her properly to prevent this type of disruption from recurring. No offers of help with Patricia were forthcoming from other staff members, only hostility – and one of these people was my direct supervisor. I also received constant calls from the police, who also wanted to know why I had not fixed the problems with Patricia's disruptive behaviours.

A solution to the waiting room problems was to make all appointments away from the centre, which I then endeavoured to do. However, the truth was that I was afraid of Patricia and did not feel comfortable visiting her at home alone and would often take a student with me on such visits. As much as possible, we had our appointments in open spaces where there were other people about. Shopping centre cafés were not ideal, due to issues of privacy and also due to Patricia begging for money and cigarettes from other patrons and abusing them if they did not give her anything. She also wanted me to buy cigarettes for her and became angry when I refused.

The situation with Patricia did gradually improve but it was a slow and difficult process. My main aim was to keep her out of the criminal justice system, which fortunately we managed to achieve through a strong collaboration with intellectual disability services, who were also working with Patricia, her mother and a caring and concerned neighbour. It was important to always be there for Patricia, regardless of the intensity of the rejection that increased the closer our working relationship became. Ultimately, progress came through Patricia's own efforts and determination to bring about improvements in her life.

Mental health social workers in private practice need to develop strong practitioner networks to support their complex work, and each other, as well as engaging in regular supervision. This is an added yet essential cost of working in private practice, unless social workers are content to spend most of their time working with the worried well. Ideally, a private practitioner is part of a group of practitioners all working from the same location with shared reception and waiting areas. The question remains as to whether or not someone like Patricia can be seen in private practice and if so what would the service funding model look like? There are many people like Patricia who end up in our prison system because services simply cannot or do not want to respond. This is not easy work but it is an essential part of the terrain of mental health practice.

There are real dangers that mental health social workers in private practice will not work with those who need their services the most, such as Patricia, due to motivations of profit, comfort and livelihood. By focusing on a narrow range of psychological strategies, social workers run the risk of losing their primary focus on social justice and human rights and working with the most disadvantaged and disenfranchised members of the community. Social workers face the risk of becoming deskilled if they only provide a limited range of psychological strategies. This is a dilemma posed by increased privatisation of services for those most in need within a capitalist system that demands that profits are made from the most disadvantaged and disenfranchised members of the community. Social work as a profession must critique itself and its practices in mental health to navigate this fraught terrain and to provide some direction on how to adhere to principles of human rights and social justice within a capitalist system that rationalises provision and funding of mental health services for profit. This is in acknowledgment that social workers want to remain in favour with governments that are funding these services. Most importantly, they must remain aligned to the principles of human rights and social justice that guide their work.

Private practitioners also provide services though mental health primary networks that are located throughout Australia. Federal government funding is allocated to these networks for private practitioners to tender for contracts for local service provision. Other community services are funded focused on using a recovery model for people to receive support post hospitalisation and to gain skills in daily living, education and employment. In-patient services are to be used as a last resort and are provided by general hospitals in emergency departments and psychiatric units. Emergency departments are not well suited to the delivery of such services; physical and mechanical restraint are often used to subdue people who are causing disruption to others. This difficult behaviour is often drug-induced. Resuscitation bays are frequently used simply because increased observations can be made by staff and not because the equipment in these bays is required. This experience is distressing for the person concerned, staff and other patients and family members. The high level of stimulation and lack of quiet spaces is problematic. In the past, psychiatric hospitals would see a person immediately in a low-stress environment. They were not restrained to the extent they are today in emergency departments and they did not endure the embarrassment of being restrained in front of members of their local community. They were not constrained by government funding models that meant they would lose money if people were not discharged from the emergency department within a specified time period regardless of their situation.

Local psychiatric units in general hospitals continue to remain problematic. Surprisingly, this promised innovative service model has basically used a very similar ward design to the old stand-alone hospitals. The main differences are that it is on a much smaller scale and people have their own bedrooms, rather than open wards to sleep in. Wards are for the most part overcrowded, with extremely high levels of disturbance and distress. The range of mental health issues people have who are admitted to these units include schizophrenia, drug-induced psychosis, mania, eating disorders, depression and anxiety. There also those referred by the courts for a psychiatric assessment prior to sentencing.

The age range is 18 years to 65 years and most have been admitted due to suicide attempts or being a danger to others. This is a toxic environment and not one in which a person can rest, relax or recover. These wards are quite contained, with a nurse's station in the middle of the ward and corridors of bedrooms, a living room and dining room. There is also a small courtyard with synthetic grass. Even though many people are admitted voluntarily, if they attempt to leave they are threatened with being made an involuntary, also known as compulsory, patient. These wards are locked at all times.

Imagine you are a young female who is having a first admission to a psychiatric unit the disbelief of what you are encountering in the name of health care. It is highly likely you will have sexual advances made towards you by older male patients and when you complain to staff you will be reminded that the person is unwell and in need of help. For those who have not experienced these units for themselves, they would not believe that these wards exist in a general hospital. These wards are often dirty with rubbish in the yards and furniture smelling of urine. Like in the old stand-alone hospitals. patients knock continuously on the window and door of the nurse's station and are generally ignored. This would never be tolerated in other wards of the hospital so why in a psychiatric unit? This question is at the heart of mental health practice. What standard of service should we expect for people with mental health issues? Some believe it is a lowered expectation due to the nature of the population and problems being dealt with. However, if you were in this situation, or it was someone you loved dearly, would you perhaps expect better than this? Again the question remains as to what level of care is appropriate.

I am definitely not arguing for the return of stand-alone hospitals but I do want to highlight the reality and dangers of construing a system as all bad and not taking forward practices that worked well.

As a social worker at that time, there was a strong organisational culture within mental heath services that rejected the stand-alone hospital system in favour of a better and more humane approach to be delivered in general hospitals in people's local communities. This situation was exemplified for me at a mental health conference I attended at the time. I have a vivid recollection of an academic doing a presentation on the horrors of the old stand-alone psychiatric hospital system and a woman putting up her hand at question time. She spoke in a quiet moderate voice and said she was well looked after at the hospital and the nurses were very nice to her. I was shocked at what happened next. Members of the audience, who were primarily academics and workers, shouted this woman down and would not let her continue to speak. The conclusion of this group think and talk was that a positive experience was not possible in the old system and such a view would not be entertained.

Community mental health services have been retained by the government for those who are seen to become unwell on a regular basis or who have disability associated with their mental health issues. It is these people who are most likely to be eligible for services under the Australian government's national disability insurance scheme. Forensic mental health services have also been retained by the government and have not been privatised. This is primarily due to issues of social acceptability; the community wants government assurance that they are safe from people who have been deemed mentally unfit to plead for crimes against the community. Politically this is important for law and order campaigns run by governments to gain votes at election times.

Even with the current problems, the overall benefits of the present system far outweigh the existing problems but we still have quite a way to go. To move forward, we must recognise that these so-called future service innovations have not always delivered a better alternative. It is important to learn from the past and continue to move forwards to look at other options that may not have even been thought of yet. Co-design, discussed in Chapter 9, and trauma-informed care, discussed in Chapter 10, offer the most promise in this regard.

Conclusion

Definitions of mental health issues and treatment methods have been debated since ancient times. This has been in accordance with dominant ideological, moral, social, political and economic views and influences. In spite of this, from the eighteenth century up until the late twentieth century the treatment of the mentally ill in the Western world has taken place mainly in institutional settings. The late 20th and early 21st centuries have seen radical changes in mental health, with the community now the main location of services. These services are increasingly delivered through private practice arrangements under government-funded programs of managed care. This development has been in response to the discovery of psychoactive medication, the human rights movement, particularly the anti-psychiatry movement in the 1960s and economic reasons. Short-term evidence-based community treatment is considered a less costly alternative to hospital care. However, both hospital and community services continue to be criticised for failing to adequately meet the needs of those with severe and persistent mental health issues.

Reflection

What are the dominant political, economic, social and cultural factors that influence the design and delivery of mental health services today?

What model of care do you think would best meet the needs of people with mental health issues?

If you were experiencing mental health issues, what kind of treatment would you like to receive, by whom, and when and where?

What discipline would your like your worker to be from?

What personal and professional qualities would you like your worker to possess? Who else would you like to be involved?

3

Recovery and Social and Emotional Well-being

The severity and high levels of disability associated with mental health issues have led to increased global efforts to address mental health issues, in particular those targeted at prevention. In recent years, mental health and well-being have been identified as priority areas by the World Health Organisation, the World Bank and government leaders worldwide.[1] This is within the context of a severe shortage of resources, particularly in low and middle income countries.[2] Mental health issues have been predicted to be the largest single source of illness globally within the next two decades.[3] Mental health issues affect all ranges of people regardless of age, gender, religion or race; however, first onset has been found to be most prevalent in young people. Three-quarters of those who develop mental health issues do so between the ages of 16 and 25, an age when most young people are likely to embark on post-secondary education and training programs or be entering the workforce.[4]

In this chapter, mental health 'recovery' and well-being are explored by examining policy, social and cultural contexts. The inter-relationship between social and emotional well-being, physical health and abuse is explored alongside issues of access and equity related to stigma, income, housing, education and employment.

Policy context

Policy changes have been influenced by dominant paradigms in community mental health, such as deinstitutionalisation, normalisation and in more recent years recovery and well-being.

In Australia, New Zealand, the United Kingdom, the United States and Canada, recovery underpins policy and practice in mental health. In these countries, mental health workers use a recovery-oriented approach. In New Zealand, advice to consumers states that mental health workers should

> show that they have hope for you and your recovery
> listen to you and treat you with respect
> involve you in decisions about your treatment and care
> support you to manage your own mental health problem.[5]

The New Zealand Mental Health Commission has identified 10 main areas of competency in recovery:

> A competent mental health worker understands recovery principles and experiences, supports

service users' personal resourcefulness, accommodates diverse views on mental health issues, has self-awareness and respectful communication skills, protects service users' rights, understands discrimination and how to reduce it, can work with diverse cultures, understands and supports the user/survivor movement, and understands and supports family perspectives.[6]

The Recovery Star is a tool developed by Triangle Social Enterprise Limited in the United Kingdom. It has 10 outcome areas as detailed in the Recovery Star diagram and is underpinned by a five-stage model of change that includes (1) stuck (2) accepting help (3) believing (4) learning and (5) self-reliance.

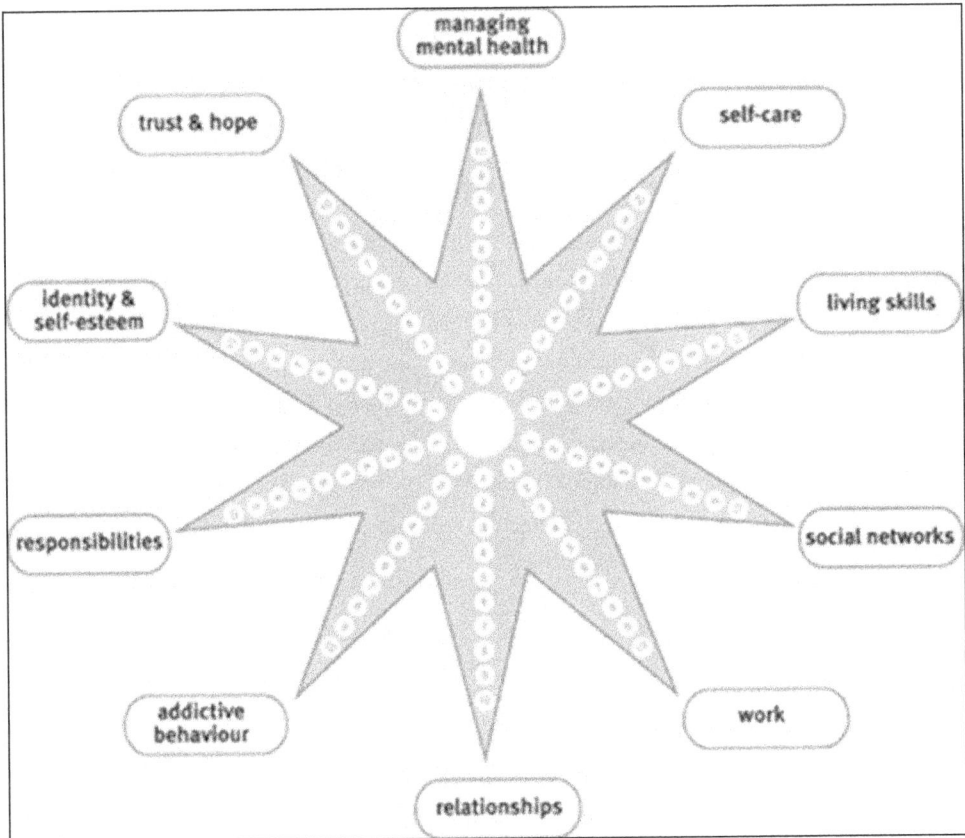

Figure 3.1: The Recovery Star (© Triangle Consulting Social Enterprise Ltd. Used under licence. See www.outcomesstar.org.uk)

Worldwide, it has been predicted that within the next two decades mental health issues will be the largest single cause of illness globally.[7] A main focus is on centralisation of governance and stronger accountability measures; population health and well-being programs are considered to be the most economically viable and equitable solution.[8] Equity of access to mental health care is a central objective of mental health systems in Canada, Australia and New Zealand and has underpinned the National Health Service of the United Kingdom since its inception in 1948. Contrary to popular belief, high levels of government funding and the privatisation of health care systems does not ensure equity, as witnessed in India, the

United States, Australia and New Zealand.[9] Equity is an ethical issue, with mental health care primarily concerned with access to hope by 'eliminating disparities that are associated with underlying disadvantage or marginalization'.[10]

Mental health services today are provided within the dominant paradigm of well-being that has seen a shift from a disease to a wellness model. The World Health Organisation defines mental health as 'a state of well-being in which every individual realizes his or her own potential, can cope with the normal stresses of life, can work productively and fruitfully, and is able to make a contribution to her or his community'.[11] The focus of wellness models is on general population health promotion and prevention activities such as nutrition, exercise and stress reduction. Well-being programs are increasingly preferred by policy makers; current health care costs under existing primary care models and projected increases are considered unsustainable in the long term.[12] However, such reforms will only succeed if the needs of those with recurring conditions are also met. This shift in funding and emphasis, from primary care to general population wellness models, has been criticised as a further means of stigmatisation of those with severe mental health issues; they are deemed 'unworthy of social investment'.[13] Richardson argues that the current focus on population health and well-being programs fails to address major inequities and system deficiencies in Australia's health care system.[14]

Social context: recovery and community living

The notion of recovery arose in the United States in the mid-1980s when consumers of mental health services began to challenge the widespread belief that severe mental health issues were chronic, and that stability was the best treatment outcome to be hoped for. This dominant belief had underpinned professional practice in mental health services since its inception.[15] Over the past two decades, considerable research and writing has been conducted by consumers, carers, academics and mental health professionals. A common research finding is that many people progressed beyond the notion of stability. Furthermore, treatment outcomes vary significantly from one person to another.[16] This has led to 'recovery' now being the dominant treatment paradigm for service provision in mental health worldwide. Central to recovery is hope and the active role taken by the individual to live well in the presence or absence of mental health issues.

With the advent of deinstitutionalisation, people with mental health issues were expected to integrate into the community. However, as Larry Davidson aptly points out, for many people with mental health issues, community living is 'a life restricted to what may be considered the psychiatric ghetto of community-based programs'.[17] Davidson alerts us to the notion of 'success' as a criterion for people with mental health issues to be included in the broader community. By this he means that people need to be seen as well and symptom-free for acceptance and inclusion in education, employment, living independently and developing relationships and friendships with others. Many people are being given double messages. On the one hand they are told that they have a severe long-term mental health condition, yet on the other hand they are told to live a normal life in the community – one that is symptom-free. While treatment and community supports are available for many people, symptoms will persist and the notion of a cure or full recovery is not real.

When applied to mental health, the notion of recovery evokes different responses in people. Recovery is a term that in the past has been used in alcohol and other drugs settings. It has been criticised for being esoteric and not evidence-based as it implies that people will no longer have mental health issues after recovery. While many people do have a full recovery, there are those who do not and who struggle on a daily basis with disturbing symptoms of mental health conditions. To tell these people they will recover could be disrespectful and undermine the efforts they are already making to improve their own lives. If applied in an individualistic way, the person who does not recover is held responsible for his or her supposed lack of effort or progress. The following definition of recovery by William Anderson is considered to be a cornerstone definition of mental health recovery. Anthony describes recovery as

> a deeply personal, unique process of changing one's attitudes, values, feelings, goals, skills and/or roles. It is a way of living a satisfying, hopeful, and contributing life even with limitations caused by the illness. Recovery involves the development of new meaning and purpose in one's life as one grows beyond the catastrophic effects of mental health issues.[18]

The concept of recovery has been further developed in New Zealand in the Mental Health Commission's Blueprint for Mental Health Services, to include the individual's social, political, economic and cultural context. The New Zealand model of recovery acknowledges diversity and challenges the dominance of the biomedical model of 'mental health issues' that was central to recovery literature in the USA.[19] A key feature of the New Zealand definition of recovery is the importance of consumer partnerships at all stages in the design and delivery of mental health services, with an emphasis on human rights and advocacy.

The past New Zealand Mental Health Services Commissioner (2000–2007) Mary O'Hagan, has been a strong advocate for a recovery approach to be led by service users and adapted to local conditions. Addressing consumers of mental health services in New Zealand, O'Hagan defines recovery in this way:

> Recovery means living well in the presence or absence of your mental health issues. It is more than just managing your mental health problem. Recovery also means getting back the things you have lost because of your mental heath problem, such as friends, your home or your job.[21]

O'Hagan's definition focuses on getting back things that have been lost. If we are truly doing our work well and intervening early on with people, our main focus is prevention of loss. Recovery is about maintaining a decent quality of life, in the presence or absence of mental health issues, where you are able to pursue your hopes and dreams and engage in purposeful education, employment and recreation; have quality housing and close relationships with family and friends. Central to recovery is 'hope' and the 'active' role taken by the individual in her or his own recovery. This includes acknowledging that medication is necessary for many people with a recurring mental health issues. The challenge is to find the right medication and be prescribed the least amount required.[22]

The emphasis on the responsibility of the individual in definitions of recovery is concerning for social workers as it does not recognise the responsibilities of government and others to provide opportunities to support the enactment of individual aspirations. A social and emotional well-being approach recognises the connectedness of the individual to the environment and acknowledges that notions of individual success are dependent upon collaboration with, and support from, others. The Western notion of individual success on your own does not fit well with such a model and is not realistic for anyone, regardless of their mental state.

There is a danger that individuals can be blamed for not achieving recovery goals and feel shame as a result. This can be demoralising and lead people to feel disengaged and become suicidal when the reality is that others have decided on the opportunities to be provided, if any, and often these carry lowered expectations and rewards. When using a recovery model, workers are not to tell people their goals are unrealistic, even if privately they hold this view, as it is deemed to be paternalistic and patronising. The challenge is how to support people in deciding on what hopes and dreams are likely to be achievable and how to go about this. Ultimately the person will decide for themselves through conversations with others to gain information and clarity, evaluative processes and taking calculated risks.

Workers must recognise there are times when people lack the confidence, motivation, energy and drive to engage with the recovery model, and they need to be supported. There are times when a person will not engage or have another hold their hope for them when they are unable to do so themselves. They may need time out and choose when they have the ability to re-engage. This does not mean the person should be discharged and get back in touch when they are ready. Patricia Deegan aptly refers to this process as 'a journey of the heart' that a person must be ready to engage in.[23] Workers must recognise that disengagement is a healthy response for those who face ongoing and cumulative rejection over a sustained period of time while also trying to manage difficult mental health symptoms and often extended periods of boredom and loneliness.

Ultimately a good quality of life is a main recovery goal for everyone and this will look different for different people at different times. It may include major changes and decisions that allow a person to move forward from distressing events and people in their past. Such decisions need to taken with care at a time when the person is thinking clearly and not during or immediately following a period of mental instability.

Ultimately, for people to succeed in their recovery goals, workers must advocate for systems change and challenge discriminatory practices that are too readily accepted as stigma of mental illness. This belief is a fallacy as the stigma is not from the mental health issues but rather discriminatory views and practices enacted by others. Workers must publicly namely and eliminate discriminatory practices if people with mental health issues are to achieve access and equity and full community participation.

People with mental health issues are often excluded from many aspects of community living. Exclusion is no longer being locked away in an asylum. It is now in more subtle forms that can generate intense feelings of loneliness and rejection. Findings of research conducted by SANE Australia reveals that 90 per cent of respondents believed that friendships were an important part of staying well yet 72 per cent said they felt lonely 'all or most of the time'.[24] While costs are high on an emotional and psychological level for those affected, the social and economic costs are also high in terms of the increased demand for social services and losses in productivity.[25] A National Mental Health and Wellbeing study found that the prevalence of mental disorders was greatest for those living alone.[26] People with mental health issues also experience high rates of unemployment. Social relationships with family and friends, and adequate support from services in the community, are important. Many people who experience mental health issues have difficulty at times being with others in a meaningful way and can experience loneliness and anxiety as a result. Social isolation in the community has been identified as a factor contributing to hospital admission.[27]

Jane was moved from a long-term psychiatric hospital ward to a hostel in the community. Jane was diagnosed as having an intellectual disability as well as personality disorder and schizophrenia. Due to Jane's difficult behaviours when she was distressed, she was evicted from the hostel and deemed not suitable to be living in close proximity to other people. She was moved to a flat on her own, located behind a house. It was here that she lived in total isolation. Her neighbours rejected her, with one woman claiming that she feared for the safety of her children and would no longer let them play in the backyard as she was worried Jane might jump over the fence and harm them. The man in the house at the front of the flat was compassionate toward Jane but at a loss as to how to deal with her. At night she would sit in her flat and scream, a piercing scream of pain and suffering. She would also harm herself by burning her arms and forehead with cigarette butts. She simply was not coping with community living and the community was clearly not coping with her.

Jane's story is an example of how community living is not just about re-location. It is about connection and quality of life.

There are many others, like Jane, who find they can no longer live in psychiatric institutions nor can they live well in the community. Those who avoid treatment can find themselves lost and alone on the streets or end up in prison, while those who accept their diagnosis may 'succumb to the weight of their disability and its stigma, and resign themselves to a shadow existence in the new back wards of social clubs, hostels and rehabilitation programs'.[28]

Loneliness and social isolation are common features of the lives of people with recurring mental health issues. The absence of social supports, particularly during times of difficulty and distress, can have a serious impact upon a person's social and emotional well-being. Loneliness is a terrible burden for many people with mental health issues. Some might identify with the social clubs and other activities focused on mental health, while others might reject these services as they feel they don't identify with, or belong in, these services. Young women in particular can find the dominance of males and their inappropriate behaviours in these settings off-putting.

Some may find appropriate groups and activities in the community, while others may find services not accepting of them if they are aware of their mental health issues. People who have developed a mental health issue in their teens or early adult years have often missed out on important aspects of socialisation. Making new friends may not come naturally and social skills may be awkward. It is important to note that gaps in skills can be addressed at any age and this may be an area where assistance is wanted so as to engage meaningfully with others. However, for those with a late onset of mental health issues, social skills are more likely to be well developed. Other aspects that may hinder the development and maintenance of meaningful relationships are stigma, fear of rejection, psychotic and other symptoms and the side effects of medication. Even when these difficulties continue, people with mental health issues overwhelmingly still long for loving and caring relationships. It is not the desire or capacity to develop caring relationships that is lacking but rather opportunities for friendships to develop. In a study focused on mental health and relationships and friendships, Davidson found that for a quality relationship to develop, 'it must be between two individuals who are on the same level and who have something of value to offer each other'.[29] In many instances, people with mental health issues are on the receiving end of services and not able, or permitted, to give anything back. The main challenge is to be 'let in' and allowed to participate in the community in meaningful activities and reciprocal relationships and to have physical, psychological, emotional, cultural, social, environmental and spiritual needs met.

Stigma

Stigma imposed by others is more debilitating than mental health issues.[30] It is not enough to have to deal with the distressing symptoms of mental health issues, but to also have to deal with unfounded fear and discrimination from a misinformed public is, for many, too heavy a burden to bear. Stigma directed towards people with mental health issues are represented by media portrayals of people to be feared or scorned. Often, mental health issues are seen as associated with acts of violence, incompetence or as a form of amusement.

Stigma is a socially constructed mark of disapproval, shame or disgrace that causes significant disadvantage through oppression and discrimination. Reidpath describes stigma as 'a mark borne by a person judged as unfit for the sharing of social resources, and stigmatisation is a process for controlling community membership or ensuring active social exclusion'.[31] Negative impacts on health and social and emotional well-being are experienced by those who are excluded. Erving Goffman's classic sociological writings on stigma highlight the central feature that the question of acceptance has in the life of the stigmatised individual and the social construction of deviant identities. The effects of stigma have been seen as contributing to an overwhelming sense of fear and isolation for the individual affected.[32] Jamison highlights how stigma insinuates itself into policy decisions resulting in institutional discrimination.[33] Mental health workers and students are not immune and many do hold negative attitudes and beliefs toward the people they work with. This is often not admitted to, due to fears of repercussions or rejection by peers and those in authority positions. A true sign of the maturity of a profession is its ability to look closely at issues such as worker stigma and to acknowledge it so that strategies can be put in place to address it.

Many people who are diagnosed with a mental health issue are members of minority groups, resulting in discrimination and oppression on multiple levels. This may be on the basis of gender, age, religious beliefs, disability, race and ethnicity, socio-economic status or sexual preference. For instance, homosexuality was not removed from the American Psychiatric Association's *Diagnostic and Statistical Manual* until 1973. Following successful advocacy and human rights campaigns from gay and lesbian activists, this diagnosis has now been removed from the DSM. However, apart from the removal of the psychiatric diagnosis from the DSM, little attention has been paid to their mental health needs. According to Uldall and Palmer, 'Mentally ill lesbian, gay, bisexual and transgender individuals face a dual stigma in society: they are frequently discriminated against by virtue of their health issues, as well as their sexual orientation and gender identity.'[34] LGBTI individuals are over-represented for diagnoses of depression and anxiety and alcohol and substance dependence.

A psychiatric diagnosis can result in discrimination and marginalisation affecting all areas of a person's life, contributing to low levels of confidence and self-esteem, with fear and ignorance often leading to the curtailment of opportunities.[35] This is because the individual is considered to be not conforming to what are considered to be 'normal' codes of behaviour. Stigma can cause those with mental health issues to avoid mixing with others or seeking assistance because they fear they may be ridiculed or misunderstood. This can lead to loneliness and isolation and the perpetuation of the symptoms.

Those who are already diagnosed may reject the label and refuse the recommended treatment. Others might refuse the treatment if they see it as inferior when compared with treatments for less stigmatised conditions, or possibly due to distressing side effects. Those who do disclose that they have a mental health issue run the risk of being rejected or treated differently, with responses varying depending upon the diagnosis. For instance, people with schizophrenia or antisocial personality disorder are stereotyped as unpredictable and prone to violence and are viewed more negatively than those with depression, anxiety disorders or eating disorders.[36] It has been found, however, that negative attitudes often do change if time is taken to get to know the person.[37] Concealment of a mental health condition can also limit opportunities as a person tries to avoid possible discrimination. Buris suggests that those who develop strategies to resist and challenge discrimination 'may actually face less stigma, experience less social harm, and be better able to cope with discrimination. At the same time they avoid the lifelong hidden distress and unhappiness experienced by people who conceal.'[38]

The stigma surrounding mental health issues and suicide can prevent people from seeking help because they do not want to be seen to be 'crazy'. Some studies have found as high as one in 10 people with schizophrenia take their own lives.[39] This figure could in fact be higher as coroners may be reluctant to give a verdict of suicide due to the social stigma and the emotional and socio-economic impacts on families and the deceased.[40] Studies on social attachment and social capital view suicide as representing individuals who are not well integrated and supported in the community.[41]

Numerous studies have found that negative stereotypes of people with mental health issues lead to discrimination in education, employment, housing and social interactions with others.[42]

Figure 3.2 illustrates mental health pathways that can result in 'disempowerment' as a result of stigma from mental health issues or 'empowerment' when support is provided and stigma is externalised with strategies developed to combat it. As shown in the disempowerment pathway,[43] a person may internalise these negative responses and experiences, either consciously or subconsciously, resulting in loss of confidence and poor self esteem. Few demands are placed on services with extremely low expectations and grave consequences.[44] Pilgrim sums up the negative impacts of stigma from mental health issues: 'The stigmatized person is set apart and they suffer the consequences of the social distance created. The person feels depersonalized, rejected and disempowered.'[45] However, as indicated in the empowerment pathway, there are those who are able to maintain or regain their confidence and self-esteem and achieve personal goals. In this pathway, the stigma of mental health issues are externalised and viewed as a means of oppression. Self-expectations are maintained and strategies developed to deal with possible discrimination, resulting in empowerment.

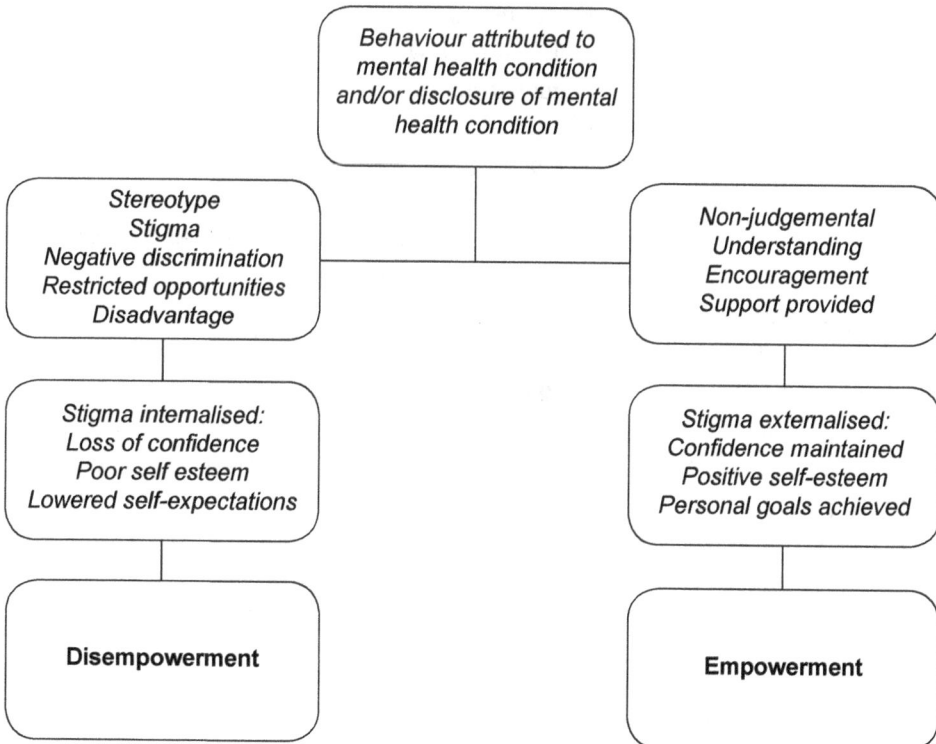

Figure 3.2: Mental health pathways

Culture

Mental health legislation and policy in Australia and New Zealand stipulate guidelines for 'powers to be exercised with proper respect for cultural identity and personal beliefs'.[46] Cultural safety is the preferred approach as it extends beyond cultural competence to a whole of system approach that embraces and is respectful of cultural diversity throughout all aspects of service design and delivery. This is reflected in the overall culture of the organisation that is welcoming and responsive to all cultural needs. Provisions are made for staff and service users to be culturally safe within the organisation. This includes all staff regardless of their duties. Culturally safe services celebrate diversity and do not reflect only one dominant culture. This comprises artwork and welcoming signs, including those that welcome first nations peoples. Cultural safety extends beyond race and ethnicity to include groups in the community who may be wary of possible discrimination in mental health services such services such as people from the lesbian, gay, bisexual, transgender, queer and intersex communities. Rainbow flags can be a sign of welcome in reception areas and help put people at ease. Culturally safe services celebrate difference and do not discriminate. This will be done in physical ways but is also very much reflected in people's attitudes and the ways they approach and treat people. In culturally safe services. discrimination of any kind is not tolerated. For this reason, discriminatory practices must be named and eradicated so that an all of service approach is possible with people feeling confident and safe with all workers.

Adriana had postnatal depression after the birth of her first child and was hospitalised. The psychiatrist had a long counselling session with her and felt things were beginning to improve. When the psychiatrist returned an hour later she found Adriana in tears. She inquired as to what was happening and Adriana replied that a member of the nursing staff was treating her very rudely and she believed that this was because she was in a same sex relationship. She said the nurse had treated her very well at the beginning yet had become quite negative toward her after she had a visit from her partner. She believed it was discrimination. Of course if the nurse was approached she would deny this and probably quite vehemently. She might even claim bullying and harassment. Thus it is the hidden nature of much of the discrimination that occurs that is most insidious. Ways to name this and at the same time bring about improvements in organisational culture and practices are required rather than the alienation of staff who may become more covert with discriminatory practices. The leadership within the organisation will generally determine the culture and put in place systems and practices throughout the organisation to promote and support this. When overt discriminatory practices are displayed in front of other staff and service users you can be sure that this is an organisation that is not culturally safe and does not pretend to be.

It has been recognised that in the past mental health services have not adequately met the needs of people from non-Western cultural backgrounds. Service provision has been characterised by longer hospital stays and greater use of involuntary treatment.[47] It has been observed that the participation of women in community mental health programs in the past has been problematic. Suggested reasons for this are the lack of bilingual staff, cultural limitations placed on interaction between females and males, the 'unwitting ethnocentric nature of service delivery' and culturally inappropriate programs.[48]

The development of culturally sensitive practices needs to be reflected at all levels of service management and delivery. This is particularly important for front-line staff whose staff development needs in this area are often overlooked. In human service organisations, it is generally assumed that all workers, managers included, embrace cross cultural approaches and understandings. The reality, however, is that workers will bring their experiences of domination and subjugation to the workplace and may wittingly or unwittingly develop and impose policies and practices that reflect this. It is not appropriate to expect people from different cultures to necessarily fit into a model of service delivery designed by, and for, people from a dominant cultural group. It is argued in this book that the model of social and emotional well-being developed for use with Aboriginal and Torres Strait Islanders is suited to people from all cultural groups.

Most students of social work and social work educators and practitioners are from the dominant cultural groups and need to be equipped to work across a range of culturally diverse settings. Ethno-specific workers are small in numbers and often experience ongoing discrimination and exclusion in the same way as those they are working with. This is reflected in the poor funding arrangements and infrastructure of ethno-specific services, particularly for new and emerging communities. There is a danger of perpetuating practices of exclusion by referring people to ethno-specific workers and agencies rather than endeavouring to create culturally appropriate responses in mainstream services. While at times it is appropriate to refer to bilingual workers, it is not appropriate to expect bilingual workers to be expert on all matters and provide all services.

Interpreters need to be made available with all staff trained to work with them.[49] Older migrants often have difficulty learning another language and it is not appropriate to expect them to do so especially if they have never received any formal education. Working with interpreters takes time and can be costly, particularly for intensive service provision in the community. It is often easier to refer people to workers who speak the person's language and this may be desirable and appropriate. However, it may not be and, because of this, the person may be denied access to services they need from mainstream agencies.

Funding constraints of human service organisations mean that people are often being required to do more for less. This means that short cuts are taken with use of interpreters. Two mental health agencies I have worked in had insufficient budget allocations for payment of interpreters. In one agency, workers were actively encouraged to use family and friends as interpreters. As a social worker on a mental health crisis response team, I recall visiting a man who did not speak English, three times daily initially. I relied solely on what I could observe, what his friends who were looking after him told me, some limited conversation with him interpreted by whoever was at the house caring for him at the times I visited, and conversations with his general practitioner. In this instance, the outcomes were positive and his friends were very supportive. However, is this model of service delivery one that is generally acceptable within the human services?

In many instances, the use of family and friends to interpret is not appropriate, particularly when sensitive and private matters are being discussed in a counselling situation. Confidentiality cannot be guaranteed and the interpretation cannot always be relied upon. In some cultures, a family member or close friend, due to bad karma, will not communicate bad news and will in fact change the message.

The reliance upon children as interpreters is particularly problematic when they are being asked to assume responsibility that is not appropriate to their age and position in the family. They can become privy to information they would not otherwise know. Role reversal can occur with the child assuming a position of authority in the family due to their language proficiency with their parents reliant upon them. Sometimes, workers will ask bilingual workers to interpret for them. This is often inappropriate, as while it may seem convenient, it is an imposition and could be seen as disrespectful. Selecting an interpreter can be more of an issue for members of immigrant groups that are small in number and fearful that problems will be shared within the community or that existing relationships may be altered, particularly if the interpreter is known to them. Due to greater cultural knowledge and understandings, some people may prefer workers of the same cultural backgrounds. However, others might want to see workers outside their culture and community for reasons of confidentiality or possible bias.[50]

Culturally inclusive practices are those where mainstream services employ bilingual and bicultural workers and forge partnerships and strong networks with community leaders and workers in ethno-specific agencies. This way, those seeking services get the benefit of the range of services available. Workers also gain from increased cross cultural knowledge and understandings and networks. Personal contact is often the most effective means of communication. Working with different ethnic-communities and providing information in community languages is central to developing culturally inclusive practices. This is often achieved through networking with ethnic community leaders and using a range of ethno-specific media such as newspapers, radio, television and notices in shops. Social media such as Facebook, Twitter, Instagram and Linked In are increasingly important for communication by human service organisations.

Workers need to continually critically reflect on whose needs they are serving and the values and ethics of the social work profession. Are these needs personal, organisational or those of the person seeking a service? In reality, all three areas of need will play some part in how workers respond. However, if personal and organisational needs dominate the service, responses will be distorted and inappropriate. Ultimately the organisational culture will be reflected in the type of services offered and the manner in which they are provided.

Aboriginal and Torres Strait Islander social and emotional well-being

Aboriginal and Torres Strait Islanders are not well engaged with heath and welfare services, have a poor prognosis and are over-represented in rates of suicide and self-harm, use of alcohol and other drugs, use of emergency health and welfare services, court appearances and detention in justice facilities.[51] Aboriginal youths are over-represented in out-of-home care services; the Victorian Department of Human Services identifies Aboriginal children as a priority population with future work focused on Aboriginal child well-being and service provision by Aboriginal agencies.

Talk about mental health issues and suicide is not encouraged in Aboriginal communities, with suicide treated as the result of family trouble, alcohol or accidental.[52] Health and well-being are viewed holistically with a social and emotional model of health and well-being considered more suited than a medical model. Spirituality is central to this approach, and physical, emotional, social and cultural aspects of a person's life are treated with equal importance.[53] The preference is to manage problems within the family and community. Aboriginal leaders claim that mental health issues did not exist in Aboriginal communities before 'European invasion'. There is often a real fear of institutions and government authorities among Aboriginal communities. This is due to the unacceptably high rates of imprisonment of Aboriginal people and deaths in custody. As well, the protection policies of forced removal of Aboriginal children from their families, with these children given new names and forced to speak in English, has resulted in many Aborigines today not knowing who their parents and siblings are, and not being able to locate them. Given social workers' part in this forced removal of Aboriginal children, it is not surprising that social work and other health and welfare mainstream workers are viewed with suspicion. 'Aboriginal people cannot trust the government where their loved ones are concerned. They fear they may be lost forever.'[54]

The role of social workers in the Northern Territory intervention has also raised concerns about social workers as agents of social control enforcing interventions that run counter to social work critical theory and community development models of community participation, leadership and empowerment. The Northern Territory intervention was introduced in 2007 by the Howard Liberal government in an endeavour to combat systemic child abuse. Since then the number of deaths of young Aboriginal girls in the Northern Territory by suicide has increased significantly. Howard Bath, the Northern Territory Childrens' Commissioner, is critical of what he refers to as the anti-intervention 'narrative down south' and calls for a greater focus on developing effective policy. This requires engagement by social workers with communities to work together to bring about improvements. Much of social work education and practice is concerned with anti-discrimination and anti-oppression. It is much harder to engage constructively and contribute effectively to major policy debates.

Only a small percentage of Aboriginal people use mental health services relative to the general community. However, services developed by the specialist Aboriginal mental health networks have seen greater usage. The success of these services is attributed to them being culturally appropriate, employing Aboriginal workers and having established effective linkages with other Aboriginal services.[55] As stated by an Aboriginal health worker in Victoria, 'The best response to mental health issues is through Koori contact. If there is no contact, the mental health issues stay longer and take longer to stabilise.'[56]

Refugees and asylum seekers

Many refugees and asylum seekers suffer from significant psychological distress due to separation from family members, often not knowing where they are or what has happened to them. For those who have survived torture and trauma, the aftermath can be post-traumatic stress, flashbacks, ongoing nightmares and fear of authorities.[57] Many asylum seekers are living in poverty without government support. Poverty is not only related to financial difficulties; poverty is a life without hope. This financial strain impacts upon relationships and quality of life. For many, experiences in refugee camps and detention centres have resulted in human rights violations that necessarily impact negatively on mental health and well-being.

Social workers play an important role in assessing needs and identifying obstacles and developing other pathways to meet these needs. This requires an ability to work effectively in a context where government policies are often hostile and contravene social work's values and ethics. Social workers must demonstrate political awareness and ethical practice with interventions that are responsive to both the personal and political dimensions of the person's situation. This involves direct service provision as well as community work and advocacy for policy improvements and legislative change directed at a more humane approach. Due to the range, diversity and intensity of needs, collaborative community-based responses are required across a range of services and workers, including refugee legal centres.[58] Issues of trust and respect are particularly important. Trusting relationships will take time and may be difficult to establish due to past experiences of violence, and abuse that may be ongoing.

A particular challenge for social workers is how to respond to both the personal and political dimensions of mandatory detention. On a personal level it may be arranging for visits and communication via newspapers or other reading materials in the person's own language, telephone, email, letters, conversation, friendship and instilling a sense of hope. It may be in advocacy and assistance in pursuing applications for asylum and appropriate representation through legal and other sources. On a political level it may be in media campaigns targeted at the abolition of mandatory detention with representations to key ministers in government for a more humane approach.

Physical health

A strong association has been found between disadvantaged socio-economic backgrounds and an increased risk of persistent mental health issues and other health problems.[59] People with persistent mental health issues have been found to have higher rates of physical morbidity and associated mortality than the general population. Often, people are not aware of their mental health issues and therefore do not seek appropriate treatment. They may also be unfamiliar with preventative approaches to health care or not be able to access these due to high costs or long waiting periods. Some may be fearful of health service providers due to past negative experiences. Long-term health risks have been associated with certain treatments for mental health condition.[60] Alcohol abuse and illicit and prescribed drug dependencies can also exacerbate health problems.[61]

The number of people with mental health issues and HIV/AIDS is unknown. Included in this group are those who have a pre-existing mental health issues and those whose mental health issues are a consequence of the HIV/AIDS infection. Specialist in-patient and community treatments are required for these people.

Physical illneses can be misdiagnosed as mental health issues due to altered mental states often characterised by confusion, hallucinations and delusions than can occur due to physical health problems and or adverse effects from incompatible medications. This is particularly an issue when working with older people who are on multiple medications. A major challenge is to keep the number and dosage of medications to the minimum required. This is not easy, particularly when medications are also prescribed to combat side effects. Social workers do need to be concerned with this, due to the impacts on quality of life as well as recognition of adverse side effects of medications. Close collaboration is required with general practitioners in this regard. For those in in-patient settings, high doses of sleeping medication at night put them at risk of falls if getting up to go to the bathroom during the night and also at risk of sexual abuse by other patients and staff.

Sexual abuse

A high proportion of women who use mental health services have been abused. Some studies estimate as many as 50 per cent of women using mental health services have been sexually assaulted.[62] The experience of abuse can result in women being fearful for their safety and having difficulty in developing trusting relationships.

A woman's personal history, geographic location, physical and intellectual capabilities and ethnic background all impact upon her survival of sexual violence.[63] Romans, Martin and Mullen's study of childhood sexual abuse and later psychological problems, highlights the importance of the family and social circumstances of the woman, and her individual experience of childhood sexual assault, both at the time of the assault and subsequently. Their findings indicate that women who had experienced childhood sexual abuse had higher representation in adverse later outcomes than non-abused women. However, they caution against simplistic assumptions about a causal relation between childhood sexual assault and difficulties in adulthood.[64] Self-destructive behaviour, anxiety, feelings of isolation and stigma, poor self-esteem, depression and drug and alcohol abuse have been found to be prevalent among women who have been sexually abused as children.[65]

Sexual abuse represents the ultimate betrayal and abuse of power. The experience of sexual assault as a child has been associated with a number of psychiatric diagnoses in adulthood. These include anxiety disorders (panic disorder and phobias) trauma, major depression, psychotic and suicidal symptoms, borderline personality disorder and dissociative disorders.[66] A strong association has been found between a reported history of childhood sexual abuse and a diagnosis of personality disorder in adulthood.[67] It is only in the past two decades that the long-term impact of childhood sexual abuse has come under investigation. A relationship has been found between early life trauma, substance abuse, crime and further abuse as an adult.[68] Outcomes identified in Alder's study of sexual abuse included

> ...frank psychiatric disorder and associated behaviours such as deliberate self harm, and range through lowered self esteem and adolescent pregnancy to increased problems with adult intimacy unrelated to concurrent psychiatric disorder and failure to advance socioeconomically.[69]

Women with mental health issues have been identified as being at risk of sexual harassment from staff and others in hospital and community settings. An issue raised in the literature is sexual relationships between male workers and female psychiatric patients. This issue is often dismissed, 'because it is seen as too controversial, or trivialised as unduly subjective or ignored as irrelevant'.[70] It is pleasing to note that recent reports by consumers of an in-patient psychiatric unit by a male staff member, often at night when under sedation, have been taken seriously and charges have been laid. The outcome of this case is yet to determined. However, to have even got it to this point is, sad to say, a remarkable achievement.

Due to the prevalence of sexual abuse among women who use public mental health services, it is important that all services are developed in ways that are non-threatening and responsive and sensitive to the physical, psychological and emotional needs of women. Workers must treat reports of abuse with the seriousness they deserve and appropriate services and responses should be put in place. Women who report or disclose abuse need to be provided with appropriate information about their legal rights and medical options.[71]

When issues of sexual assault are raised, appropriate support and follow-up is needed to assist the woman to deal with the intensity of emotions that are aroused. Women who are acutely mentally unwell are very unsafe and vulnerable to sexual assault from both males and females. Sexual abuse can sometimes cause psychosis as the woman's internal defence mechanisms take over from a reality that is too hard to bear. If the possibility of ongoing abuse is an issue within the setting the woman is living in or is likely to return to, this needs to be addressed. Specialised staff training and supervision in this area is required. It is important that workers respond in a timely and appropriate manner to reports of abuse in consultation with the police and specialist services, particularly centres against sexual assault. Sexual abuse is a serious crime that needs to be investigated by the police. The decision as to whether or not to report claims of sexual assault to the police in in-patient settings should not be in the hands of medical staff. All complaints must be reported and the police can then decide on appropriate follow-up.

Housing

Mental health issues can cause a person to become or remain homeless and subsequently not have economic and social supports. Likewise, a person may become homeless for other reasons, such as violence and abuse within the family home. Some argue that this is a main cause of homelessness rather than mental health issues. A polarised debate has developed between some academics, who claim to be the experts, and some practitioners. These academics argue that there is not a high representation of people with mental health issues in the homeless population. Workers acknowledge, however, that if reasons for becoming homeless are attributed to other sources, such as violence and abuse, the stress of homelessness is likely to increase the risk of developing mental health issues. To say mental health issues are not relevant to the homeless population is simply wrong and is a major injustice. Issues faced by women prisoners post release, discussed in Chapter 14, highlight the emotional, economic and social problems arising from difficulties accessing appropriate and affordable housing. A mother whose son had severe mental health issues and was homeless commented, 'It is not poverty that causes mental health issues, but mental health issues certainly cause poverty.' Poverty, in turn, is a risk factor for homelessness, as people simply cannot afford to pay rental and power bills. Increases in rental and amenities charges can be out of reach, especially for those who have recently lost employment and do not have savings to fall back on. Older women in the retail sector are a particularly vulnerable group. The lack of parity in price increases and wages across is a major concern for housing affordability. Homelessness can affect anyone; it is true that it is not always due to mental health issues but it will certainly trigger and exacerbate them. Housing needs to be safe, appropriate and affordable.

Another mother told me that often she does not know where her son is. He may be unwell and living on the streets but she is not to know. He is often too unwell to contact her and she told me in a matter of fact way that services do not contact her due to confidentiality. She told me that even though he has been under mental health services for many years, she has never been told his diagnosis. She seemed to accept this and when I told her services were obliged by law to include her if she is the nominated primary carer, she didn't seem to show much interest. I left her feeling disheartened and somewhat naïve in my response to her.

Even though we have made progress with human rights and laws in relation to the inclusion of primary carers, it is up to workers to implement this and they may or may not do so. This highlights the powers of workers and the difficulties of bringing about substantive changes in the mental health system, particularly in relation to the inclusion of primary carers. It highlights the importance of service responses that enact legislation that supports the inclusion of key people in a person's life in their recovery journey. Australian law requires that primary carers are provided with information essential for looking after the person in their care and any worker who says otherwise is not only in breach of the legislation but also denying a person of proper care. Whatever the reasons given for the exclusion of a primary carer, they need to be challenged. Social workers must enact this legislation and model carer-inclusive practices for best outcomes to occur in the lives of those they are working with. Carers often have greater influence than workers due to the nature of the relationship and emotional attachment. It is carers and family and friends who provide the love and reassurance and spend the time listening to, encouraging, socialising and exercising with a person that is so important for their recovery. These formal and informal support needs must all be attended to and not only one at the expense of the other. Carers are key members of the treatment team and must be included as such. They will only be excluded when there is evidence to support this such as abuse, keeping in mind that if a person is prone to paranoia they may accuse their primary carer of terrible things that were in fact not real, even though they seemed very real at the time. The closeness and intensity of this relationship can mean that the carer is likely to feature in a person's distorted thinking that is often associated with psychosis. A thorough assessment of the relationship is required before the person develops negative views towards their carer and the circumstances immediately following. Nonetheless, perceptions of harm need to be taken seriously in intervention planning, as this can impact upon a person's willingness to receive care. For instance, a person may stop eating food prepared by a carer if they believe they are poisoning them.

Appropriate housing is critical to recovery from mental health issues. People must be satisfied that they can live a fulfilling life in what is not simply housing or accommodation but rather their home. People's homes are central to quality of life, sense of identity and place within the community. Housing is contingent upon affordability and gaining and maintaining suitable housing is strongly influenced by the person's mental health. At a policy and service design and delivery level, shared understandings of recovery by mental health, housing and income support services are required. This common view promotes collaborative teamwork that is coordinated across these three service sectors rather than simply referring or networking between services. Workers in these areas need to develop a full understanding of the discrimination that people with mental health issues face as well as those on a low income. This includes overt and covert types of discrimination toward people with mental health issues. This may be systemic discrimination or individual practice. Some policies and practices are unwittingly discriminatory while others are more blatant.

Levels of tolerance and acceptance are generally context specific. While people may express support and positive attitudes to people with mental health issues this does not always translate into positive interactions. Housing managers may profess support for taking in people with mental health issues, yet when faced with an actual request they will often be ambivalent. For those who do succeed in gaining accommodation after declaring they have a mental health issue, lease agreements or planning and building rules may be more stringent than for others. Likewise, people may express broad sentiments in favour of community living yet be opposed to community housing in their street or neighbourhood. The often unspoken message is 'Yes, but not in my backyard.'

Workers in mental health, housing and income support services need to be aware of risks to people's housing and take appropriate action to prevent housing loss, protect access to housing, and promote access to a range of suitable housing options that are in accordance with the individual's needs and wishes. Inappropriate housing and homelessness significantly contribute to the stress in the daily lives of people with ongoing mental health issues and those who are dependent upon them. Adequate housing is a major factor for providing a stable environment for families to be able to adequately care of their children.[72] Both local and international studies have shown a direct correlation between stable and suitable housing with the provision of appropriate supports, and improved outcomes for people experiencing mental health issues. A significant proportion of homeless people have a history of mental health issues.

People experiencing mental health issues can be at risk of losing their housing due to loss of income, discrimination from landlords or co-tenants, and, particularly in cases of unplanned hospitalisation or imprisonment, their inability to organise payment of rent and bills for essential services. It is not only housing that they are at risk of losing but also household goods and personal possessions. For parents with sole responsibility for dependent children, the loss of appropriate housing can preclude them from regaining care of their children. This then affects their income and ability to re-establish suitable housing. People caught in this poverty trap cannot get their children back without appropriate housing and they cannot afford adequate housing because they do not have their children to receive the additional income from family allowance payments. Regardless of a person's family circumstances, where they have adequate and appropriate housing, every effort must be made to prevent loss of that housing.

Workers need to protect people's access to suitable housing options by breaking down the barriers that people experiencing mental health issues face. These barriers are formed by discriminatory practices and beliefs about what is considered appropriate housing by consumers, family and workers, and discrepancies in these beliefs. Implicit in choice of housing are assumptions about what type of housing is suitable; people experiencing mental health issues are sometimes denied access to the range of housing options available to members of the general community. Supported housing options and private rentals frequently leave people with inadequate levels of disposable income. This not only impacts on issues of survival but can also hinder involvement in leisure and other activities where a financial cost is involved.

The lack of an appropriate range of suitable housing options, coupled with inadequate mental health services in the community has resulted in an over-reliance by mental health services upon group homes, hostels and special accommodation style housing. Accommodation options in the community, including women's refuges, are often considered by managers of mental health services as a preferred option to hospital admission.

Funding and service configurations can limit people's housing options to those that allow for easy access to particular mental health services. Workers need to promote access to a range of suitable housing options that are in accordance with individual needs and wishes and to design strategies and activities to assist people to gain and maintain suitable and affordable housing.

These may include assistance with finding public or private housing and support services, rental assistance and other income supplements and assistance with home maintenance if required. Inappropriate or unsafe housing can increase a person's vulnerability to abuse. It can also reduce a person's life chances of getting an appropriate education and employment.

Education

Many individuals who experience mental health difficulties want to undertake post-secondary education.[73] A person may have a pre-existing mental health condition or they may experience stress that can trigger a first episode of mental health issues. The nature of the studies and major life changes may generate stress that can lead to mental health difficulties. Given the importance of education in relation to career opportunities, income and lifestyle, it is essential that education providers support people experiencing mental health issues during their studies. This is particularly important for maintaining engagement during secondary school, when mental health issues may first become noticeable. Without appropriate assistance and support, it is highly likely the young person will not complete their schooling. People need to be offered pathways into post-secondary education and this includes provisions to assist the person to remain engaged in their studies when they are experiencing mental health difficulties. In the past, students were told to have a break from their studies during such times and subsequently did not complete their studies. It used to be that students with mental health issues had the highest non-completion rates. In recent years, however, there is increased acknowledgment of the rights of people with mental health issues to full participation in post-secondary education. Discrimination is no longer tolerated and disability provisions are put in place to assist people to do their best work regardless of their mental health status.

We have come a long way in post secondary education in the past few years and this is to be applauded; increasing numbers of people with mental health issues are engaging is social work and other post-secondary education programs. Anecdotally, however, there is an undercurrent of social workers who question the suitability of people with certain mental health issues to effectively practice as social workers. This stigma within the profession is never openly talked about as it is not considered politically correct, or indeed lawful, to exclude people on the grounds of mental health issues or disability. What has happened instead is the introduction of inherent requirements that stipulate what is required of a student entering into a degree program. Students who develop mental health issues during their studies may no longer meet these inherent requirements and not apply for disability provisions to support their studies in fear of discrimination or even the loss of their place at the university. It seems universities are making decisions as to who is desirable in the social work profession, and who is not, without informed discussion and debate within the profession itself. It is important that students are aware of their rights and challenge anything that appears discriminatory while at the same time attaining the rights they are entitled to. Student rights officers play a particularly important role in terms of advocacy in this space.

The incidence of mental health issues amongst students enrolled in post-secondary education is steadily increasing, with estimates of between 10 and 20 per cent.[74] Of particular concern are reports that these students have lower completion rates than all other disability groups.[75] The integration of student well-being programs in high-stress academic vocational programs has resulted in reports of marked improvements in overall student mental health.[76]

As mentioned earlier in this chapter, the stigma associated with mental health issues, and the hidden nature of the disability, constitute powerful barriers to seeking and receiving assistance. Nevertheless, there is increased evidence that students' with mental health issues who receive appropriate support are successful in post-secondary education, experience decreased hospitalisation rates and increased levels of self-confidence, self-efficiency and empowerment.[77]

The period of mid to late adolescence and early adulthood is a time of major change and adjustment, not only in relation to the challenges and obligations of studies but also in terms of general expectations of increased self-reliance. This situation is poignantly depicted in Conger's description of adolescence, highlighting not only change but also the confusion and self doubt that can occur:

> Adolescence can be the time of irrepressible joy and seemingly inconsolable sadness and loss; of gregariousness and loneliness; of altruism and self-centeredness; of insatiable curiosity and boredom; of confidence and self-doubt. But above all, adolescence is a period of rapid change; physical, sexual and intellectual changes in the nature of the external demands placed by society on its developing members.[78]

These demands have increased in recent years, with young people exposed to higher rates and different types of stressors than previous generations, even though many adults fail to recognise it.

Models of post-secondary education are based on adult learning principles that require considerable autonomy and resourcefulness from students. The move from secondary school to further education can be both exciting and stressful as students learn to adapt to a new learning environment, workload and relationships with both staff and students and juggling paid employment. This situation is exacerbated for those who are studying away from home and for international students often studying in a new culture and language medium. It is generally assumed that young people who are offered a university place are capable and well organised, not only in their studies but also their self-management. A person's ability to manage stress and respond to change is a key aspect of mental health adjustment.

A barrier to successful educational outcomes is the common assumption that if a person is mentally unwell they should not be attending classes, whether at school, or university. This reflects the dominant view that people must be symptom-free before they can participate or be 'let in'.[79] Thus for many people, education is not an option as they may experience psychotic symptoms several times a day. For others, days lost from class will mean lack of engagement and continuity and may result in an inability to successfully complete study requirements.

This is a major loss for the young person, her or his family, the institution losing talented students and the broader community. On a personal and family level, those not studying or working run the risk of social exclusion and a life of poverty, and this is compounded by a diagnosis of mental health issues. Loss of productivity results in an increased tax burden through welfare payments, with government pensions or payments the main income source for those with mental health issues.[80] An increased financial burden is placed on the family at a time when increased financial independence is expected.

In social work, students are taught anti-discriminatory practice and can demonstrate commitment to this in class discussion and in written work. However, when they encounter a student or co-worker who is experiencing mental health issues, the response is often one of rejection. It is almost as if it is acceptable to work with people with mental health issues as 'clients' or 'consumers', but that it is not so acceptable for a peer or colleague to have a mental health issue. Responses tend to vacillate between sympathy and anger.

I had a student in my mental health class who was exhibiting unusual behaviour. She appeared totally distracted and was giggling and talking to herself during the class. After the class some students approached me and demanded, 'You need to do something with her. She is obviously unwell.' They did not offer any advice on what they wanted me to do or offer to do anything themselves. I spoke with the student privately after class, as had been my intention, and she spoke about the difficulties she was experiencing with auditory hallucinations. This was in the context of a diagnosis of schizophrenia and ongoing treatment, and the stressors of extremely long hours of paid work as well as full-time study and a lack of social supports. She agreed to contact her mental health worker that day for an appointment. While this student experienced ongoing mental health difficulties, she attended all classes and passed the course. She managed to get appropriate treatment and her mental health improved without having to miss classes. This continuity was very important for her to remain connected with her studies at university. She has now successfully completed the degree and is employed as a social worker.

On a previous occasion as a mental health social worker on a community assessment and treatment team (CATT) I was asked to try and find a young woman who had 'absconded' by leaving the hospital grounds without permission. Hospital staff believed that she was not well enough to leave hospital. I remember going to her flat and finding her there working on an assignment for her Masters degree at university. She said that she had left the hospital because she needed some sanitary items from home and would return to the hospital that evening after she had completed her assignment, which she did do. On other occasions she left the hospital of her own accord to do her assignments at home and then returned to the hospital of an evening. She achieved first class honours for the assignments she did at the time she was deemed most unwell by hospital staff. Her experience is a good example of how people can function well despite symptoms of mental health issues. However, this is not always the case and measures are required to support the person achieve their educational goals.

As a social worker in mental health, I once worked with a colleague, employed as a psychiatric nurse, who was diagnosed with schizophrenia. While some people were very accepting of this, others were antagonistic. He ultimately resigned because this workplace stress and pressure exacerbated his mental health issues.

Employment

Paul Keating, former prime minister of Australia, asserts that there are three factors underpinning poverty in Australia.[81] These are social isolation, lack of suitable or affordable housing and unemployment. He argues that if a person is able to gain suitable employment this provides access to social opportunities and finances to support housing costs. According to Keating's view, employment and appropriate income are at the forefront of addressing poverty. Poverty, insecure housing, economic disadvantage and abuse are common experiences of people with mental health issues.[82] A lack of access to flexible paid employment often results in poverty and extra health care costs are often accrued due to mental health issues.

People with mental health issues experience high rates of unemployment. Many people spend lengthy periods, sometimes decades, in pre-vocational training programs. In such instances, 'pre' has become synonymous with 'never'.[83] As with education and other areas of community participation, given the long-term nature and severity of many mental health issues, the expectation that people are symptom-free prior to gaining employment is unrealistic.

Employers may endorse employing people with mental health issues yet, when faced with the reality of an appropriately qualified candidate for a position who declares having a mental health issue, they may not offer them a position. Discrimination and stigma are often covert and can be difficult to deal with because of this. In this instance, the employer is not likely to name the person's mental health issues as a factor for not offering them the position. Employment opportunities are relative to the discrimination the person may face due to their mental health issues. As mentioned previously, discrimination may also be occurring due to other factors such as gender, ethnicity, age and sexual preference, not only because of mental health issues.[84]

Numerous studies, including one by Freud in the 1930s, have reported the benefits of employment for people with mental health issues.[85] Some of these include structure, social interaction and meaningful activity. However, if the person is not supported within their organisation, they may experience rejection and discrimination in the form of bullying and social isolation. Up until the past couple of years people with recurrent mental health issues were reliant upon the disability pension and were not in paid employment. This situation has now changed markedly, and many of these people are now deemed ineligible for disability pension payments and told they are now required to get paid employment. This in part has contributed to the rise in the number of people with mental health issues now engaged in post-secondary education programs, including social work. This raises the question of what education and work mean to people with mental health issues and how it impacts upon quality of life. I recall several people I worked with who gained employment that they found totally meaningless and of little more financial benefit than being on a pension. For those on a disability pension, the risks associated with getting a job may mean a transfer to unemployment benefit if the job does not work out and the loss of the preferred disability pension entitlements and safety net.

A woman I once worked with spoke of the relief and stability that she gained from being on a disability pension. She no longer needed to do stressful and meaningless jobs that seemed to be all she could get despite being educated, intelligent and articulate. A young man I worked with got himself a job at a peanut factory with the unfortunate name The Nut House. The constant jibes by family and friends, the routine nature of the work, his regular use of drugs and persistent hallucinations resulted in him lasting only a short time. In both of these instances, a stressful workplace led to deteriorating mental health resulting in a cost transfer from income security to health care systems.

In the workplace, stress means different things to different people. For some people, a busy environment can create a lot of stress, while for others a quiet work environment without enough to do can be far more stressful. Some people fear the stress of paid employment will increase symptoms of mental health issues. However, the opposite is often true, with symptoms tending to decrease and mental health outcomes improving. A positive work environment can serve as a distraction from worries and persistent psychotic symptoms.[86] This is also the case with the general population, as work status is often a strong predictor of life satisfaction as it brings status, income and social opportunities.[87]

People with ongoing mental health issues often have low self-esteem and poor quality of life. Confidence is often low as a result of stigma, long-term unemployment, poverty, disturbing symptoms associated with the mental health issue, side effects of medication and hospitalisations. A higher number of hospitalisations is often associated with poor work adjustment and higher unemployment.[88] In a study of quality of life and self-esteem in working and non-working persons with mental health issues, Van Dongen found positive attitudes towards psychotropic medications by both workers and non-workers who were taking these medications.[89] Other studies have found that side effects of anti-psychotic medications have contributed to non-compliance, and also claim that side effects can impair work capacity.[90] However, Van Dongen's findings suggest that people with mental health issues are less concerned with medication side effects than previously thought. This is within the context of improved medications in recent years with markedly reduced side effects for some people.[91]

Positive work experiences increase self-esteem and life satisfaction but negative experiences and chronic unemployment contribute to feelings of poor self-worth. The meaning of work, including perception of work and the value attached to it, is an important consideration. In a study of roles most valued by people with mental health issues, Hachey found that the most valued positions were friend, worker and family member even though most participants were not working.[92] Most people in Hachey's study wanted paid employment. It is important that support is provided for people with mental health issues to gain and maintain appropriate employment.

Voluntary work is often seen as preparation for paid employment and less demanding. However, paid employment is quite different in terms of commitment and performance expectations. Appropriate job matching is required on a number of continuums, including qualifications and training, personality type, career aspirations, pay and conditions, location and support. Factors contributing to job satisfaction are no different to anyone else and include mutual respect and acknowledgement, predictability, clear expectations, having sufficient time to complete work and social opportunities with co-workers.[93]

Conclusion

Recovery and well-being are concerned with quality of life and living well in the presence or absence of disturbing signs and symptoms of mental health issues. Community living requires the addressing of stigma and discrimination for full acceptance of, and participation by, those considered to be experiencing mental health issues. This includes adequate income, access to appropriate and affordable housing, education and employment and leisure activities. It is about being able to fully participate and engage in daily activities, even though symptoms of mental health issues may vary in intensity at different times, confident that appropriate services will be available if and when needed. It is about 'the kindness of strangers' who will provide opportunities rather than judge, ridicule or discriminate. Ultimately, recovery is about acceptance and appreciation of people for who they are beyond their mental health issues.

Reflection

What are the main areas that impact upon a person's quality of life and the ability to live well in the community?

How do you look after your own mental health and well-being?

How does stigma impact upon quality of life?

What are some of the features of recovery-oriented mental health services?

Why do you think Aboriginal and Torres Strait Islanders are not well engaged with health and welfare services, have a poor prognosis and are over-represented in the use of emergency and forensic services? What can you do about this?

What are the main mental health and well-being issues for refugees and asylum seekers?

4

Legislation, Policies and Practice Standards

Social work practice in mental health is governed by legislation, policies, practice standards and professional ethics. In Australia federal, state and territory legislation and policies guide social work practice in mental health.[1] The federal government controls fiscal resources and sets overriding standards for mental health services that the states and territories must adhere to.[2] Each state and territory government has developed polices and practices consistent with these overriding national standards for mental heath service provision. Legislation governing the design and delivery of mental health services is discussed, followed by consideration of the policy context, practice standards and rights review and complaints procedures.

Legislation

In Australia before the 1980s, the main location of treatment was in institutions, often located on the urban fringe, in rural areas or in discreet metropolitan locations. These institutions were a world unto themselves hidden away behind high fences, or walls of pine trees, with all of the services required from cooking to laundry, maintenance and psychiatric treatment provided within. Goffman aptly described such institutions as 'total institutions' and 'closed communities'. As discussed in Chapter 2, Goffman and others were part of a civil rights movement that came to be known as the 'anti-psychiatry movement'. The civil rights movement arose in many areas where people were experiencing discrimination and oppression, including women, cultural and ethnic minorities, gay and lesbian communities and people with mental health issues and disabilities. The civil rights movement was formalised in the United Nations Declaration of Human Rights in 1957. This coincided with the medical discovery of psychotropic medication in the 1950s that created opportunities to treat people with mental health issues in the community, disenchantment with treatment in institutional settings, and the high economic costs of sustaining this service model. Others preferred alternatives to the dominant medical model.

In Australia today each state and territory has its own mental health legislation.[3] This legislation defines who is deemed to be mentally ill, as well as criteria for involuntary treatment and detention in both hospital and community settings. Legislative and systemic reforms supported deinstitutionalisation and the separation of intellectual disability and mental health services in the 1990s. The separation of mental health and disability services meant that models of treatment and care could be tailored to the specific needs of both areas with the establishment of separate review boards. The dominant view was that a person had either a mental health issue or an intellectual disability, and no provision was made for those who had both. This was due to the erroneous belief that a person with an intellectual disability did not have the mental capacity to have a mental health issue as well.[4] In the mid-1990s a state-wide dual disability service was established in Victoria. A further state-wide service has been developed in Victoria for dual diagnosis of mental health and alcohol and other drugs. This is referred to as a dual disability service in other jurisdictions in Australia and elsewhere. Hence much confusion abounds in the terminology used concerning mental health and disability. An important further distinction is the difference between intellectual disability and disability that may be due to, or an outcome of, mental health issues.

In addition to state and territory mental health legislation, other key pieces of legislation are also in the areas of human rights, equal opportunity and anti-discrimination, income security, housing, education and general health. Relevant legislation also relates to carers, children, youth and families, and includes provisions for child well-being and safety, and family violence and protection. More recent mental health legislation has a much stronger human rights focus although it still has considerable involuntary functions that are now referred to as 'compulsory'. This more recent legislation names social workers as mental health service providers for the first time and bestows upon them a range of powers to enact compulsory interventions. This includes restraining a person, transporting a person to a mental health service against their wishes, searching a person and their property and entering premises without permission. These new powers do not sit well within a framework of human rights. A main consideration is implications for social work education. There has been silence from the social work profession and universities here. Was the nurse mentioned in Chapter 2 quite right to be annoyed that he had to work with a social worker who had not been trained in restraint? A major question concerns whether or not these are practices that social workers should be required to, or want to be trained to, do? In hospitals, restraint is now left to security staff, who may call police for assistance, and nursing and social work staff are not required to participate. This may be different in practice in an emergency situation when security staff are delayed. In forensic in-patient settings, all medical and allied heath staff are required to assist with restraint. This is premised on the view that nobody wants to do this and if some workers refuse to participate they could be putting others in danger, including the person who is deemed necessary of restraint.

Social workers need to carefully consider their roles and practices with these new powers. If they are to enact them, they need to be properly trained. If they are not going to engage with these powers, others need to know so that they are quite clear, even though the legislation permits this, that these are not practices that social workers will engage in due to issues of human rights. A main consideration is whether or not these practices contribute to improved social and emotional well-being for the person and uphold their human rights. This is not likely. These powers suggest there are times when people need to be protected from themselves. Students of social work are generally horrified about these powers and not inclined to use them. Those with experience in youth services, however, have many stories to tell of use of restraint.

In my own practice as a worker on a crisis team, and also in community mental health, at the risk of being judged, I have engaged in all of these practices without the protection of the law. This would be the same situation for most social workers who work in crisis mental health services. This does not necessarily make it right and, on reflection, my view today is that these practices should not exist nor be supported in mental health care. The focus must be on maintaining the dignity of the person at all times. For a skilled practitioner, this requires creating a safe space, listening and talking and intervening from our professional knowledge and skill base. This does not include involuntary, or what are now referred to as compulsory, practices and social workers need to take a stand against this. It is hoped that co-design will create safe spaces that eradicate such practices and instead focus on environments and approaches that provide comfort and kindness and support the recovery journey.

Additional legislative requirements are set out under the children, youth and families legislation.[5] This legislation requires designated professionals to report to Protective Services where they form a belief on 'reasonable grounds' that a child, or young person has suffered, or is likely to suffer, harm as a result of physical injury or sexual abuse. Designated professionals referred to in the Act are medical practitioners (including psychiatrists) nurses, primary and secondary school teachers and principals and police officers.[6] Social workers are not named as designated professionals; however, they still have a 'duty of care' and a professional responsibility to notify Protective Services if abuse is suspected. Reasonable grounds for notification are if a young person or a third party tells a worker they have been abused or feel unsafe, as well as workers' own observations. The notification may not result in investigation by Protective Services. If an investigation does occur, the risk of significant harm may or may not be substantiated, with or without any further risk. Substantiation involves confirming that the child has suffered, or is likely to suffer, significant harm and that the child's parents have not protected, or are unlikely to protect, the child from such harm. If a person has a file with Mental Health Services, this must be provided to Protective Services workers if requested by them in the conduct of their investigations, if it is considered critical to their work. The identity of a worker referring to Protective Services is protected under the children, youth and families legislation. While this protection is provided by the legislation, social work ethics and practice standards require that social workers involve consumers in all aspects of their treatment and care as much as possible. This means open and frank discussions about both voluntary and involuntary interventions and procedures. Social workers need to stand by their assessments and interventions and to be held professionally and publicly accountable for them. However, it is acknowledged that in certain situations protection of the identity of the social worker may be required.

Other significant laws relate to guardianship and administration, freedom of information and privacy, and occupational health and safety. Migration legislation, now known as border protection legislation, is pertinent to refugees and asylum seekers experiencing mental health issues. Crimes, sentencing and mental unfitness to be tried legislation is relevant to people with mental health issues involved with the criminal justice system, with provision for compulsory treatment in both mental health and sentencing legislation.

Mental health legislation in each state and territory of Australia has fundamental similarities. These include definitions of mental health issues and the provision of mental health services in the 'least restrictive environment'. This has been particularly so since the early 1990s, when all states and territories were required to conform with the United Nations Principles for the Care and Protection of Persons with Mental health issues.[7] According to Principle 9.1, treatment must be provided 'in the least restrictive environment and with the least restrictive or intrusive treatment appropriate to the patient's health needs and the need to protect the physical safety of others'.[8] Provision is made for internal and external review processes for involuntary detention and treatment in both hospital and community settings.[9]

Involuntary detention and treatment: hospital and community

The criteria in the legislation as to what is deemed to be mental illness in the legislation are very broad and subject to interpretation, particularly the judgement that a person 'appears to be mentally ill'. Due to the level of professional judgement required when assessing a person for a 'compulsory psychiatric admission' a lot is left to the discretion of psychiatrists and medical practitioners. This places them in a position of considerable power over the lives of the people they place on such orders as well as other mental health workers. Psychiatrists and medical practitioners are in effect the gatekeepers of mental health services and ultimately determine who social workers work with.

Decisions on eligibility for mental health services are based on diagnostic criteria for mental health issues specified in the *Diagnostic and Statistical Manual* (DSM) of the American Psychiatrists Association or the *International Classification of Disorders* (ICD) of the World Health Organisation. Not only does the person need to appear to be in need of psychiatric care, treatment must be available for them to remain 'involuntary'. The issue of refusal of treatment is contentious as it refers to 'necessary treatment'. 'Treatment' is frequently referred to in mental health legislation and policy. In practice, 'treatment' is often synonymous with 'medication'. Again this is open to interpretation; medical practitioners often disagree as to the most appropriate treatment regime.

The Supreme Court of Western Australia found in favour of a woman who was appealing against her involuntary hospitalisation due to 'refusal of treatment'. The court revoked her involuntary status, finding that treatment also included vitamins, food and accommodation that could be provided in the community. Thus refusal of 'necessary treatment' may simply mean a person is requesting 'different treatment'. Most psychiatrists and medical practitioners in Australia operate within a Western medical model. This leaves little room for alternative 'treatment' approaches that may be more consistent with different cultures, lifestyles and beliefs. The provision 'danger to self and others' can also be applied quite broadly, with 'self-neglect' constituting 'danger to self'.

Under more recent legislation, temporary treatment orders are used to access assessment and treatment initially; this order is reviewed by the Mental Health Tribunal, who will decide if a person is to be put on a treatment order in the community. The tribunal panel includes a psychiatrist, lawyer and community member. Community members are sometimes social workers.

A treatment order must specify

treating psychiatrist
medical practitioner
reporting timelines by medical practitioner to psychiatrist
duration of the CTO – must not exceed 12 months
where the person lives.[11]

The ability to stipulate a person's place of residence means that if a person wishes to move or simply go on a holiday this must be approved, or they are in breach of the treatment order. The penalty for breaching a treatment order is compulsory hospitalisation. However, this power is not often invoked. A person could be regarded as a criminal if in breach of such an order and be apprehended by the police. This is particularly concerning for those who may not even be aware they are still on a treatment order. At times, workers think and behave as if a person is on a treatment order when in fact this is not the case. This is illustrated in a case where the Mental Health Review Board extended a treatment order for a man who claimed he was not on such an order. The Supreme Court of Victoria eventually revoked the decision of the board.[12]

Treatment orders can have positive effects by providing regular and ongoing treatment and interventions than can assist with stability and overall improvements in quality of life.[13] Yet it is the involuntary imposition of such orders that is most problematic and raises considerable ethical and human rights concerns.[14] The restrictions placed on people who are deemed mentally unwell, under the guise of health care, are extreme and in some cases more severe and lengthy than sentencing provisions in criminal legislation.

As a social worker in mental health, it soon became apparent to me that there was very little consistency in the manner in which psychiatrists and medical practitioners invoked their powers to detain someone involuntarily under the mental health legislation. Given similar circumstances, one medical practitioner would always admit while another would not. I soon learnt that much was left to the subjective decisions of medical practitioners as to their assessment of mental health issues and associated risk, with the consultant psychiatrist having overall clinical responsibility. This can cause conflict for social workers, who can be directed to follow the orders of medical staff as illustrated in the following story of Anna.

Anna was referred by her medical practitioner who believed she was psychotic and in need of psychiatric care. I visited Anna and her parents at the family home with a psychiatric nurse for an assessment interview. Anna was extremely fearful and our assessment was consistent with that of the referring medical practitioner that Anna was experiencing auditory hallucinations. After some time, Anna and her parents told us her story about how she had been having a relationship with her employer, an older married man, and how she had become pregnant to him. He had organised and paid for her to have an abortion, and soon afterwards made her position redundant. Anna was 18 years of age and the only child of an Eastern European couple who had adopted her as a baby. It was clear she meant the world to them and they were grief-stricken by what had happened. The walls of the house were covered with pictures of her holding trophies at the many beauty contests she had won over the years. Both of her parents sobbed as they told us what had happened to Anna. They feared for her future and were very embarrassed and ashamed. Anna's parents were devout Catholics and strongly opposed to abortion.

Our assessment was that the family was traumatised by what had happened and that Anna was experiencing post-traumatic stress following the abortion. We believed that in the short term a crisis intervention approach was required with intensive counselling and support.

The following day Anna was reviewed by a psychiatrist who gave her a provisional diagnosis of schizophrenia. He argued that her natural parents were quite likely to have had psychiatric problems leading to her being put up for adoption. Anna's adoptive parents started to wonder about this themselves, as they knew very little about Anna's family of origin. The psychiatrist prescribed anti-psychotic medication. Anna commenced this medication but experienced strong side effects and stopped taking it. Her parents were unhappy about the amount and strength of the medication and side effects and wanted to explore more natural remedies. The psychiatrist insisted she must take this medication as prescribed. Much of the focus of subsequent daily visits was to convince Anna to take the medication and to supervise her taking it. Very little focus, if any was on counselling about the trauma she had experienced.

It became quite apparent that Anna was not going to take the medication, unless she was doing so under supervision from mental health workers, and that her parents were supporting her in this behaviour. At this point, Anna was deemed uncooperative and her parents were no longer seen as allies or even carers but rather as 'colluding' with her. The psychiatrist decided that he would hospitalise Anna for 'refusing necessary treatment'.

Not surprisingly, Anna refused to go to hospital and her parents again supported her in this decision. In fact, at this point they said they no longer wanted our service to visit and that they would organise for a private psychiatrist to see Anna. The psychiatrist did not feel confident that this would happen and made Anna a compulsory patient under the Mental Health Act. Still she refused to go to hospital. The psychiatrist then ordered the psychiatric nurse and me to arrange for Anna's hospitalisation and to simply tell her she had no choice in the matter. Anna still refused and again the family asked us not to return. We reported back the psychiatrist what had happened and he ordered us to return, against Anna's and her parents' wishes, with the police, to enforce the order for her compulsory hospitalisation.

Neither the nurse nor I wanted to do so and told the psychiatrist this. He became angry at our questioning of his decision and insisted we go immediately and bring her into the hospital. We very reluctantly arranged to meet the police at the house and took Anna to the hospital. This caused further trauma and humiliation to Anna and her parents as she was taken by the police from her home and escorted to hospital.

Anna was put in a ward for young people who were experiencing a first episode of psychosis. This was an 'open' ward, as opposed to a 'closed or secure' ward that is locked at all times. Even though she was on an open ward, she retained her involuntary patient status. When her parents came to visit , they simply took her home in the car with them. The family were once again referred back to us to arrange for Anna's return to the hospital. Her parents said that they took Anna home because she was frightened when other patients had told her that if she upset the nursing staff they would put her in a cage. It seems Anna confused 'cage' for 'Cade', the name of the hospital's secure ward.[15]

Interestingly, even though her mental state remained the same as when she was hospitalised, the psychiatrist no longer took any particular interest and did not insist she be returned to the hospital. The family was left to make their own private arrangements and we had no further contact with them.

Mental health policy

The 1990s saw the integration of psychiatric services with mainstream public general hospital services and the closure of stand-alone psychiatric hospitals. In Victoria, Royal Park Psychiatric Hospital was, in 2000, the last psychiatric hospital to close. It was argued that services delivered in mainstream community settings reduced the stigma associated with mental health issues. The result has been major changes for users of mental health services, their families and staff, nursing personnel in particular. While some patients had not lived in the community for many years, likewise some staff had never worked in community settings. In 1993 a review of Australian mental health services by the Human Rights and Equal Opportunity Commission found that the inadequacy of existing community services was 'disgraceful'.[20] This led to more targeted community mental health service development as well as an increased focus on accessibility to general community services.

Of those who were identified as experiencing a mental disorder in the 1997 National Mental Health and Wellbeing profile, less than half (38 per cent) had used a health service for their mental health issues in the 12 months before the study.[21] Women were far more likely to seek assistance for mental health issues than men. Assistance was sought mostly for affective disorders and the most common health service used by both men and women was medical practitioners.

While in the past institutions were criticised for not providing adequate standards of care, community treatment has also received harsh criticism predominantly due to inadequate funding to provide the range and quality of services required in the community. Public psychiatric hospitals have now been replaced by a predominantly privatised system. Residential facilities include a limited number of 'acute' psychiatric beds in general hospitals and community-based housing that provide 'continuing care' and 'psychosocial rehabilitation'. Specialist in-patient facilities are provided in the area of psycho-geriatrics and forensic psychiatry. Community services include crisis assessment treatment teams (CATT) mobile support teams (MST) and community mental health centres. There are also a small number of statewide specialist services for dual diagnosis, dual disability, personality disorder and torture and trauma. In Victoria, ambulance services have responsibility for transporting people for a psychiatric hospital admission rather than the police unless the person is deemed dangerous. Some areas have crisis mobile response teams that include both the police and mental health crisis workers. These services are called Police and Community Emergency Response (PACER) and are viewed favourably by the police. Response times are reduced when compared with those of mental health crisis services and if a person is hospitalised they can usually be admitted directly to the ward, bypassing the Emergency department. The police vehicles have immediate access to both police and health records. The police are very much in favour of these services yet in some jurisdictions concerns have been raised about police and mental health workers arriving together in a police vehicle as too heavy handed. Discretion needs to be applied, with these PACER services only used when a police response is deemed necessary. This is a more transparent approach than having police and mental health workers arrive separately with cars hidden from the view of a person's home. Workers need to be up front when they work with police rather than trying to pretend they have had no involvement in fear of damaging their therapeutic relationship. The reality is that regardless of a person's mental state they are quick to pick up on the duplicity of workers and this is what is most damaging to the provision of appropriate mental health care.

Katrina was in a secure psychiatric ward in a general hospital on the evening of your daughter's 21st birthday. Unbeknown to her, the school which her younger children aged six and eight years sporadically attended called Child Protection, as they believed she was not caring appropriately for her young children because she was not requiring them to attend school. When Child Protection visited, they expressed concern about the clutter and mess in Katrina's house. Katrina explained that she had been feeling physically and emotionally exhausted and was grieving the recent death of her husband. Much of the so-called clutter in the house was his belongings that she needed to sort through. Katrina did not have anyone to help her care for the children, or herself for that matter, since her husband died. She was angry and disappointed with the school and the Child Protection workers for their criticisms of her as a mother. On the evening of the visit by Child Protection workers, an ambulance and the police came to her house and forcibly took her to the local hospital, where she was admitted involuntarily in the acute secure psychiatric ward. She was completely taken by surprise as no one had told her they were coming. She guessed that they had been called by the social worker from Child Protection. Katrina felt extremely distressed and let down by all of the workers involved with her and her children.

She asked to see the hospital social worker and had a number of questions she wanted answers to, including

Why was I treated with such disrespect by the school, police and Child Protection workers?

Why did these people attack me when I was at my lowest point?

> Rather than criticising me for having a messy house, why didn't they offer help to get it sorted?
>
> Why didn't the school appeal to the community and say, 'There's a family that needs assistance. Can anyone help?'
>
> Why can't I be with my daughter on her 21st birthday?
>
> How might you respond to Katrina using a recovery approach?

Community treatment, and the integration of psychiatric services within the general hospital system, has both advantages and disadvantages. The advantages are that it may be less stigmatising and more socially acceptable to be admitted to a general hospital rather than a psychiatric hospital. It is also much easier for family and friends to visit. However, it is much harder to get admitted. This is due to the relatively small number of psychiatric beds now available. While in the past people had lengthy admissions to psychiatric hospitals and often found it difficult to get out, the reverse is true today, with people finding it difficult to get in to hospital. Once in, it is difficult to stay for more than a week due to pressures for early discharge. This is particularly problematic in instances of changes of medication, with some medications for depression taking up to a fortnight for any therapeutic benefit. Admissions to psychiatric hospitals in the past were relatively easy if a bed was available. However, integrated services generally require that people be admitted through the accident and emergency department and wait in line.

Recent legislation makes provision for advance directives that a person completes when mentally competent. This directive details the treatment they do and do not want to receive when mentally unwell. This can be helpful for knowing a person's wishes but unfortunately these directives are often over-ridden at the discretion of the treating medical officer during a hospital admission. Nonetheless, workers should encourage people to complete these advance directive statements and have them lodged on their health records and advocate for the plan to be followed wherever possible. If a person's advance directive is not followed, reasons must be provided by the treating practitioner.

People are now living in the community with greater levels of mental disturbance. Increased pressure is put on family and friends and general community health and welfare services to provide care that was the responsibility of psychiatric hospitals in the past. Stigma may be increased rather than decreased due to the public display of disturbed behaviours that can cause extreme distress and embarrassment for the person affected and family members.

The dominant model of mental health service delivery is primary care partnerships in the community, with services provided primarily by medical practitioners with assistance from other health care workers or counsellors. However, only a small minority of people treated for mental health concerns are actually referred on to specialist mental health services, and this is often for a short-term intervention only.[22] This may occur in the community or a short-term acute hospitalisation, with the person soon returning to the primary carer.

Five main target areas for action were identified in the Council of Australian Governments (COAG) National Action Plan on Mental Health 2006–2011:

promotion, prevention and early intervention;

integrating and improving the care system;

participation in the community and employment including accommodation;

coordinating care; and

increasing workforce capacity.

Each state and territory of Australia has developed an Individual Implementation Plan, identifying priority areas for service development and investment. The COAG plan was a further step in the mental health service reform agenda in Australia supporting the shift of mental health services from psychiatric hospitals to the community. Subsequent iterations of the COAG plan were focused on similar priorities to progress this agenda.

Medicare agreements under the federal health insurance scheme provided funding to each state and territory to develop this new service system resulting in a range of mental health reform strategies, such as *Because Mental Health Matters; The Victorian Mental Health Reform Strategy 2009–2019*. A focus of all these strategies is on the integration of mental health services with mainstream health and human services with psychiatric in-patient units re-located to general hospitals. Unfortunately, the development of community-based services across Australia has not met the needs created by the deinstitutionalisation of mental health services with state and territory variations disparate and ad hoc. Australian Mental Health Social Work advocate Dr. Valerie Gerrand is critical of the overall Australian service system for a lack of agreed implementation measures, and on behalf of the Australian Association of Social Workers (AASW) has called for a national blueprint to identify where the gaps in services are in each state and territory and how these will be addressed. This blueprint would include both public and private clinical treatment and disability support services.

This changing policy context has seen the expansion of the role of social workers in mental health as both providers of public and private services to include comprehensive needs assessment focusing on psychological responses to mental health issues, housing, education, employment, consumer and carer rights, and participation as equal members of the treating team. Social workers understand the broader political and socio-economic context of consumers and carers and are skilled at strategies that engender hope using a strengths perspective.

Evidence-based practice and managed care

Alongside these expanded settings has been an increased emphasis on evidence based practice. Evidence-based practice has strongly influenced what has come to be known as managed care. The main features of managed care are time limited services and outcome measures to control accessibility, utilisation and costs. Various types of managed care can be seen in operation in Britain, the United States and Australia. This is amidst widespread concerns that an already vulnerable population, those with severe and persistent mental health issues, such as persistent schizophrenia will be placed at increased risk rather than being provided long term care and integrated services. It is generally acknowledged that the expertise for working with these people lies in public, rather than private mental health services. In her longitudinal study of social workers in a public-managed care service in America, Scheid found that they were all 'deeply concerned about the quality of care received by their clients and denials for needed services'. Critical attitudes to managed care, lack of professional autonomy and disagreement with service priorities contributed to emotional exhaustion, and ultimately burn out.

Rather than cost savings, Mechanic argues that what is occurring is in fact cost shifting to the community, borne by clients and their families and workers. He also notes the resultant changes in the nature of relationships brought about by managed care in the relationship between mental health consumers and service providers as workers perform the role of gatekeeper to reduce costs. Relationships between service providers are altered with services rendered reviewed by third parties. Scheid's study findings suggest that whilst third party reviews may increase accountability they decrease autonomy and limit the worker's ability to provide quality care, impacting negatively on the development of a trusting relationship. In their work on stigma and mental health issues, Link and Phelan highlight the structural disadvantage that can occur with policies that provide more coverage for some services or people over others. The Better Outcomes and Better Access federal government initiatives are two examples of managed care in Australia.

Better outcomes and better access

In 2001 the federal Liberal government introduced the Better Outcomes in Mental Health Care initiative. The aim was to improve the quality of care provided through general practice to people with mental health issues, particularly those with chronic and complex mental health needs. Medical practitioners could refer to allied health professionals for approved focused psychological strategies (FPS) under the Access to Allied Psychological Services (ATAPS) program.[23] Allied health professionals included accredited mental health social workers (AMHSWs) psychologists, mental health nurses and Aboriginal and Torres Strait Islander health workers. Successive budgets of the federal Labour government have continued to support the Better Outcomes program. Funding for these services was provided to Divisions of General Practice to broker allied mental health services for patients with severe mental health issues. The funding model was to allow for flexibility in the development of service delivery models best suited to local needs. As a result, a range of diverse models have developed and continue to operate around Australia.

In 2005, serious concerns were raised about access to appropriate mental health services by the Mental Health Council of Australia, the Brain and Mind Research Institute and the Human Rights and Equal Opportunity Commission. These were particularly in relation to the legislative context used to determine a person ineligible for treatment by mental health services, if they did not meet set psychiatric diagnostic criteria. For those deemed eligible for services, these were considered to be difficult to access and of varying quality; this situation was exacerbated for those living in rural and remote locations.[24]

The Better Outcomes initiative provided a foundation for the Mental Health Better Access program under the National Action Plan on Mental Health 2006–2011. On 1 November 2006, the Howard Liberal federal government introduced the Medicare-funded Better Access to Mental Health Care program to extend the role of medical practitioners, and allied health workers, in the early intervention and management of people with mental disorders. Under the plan, diagnostic categories for service eligibility were also extended. Referrals could now be made to social workers under a GP mental health care plan, or directly by psychiatrists or paediatricians from eligible Medicare services.[25] The professional body, the Australian Association of Social Workers (AASW) welcomed these policy developments highlighting the important role of social workers in assisting people to live meaningful and productive lives in the community.[26] Central to this role is the development of effective relationships between consumers, carers and service providers in all aspects of mental health care.[27]

Concerns have been raised about the reduction in the numbers of services to be funded. For many, particularly those experiencing major difficulties, more long term interventions are required. The 2006 National Action Plan further emphasised promotion and prevention as well as early intervention. This included improved access to mental health services for Indigenous people and rural communities, stable and supported accommodation and meaningful community participation.[28] A focus was on recovery and living well in the community, with full participation and opportunities in education, employment, recreation and social activities.

Improved coordination of mental health services and building workforce capacity was also a main feature of the plan. Medical practitioners continue to play a central role in the provision of mental heath care, and referrals to allied health professionals, and are the first point of contact for many people experiencing mental heath difficulties. Opportunities arose for social workers in psycho-social rehabilitation services and in particular supported education and employment services, as well as being providers of Medicare-approved FPS.[29]

Under the Medicare Better Access program, accredited mental health social workers (AMSHWs) are eligible to apply to Medicare Australia for a provider number and receive rebates for a limited number of FPS delivered to individuals and/or groups. Upon registration with Medicare, AMHSWs are automatically eligible to claim benefits for allied health services provided under the federal government Better Outcomes in Mental Health Care and the Better Access initiatives. FPS services are also provided by AMHSWs to entitled veterans registered with the Department of Veterans Affairs as well as non-directive pregnancy support counselling services. AMHSWs are registered with Medicare as having the knowledge, skills and experience to competently deliver approved focused psychological strategies (FPS) services.[30]

Mental health practice standards

The AASW has developed Mental Health Practice Standards[31] in response to paradigm shifts in mental health, the challenge of evidence-based practice models, increased recognition of human rights and collaborative work with consumers and carers.[32] These include standards for direct practice, service management, organisational development and systems change, policy, research and evaluation, and education and professional development. Calls for a national mental health curriculum have resulted in the AASW developing specific mental health curriculum content for accredited social work education programs[33] as well as introducing mandatory continuing professional development requirements.[34] Accredited mental health social workers are required to possess knowledge of mental health legislation, policy, programs and of the broader network of services. They are to be familiar with currently used diagnostic frameworks and treatment approaches and the implications of these. Also they are to be aware of interdisciplinary team functions including the roles of other disciplines.[35] Evidence of these practice standards is now required for accreditation to practise as a mental health social worker for registration with Medicare Australia.[36]

Since 1992, the National Mental Health Policy has laid the foundations for the development of national practice standards in mental health, as part of the National Mental Health Strategy. The focus of these practice standards is on outcomes, quality assurance and independent review. The development of national standards has been endorsed by federal state and territory health ministers in the National Mental Health Plan.[37] On 3 December 1996, the Australian Health Ministers Advisory Council National Mental Health Working Group announced national standards for mental health applicable to all mental health services in Australia. The intention of the standards was to reflect a strong commitment to human rights, dignity and empowerment. Standards were included for rights, safety, confidentiality and privacy. Consumer participation and carer participation were to occur at all levels of service planning and delivery with sensitivity to cultural differences. Services were to be developed in an integrated manner that focused on mental health promotion and community acceptance.[38]

A distinction was made between 'mental disorders' and 'mental health problems'. According to the National Mental Health Practice Standards, a 'mental disorder' is a significant impairment of an individual's cognitive, affective and/ or relational abilities, which may require intervention and may be a recognised, medically diagnosable illness or disorder. A 'mental health problem' is a disruption in the interactions between the individual, the group and the environment producing a diminished state of mental health.[39]

The United Nations Principles for the Protection of Persons with Mental Health Issues guided the development of these standards.[40] Recommendations were made for implementation and monitoring. However, the application of these standards was to be determined by local relevance and applicability with the standards to be used 'as much as possible.' Thus, much was left to discretion at a local level.

The following story of Julie describes an incident that challenged my professional social work ethics and practice standards and those of my nursing colleague.

Julie was a young pregnant woman in her late teens to early twenties who had recently arrived in the area. A woman who ran a boarding house referred Julie to the local mental health centre. A medical practitioner at the centre assessed her. She reported that Julie was 'hallucinating' and experiencing 'paranoid delusions'. She called a psychiatric nurse and myself into her office and told us that she was concerned about Julie's mental state and stage of pregnancy. Julie appeared to be close to the end of the first trimester. The medical practitioner told us that she had arranged for Julie to have an abortion the following day and we were to take her.

When we asked about the woman's consent to the abortion, we were advised that she was unable to give it due to her mental state. When I expressed my concerns about having the pregnancy terminated without Julie's consent, I was construed as being difficult. The medical practitioner took me aside and said in private, 'It is highly likely she has schizophrenia. For all we know, the father also has schizophrenia. She is obviously not caring for herself and the foetus, so what hope does this baby have if it does survive?' I then went and spoke to the consultant psychiatrist, who I hoped might see things differently. However, he supported the view of the medical practitioner and it was arranged that the nurse and I would take Julie for an abortion the following morning.

That evening, the nurse and I spoke at length over the phone about our ethical concerns. We both felt strongly that Julie should have a say in the decision to terminate the pregnancy and if she was unable to do so the termination should not proceed. We decided not to follow the medical practitioner's orders and did not arrive to take Julie to the scheduled appointment.

The next morning we were both called in to see the psychiatrist, who was obviously angry we had not followed his instructions. When I said we had discussed it that evening and decided we could not ahead without Julie's consent due to our professional ethical concerns, he replied that he had obviously sent the wrong people to do the job. He then referred to my own advanced stage of pregnancy at the time and used this as his justification. We later found out that Julie had moved out early that morning and was no longer at the boarding house when we were scheduled to arrive.

The stories of Julie and of Anna, earlier in the chapter, highlight the power of psychiatrists in mental health settings.

Clearly, Anna and her family were not allowed to reject mental health services and the treatment prescribed even though this was their expressed wish. The dominance of medical interventions over psychological and social interventions was evident in both situations. With Anna, the battle over the medication took precedence over counselling for the trauma she had experienced, as well as industrial issues related to her unfair dismissal.

In Julie's case, I was so preoccupied with the dilemma around the termination of the pregnancy that I did not have the opportunity to even meet with Julie to establish a working relationship with her to be able to conduct a social work assessment, or to try and find any family or friends or health and welfare agencies that might have been able to assist.

Both Anna and Julie were simply denied many basic human rights.

Confidentiality and documentation

According to mental health legislation, the National Mental Health Practice Standards, social work practice standards and the social work code of ethics, confidentiality is to be respected and maintained. Personal information is only to be provided to health professionals outside the mental health service, carers and other agencies or people with the informed consent of the person concerned.[41] Both clinical and service development activities are to be recorded to assist in the effective management and delivery of services. The 'individual care plan' of each person is to be documented to include 'relevant history, assessment, investigations, diagnosis, treatment and support services required, other service providers, progress, follow-up details and outcomes'.[42] This information is to be factual and comprehensive to serve as a sequential record of the person's mental health state, treatment and care provided and outcomes. It is to be accessible throughout all components of the mental health network involved in the person's care and people are provided with opportunities to access their records. Confidentiality is to be maintained; this information is only accessible by authorised persons.

Confidentiality in social work is qualified and therefore necessarily not absolute. Social workers need to be honest with the person from the start about the limits to confidentiality including the duty to warn of danger to self or others and bureaucratic disclosures within and between agencies. Unwarranted disclosures are not to be made particularly those that might affect the person's interests, autonomy, reputation, standing and feelings.[43]

If confidentiality is to be breached, it is important that this is done under legal or authorised directives through the civil duty to prevent harm. The AASW Code of Ethics refers to the revealing of information for a lawful excuse when 'compelling legal or ethical issues prevail'.[44] This is done within an assessment of the level of perceived risk in doing so.

The application of confidentiality is complex particularly if under the mental health legislation a person is deemed mentally unfit. Information about a person can be given without consent in the following situations:

> to a primary carer because the information is reasonably required for the care of the person to whom it relates in connection with further treatment of the person
> to a court in the course of criminal proceedings
> under prescribed circumstances to the Secretary of the Department of Human Services.

Confidentiality is often not fully understood or applied in relation to the provision of information to carers. Carers are still often denied information because it is seen as confidential, particularly if the person has requested they not be told. This is particularly problematic in situations where a person has portrayed the primary carer as a problem or hostile. This is not unusual when people are experiencing paranoid delusions as often those who are closest to them are the subject of such delusions. In these circumstances, third-party accounts are useful as well as a detailed history of relationships prior to the person becoming unwell. Gary's account in Chapter 9 illustrates the frustration and impotency he and his family experienced before his brother Ian's death by suicide. Apart from regular appointments with a psychiatrist, Ian spent most of his time at home alone in his bedroom. Family contact with the psychiatrist occurred only after his brother's death. The warning here is 'Do not take confidentiality to the grave'.[45]

Likewise, the account of the mother in the previous chapter who did not know where her son was when he was in greatest need, and sleeping on the streets and mentally quite unwell, also highlights the harm caused by workers not contacting and collaborating with carers. Even though the legislation has been strengthened for the provision of information to carers, workers still refuse to do so, referring to confidentially guidelines they are following that are in actual breach of current mental health legislation. Such practices are causing considerable pain and harm to consumers, carers and families. Workers need to be held to account for this terribly misguided basic denial of a person's human rights and access to the care and supports they need outside of mental health services.

In accordance with the AASW Code of Ethics, social workers must respect the right of clients to a relationship based on trust, privacy and confidentiality and to use information gathered responsibly. This includes gaining informed consent for the use, collection and sharing of information about the client. Often this is in writing and includes consideration of the person's mental capacity to make an informed decision. It is important that the person fully understands what they are consenting to and freely agrees to this. Confidentiality is underpinned by privacy issues. When collecting and recording this information, it is essential that social workers take care to respect the client's rights to privacy and only collect and record necessary information.

Privacy and safety

A safe environment for consumers, carers, family, staff and the community must be maintained. This includes physical, psychological, emotional, spiritual, environmental and cultural safety. Treatment and support services need to ensure that the person is protected from physical, sexual and financial abuse and exploitation. Consumers are to be given the opportunity to access a worker of the same gender if this is preferred. Adequate personal space is to be provided with control over, and safety of, personal belongings in in-patient settings. In hospital and residential settings, people are to be given choices concerning surroundings and daily routine, and control of these, where possible. Adequate private space, with appropriate flexibility, is to be provided in hospitals for visits by family, friends, workers and others who are providing support with adequate play space for children. Likewise, appropriate space and privacy is to be provided for people in order to practise their religious, spiritual and cultural beliefs.

Safety for workers includes policies, procedures, security measures and appropriate resource allocations. Policies and procedures relate to staffing levels, debriefing processes, transport, complaints and critical incident reporting. Access to another staff member is to be provided at all times to lone workers. This creates a dilemma for social workers in private practice who may be working alone. Continuing education on understanding and managing difficult behaviours is to be provided so that workers can respond safely and appropriately.

While the national and social work practice standards provide for safety and privacy, women continue to report feeling vulnerable in mixed-gender hospital wards.[46] Attention to issues of safety and privacy are particularly important due to the high levels of past abuse many women have suffered, combined with the vulnerabilities arising from their current mental and emotional state. The possible risks of further abuse, harassment or intimidation within the hospital setting need to be minimised if a positive therapeutic environment is to be provided. This includes the physical environment, such as the design of sleeping areas, bathroom facilities, recreational areas, visiting areas and high-dependency areas.[47]

For many years now, women have complained about sexual harassment and assault by both patients and staff in mixed psychiatric wards, but these complaints have fallen on deaf ears. This is even more disturbing when such assaults are occurring in 'closed' or secure wards. The combined factors of lack of privacy and use of sleeping medications, often in conjunction with the sedation effects of major tranquillisers to treat psychosis, increase levels of vulnerability, particularly during evenings when staffing levels are reduced.[48]

While review and complaints processes are in place, a major obstacle to a fair hearing is lack of credibility. A person who is deemed 'mentally unwell' is often not believed.[49] If rights violations have occurred in situations where there are no witnesses or the only witnesses are other people deemed to be mentally unwell, the likelihood of a complaint being treated seriously is negligible.

Rights, review and complaints procedures[50]

Mental health legislation provides psychiatrists with extraordinary powers to limit or deny a person's civil liberties. The Victorian Mental Health Legal Service draws attention to the denial of basic human rights to people with a mental health issue that members of the general community often take for granted.[51] This includes rights to freedom and to be treated as an equal member of society, to receive assistance when you want it and to be cared for and protected, but also to be able to reject help if you do not want it. Other basic rights include the right to be believed and defend yourself against allegations, while not being held accountable when deemed to be less competent.

The National Mental Health Practice Standards make provision for the protection of the rights of individuals with mental health issues. A written statement, in language that the person and carer/s can understand, of a person's rights and responsibilities must be provided as soon as possible after commencing with a mental health service. Also, information is to be provided to consumers and carers about mental health and support services, mental disorders, mental health issues and treatments. Rights include access to interpreters and advocacy services, and choice of health care practitioners. This is not always possible, as choices, particularly in in-patient settings, are often limited to staff available. These are to be reflected in policies and procedures at all levels, with information on complaints processes readily accessible. It is the responsibility of workers to inform consumers of decisions that have been made and their rights. This includes information about review and complaints mechanisms and processes, and how to lodge an appeal against treatment or involuntary detention. The United Nations Principles for the Care and Protection of Persons with Mental health issues require a second opinion and review of decisions for involuntary detention. Recent mental health legislation makes provision for an independent second opinion. However, in practice this is provided by the staff in the hospital the person is admitted to and as such cannot be truly considered to be independent. Each state and territory of Australia has a mental health review tribunal that hears appeals from people who have been placed on a temporary treatment order or hospitalised involuntarily.[52] Mental health review boards consist of three members whose backgrounds include law, psychiatry and the community. The Supreme Court hears appeals against decisions of the mental health review boards.

In addition to general review procedures, complaints procedures need to be in place to provide an immediate response to threats of intimidation or abuse.[53] Internal avenues of complaint are the case manager, service manager or complaints officer. External avenues of complaint include the Mental Health Services Commissioner, who investigates complaints about health services; the Ombudsman determines complaints about government departments and agencies. Under mental health legislation, the Chief Psychiatrist has powers to investigate complaints about mental health services; community visitors attend mental health services to assess standards of care. Mental Health Legal Centres can arrange representation before the Mental Health Review Board and assist with other legal matters; the Office of the Public Advocate is also available to assist and advise people with mental health issues. Nonetheless, even with such an array of complaints mechanisms it is difficult to complain about those who are more powerful, particularly when you are vulnerable and reliant upon their care. Often people feel more confident to complain once they have left a service due to fears of retribution. Given the local focus of mental health services a person with ongoing mental health issues may always rely on such services.

Conclusion

Social work practice in mental health is guided by legislation, policy, practice standards and professional ethics. Mental health legislation and policy bestows extraordinary powers on psychiatrists and medical practitioners to determine who is deemed mentally ill and methods of treatment. Both the national and social work practice standards in mental health validate the importance of social assessments and interventions and provide a useful guide for social work practice in mental health. Due to the involuntary nature of many of the practices in mental health, issues of human rights are paramount. Multidisciplinary collaboration with individuals and families, utilising a range of services, is required for the achievement of best outcomes. A particular challenge for social workers is how to work in a manner that is consistent with practice standards, professional values and ethics, in the best interests of the client, in instances where involuntary interventions are deemed necessary and basic human rights are denied.

Reflection

What is the main legislation relevant for your practice as a social worker?

If you were experiencing mental health issues and were in need of assistance, how would you like to be treated? Would this include restrictions on your liberties and denial of rights and interventions using force such as restraint?

As a social worker, how might you implement the provisions in the legislation to apprehend, search, enter premises, transport and restrain people against their wishes? Is this something that you might do as a social worker? If not why not?

Should Julie have been allowed to keep her baby? Whose decision is it if she is assessed as not mentally competent to make this decision herself?

5

Theory

Many social workers find it difficult to establish meaningful links between theory and practice, or to acknowledge the important contribution of theoretical frameworks in their daily work. In order to be effective social workers, we need to have a view about what we are doing that will guide our practice. Theories provide us with different ways of viewing and explaining the same phenomena. It is important that social workers can clearly articulate what they are doing and provide reasons why. Social workers cannot afford to make and use generalisations that are not grounded in the bodies of knowledge relevant to social work and social and emotional well-being. Theory offers accumulated understandings of problems and issues that can lead to improvements in policies and practices in social and emotional well-being. The clear articulation of different approaches to, or perspectives on, mental health allows others greater insights and understandings about the basic premises informing the social work approach as well as likely outcomes. Explanations provide reasons for outcomes with accountability to those using services, service managers, politicians, bureaucrats and the general public. This in turn provides justifications for approaches to social work practice and interventions used.[1] Personal reflection and the application of relevant theory provide insights and understandings that inform a professional response.

In this chapter, the social theories that guide practices in mental health services today are discussed. This includes consideration of Marxist, structural, feminist, anti-oppressive and anti-discriminatory, and postmodernist critical theories.

Biological

Human service workers need to consider how dominant medical models impact upon their work with people using mental health services. According to biological or physiological theories, certain people have a genetic predisposition to developing mental health issues. Physical, psychological and social stressors can trigger this. Heredity determines our physiological make-up including skin, hair and eye colour and physique. Heredity also determines personality and temperament. These will also be affected by social interactions, but each of us has a genetic endowment at birth. This includes our neurological system. The central nervous system sends and receives messages via neurotransmitters from the body's tissues and organs. Neurotransmitters are biochemical substances that influence human drives for food, sleep and sexual gratification. They also influence tolerance of stress and anxiety and associated emotional responses. Adrenalin and serotonin are two of the more commonly known neurotransmitters.[2] Research studies have found subtle, yet distinct biochemical differences between people with mental health issues and those seen as not having mental health difficulties. It is unclear, however, whether or not these biochemical differences develop before or after the onset of mental health issues.[3] People with schizophrenia have been found to have higher levels of the neurotransmitter dopamine.

Before the 1970s, social work relied upon therapeutic models of intervention heavily influenced by psychodynamic theory and systems and ecological perspectives.

Psychological

A focus of psychodynamic theory is on personality and interpersonal relationships. An emphasis is on developmental stages, personality development and unconscious processes. Developmental theory sees schizophrenia developing as a result of emotional deprivation by significant adult figures during childhood.[4] Gertrude Mahler emphasised the importance of psychological development in the first two and a half years of life. She stressed the importance of love and consistency in the caring relationship during this time from an adult figure, preferably the child's mother for emotional security in later years. Erik Erikson has developed a concept of personality development linked with biological development. He argues that psychological and physical development are linked and has identified stages of physical development and associated psychological tasks at each stage.[5]

The stages and associated developmental tasks identified by Erikson are presented in Table 5.1.

Stage		Task
early infancy	birth–1 year	trust vs mistrust
later infancy	1–3 years	autonomy vs shame and doubt
early childhood	4–5 years	initiative vs guilt
later childhood	6–11 years	industry vs inferiority
puberty and adolescence	12–20 years	ego identity vs role confusion
early adulthood	20–40 years	intimacy vs isolation
middle adulthood	40–60 years	productivity vs stagnation
late adulthood	60 years and over	ego integrity vs despair

Table 5.1: Erikson's stages of psycho-social development and developmental tasks

The ages specified by Erikson for each developmental stage are an approximate guide allowing for wide variation according to individual differences. He also saw each of these stages overlapping. Tasks are stipulated for each stage of development but Erikson's model allowed for these stages to be completed at a different time in a person's life. In early infancy, from birth to approximately 12 months, trust is established, with caring adults demonstrating love and responding to the baby's needs. In turn the baby learns to trust and love others. Many people with schizophrenia report feeling unloved and unwanted in childhood with difficulty establishing trusting and loving relationships with others in later life.[6] During later infancy, approximately one to three years of age, the child becomes more autonomous while also conforming to rules and routines. At approximately four to five years of age, early childhood, the child demonstrates increased initiative and exploration of her or his environment. Fantasy and role play of adult activity occurs, with the child often copying the parent of the same sex and adopting similar behaviours and attitudes. Positive self-esteem develops by engaging in new tasks and receiving positive feedback from significant others.

Later childhood, around six to 11 years, is characterised by industry and accomplishment, with the child having seeming boundless energy. During this stage, the child learns new intellectual, practical and social skills. The child is to be encouraged to participate in a range of group activities and interests and learn skills in cooperating with others and competing in appropriate ways. The child's self esteem develops through the positive feedback received from her or his efforts and accomplishments. In puberty and adolescence, from approximately 12 to 20 years, major changes are occurring physically and emotionally with increased sexual feelings and attractions. This period is distinguished by a desire for increased independence often associated with feelings of self-doubt and confusion. Association and identification with peers takes on increased importance with temporary rejection of parents' standards. This is seen as necessary for the development of an independent identity. In early adulthood, between the approximate ages of 20 and 40 years, the main developmental task is intimacy. This requires trust and commitment between two people. In a sexual relationship, this is characterised by love, concern and compassion. Intimacy is also a feature of long-standing friendships. Those who do not relate with others on an intimate level can be seen as aloof and unfriendly and can have difficulty establishing relationships. The main task of middle adulthood, between 40 and 60 years of age, is productivity and giving back to others. This may be in relation to children, grandchildren, mentoring younger colleagues or community action and involvement. Those who do not successfully achieve this stage are seen to be self-interested and preoccupied with their own needs to the exclusion of others'.

Erikson's final stage is late adulthood, for those aged 60 years and over. Integrity is the main developmental task and living with dignity. This requires having a sense of meaning and purpose in life as well as order. Integrity results in joy for living in contrast to despair that can develop in older people due to unresolved issues of loss and grief.

Abraham Maslow, a founding humanist psychologist, developed a hierarchy of human needs that must be met for a person to achieve psychological maturity. Maslow's hierarchy of human needs in order of attainment is

physiological needs
safety needs
love and belonging needs
esteem needs
self-actualisation needs.[7]

Physiological needs include food, water, oxygen, clothing and shelter, sleep and excretion.

Safety needs comprise predictability and reliability in physical, psychological and social arrangements. The need to love and be loved and to have a sense of belonging and emotional security is important for the development of trust, emotional security and intimacy. Self-esteem is about having a positive self-image. This develops from feelings of love and acceptance from significant others. It involves feeling competent and having a good reputation. Self-actualisation needs are concerned with achieving one's full potential.

For Maslow, it was necessary to successfully attain each level before moving to the next. This may be relevant for basic physiological needs for survival, but the other needs are not necessarily met in a chronological order. For many of those who are with mental health issues, there are often huge gaps in the areas of need identified by Maslow. In many ways it is an ideal typology only achieved by a very few. There is a temptation for workers to unwittingly judge and pathologise a person according to whether or not they have passed a particular stage. However, if Maslow's hierarchy of needs is applied more liberally, it acknowledges the complexity of people's lives, including strengths as well as areas of need.

In the 1960s, systems and ecological perspectives were used in therapeutic social work as a way of conceptualising reality. The focus was on principles of complex, adaptive systems that were continually changing, and generating new patterns of actions, interactions and meanings. Explicit assumptions were that people have a right to control their own lives. Society has an obligation to ensure that people have access to resources, services and opportunities that they need to meet various life tasks, to alleviate distress and realise their values and aspirations. When providing services, the dignity and individuality of the person must be respected, with interventions maximising client participation and self-determination. Social problems were viewed as manifestations of a breakdown in the interactions between people and their environments.[8]

Key concepts in a systems approach were 'interaction' and 'problems in living'. Interaction was seen as dynamic and constantly changing with a focus on the interconnectedness and interdependence between the person and her or his 'whole' environment and adaptation or 'goodness of fit'. The emphasis of problems in living was on life transitions, environmental pressures and interpersonal processes. The aim of interventions was to achieve balance or a 'steady state' that alleviated tensions and provided stability. This steady state was also referred to as 'homeostasis' and was likened to the thermostat on a heater. Many of the concepts and examples used were from engineering and the physical sciences.

Difficulties were seen as having a variety of causes, with multiple ways of achieving goals. The family was divided into the marital, parental and sibling sub-systems. A focus was on boundaries and transactional patterns between the three sub-systems. The idea of reciprocity was important in that if change occurs in one subsystem, change is likely to occur in another as a flow-on effect. Genograms and eco-maps were tools used for plotting family and social connections. Systems theory was used in family therapy, and social workers and other allied health professionals in mental health called themselves family therapists. Social workers in mental health were endeavouring to position themselves as professional experts in mental health alongside colleagues in psychiatry, nursing psychology, particularly in family therapy. However, in their efforts to do so, some social workers in mental health lost sight of the social aspects of their work beyond the individual and the family and the person's immediate social environment. These early writings on systems and ecological perspectives were generally from a white middle-class perspective in language that was disrespectful and disempowering.[9] Families were described as 'dysfunctional' and mothers were often blamed for being too 'enmeshed' or 'disengaged' and held responsible for family problems. Fortunately, more recent developments in family derive from a strengths approach that focuses on relationships and attachment and does not blame family members for deficits. This is particularly so in attachment-based family therapy that is showing promising results in family work with suicidal young people. The emphasis is on relationships and attachments rather than problematic behaviours.

Neither psychotherapy nor family therapy address the broader social, political and economic structures that influence issues of power and subsequent disadvantage.

Social

Critical social work theory was developed in response to the failure of psychodynamic and family systems perspectives to take adequate account of social contextual factors. These included poverty, exploitation and deprivation. Social workers have engaged, at times uncomfortably, with critical theories in the social sciences. This is particularly evident in the sociology of deviance literature that attacked social work in psychiatric settings as a form of social control under the guise of humanitarian caring.[10] I was acutely aware of this social control aspect of my work and the power imbalance, particularly when working with people on the locked ward of a psychiatric hospital. Most of these people were involuntarily hospitalised and wanted to leave. The fact that I held a key clearly made me part of a system that they saw as oppressive. Thomas Scheff criticised the professional–client relationship and the perceived superior status assumed by the mental health social worker in knowledge, attitude and influence. According to this view, social workers were defining 'pathology' against norms of 'mental health' predominantly determined by white middle-class male psychiatrists. Scheff argued that the emphasis on the professional relationship encouraged neutrality and emotional distance that had disastrous effects at both the personal and political level. At the personal level, social workers were seen as aloof and uncaring. At the political level, neutrality could imply that the social worker was aligned with the dominant social institutions and forces of oppression.

Critical theories focus upon social and structural inequalities and causes of oppression that are a part of the social context within which we all live. A critical theoretical analysis of inequalities and inequities focuses on power imbalances and how these impact upon those with mental health issues.[11] It provides a critical analysis of power relationships particularly in terms of health and social and emotional well-being, gender, age, class, ability, race, ethnicity, culture and sexual preference. A major contribution of critical theory to social and emotional well-being is the focus on issues of power, human rights and social justice. Critical social work theories include Marxist, structural, feminist, anti-oppressive and anti-discriminatory and postmodern theories.

Marxist theory

According to Marxist theory, mental health social workers are agents of 'social control'.[12] Mental health services are seen as a tool of capitalism to appease the poor, ease the consciences of the wealthy classes and ward off possible rebellion. Capitalism demands a mobile and autonomous labour supply with relationships based on the selling of individual labour power. One of the terrible costs of capitalism is the alienation and privatisation of the individual, with individualism replacing reciprocal social relationships between people. The privatised individual is necessary for both production and consumption. Increased alienation, separation from others and loneliness has increased the importance of compensatory consumption of material goods, a basic requirement of capitalism.[13] It has also led to greater prevalence of mental health issues as people are placed under more pressures with fewer supports. A Marxist analysis sees the mentally ill as victims of individualistic capitalism. Mental health social workers are regarded as a tool of capitalist welfare to contain individual and collective pressure for change, especially by rationing services and benefits to those deemed deserving. This occurs in the application of medical psychiatric diagnostic categories to determine eligibility for mental health services, including those provided by social workers.[14]

Structural theory

The goal of structural social work is to help people develop a social praxis. In other words, the aim is to assist the person to critically reflect on the personal, social, economic and political situation they are in by looking at who benefits and who suffers due to the labelling of behaviours, values, ideas or feelings as undesirable. The key task of a structural approach is analysis of how the dominant institutions define and interpret specific situations. For example, counselling women in mental health settings involves examining the relationship between what are presented as personal problems, and a capitalist social structure that perpetuates the sexist, ideological and economic oppression of women.[15]

Structural theory focuses on the power dimensions in relationships. A dialogical relationship is formed that does not involve the imposition of power by social workers over those they work with. A structural approach requires willingness by social workers to give up positions of power and privilege. This is particularly challenging, and in some situations impossible, given the statutory requirements of social workers in mental health settings and the resultant enforcement of legislation for involuntary hospitalisation or treatment orders. Workers may be instrumental in bringing about actions, such as arranging an involuntary hospitalisation of the person they are working with against the person's expressed wishes or making a referral to protective services where issues of child abuse and neglect are present. Although equality is a noble aspiration, it is sometimes not achievable in practice, particularly in mental health settings. However, the personal discomfort created by structural theory through critical reflection on the exercise of power and control means that social workers will only engage in coercive practices as a last resort and be cautious with any exercise of power. It is important for workers to be well aware of the power dimensions in their work and to openly and honestly convey these to those they are working with. To deny the existence of differences in power, and assume a relationship of equality, is denying the reality of your relationship with the person.

Many social workers find it difficult to tell a person when they plan to engage in actions against the person's wishes. A worker may make a referral to a crisis service, child protection unit or the police and not inform the person of this.

Brian was a 56-year-old man who ran his own small business. He had a long-standing diagnosis of schizophrenia and had a social worker regularly visit him and his family. The worker considered she had become a family friend, equalising power relationships, and often shared a meal with Brian and his family. On one of these visits, the worker became concerned about Brian's mental state in that he seemed to be hallucinating and delusional. Without informing Brian or his family, she contacted the local crisis team and asked them to visit him. Brian was annoyed that the crisis team had been called and assumed the social worker had contacted them. He rang the worker and angrily accused her of betraying his trust and hospitality. The worker made further contact with the crisis team, this time saying that Brian had threatened her. Brian received a visit from the crisis team and was escorted to hospital by the police and told he was considered 'a danger to others'. Brian was denied access to a lawyer at his assessment interview, even though he requested one, and was held in a locked ward against his wishes for two weeks. This was very stressful personally and financially as a small business owner. On the evening he was involuntarily hospitalised, Brian had been working all day. The day he was released he immediately returned to work. This social worker had not revealed her actions to Brian or his family, as she did not want to interfere with her relationship with him and his family. This was the worst thing she could have done, as the family felt betrayed by her and she feared for her safety. Brian admitted being angry and threatening her, but he claimed he never intended to harm her.

One way of avoiding such damaging situations is to be honest and open about statutory powers from the very start of the relationship and the exercise of these powers. This is something that needs to be continually addressed throughout the working relationship. As mentioned earlier in this chapter, people using mental health services are often on regular medication. Workers may be aware that the last time a person decided to stop taking medication, disturbed and disruptive behaviours led to an involuntary hospitalisation. It is the worker's professional responsibility to remind the person of these past events and concerns, as well as statutory powers for arranging a further involuntary hospitalisation if the situation becomes unmanageable. It is crucial that this is done in a way that conveys respect, sensitivity and understanding rather than in a threatening or coercive manner. A structural approach also requires workers to question the inappropriate use of medication and to challenge the use of medication as a means of restraint. It also highlights economic factors and the role of business, particularly questioning the influence multinational drug companies have on prescribing practices in mental health.

Social workers generally will feel very uncomfortable with both the care and control aspects of work in mental health and may ignore one or the other. I have worked with colleagues at both ends of the spectrum. I once worked with a doctor who admitted everyone we saw to hospital and another who did not admit anyone. This was more a reflection of their philosophical differences and seemingly nothing to do with levels of psychiatric disturbance. This illustrates the power of general practitioners and psychiatrists in mental health and in society, with very few successful challenges to the exercise of their powers.

Due to the discrepancies between the ideal of equality embodied in structural theory and the realities of practice, it is crucial that workers address this power dimension. It is only when workers honestly and openly address the issue of power in the relationship with those they are working with that an atmosphere of trust and respect can ensue.

Feminist theory

Feminist theory highlights the patriarchal and sexist practices in dominant social institutions, including mental health settings. Feminist social work rejects conservative determinism that women are subordinate to men due to nature. Four broad approaches to feminist theory used by social workers are liberal feminism, traditional Marxist feminism, radical feminism and socialist feminism. Liberal feminists seek opportunities for the education and professional advancement of women, equal to men, within the existing social structures. Marxist feminists assert that the oppression of women is inextricably linked to capitalism and the class system. Radical feminism focuses on the social institution of gender as the source of women's oppression. Socialist feminists argue that capitalism and sexism are inseparable and reinforce each other.[16]

Although different theories of feminist social work exist, feminist social workers have focused their efforts in five main areas. These are the manner in which social problems are defined, the development of feminist campaigns and networks, social work in statutory settings, counselling and therapy and feminist working relations.[17] In feminist social work, personal problems are defined as political, thereby focusing on social justice campaigns to increase the allocation of resources to gender specific programs and campaigns. Feminist social work in mental health identifies issues that are particularly relevant to women. These include violence, rape, incest, women's emotional welfare and women's labour. A feminist analysis highlights the fact that a high proportion of women who use mental health services are survivors of physical and/or sexual abuse as discussed in Chapter 3.

The DSM and the ICD diagnostic categories used in psychiatry do not take account of gender differences; the DSM is criticised as a 'gender-biased social construction'.[19] Similar gender patterns of psychiatric diagnoses have been observed across studies in Australia, Britain, the United States and Canada. Women are more frequently diagnosed as depressed, while men are more likely to be diagnosed as having an alcohol or other drug disorder, or a personality disorder. When women are with personality disorder, it is most likely to be a diagnosis of histrionic or borderline personality disorder.[20] The most common primary diagnoses of women using public mental health services are schizophrenic disorders, major affective disorders, other affective and somatoform disorders and acute stress disorders.[21] Women using services in the private sector are more likely to be treated for eating disorders, post-natal disorders, anxiety, affective and somatoform disorders.[22]

Sex stereotypes are reflected in the psychiatric diagnostic categories assigned to women; those women who do not conform to traditional stereotypes are often viewed as experiencing an even greater level of disturbance.[23] Women prisoners do not conform to stereotypical diagnostic categories and have an overwhelming representation in the diagnostic categories of substance abuse and personality disorder generally associated with males.[24] The higher rate of antisocial personality disorder generally assigned to men is sanctioned by society's greater tolerance, and expectation that males engage in aggressive and acting out behaviours. Yet women do not receive this sanction.[25] Female socialisation and the traditional role of caring for the emotional needs of other family members can lead women and society to blame them when things go wrong. The relationship between the diagnosis of clinical depression in women and their life circumstances has often been ignored, resulting in the woman feeling not heard and misunderstood.[26] A correlation has been found between depression in women and the combined factors of inadequate housing, low income, caring for dependent children and lack of emotional support as discussed in Chapter 3.[27] This reflects the importance of viewing women's lives within their proper context. Gerrand comments,

If a woman's life circumstances are ignored, then the opportunity for an accurate and comprehensive understanding of her problems is thereby diminished and, presumably the development of an appropriate range of responses curtailed.[28]

Research studies have found that some general practitioners and psychiatrists, particularly males, become more anxious and frustrated when treating women than they do with men. Women have been seen as presenting with vague and difficult to understand complaints.[29] Many women have also expressed feelings of frustration, feeling patronised and not taken seriously by their general practitioners.[30] This frustration appears, in part, to be related to the individual focus of diagnostic categories that are not inclusive of the broader social context of women's lives.[31]

The prescribing of psychotropic drugs for women and the use of electro-convulsive therapy are significantly higher, with more than twice the amounts, for women than men across a number of studies conducted in Australia, Britain and the United States.[32] High rates of prescription drugs used by women in the community generally are an area of major concern, with one study finding that females were twice as likely as males to be prescribed tranquillisers for the same symptoms.[33] It has been suggested that medication is routinely dispensed to women in lieu of counselling or other support.[34] On this point Raeside comments,

> The 'quick fix' of targeting specific symptoms (e.g. insomnia) is very attractive. However, this recreates what the patient has been doing for most of her life, namely using psychotropic substances to avoid painful affects and memories.[35]

Insufficient attention has been given to the physical health needs of long-term women psychiatric patients. Concerns have been raised about women's physical complaints too often being attributed to psychological causes and inadequate physical investigations undertaken as a result.[36]

Feminist social work identifies and confronts issues of gender inequality and discrimination in the workplace that impacts both upon female social workers and women using their services. The majority of social workers are women, although most senior managers in mental health and other human services are men.[37] This includes social work education, where males are also over-represented in terms of numbers and seniority. Feminist social work challenges this dichotomy and questions the impact this has on policy and service design and delivery for social work as a profession and for service users.

Anti-discriminatory and anti-oppressive theory

Anti-discriminatory and anti-oppressive theory addresses the stigma and lost opportunities people experience due to mental health issues. This includes recognition of other areas of possible discrimination, including gender, age, race and ethnicity, sexuality, family situation and economic status.[38] According to anti-oppressive and anti-discriminatory theory, there is a causal and interconnected relationship between discrimination and oppression. It is therefore necessary to deal with discrimination before oppression can be challenged. This requires openly naming injustices and discriminatory practices. However, this is often difficult, as discrimination is generally covert and people will not openly reveal discriminatory practices as discussed in relation to employment in Chapter 3.

Contemporary anti-oppressive practices are occurring within the context of globalisation, economic rationalism, the privatisation of welfare services and an increasing gap between the rich and poor in Western industrialised nations. An anti-oppressive approach requires commitment and engagement by social workers with the harsh realities of the lives of those they work with. This requires them to recognise strengths and facilitate both change and coping strategies. Access and equity and equal opportunity are central to the development of a fully inclusive society for those with mental health issues.[39]

Self-knowledge and the valuing of difference are essential for engaging in anti-oppressive practices that challenge inequality. Anti-oppressive practice requires commitment at both an intellectual and emotional level as well as practice skills for implementation. Anti-oppressive theory challenges notions of professionalism focusing on power sharing and egalitarian relationships based on shared values.[40] Anti-oppressive practice requires social workers to form strong alliances with consumers and other professionals who advocate anti-oppressive practices and activists involved in the 'new social movements'.[41] The ideas expressed in anti-discriminatory and anti-oppressive practice have been further developed, particularly within critical postmodernism. A focus is on issues of power, knowledge and difference.

Postmodern theory

It is difficult to begin a discussion of postmodernism without firstly considering 'modernism' or 'modernity'. Modernity is the term used to describe what was regarded as rational, objective knowledge of the physical and social world. It had its origins in the early seventeenth century during a period that has now become known as the European Enlightenment. The disorder, superstition and cruelty of the Middle Ages, discussed in Chapter 2, was to be replaced by order, reason and universal knowledge. The application of reason to both the natural and social world saw the development of disciplines and professions such as physical sciences, medicine, economics and engineering. This enabled new methods and means of capitalist production that were transforming Western countries. Social problems were seen as an inevitable consequence of social change. Scientific knowledge of the social world was derived from the social sciences and used to manage these social problems. Grand theories were developed to explain this new social order and the negative effects of industrialisation, including disease, poverty and the exploitation and alienation of people. These include grand theories on mental health issues, racial purity, the market economy, the inferiority of women, the family and more recently globalisation and the new world order. These dominant beliefs have been incorporated into policies and professional practices such as psychiatric classification and diagnosis and psycho-social models of family dysfunction.

Postmodern critiques of modernism have focused on its claims of Western reason, universality and objectivity, as well as its totalitarian features. Postmodernism focuses on difference, emphasising the experiences of those who have been excluded from modernist critiques. This includes the views of ordinary people, non-Westerners, women and members of lower socio-economic groups.[42] Examples throughout history are used to document the exploitation, cultural destruction, devastation, genocide and impoverishment that has occurred as a result of what has been viewed as progress under the guise of colonialism, imperialism and economic development.

Postmodern theory provides valuable critiques of modernity; however, it has been criticised for providing 'cultural logic' for late capitalism.[44] Much of postmodern writing reflects cynicism, disenchantment and despair with late capitalism and modernist attempts to impose reason and order. The reductionist and relativist perspective of postmodernism reduce the possibility for collective action and mass movements due to the focus on difference. It has also been criticised for reflecting the interests, concerns and lifestyle of middle-class professionals, particularly academics. The complex language of postmodernism also suggests this.

Critical postmodernism was developed in response to the self-interest and conservatism of postmodernism. It was argued that the relationship between power and knowledge required close attention by social workers.[45] In particular, it required social workers to focus on the contradictions of emancipation and domination within modernism. Critical postmodernism questioned the meta-narratives used in social work according to issues of power and control, including assumptions about social justice, rationality and equality and new forms of power, particularly professionalism and cultural production. It opposes the view that global economic and cultural modernisation espoused by corporate capitalism will result in human progress. Social work engagement is with new concepts that are neither absolute nor relativist. It is through narratives, or discourses, that knowledge is developed. The result is interactive multiple views and realities that connect with and inform the broader political, economic and social structures. In mental health, consumers' stories of their experiences of mental health services have informed the process of deinsitutionalisation and the development of mental health policy and service design and delivery. People's stories give life and humanity to clinical diagnostic categories and brusque treatment. A so-called 'schizophrenic' becomes a person with feelings, wishes and dreams rather than a patient to be treated or managed.[46]

Critical postmodernism requires social workers to recognise and respect difference while also acknowledging commonalities among diverse groups. This requires engagement with consumer groups and issues excluded by modernism including mental health, feminist, anti-racist and anti-colonial, environmental and socialist. Specific campaigns may be organised around mental health, age, class, ethnicity, gender, race, ability and sexuality.

Conclusion

Critical social work practice has been informed by Marxist theory and has its origins in the radical critique of social work in the 1970s. It has been further developed by structural social work, feminist social work and anti-discriminatory and anti-oppressive social work and postmodernism. A Marxist analysis highlights the contradictions inherent in the welfare state and the functions within it. Revolutionary change is advocated by radicals, with social workers called upon to have a far greater social and political awareness. The goal of structural social work is critical reflection on the interplay between personal, social, economic and political processes. Of central concern to structural social workers are ways in which the rich and powerful within society constrain and define the less powerful. Structural social workers focus on issues of class, gender, race and ethnicity, ability, age and sexual preference. A primary focus of social work is addressing structural inequalities as well as recognising a role for interpersonal work.

Feminist social work stresses the importance of issues of gender inequality and the connection between the personal and political. The focus of developments in anti-discriminatory and anti-oppressive practices on issues of inequality has further enriched critical social work. Postmodernism, particularly critical postmodernism, calls upon social workers to critically examine the relationship between power and knowledge and the dominant discourses used in social work practice. A central theme common to all of these approaches is the concern of social work with issues of social justice and human rights.

The next chapter presents a mental health assessment interview framework that is inclusive of biological, psychological, social, cultural and spiritual aspects of a person's life.

Reflection

What are the main contributions of theory to practice in mental health?

What theories, or aspects of theories, do you find most appealing and why?

What theories, or aspects of theories, do you have difficulty with? Provide reasons for this.

How do you integrate your own personal reflections and theory to inform your practice as a mental health social worker?

What are the potential benefits of being able to articulate your theoretical approach to others?

6

Assessment

Social workers are employed in mental health settings due to their knowledge and expertise in psycho-social assessments and interventions. This is within the context of a holistic approach that includes cultural, economic, emotional, spiritual and environmental aspects of a person's life. The social work interview is the main assessment instrument. The assessment is multidisciplinary; however, a lone worker generally conducts it. It is therefore important that the worker is able to conduct a comprehensive assessment that will result in an intervention plan including areas of further assessment and referral to workers from other disciplines as required. In this chapter, the assessment interview is discussed using a holistic approach. A guide to conducting a mental status examination is presented from a social work perspective followed by a formulation of assessment and social work diagnosis to inform intervention planning.

Assessment interview[1]

It is important that the social worker behaves in a manner that encourages the person to discuss what is happening currently, including future aspirations as well as significant contextual information and past events. It is crucial that an environment of trust and confidence is established for the person to feel as comfortable as possible disclosing personal and intimate information to a relative stranger. Once an assessment has been conducted, it is important that the social worker explains to the person, and significant others, what they think is happening and to discuss possible courses of action and likely prognosis. This component of the interview is crucial yet it is frequently overlooked or not managed well. If this does not happen, the person is likely to feel dissatisfied and not accept proposed interventions and treatment recommendations.

Consideration needs to be given to the time and place of the assessment interview as well as who should be present. A safe and relaxed atmosphere is required to encourage people to discuss fears and concerns. Sufficient time is necessary for concerns to be addressed and questions answered. Skills in interviewing are important if this is to be done well. Precision is required in eliciting critical information pertaining to the onset of problems and the relationship between onset and possible aetiological factors. Subjective meanings and interpretations are important. When people say things such as 'I'm having trouble with my nerves', or 'I'm having a breakdown', it is important to elicit the particular meaning such a statement has for them, rather than what the worker thinks it might mean. If statements such as these are not checked with the person and clarified, it is likely that false impressions will be gained resulting in misinformation and inappropriate interventions.

Non-verbal communications are important, particularly when they are reflecting strong emotions. Many workers become concerned and anxious when faced with strong emotions in an interview situation and often ignore or try to avoid addressing them. Some workers have said they simply do not know how to respond in such situations, while others are fearful that they will make the person become even more distressed and lose control of the situation. Self-knowledge and an understanding of your own personal responses in such situations is the first step in skill development in this area.

Assessment interview questions are often asked in a manner that makes them difficult to answer or that elicit a closed response and discourage open discussion. Sometimes a number of questions are put to the person at the same time, with the person generally only responding to one element of such questions. Interviews conducted in this manner result in people answering questions put directly to them in monosyllabic responses, without having the opportunity to tell their story in their own way.

It is surprising and a cause of dismay to see the number of interviews that are conducted where mental health workers neglect to introduce themselves, their workplace context, professional role and the referral information they have received. The purpose of the interview is often not stated and confidentiality, note keeping and files are not addressed. Full attention is often lacking, and workers give the impression, usually unwittingly, of lack of interest or concern, boredom, irritability or detachment by not attending appropriately to body language, including appropriate eye contact. Other concerns are a lack of tolerance of silences, avoidance or lack of time devoted to exploration of feelings and social and contextual issues. There is a danger of mental health workers only responding to concerns specific to their discipline area; for example, social workers focusing only on social issues, psychologists the inter-psychic and interpersonal, and psychiatrists and medical officers selectively responding only to physical concerns.

Referral information is an important component of an assessment. However, if referral information is too readily accepted, decisions can be made prematurely about what the person's problems are and the causes, and this may lead to inappropriate closure of the interview. All of these practices serve to distance health professionals emotionally from the people they are working with, either consciously or unconsciously. Professional distancing, however, serves a number of purposes for mental health workers. It protects them from eliciting emotional information that cannot be readily dealt with or resolved, and from being asked questions that are difficult to answer or that may not have an answer. The worker may become emotionally affected by the person's situation, feeling angry, sad or overwhelmed and personally threatened. It is 'safer' for workers, particularly psychiatrists and medical practitioners, to focus on symptoms that can be treated medically rather than risk getting out of depth in exploring a person's emotions. A consequence of responding to symptoms is the lack of acknowledgment of the person's emotional and psychological state, social situation and the function served by the symptoms. This approach is particularly problematic in cultures where psychological and emotional concerns are almost invariably expressed as physical symptoms. Poor compliance with medical treatment and interventions has been linked with this distancing or business-like approach. A lack of acknowledgment of psychological, social, environmental and spiritual factors, coupled with a lack of feedback and poor explanation of diagnosis and prognosis, renders much of the treatment and interventions offered ineffective. This situation is particularly concerning given the increasing responsibilities general practitioners now have for early detection and management of mental health issues under primary care partnership models.

Social work interview

The social work interview deals with power imbalances, changes in perception of issues, and patterns of communication. This practice relies upon the person telling her or his story, listing issues in order of priority and making decisions and commitments. The social work interview is concerned with both personal and social change and development.[2]

Interviewing skills for assessment include skilled observations, effective listening, non-verbal communication, empathy, paraphrasing and questioning.[3] Mirroring is a particularly useful skill.

Skye was referred to the crisis team by her general practitioner. I visited her at home with a nursing colleague, Laura. Skye was 18 years of age and was experiencing a first episode of psychosis. Skye's parents let us in the house to find Skye curled up in a ball on the floor in the lounge room with her head tucked in between her legs. She did not respond to any efforts we made at communicating with her. I went into the kitchen with Skye's parents and watched as Laura also curled herself up in a ball next to Skye and just sat there with her in the same position, head tucked between her legs. Eventually Skye started to gradually unfurl and as she did so Laura did as well. Sitting on the floor together, Laura was able to develop Skye's trust, with Laura opening up and telling her how she was feeling and what had happened to her as well as the disturbing thoughts and voices she was experiencing.

Other skills consistent with a critical theoretical approach to practice include believing the person and clear contracting about your work with them.[4] Being believed is something that we generally take for granted yet unfortunately this is not so for people who use mental health services as discussed in Chapter 4. It is therefore important for workers to believe what a person is saying and try to understand the meaning of this. Creating a safe space requires attention to the time and place of interview, who is present or absent, and creating an environment of trust and respect. Limits of confidentiality must be clear so that a person is aware of the consequences of sharing information with a worker.[5]

Demystifying the social work contact is a skill that requires social workers to communicate directly with those they are working with in language that is appropriate and easily understood and demystifying so-called professional behaviours. Psychiatrists use a range of unfamiliar terms when conducting an assessment, particularly a mental status examination. The danger in adopting this language is that the person is objectified and compartmentalised into categories. However, if this language is not known or understood, it is difficult for social workers and other mental health workers to communicate with psychiatrists in language with shared meanings and understandings. It is important that examples are offered to illustrate the terms used. However, if social workers do not comprehend the terms, it means that consumers who are not medically trained are also not likely to understand them. It is therefore the responsibility of social workers to communicate in language that is appropriate and will be understood and beneficial to those they are working with. Many people who use mental health services describe a process that is often very disempowering and alienating. It is important that assessment interviews are conducted in a manner that is respectful and empowering. This includes the appropriate sharing of information, resources and file notes.[6] Critical questioning is a useful skill for asking questions in a way that gets the person to think about their situation in a way that goes beyond information collected from open and closed questions and is particularly useful when conducting a mental status examination. It is about looking for meanings and understandings for particular behaviours and symptoms.

Holistic approach to assessment

A bio-psycho-social assessment is done with consideration of a person's gender, age, cultural background, spiritual beliefs and environmental and social context. As mentioned in the previous chapter, one of the main criticisms of the DSM is that diagnostic and assessment criteria do not take adequate account of gender, cultural and spiritual differences and a person's social circumstances and environment.[7] In this chapter, the assessment pro forma generally used within adult mental health services is further developed to allow for the addition of these crucial dimensions of assessment and is presented in the Appendix. Each of the categories included in the assessment is discussed below.

Presenting situation

Assessment of the presenting situation includes reasons for referral and circumstances that have precipitated the referral. The onset, cause and duration of problems and symptoms are examined, as well as current thoughts and behaviours, and attempted solutions and responses. The person's general health and eating and sleeping patterns at the time of assessment are explored. This assessment is within the social context of the person's housing and income, family and significant relationships. A focus is on getting to know the person and their strengths and resources and the reality of their lives.

Physical health

A full physical examination is a part of the assessment in a hospital setting to consider possible biological explanations for current thinking and behaviour. Confusion and changes in behaviour, that may appear to be signs and symptoms of mental health issues, may simply be the result of a physical complaint such as a urinary tract infection or an adverse reaction to a combination of medications. However, with most people now being cared for in the community rather than in hospital, these physical assessments are no longer routinely conducted. Social workers therefore need to be alert to the person's physical health, current medications and call in the expertise of medical practitioners and other allied health staff as required. In the community, it is generally the person's general practitioner, if they have one, who is likely to have a comprehensive knowledge and history of the person's health.

Personal and social history

Assessment of personal and social history includes the person's cultural and spiritual background, developmental history, sexuality, education and employment, housing, social history and pre-morbid personality. Cultural background is focused on dominant beliefs and practices and how these impact upon daily life. Developmental history includes information on the person's overall development. A detailed developmental history will cover pregnancy and birth, early childhood development, milestones, childhood illnesses and family functioning. Sexuality is an area that is often overlooked in assessment and intervention. Few mental health workers understand the issues associated with trans-sexuality or gender dysphoria. This can result in inappropriate assessment resulting in people not being referred to appropriate services.[8] Education and employment is focused on schooling, further education and training and work history. Social history includes friendships, relationships and leisure interests. The focus of assessment of pre-morbid personality is on dominant traits and features, impulse control and anger management.

Past history involves assessment of past psychiatric and medical history as well as issues of violence, use of alcohol and other drugs and forensic history. For both the psychiatric and medical histories the focus is on diagnosis, prior hospital admissions and community treatment, interventions and treatments, with allergies and adverse side effects from medications noted. Previous suicide attempts, instances of deliberate self-harm and situations of violence and sexual abuse are explored. The alcohol and other drugs history involves discussion of substances used, amounts, frequency and setting. Issues, problems and treatments are explored. This includes effects of the substances used and eliciting the person's view as to perceived benefits and harm, as well as the impact the substances are having on the person's life generally.[9] Forensic history is concerned with past police involvement, charges, court appearances and sentences, as well as the person's current legal status.

Family history

Family history involves mapping the person's family tree and presenting it in a genogram.[10] It is useful to record the genogram across three generations for maximum benefits to be obtained. For instance, in schizophrenia there is often a pattern across the generations; biological theories discussed in the previous chapter claim that some people have a genetic endowment that makes them susceptible to developing this condition when placed under severe or prolonged stress. Likewise there is often a strong family history with endogenous depression as well as other disorders. Patterns of physical illnesses and causes of death can also be observed, as well as transactional interactions currently and across the generations. Strengths and resilience and levels of support and stress within the family are also assessed.

Spirituality is an area that is often overlooked in assessments and interventions in mental health even though much of the content of hallucinations and delusions has spiritual or religious themes.

Spirituality

As mentioned in the discussion in Chapter 1, spirituality is one of the few areas where altered states of perception and cognition are socially acceptable. Spiritual content is highly represented in the hallucinations and delusions of people with mental health issues. This is generally interpreted as people trying to make sense of their experiences by seeing them as coming from supernatural causes when no physical cause can be detected. This, however, avoids the question of the sequence of events and does not explain the spiritual content of the hallucinations and delusions that has occurred prior to this interpretation. It is after people experience altered states of perception and cognition that they seek explanations and solutions. In times of adversity, people will often resort to a higher being for support and guidance. Another explanation is that this altered reality state is not mental health issues but is in fact a spiritual experience. Most of the world's population subscribes to spiritual or religious beliefs. For most, the experience is comforting and rewarding, yet for many it can be a source of guilt and intra-psychic conflict, particularly if people have not followed the teachings of their spiritual or religious leaders.

Mental health issues are often triggered by traumatic life events and for many women such an event is sexual assault. Many of these women experience religious and spiritual hallucinations and delusions. Trauma-informed care and practice, discussed in Chapter 10, provides a useful framework for assessment and intervening with women who have experienced the trauma of sexual assault.

Whether spirituality is a source of tension or comfort it is an important area to consider as it will often impact upon how people understand and interpret their situation. The way spirituality is dealt with will necessarily impact upon a person's recovery. If workers ignore spirituality, they run the risk of ignoring underlying tensions or conflicts or important sources of support and solace.[11]

Mental status examination

The mental status examination is unique to mental health assessments. It is intended to provide a snapshot of the person's mental state at the time of assessment. The mental status examination is augmented by information in the individual and family history, reports from others, rating scales and biological markers, leading to an overall formulation of an assessment and management plan. Areas covered in the mental status examination include appearance, relationship with interviewer, mood and affect, thought processes, and verbal and non-verbal communication. In children, coping mechanisms and major defences are assessed as well as conscience development, concept of self and fantasy. An appraisal is also made of cognitive functioning and awareness of problems.[12]

Some social workers argue that it is not their role to conduct a mental status examination as they are labelling and making judgements about the person, and this is inconsistent with a critical theoretical approach. These criticisms come predominantly from those who have no direct practice experience of social work in mental health and who are applying abstract theory. Social workers, like other workers from various disciplines working in mental health, need to be able to conduct a thorough assessment that includes a mental status examination as one component of the assessment. This can be done in a manner that is informed by critical theory and that is sensitive to the adverse effects of inappropriate labels or judgements. What is required is detailed descriptions of observations that are respectful and can easily be understood by other workers, consumers and carers. It is not enough to simply fill out a form saying the person is 'delusional' without giving any details of the content of what the worker considers to be a delusion.

> Dave was working as a barrister and solicitor prior to developing schizophrenia. On one of his numerous psychiatric hospital admissions he mentioned that he had had lunch with a High Court judge that afternoon before being hospitalised. This was mistakenly written in his file as 'delusional'. The psychiatric registrar simply did not believe that this occurred.

A simple rule of thumb is only to use language that you would be happy to have used about yourself, or a loved one, in similar circumstances. Ultimately this is language that clearly conveys what appears to be happening and is respectful and helpful. It is useful to ask yourself, 'How would I feel if I was reading these notes written by someone else about me?' Personally I would not like to read that my appearance was 'fixed', that I was considered 'foul-smelling' and had 'unkempt hair', that I had 'pressure of speech' because I was speaking quickly or that I was considered 'suspicious' or 'guarded'. Nor would I consider it helpful to have my thoughts described as 'flight of ideas' if I was jumping from one topic to another or 'word salad' if it was hard to elicit meanings and intentions or 'drivelling' if I didn't make sense to the worker or that my thoughts had actually 'derailed'. I also would not appreciate being asked who is the president of the United States and being asked to count in threes. I would not like to be considered 'hysterical' if I became so frustrated with the assessment interview that I lost my temper or that I had 'impaired judgement' because I appeared agitated and distressed.

Ultimately what is required is a thorough assessment to be able to assist the person in the most beneficial ways possible. If there are gaps in the assessment, best intentions are most likely to be misdirected when it comes to intervention. The mental status examination provides baseline information that can be used to assess any significant changes in the person's usual appearance, thinking and behaviour. This includes information from the person as well as reports from significant others that are crucial to gaining a sense of the person's usual appearance and behaviour. The focus is on changes in usual appearance, perception, cognition, thinking and behaviour, particularly change that is seen to be problematic.

The main components of the mental status examination are presented in Figure 6.1, followed by further discussion of main areas of assessment under each category as well as some useful questions to consider when conducting an assessment.[13]

General appearance and behaviour
physical characteristics, dress, grooming, hygiene, demeanour, manner, posture, gait, motor activity, level of cooperation and engagement during the interview

Speech
rate, quality, volume, tone, content, flow

Affect
quality, range, appropriateness, congruency with verbal content

Thought
stream, form, content, possession, delusions

Perception
hallucinations, illusions, phobias

Cognition
orientation, memory, conscious state, arousal/wakefulness, attention, concentration

Insight and judgement
recognition of illness, attribution, acceptance of treatment

Figure 6.1: Adult mental status examination

General appearance and behaviour

The appearance and behaviour of the person may change over time and reflect what is happening for them mentally. A person who is hypomanic may dress in a flamboyant and colourful manner, demonstrating extrovert type behaviours in comparison with a person who is depressed who may be dressed in darker colours, and present as more introverted and withdrawn. Of course this is a gross generalisation and what is most important is to have a sense of the 'usual appearance' of the person and how this may have changed.

Melanie's husband John had lived with bipolar for many years. An early warning sign for her of when he was becoming manic was when he simply wore a flower in the buttonhole of his jacket. She learnt from past experience that this was the start of his mood rapidly escalating. John had a past history of hospital admissions due to mania. By noting such a subtle change in his appearance Melanie was able to call mental health workers, with

105

If the person is not willing, or is unable to be involved in the interview process it is important that the worker notes this, due to the implications for the overall assessment. Likewise it needs to be recorded if the person is heavily sedated, or under the influence of alcohol or other drugs, as a full assessment cannot occur under these circumstances. Following these introductions some possible opening interview questions are

What were you told about seeing me today for this interview?
What do you think is the purpose of us meeting here today?
Is there anything particularly worrying you at the moment?
Is anyone else worried about you at the moment?
If yes, what do you think they are they worried about?
Who brought you to see me today?
If different person, ask, What do you think they are worried about?
How are things going for you at the moment?
Have things been like this before?
How are things for you usually?

Speech

Assessment of speech is concerned with how a person is communicating rather than the content of what is being said. It is concerned with the rate, volume, modulation and flow, and the ability to produce words. Again this is in the context of what is considered usual for this person. The term 'pressure of speech' is commonly used when a person is speaking in a rapid and intense manner, with little time devoted to listening or sitting quietly. It is often associated with mania. However, we all know people not with mania who also communicate in this manner.

Affect

A person's mood may be elevated, lowered or labile alternating between the two within a limited period of time. Schizophrenia is often associated with mood states that are flat or blunted, suspicious or guarded and is often influenced by the presence of hallucinations or delusions as well as side effects of medication. It is important to check if the person's mood state is congruent with the verbal content. For instance, a person may be laughing while recalling extremely sad events. Depression is generally characterised by lowered mood and a decreased range of emotional reactions to situations. Self-criticism and feelings of hopelessness and helplessness can often co-exist with suicidal thoughts and ideas.

Mania is distinguishable by labile, elated, excitable, loud, denigrating, contemptuous and disinhibited emotional states. Hypomania is when the person's mood is elevated but not to the extent witnessed in mania. Anxiety in heightened states can result in the person being tense, fearful and phobic. Panic attacks are when the person feels an overwhelming anxiety state. They are generally associated with a particular activity or social context. These will vary according to individual circumstances. Some people experience panic attacks when alone in a crowd, others in enclosed spaces or at a particular height, and others when in situations of intense conflict. Some possible interview questions on how a person is feeling are

> If you were to rate yourself on a scale of 1 (most miserable) to 10 (happiest) how would you rate yourself at the moment?
>
> If you were to rate yourself on a scale of 1 (most miserable) to 10 (happiest) how would you rate yourself usually?
>
> What things make a difference to how you are feeling?
>
> Can you tell me about a time when you were really happy, what was it like for you? What were you doing?
>
> (Ask these same questions, replacing happy with other emotions such as bored, worried, frustrated, angry, irritable, sad, anxious and miserable.)

Possible questions to assess a person's coping mechanisms are

How do you deal with feeling _____ (bored, worried, frustrated, angry, irritable, sad, anxious, miserable)? Check for substance use.

Does this work for you?

Who knows about this?

What do you do when you get really distressed?

How have you been feeling lately?

What have you been doing?

Questions to assess possible suicide or self-harm are

Have there been times when you have felt so bad that that you thought of killing yourself?

If yes, what did you do?

Did other people know how you were feeling?

What helped you to overcome these feelings at the time?

Do you have any plans at the moment to kill yourself? (Check access to means to carry out plan, e.g. pills, guns etc.)

Who knows how you are feeling at the moment? Who can you talk to about how you are feeling?

Are there times of the day when you feel better or worse?

Are you able to concentrate as well as you used to?

Do you have as much, or more, energy than you used to?

How have you been sleeping?

If the person is experiencing disturbed sleep, ask,

What time/s do you usually wake up?

How difficult is it for you to get back to sleep again?

How have you been eating lately?

Have you lost or put on weight recently?

If yes, how much and over what period of time?

These questions are a guide for areas to cover in an assessment. It is important to use a range of skills and not ask too many questions as this can be aggravating. Use appropriate eye contact and body language, listening and assertiveness skills, empathic responses, reflective statements and minimal encourages to engage the person to develop a trusting relationship so they are comfortable sharing private and personal information with you. Critical social work interview skills are discussed further in Chapter 10.

Thought

The content of people's thoughts is generally a reflection of how they feel about themselves and the world around them. At times there are areas of unresolved conflict that result in unwanted thoughts that are intrusive and disturbing. A person's thought processes may be rapid and pressured or slower than usual with ideas not clearly expressed. The sequence of ideas may appear disjointed and unclear. Some people have compulsive thoughts that result in obsessive actions. We all engage in some of these from time to time, such as checking that the stove is turned off or that the front door is locked, sometimes more than once, before leaving the house. However, for some people these actions can turn into lengthy and prolonged rituals that can cause severe disruption to their daily lives.

Briony was close to losing her job for regularly being late for work. In fact, she was not arriving late but was getting there early. Her difficulty was a compulsion to continually go back and check that her car was locked, a ritual that was taking half an hour or more, that she felt absolutely no control over in being able to stop herself. She felt immobilised and could not leave the car park. This behaviour had increased in the context of escalating anxiety due to her husband moving interstate for work and the associated withdrawal of his assistance and support with the care of the children.

Interview questions to assess thoughts might be

Do you feel in control of your thinking?

Are there times when you feel that your thinking is not under your control, or that other people can read your mind?

Are there times when you feel you can control other people's thinking?

Are there times when you find your thinking is slowed down or sped up?

Have you had any weird, unusual or frightening thoughts lately?

Bill was referred to the crisis team for assertive follow-up over the weekend by his case-manager who was concerned about his 'deteriorating mental state'. I visited Bill with a nurse colleague, Jack, and found him to be quite okay. He was not sure why we were visiting him and after talking with him and conducting an assessment, neither were we. On all counts he seemed to be managing well and did not demonstrate any overt signs or symptoms of mental health issues or any need of assistance from us. As we were about to leave, my nurse colleague asked, 'Have you been receiving any special messages from your television or radio?' Bill looked very surprised and then went on to tell us at length about the special messages he was receiving not just from the television and radio but from his toaster as well.

Sometimes when people are referred to mental health services they appear to be quite okay and it is only when probing questions that may seem unusual are asked that information such as in the situation of Bill is gained. People may hide delusions or suicidal thoughts for fear of workers not understanding or intervening against their wishes. This can be extremely frustrating for family and friends who have requested assistance from mental health workers only to find the person appears quite well at the time of the assessment interview. It is often difficult, though, to sustain this for an extended period.

Three types of delusions are often observed. These are delusions of grandeur, reference or persecution. Delusions of grandeur are when people have exaggerated beliefs about their abilities or sense of importance. Delusions of reference are when people falsely believe that they are the focus of other people's attention or conversations. Delusions of persecution are false beliefs that others are going to cause harm or serious injury.[14]

Perception

As mentioned in Chapter 1, perception involves the sensory experiences of illusions and hallucinations. Illusions involve the misrepresentation of an external stimulus that is regarded as a normal everyday experience. Illusions are associated with severe anxiety, depression and delirium. Hallucinations are perceptions without an external stimulus. They involve one or more of the five senses of sound, sight, taste, touch and smell.

Auditory hallucinations may be voices, noises or music. Those commonly associated with schizophrenia are voices talking to or about the person in the third person, two or more voices arguing, or thoughts spoken out loud. These voices are often critical and demeaning yet voices can also be positive at times for some people. The voices of severe depression are generally harsh, abusive and critical. It is more often that music and noises will be heard in organic states.

Visual hallucinations include patterns, lights, colours or identifiable people and objects. They are generally associated with substance misuse or abuse. In cases of delirium, these hallucinations can seem very real and can be extremely frightening. Visual hallucinations may be accompanied by auditory hallucinations for those with temporal lobe damage to the brain with some people seeing flashes of light prior to having a fit.[16]

Olfactory hallucinations can be found in schizophrenia and are common with persecutory delusions. In cases of severe depression, these hallucinations of smell are often focused on the person's own body. Olfactory hallucinations sometimes occur before a fit for those with temporal lobe damage.

My nursing colleague Adrian and I were asked by Rose's case manager at the community mental health centre to see her over the weekend to check that she was okay. Rose had just shifted into a new flat and we were told her mental state had deteriorated due to the stress of the move. When we knocked on the door, Rose did not answer for quite some time. Eventually she spoke to us through the door and said she was okay and did not want to see us. After some persuasion she agreed to let us in. She made us a cup of tea and told us how happy she was with her new flat. We sat in the lounge room of her upstairs flat and enjoyed the lovely view and sunshine that streamed in through her large window. She said people were worried unnecessarily and that she was fine. However, she did complain of being able to smell gas and seemed quite concerned about this. Adrian and I diligently checked her gas stove and said it seemed fine and that we could not smell any gas. Rose still seemed doubtful yet we reassured her there was no gas smell and not to worry. That evening, Rose pushed her lounge suite through the window and was admitted as an involuntary psychiatric patient. What Adrian and I did not know was that when Rose became unwell she usually had olfactory hallucinations that generally led to her being hospitalised in distressing circumstances.

This unfortunate experience was a reminder to Adrian and me of the importance of having as much knowledge as possible about a person before seeing them, particularly if they are regarded as being in a crisis situation. Often there are patterns of behaviour that can be observed each time a person becomes unwell. Good practice is being familiar with this pattern and knowing when and how to best intervene. Often it is carers rather than workers who are the first to observe when things are not quite right. It is therefore crucial that workers listen to carers' concerns and learn from them about how crisis situations have been successfully resolved in the past. Unfortunately, Rose lived alone and did not have anyone to care for her apart from workers.

Gustatory hallucinations involve taste and are commonly associated with persecutory delusion in schizophrenia as well as with delirium.[17]

Tactile hallucinations include sensations of pain, sexual experiences or feelings of the person's body being infested. This, as presented in Chapter 5, was the situation with Janet, who was suffering with post-natal depression and had the extremely distressing sensation of small animals crawling about, both inside and outside her body. Tactile hallucinations are frequently associated with delirium.[18]

Possible interview questions are

Do you ever hear, see, feel, smell or taste things you cannot explain?
If yes, can you tell me what happens?
When is the last time you had an experience like this?

Where were you at the time?

Who were you with?

What were you doing?

How were you feeling?

How often do you have these experiences?

Cognition

A cognitive assessment involves orientation to time, place and person. In other words, does the person know who they are, where they are and how they got there? Do they know the day of the week, date and year? Areas of assessment include intellectual manipulation, planning, identification and naming of objects, skills in writing and interpretation. General knowledge is assessed as well as knowledge of past and recent events. The manner in which a cognitive assessment is approached is strongly influenced by the practitioner's professional background and training. For instance, psychiatrists often assess intellectual manipulation by asking the person to count in number sequences such as serial sevens or threes. They may ask general knowledge questions about political parties and prominent politicians, events in the news recently, and possibly ask the person to interpret some proverbs. Social workers, on the other hand, will generally approach this area of assessment in a manner that is integrated with events happening in the person's life. They will ask questions directly related to the person's environment rather than in a more clinical and structured format. Regardless of approach, what is important is that an indication is gained of the level of cognitive functioning at the time of the assessment. This is then compared with the person's level of cognitive functioning generally, including intelligence quotient if this has been assessed by psychologists in the past, level of education, written and verbal language skills and cultural background. For instance, if the person is from a non-English speaking background and has not had any formal schooling, this needs to be taken into consideration. The person simply may not have ever known the answers to some of the questions asked, and English proverbs may seem very strange and unfamiliar!

Both long-term and short-term memory is assessed, including the potential for amnesia, distortion of memories and recognition. Amnesia may be psychological or organic. Psychological amnesia is frequently anxiety-based, while acute organic amnesia is often due to trauma or intoxication. Sub-acute and chronic amnesia is generally associated with dementia. Distortion of memories might include retrospective falsification by the modification of memories of recent or past events. Confabulation is detailed false descriptions of past events and is often present with dementia. Distortion of recognition may involve déjà vu – the feeling of already having had an experience prior to it happening. This often occurs when a person is stressed or tired.[19] Again these are experiences within the realms of 'normal' everyday experience. We all forget things, names of people, the date and so on and exaggerate and change stories to add interest and excitement. However, it is when these behaviours are exacerbated and result in problems in daily living that they may come to the attention of mental health professionals. The mini mental health status presented in Figure 6.2 is used to assess cognition, particularly in older people.

Orientation

Score one point for each correct answer:

What is the time, date, day, month, year? Maximum: 5 points

What is the name of this ward, hospital, district, town, country? 5 points

Registration

Name three objects only once. Score up to a maximum of 3 points for each correct repetition. 3 points

Repeat the objects until the person can repeat them accurately (in order to test recall later).

Attention and calculation

Ask the person to subtract 7 from 100 and then 7 from the result four more times.

Score 1 point for each correct subtraction. 5 points

Recall

Ask the person to repeat the names of the three objects learnt in the registration test. 3 points

Language

Score 1 point for each of two simple objects named (e.g. pen and a watch). 2 points

Score 1 point for an accurate repetition of the phrase 'No ifs, ands or buts'. 1 point

Give a three-stage command, scoring 1 point for each part correctly carried out; e.g. 'With the index finger of your right hand, touch your nose and then your left ear.' 3 points

Write 'Close your eyes' on a blank piece of paper and ask the person to follow the written command. Score 1 point if the patient closes the eyes. 1 point

Ask the person to write a sentence. Score 1 point if the sentence is sensible and contains a noun and a verb. 1 point

Draw a pair of intersecting pentagons with each side approximately 1 inch long. Score 1 point if it is correctly copied. 1 point

TOTAL MAXIMUM SCORE 30 POINTS

Figure 6.2: Mini mental status examination[23]

Insight and judgement

Assessment of the extent to which a person's judgement is affected, including the ability to make reasoned and informed decisions, is made on the basis of the information gained in the previous sections of the mental status examination. If a person is thinking clearly, managing emotionally and is cognitively aware, they are not likely to have impaired judgement. Assessment of a person's judgement is particularly important for issues of safety, especially when suicide is an issue, and also the well-being of those in the person's care. Insight into the presence, nature and cause of problems is assessed, as well as the person's willingness to accept and engage in treatment. Unfortunately, insight is often quite narrowly defined – as whether or not the person agrees with the psychiatric diagnosis assigned to them. In cases of disagreement, 'No insight' is often recorded on the person's file. Insight is much broader than acceptance of a diagnosis and includes recognition of problems in daily living without necessarily making any concessions about diagnosis. A person may not agree with a particular diagnosis for a range of reasons but still willingly engage in treatment and interventions if they perceive that direct benefits will be obtained. Insight resulting from acceptance of a diagnosis may be beneficial in getting the person to comply with treatment. On the other hand, it may be extremely distressing and disabling as the person faces the prospect of living with the stigma of mental health issues, which may be perceived as more disabling than the mental health issues itself. In such instances where insight has overwhelming negative connotations, it may be associated with suicidal thoughts and actions.

Possible interview questions are

What do you make of what is happening to you?

What sort of, and how much, help do you think you need at the moment?

If I suggest you are experiencing difficulties in these areas _____ at the moment, what would you think?

If the problems you have talked about continue, what do you think will happen?

Formulation and provisional diagnosis

An assessment is made following personal reflection and integration of relevant theory. A brief summary of the person's current and past history is recorded, including predisposing, precipitating, perpetuating and protective factors across the continuum of biological, psychological and social indicators. This includes a summary of risks and is followed by a provisional social work diagnosis.[20] Recommendations are made as to other areas of assessment required and most appropriate interventions. Communication with other team members, including psychiatrists, general practitioners, medical officers, nurses and occupational therapists and psychologists and carers, is essential for comprehensive assessment and intervention planning.

Assessment of older people

People in Western countries are living longer due to the decline in infant mortality, the control of infectious diseases and improvements in nutrition and living standards. Ageing reflects trends in mortality, frequency of chronic disease and maintenance of autonomy. Attention to these independent, though related, variables will increase the proportion of the population surviving disease free to an advanced age. The expected lifespan of individuals is not only likely to increase but the number of years that one is disease free is also likely to increase. However, the number of years that an older person is expected to live with loss of independence and loss of autonomy is also likely to increase. Of specific importance to older people are disorders that affect hearing and vision, dental problems, incontinence of urine and faeces, and intellectual failure, particularly dementia.

One-third of those aged 65 years and over and three-quarters of those aged 75 years and over are taking medication on a regular basis. It is not unusual for an older person to be discharged from hospital on 10 or more medications. Older people are a more diverse physiological group and are therefore much more prone to adverse reactions of drug therapy. The family is the greatest single source of support for older people. Loneliness is a key factor in compounding health problems, especially in older women.

Health care workers have been criticised for their controlling role in access to services and for fostering a dependency view of older people, with policy and practices dominated by risk management. A postmodern view of ageing rejects life cycle theories, preferring to focus on living well in the community with particular regard to

choice
control
coordination (and)
empowerment.

Social workers as 'care managers' struggle between acquiring value for money and appropriate care packages and an increased focus on assessment documentation with service provision seen as a separate function. Assessment of older people requires consideration of hopes and dreams and strengths and resources in addition to needs and risk factors. Positive choices need to be highlighted in relation to the type and quality of care required. Older people who are also carers need to be seen as people with their own needs and desires not purely as resources. The relationship developed between the worker and the older person is paramount. Relationships based on trust and mutual respect are essential for developing meaningful partnerships with older people to conduct accurate assessments and intervention planning.

The social work assessment of an older person requires that

the older person is seen in the context of a particular social network and environment (and)
the older person is the central decision maker in the choices required in relation to health and
social status.

Assessment is a collaborative exercise with the older person and family members and significant others which occurs in the context of a helping relationship directed towards actions aimed at alleviating or ameliorating the older person's presenting and underlying difficulties.[21]

A social work assessment with the older person involves

1. an initial request for service
2. engagement and contracting as to the nature of help required and offered
3. evaluation of the presenting difficulty in terms of both the older person's strengths, desires,

capabilities and available resources (and)

4. the development and implementation of an appropriate intervention plan.[22]

The assessment is rarely a one-off exercise and usually requires on-going negotiation and adjustment by both the older person and the worker to changing needs and shifts in resources available. The mini mental status examination (see Figure 6.2) is often used to assess cognitive function.

It is generally considered that if a person scores 23 or less they may have a cognitive impairment. However, it may also indicate that the older person thought it was a complete waste of time and did not understand the purpose or significance of the testing. A low score could also reflect level of educational attainment and/or cultural inappropriateness. People on heavy doses of medication who have perhaps been transported by ambulance may have good reason not to know some of the answers to these questions. It is when these scores are used to deny people services that social work advocacy is important even if simply to have the test re-administered under more conducive circumstances so as to gain a more accurate assessment.

Child and youth assessment

Three principles guide the assessment of children and youths. These are

1. The acquisition of skills, such as the use of language, or particular ways of thinking proceeds in stages. Because of this, there is a lower age level for the appearance of most developmental phenomena. This limit is primarily determined by the maturation of the central nervous system.

2. The child is an important shaper of the environment. While children react to their environment the environment reacts to them as well. Parents have their own needs, and whether or not their particular infant meets these needs will affect the parent's response and therefore the environment in which the child grows.

3. Development is the sum total of biological, intellectual, emotional and social behaviour and their constant interaction. Therefore all areas of development should be examined in any assessment of either children or adults.

In the past, assessments in child psychiatry settings are generally conducted over four sessions:

1. The first session is conducted with all family members present.
2. The second session is conducted with the parents.
3. The third session is conducted with the child.
4. The fourth session is conducted with all family members present.

The first family session includes

introductions
reasons for being at the interview

different family members perceptions of issues the family is dealing with

patterns of problem solving

family lifestyle

family culture.

The parent interview includes the

child's complete personal history

parent's relationship history

personal and family history of each parent.

The third session is conducted with the child alone and includes assessment of the child's mental state (see Figure 6.3).

1. Appearance
2. Mood or affect
3. Orientation and perception
4. Coping mechanisms:
    a. major defences
    b. expression and control of affectional and aggressive impulses
5. Neuromuscular integration
6. Thought process and verbalisation
7. Fantasy:
    a. dreams
    b. drawings
    c. wishes
    d. play
8. Superego
    a. ego ideals and values
    b. integration into personality
9. Concept of self
    a. object relations
    b. identifications
10. Awareness of problems
11. Intelligence quotient estimate
12. Summary of MSE

Figure 6.3: Child mental status examination

The fourth session is a second family interview with a summary of the assessment provided to the family with a recommended intervention plan. In child and youth mental health services today, the assessment interview is often condensed into one or two interviews with family members who are willing and able to attend.

Assessment tools

An evidence-based approach has seen the introduction of national outcome measures by the federal government of Australia. The national collection of consumer level outcome data is considered to be systematic evidence regarding whether or not people using public mental health services improve.

Assessment tools can be useful for data collection on outcome measures for assessment purposes as well as for noting changes in behaviours or new outcomes. However, it is when social workers spend more time compiling and entering data than engaged in meaningful work with clients that the utility of these measures must be questioned. The five assessment tools presented below are frequently used by medical practitioners to assist in history taking in a short time frame. These tools can provide a shared reference point for multidisciplinary teamwork with these assessments done collaboratively where possible to increase reliability measures and shared understandings across all members of the treatment team. These tools provide brief, easy to score and clear outcome measures with proven reliability from evidence-based research to supplement but not replace a full assessment.

SF12

The SF12 was developed from a two-year medical outcomes study in the United States for adults 18 years and older and is used to assess symptoms, functioning and quality of life (see Figure 6.4 overleaf). It can be self-administered or used in interviews with people with limited skills in reading English, taking approximately five minutes to complete. A particularly useful feature of this tool is that it provides two scores for mental and physical disability and draws attention to the co-existence of both. For instance, a person with kidney failure may also suffer with depression.

40+ indicates mild disability
30–39 indicates moderate disability
under 30 indicates severe disability.

Kessler Psychological Distress Scale (K10)

The Kessler Psychological Distress Scale (K10) was developed in 1992 as a screening scale for mental disorder and to measure non-specific psychological distress to assist with clinical judgment as to whether the person requires intervention (see Figure 6.5 overleaf). It is used as a standard outcome measure in mental health services in New South Wales and in Australian National Mental Health and Wellbeing surveys. The K10 is a questionnaire with 10 items that provides a single score that is an indicator of whether or not the person may have a mental disorder.

Advantages of the K10 are its brevity – taking only two minutes to complete – and that it can be administered to people who are unable to read English. Scores range from 10 to 50:

under 20: likely to be mentally well
20–24: likely to have a mild mental disorder
20–25: likely to have a moderate mental disorder
30 and over: likely to have a severe mental disorder.

1. In general, how would you describe your health?

__ excellent (5)

__ very good (4)

__ good (3)

__ fair (2)

__ poor (1)

Questions 2 to 8 are about activities you might do during a typical day. Does your health now limit you in these activities? If so, how much?

2. Moderate activities such as moving a table, pushing a vacuum cleaner, bowling or playing golf.

__ yes, limited a lot (1)

__ yes, limited a little (2)

__ no, not limited at all (3)

3. Climbing several flights of stairs.

__ yes, limited a lot (1)

__ yes, limited a little (2)

__ no, not limited at all (3)

4. During the past four weeks, have you accomplished less than you would like as a result of your physical health?

__ yes (1)

__ no (2)

5. During the past four weeks, were you limited in the kind of work or other regular activities you do as a result of your physical health?

__ yes (1)

__ no (2)

6. During the past four weeks, have you accomplished less than you would like to as a result of any emotional problems, such as feeling depressed or anxious?

__ yes (1)

__ no (2)

7. During the past four weeks, did you not do work or other regular activities as carefully as usual as a result of any emotional problems such as feeling depressed or anxious?

__ yes (1)

__ no (2)

8. During the past four weeks, how much did pain interfere with your normal work, including both work outside the home and housework? Did it interfere not at all, slightly, moderately, quite a bit, or extremely?

__ not at all (5)

__ a little (4)

__ moderately (3)

__ quite a lot (2)

__ extremely (1)

Questions 9 to 12 are about how you feel and how things have been with you during the past four weeks. For each question, please give the one answer that comes closest to the way you have been feeling.

9. How much time during the past four weeks have you felt calm and peaceful?

__ all of the time (6)

__ most of the time (5)

__ a good bit of the time (4)

__ some of the time (3)

__ a little of the time (2)

__ none of the time (1)

10. How much of the time during the past four weeks did you have a lot of energy?

__ all of the time (6)

__ most of the time (5)

__ a good bit of the time (4)

__ some of the time (3)

__ a little of the time (2)

__ none of the time (1)

11. How much time during the past four weeks have you felt down?

__ all of the time (6)

__ most of the time (5)

__ a good bit of the time (4)

__ some of the time (3)

__ a little of the time (2)

__ none of the time (1)

12. During the past four weeks, how much of the time has your physical health or emotional problems interfered with your social activities like visiting with friends, relatives etc?

__ all of the time (6)

__ most of the time (5)

__ a good bit of the time (4)

__ some of the time (3)

__ a little of the time (2)

— none of the time (1)

Figure 6.4: SF12 Short Form[24]

	Rating	Score
1. In the past four weeks, about how often did you feel tired out for no good reason?	1 2 3 4 5	
2. In the past four weeks, about how often did you feel nervous?	1 2 3 4 5	
3. In the past four weeks, about how often did you feel so nervous that nothing could calm you down?	1 2 3 4 5	
4. In the past four weeks, about how often did you feel hopeless?	1 2 3 4 5	
5. In the past four weeks, about how often did you feel restless or fidgety?	1 2 3 4 5	
6. In the past four weeks, about how often did you feel so restless you could not sit still?	1 2 3 4 5	
7. In the past four weeks, about how often did you feel depressed?	1 2 3 4 5	
8. In the past four weeks, about how often did you feel that everything was an effort?	1 2 3 4 5	
9. In the past four weeks, about how often did you feel so sad that nothing could cheer you up?	1 2 3 4 5	
10. In the past four weeks, about how often did you feel worthless?	1 2 3 4 5	
TOTAL (10–50):		

Figure 6.5: Kessler Psychological Distress Scale (K10)[25]

It is estimated that approximately 13 per cent of the adult population will score 20 and over; this increases to 25 per cent of people seen in primary care services. Scores will decline over time with effective interventions. However, it is recommended that if a person's score remains over 24 following intervention, a specialist referral should be considered.

Distress is measured on a five-point scale (1,2,3,4,5).

1 = none of the time
2 = a little of the time
3 = some of the time
4 = most of the time
5 = all of the time.

Health of the Nations Scorecard (HoNOS)

The Health of the Nations Outcome Scale (HoNOS) Scorecard (see Figure 6.6 overleaf) was designed in the United Kingdom in 1994 to measure types of problems people present with at mental health services. The HoNOS Scorecard was initially intended for use with people with severe mental health issues. Specialist training is required to ensure common definitions of terms and reliability. It provides a brief profile of severity rating in 12 key areas to supplement a full assessment, with each item assessed only once each time. For instance, aggression is only ranked in 1 and not included in other ratings. When two problems are present on the same scale, the rating is made for the problem of greatest severity during the rating period; severity is not to be confused with frequency. A ranking of 2 to 4 for an item often indicates a need for intervention. Ratings are often made on a few scales only that are relevant to the person.

The HoNOS Scorecard is used to measure health outcomes not health care outcomes and

Name:
HoNOS Scorecard completed by:
Assessors Professional background:
HoNOS Scorecard Rating:
Specify Disorder (if known):

Completion Time 1 (insert date):
or
Completion Time 2 (insert date):
Time frame (in weeks):

Severity is measured on a five-point scale (0,1,2,3,4).
0 = no problem within the period rated
1 = sub-threshold problem
2 = mild but definitely present
3 = moderately severe
4 = severe to very severe
9 = unknown (not included in total score)

	Rating	*Score*
1. Overactive, aggressive, disruptive behaviour	*1 2 3 4*	
2. Non-accidental self-injury (including suicidal thoughts)	*1 2 3 4*	
3. Problem-drinking or drug-taking (associated with health or social problems)	*1 2 3 4*	
4. Cognitive problems (memory, orientation and understanding of problems)	*1 2 3 4*	
5. Physical illness or disability problems	*1 2 3 4*	
6. Problems with hallucinations and delusions	*1 2 3 4*	
7. Problems with depressed mood *Specify disorder (if known):*	*1 2 3 4*	
8. Other mental & behavioural problems (e.g. panic, phobias, obsessions, eating or sleeping disorders)	*1 2 3 4*	
9. Problems with relationships (e.g. problems developing and maintaining supportive relationships)	*1 2 3 4*	
10. Problems with activities of daily living (e.g. self-care)	*1 2 3 4*	
11. Problems with living conditions (e.g. housing, finances)	*1 2 3 4*	
12. Problems with occupation and activities (e.g. education employment and recreation)	*1 2 3 4*	

TOTAL (0–48):

Figure 6.6: The HoNOS Scorecard[26]

is a guide for when interventions may be required. It is not to be used as an indicator of overall functioning. It does, however, provide a record of change in certain areas. Outcomes are measured by comparing ratings for two set time periods. The initial rating is based upon the previous two weeks. This does not apply if the second rating occurs less than two weeks from the initial rating. As a general rule, the HoNOS Scorecard is completed in collaboration with the person being assessed, carers and other mental health practitioners wherever possible to get accurate and reliable measures. It is important that a clinical judgement is recorded and

91-100	Superior functioning in a wide rage of activities, life's problems never seem to get out of hand, is sought out by others because of his or her many qualities. No symptoms.
90-81	Absent or minimal symptoms, good functioning in all areas, interested and involved in a wide range or activities, socially effective, generally satisfied with life, no more than everyday problems or concerns.
80-71	If symptoms are present they are transient and expectable reactions to psychosocial stresses; no more than slight impairment in social, occupational, or school functioning
70-61	Some mild symptoms OR some difficulty in social, occupational, or school functioning, but generally functioning pretty well, has some meaningful interpersonal relationships.
60-51	Moderate symptoms OR any moderate difficulty in social, occupational, or school functioning.
50-41	Serious symptoms OR any serious impairment in social, occupational, or school functioning.
40-31	Some impairment in reality testing or communication OR major impairment in several areas, such as work or school, family relations, judgment, thinking, or mood.
30-21	Behaviour is considered influenced by delusions or hallucinations OR serious impairment in communications or judgment OR inability to function in all areas.
20-11	Some danger or hurting self or others OR occasionally fails to maintain minimal personal hygiene OR gross impairment in communication.
10-1	Persistent danger of severely hurting self or others OR persistent inability to maintain minimum personal hygiene OR serious suicidal act with clear expectation of death.

**Figure 6.7: The global assessment of functioning (GAF-Scale)
reproduced from DSM IVTR**

not perceptions. It is recognised that this is not always possible, particularly if the person is acutely unwell at the time.

The Global Assessment of Functioning (GAF-Scale)

The Global Assessment of Functioning (GAF-Scale) in the DSM (see Figure 6.7) is widely used to assess overall functioning and measurement of change.

Life Skills Profile (LSP)

The Life Skills Profile (LSP) was developed by Australian psychiatrist Alan Rosen as a strengths-focused ranking scale to assess basic life skills over the previous three months.[27] Three versions of the LSP have been published, each of them indicating the number of questions on the scale, starting with the LSP39, followed by the LSP20 and the abbreviated LSP16 (see Figure 6.8 overleaf). The LSP is not to be used if the person is in crisis or mentally unwell. The intention was to develop a scale that emphasised a person's life skills and took account of the person's age and social and cultural context. This strengths approach was evident in the

1. Does the person generally have difficulty with initiating and responding to conversation? Measures the ability to begin and maintain social interaction, ensuring the flow of conversation; taking turns in conversation, silence as appropriate.
Assessment sub-scale: Withdrawal

2. Does the person generally withdraw from social contact? Does the person isolate themselves when part of a group? Does the person participate in leisure activities with others? Spend long hours alone watching TV or videos?
Assessment sub-scale: Withdrawal

3. Does the person generally show warmth to others? Does the individual demonstrate affection, concern or understanding of situation of others?
Assessment sub-scale: Withdrawal

4. Is this person generally well groomed (eg, neatly dressed, hair combed)? Does the person use soap when washing, shave as appropriate/ use make-up appropriately, use shampoo?
Assessment sub-scale: Self care

5. Does this person wear clean clothes generally, or ensure that they are cleaned if dirty? Does the person recognise the need to change clothes on a regular basis? Are clothes grimy, are collars and cuffs marked, are there food stains?
Assessment sub-scale: Self care

6. Does this person generally neglect her or his physical health? Does the person have a medical condition for which they are not receiving appropriate treatment? Does the person lead a generally healthy lifestyle? Does the person neglect their dental health?
Assessment sub-scale: Self care

7. Is this person violent to others? Does the person display verbal and physical aggression to others?

8. Does this person generally make or keep friendships? Does the person identify individuals as friends? Do others identify the person as a friend? Does the person express a desire to continue to interact with others?
Assessment sub-scale: Withdrawal

9. Does this person generally maintain an adequate diet? Does the person eat a variety of nutritious foods regularly? Do they watch their fat and fibre intake?
Assessment sub-scale: Self care

10. Does this person generally look after and take her or his own prescribed medication (or attend for prescribed injections on time) without reminding? Does the person adhere to their medication regimen as prescribed? The right amount at the right time on a regular basis? Does the person need prompting or reinforcement to adhere to their medication regimen?
Assessment sub-scale: Compliance

11. Is this person willing to take prescribed medication when prescribed by a doctor? Does the person express an unwillingness to take medication as prescribed, bargain or inappropriately question the need for continuing medication?
Assessment sub-scale: Compliance

12. Does this person cooperate with health services (eg, doctors and/or other health workers)? Is the person deliberately obstructive in relation to treatment plans? Do they attend appointments, undertake therapeutic homework activities?
Assessment sub-scale: Compliance

13. Does this person generally have problems (e.g., friction, avoidance) living with others in the household? Is the person identified as difficult to live with? Do they have difficulty establishing or keeping to 'house rules' or are they always having arguments about domestic duties?
Assessment sub-scale: Anti-social

14. Does this person behave offensively (includes sexual behaviour)? Does the person behave in a socially inept or unacceptable way demonstrating inappropriate social or sexual behaviours or communication?
Assessment sub-scale: Anti-social

15. Does this person behave irresponsibly? Does the person act deliberately in ways that are likely to inconvenience, irritate or hurt others? Does the person neglect basic social obligations?
Assessment sub scale: Anti-social

16. What sort of work is this person generally capable of (even if unemployed, retired or doing unpaid domestic duties)? What level of assistance/guidance does the individual require to undertake occupational activities?
Assessment sub-scale: Self care

Ratings are tailored to individual questions and generally indicate:

0 Not a problem
1 Slight problem
2 Moderate problem
3 Extreme problem

Figure: 6.8: Life Skills Profile 16 item elaboration and clarification, developed as part of the training materials for the Victorian Mental Health Outcomes Strategy

labelling of categories and the four-point scoring system. However, some of the sub-scales used for different versions of the LSP still have negative connotations such as 'bizarre', 'anti-social' and 'withdrawal'. In the first version, the LSP39, higher scores mean higher levels of functioning. Confusion has arisen with the application of the LSP as higher scores from other scales, such as the GAF-Scale and the HoNOS, mean lower levels of functioning, and the different scoring systems used on different versions of the LSP. The scoring for the most recent version, the LSP16, has been reversed so that high scores indicate increased difficulty.

Conclusion

A social work assessment in mental health requires knowledge and skills in assessment of the social as well as environmental, cultural, spiritual, emotional, psychological and biological factors. Social workers need to be equipped to conduct a comprehensive and holistic assessment of the person in context. This is in relation to personal, family and social issues that are respectful of gender, culture and different belief systems. A humane approach to assessment and intervention is required that is respectful of the person and the difficulties they are experiencing while at the same time acknowledging their strengths and resources and getting to know them as a person. Information is shared and language used that demystifies the worker and consumer relationship. Skills in engagement and listening are paramount as well as critical questioning, so that an effective working relationship can be established to facilitate a thorough assessment that will inform appropriate interventions. Social workers need to know the various tools of assessment used in mental health. However, these are to be used discerningly and always in the best interests of the consumer. The assessment framework presented in this chapter is illustrated in the assessment of Luisa in Chapter 8.

Reflection

What are the main contributions of social workers when conducting a mental health assessment? What are the main contributions of other disciplines?

What is the purpose of a mental status examination? What is the relationship of the MSE to a full mental health assessment?

Who would you include when conducting a mental health assessment? Provide reasons.

How can you ensure that a mental health assessment (including MSE) is conducted in a respectful and appropriate manner?

Do you think you will use an MSE in your practice as a social worker? Provide reasons.

7

Diagnosis

Eligibility for mental health services is determined by whether or not a person is deemed to have a psychiatric diagnosis in accordance with those identified in the *International Classification of Diagnoses* (ICD) by the World Health Organisation[1] or the *Diagnostic and Statistical Manual* (DSM)[2] by the American Psychiatrists Association. It is therefore essential that workers in mental health settings are aware of these major diagnostic categories and assessment and treatment approaches. Some social workers can be seduced by these psychiatric diagnoses and assume a paramedical status by adopting the language of psychiatry. Others reject them entirely. It is important, however, to understand the ways that each discipline works for effective inter-disciplinary collaboration. This can be challenging particularly for social workers and psychologists as in many instances they are sole workers on multi-disciplinary teams that are dominated by medical personnel, mostly psychiatric nurses, with overall clinical responsibility resting with the consultant psychiatrist. The diagnoses discussed in this chapter are psychotic disorders, mood disorders, trauma, personality disorder, eating disorders and organic brain disorders.[3]

Diagnosis and recovery

Up until the mid-1970s, diagnosis was a term used by allied health professionals. Since then, however, in the mental health field, diagnosis has become synonymous with psychiatry and the psychiatric diagnoses in the DSM and ICD.[4] For some social workers, there is confusion between assessment and diagnosis, with both terms used interchangeably. Critics of diagnosis argue that it is negative and problem or illness focused, and have rejected the term and replaced it with 'assessment'.[5] This is problematic as both are closely related, with diagnosis built on an assessment and informing the management plan. Assessment is concerned with gaining an increased understanding of the person and situation, and diagnosis is the formulation of a judgement, with or on behalf of the person, as to what is of particular significance in the current situation.

Turner is highly critical of the rejection of the term diagnosis and refutes claims that it is the prerogative of any one profession and that it is a search for pathology and problems. He argues that diagnosis is not applying labels or categorising in a unitary sense and acknowledges that a single term or label cannot do justice to the multidimensional complexities of the individual and her or his world. However, labels and categories are useful, if not necessary, for communicating information and assuring appropriate interventions as well as drawing attention to areas of uncertainty requiring further assessment. Turner cautions social workers, 'In our appropriate and strongly justified concern about the misuse of labels we need to keep in perspective that they are also powerful agents of help and reassurance.'[6] There is a professional responsibility to convey judgements made in terms of accountability. The focus of a diagnosis will vary according to the professional background of workers involved. For instance, social workers will focus more on a social diagnosis, while psychologists focus on psychological content and processes.

The term diagnosis is powerful and if misused or incorrect can cause considerable harm. However, an accurate diagnosis can bring about increased allocation of much-needed attention and resources that can empower individuals and bring about improvements in quality of life.[7] The New Zealand Mental Health Commission advises consumers, 'Your psychiatrist may give you a diagnosis. A diagnosis can be helpful but sometimes service users feel put down and labelled by them. Not everyone agrees with the diagnosis they are given.'[8]

Louise is a community educator who has lived with schizophrenia for the past 20 years. She was giving a lecture to students in mental health about how schizophrenia has affected her life. One of the students asked her what had empowered her the most and her response was 'When finally I was told my diagnosis.'[9] It was nearly two years of involvement with mental health services, including involuntary hospitalisations, before anyone mentioned to Louise what her diagnosis was. She felt there was then, and still exists today, a general reluctance by mental health workers to inform people of their diagnosis. Once she was aware of her diagnosis, she was able to read about schizophrenia, talk with people about it and look at ways of effectively managing the distressing symptoms she was experiencing as well as reflecting on all aspects of her life. She now shares these experiences with others to help educate people about responsible and respectful practices in mental health settings and the community in general.

Some may argue these symptoms could have still been treated effectively without Louise being told she was diagnosed with schizophrenia. However, there is something about human nature that when something is not quite right, and particularly when people are hospitalised and undergoing medical treatment, they and those close to them want to know what is wrong. This is certainly the case with physical illness and should be the same with mental health issues. This code of silence, or mystery surrounding diagnosis, can be very disempowering, as aptly pointed out by Louise. She also highlighted the further problem of multiple diagnoses, which I have also observed in my own practice. It seems that if a person is hospitalised on numerous occasions this can result in varied diagnoses. I know a woman who has been hospitalised several times in the past year with diagnoses of depression, schizophrenia and personality disorder at different admissions. Herein lies a tremendous frustration with the accuracy of psychiatric diagnoses. It seems that if a person has multiple hospitalisations they may receive multiple diagnoses. This is generally contingent upon who conducts the assessment and gives the diagnosis, rather than upon any marked change in the person's presentation. This situation would be seen as negligent in the treatment of physical conditions. However, it continues unchallenged in mental health settings. This is a reflection of how much we still really do not know about mental health issues. However, much is known about effective methods of treatment and interventions to alleviate symptoms of mental health issues and bring about improvements in a person's quality of life.

Psychosis

The ability to recognise the early signs of psychosis is essential for early intervention and to prevent loss in accordance with mental health recovery. Early signs may be an indication that things are not quite right across a range of areas and there may be a lack of clarity surrounding this. Early intervention requires a response rather than dismissing these signs due to lack of severity or attributing them to other causes such as substance use. These changes be subtle and occur gradually over a period of time or appear more rapidly.

Changes will be observed across thinking and perception, emotion and motivation and behaviour. Issues with thinking and perception are likely to be associated with concentration and attention. The person may develop an altered sense of reality in relation to her/himself, others or their environment. These are generally considered to be 'odd ideas'. Unusual perceptual experiences may be a reduced or increased intensity in sensory experiences such as sound smell and colour. Changes in emotion could be reduced energy and motivation, irritability, anxiety, lowered mood. The person's affect may seem to be lowered, with a reduced range, sometimes referred to as blunted affect. Changes in appetite and sleep may also be present. Behavioural changes may include social withdrawal and isolation and difficulties performing usual family, social and vocational roles. It is not likely that the person will be seeking assistance and they may deny that there are any issues of concern.[10]

The main features of a psychotic disorder are the presence of hallucinations, fixed delusions (false beliefs) illogical or disordered thinking (thought disorder) and labile or incongruent emotions.[11]

When psychosis is more established, it is likely that hallucinations and or delusions will be present. Delusions are false beliefs from thought processes that are not consistent with the person's usual cultural or religious beliefs and cannot be changed by reasoning or the presentation of contradictory information. Hallucinations are sensory experiences that occur without sensory stimuli and result in profound distortions to a person's sense of perception. These distortions may be related to one or more of the five senses of sound, sight, touch, smell and taste. It may be that they are hearing voices or feel that bugs are crawling under their skin and so on. These hallucinations can vary in intensity and the level of distress and at times support generated from these hallucinatory experiences. Beginning workers often confuse hallucinations and delusions and it is true that often the two are related and connected in some way. The main distinction is that delusions are a thought process and hallucinations are related to perception. It is important to remember that these experiences are very real for the person and it is inappropriate to argue with the person and to dismiss or minimise the experiences.[12]

The main mental health issue where psychosis, characterised by hallucinations and delusions, is likely to be evident is schizophrenia. However, it can also be seen in depression, bipolar affective disorder and drug-induced psychosis.

The incidence of schizophrenia is relatively low, with estimates of 15 people per 100,000 in the population of Australia with schizophrenia each year. However, it is identified by the World Health Organisation as one of the main contributors to the 'global burden of disease' due to the frequency of onset in early adulthood, between 16 and 30 years of age, with an earlier onset usually for males, and the persistence of disturbing symptoms. It is estimated that one person in every hundred is affected in some way by schizophrenia.[13] Prevalence studies indicate that there is considerable variation amongst different populations and that these change over time.[14] Higher rates of schizophrenia have been found in males, immigrant groups and urban populations.[15] For those diagnosed with schizophrenia, one-quarter will have one or two episodes and then be symptom free. Fifty per cent will have recurrent episodes and require ongoing treatment and support to assist them to maintain a good quality of life. A further 25 per cent will experience more persistent and ongoing issues.[16]

Symptoms of schizophrenia are classified as 'positive' and 'negative'. These terms do not have usual everyday meanings. 'Positive symptoms' relate to psychotic behaviours and 'negative symptoms' include lethargy and difficulty with motivation. Positive symptoms of schizophrenia include hallucinations, delusions and what is referred to as 'thought disorder'. Delusions experienced in schizophrenia are false beliefs around persecution or guilt, being under the control of an external source or of grandeur. These false beliefs may cause the person to withdraw from people or situations to avoid imagined persecution.[17] Thought disorder is when a person jumps from one topic to another without any logical connection, with the person's thoughts and speech disjointed. Negative symptoms of schizophrenia include loss of drive and motivation, blunted expression of emotions and social withdrawal.[18]

The cause of schizophrenia is still unknown, although it is generally believed that it is caused by a chemical imbalance in the brain, particularly a neurotransmitter called dopamine. However, psychiatrists are not able to provide details of what the balance actually is and what it should be corrected to. It is generally recognised that some people have a genetic susceptibility to developing schizophrenia, and children of a parent with schizophrenia are seen as having a 10 per cent chance of developing this condition.[19] However, in the majority of cases of schizophrenia, this is not supported. Eighty per cent of those with schizophrenia do not have an immediate family member with the same diagnosis, while approximately 60 per cent do not have an immediate or extended family member with schizophrenia.[20]

Schizophrenia is generally understood according to the vulnerability-stress model, introduced by Zubin and Spring,[21] and further developed by Nuechterlein[22] to include coping resources. According to the stress-diathesis model of schizophrenia, the likelihood of an individual developing schizophrenia is the result of stress acting upon a genetic 'diathesis' to develop schizophrenia.[23] Although stressful events often precede the onset of schizophrenia, it is not always clear if stress has caused schizophrenia to develop. Schizophrenia is generally assessed as having either a chronic or an acute onset.

Stage models of schizophrenia see most cases of schizophrenia ending with the development of psychotic symptoms rather than beginning with them. The focus is on the process that generally begins with social withdrawal rather than the onset of psychotic symptoms.[24] Individuals with acute onset of psychoses usually have better outcomes than those who have a slower more sinister onset.[25] Approximately 20 to 30 per cent of people with schizophrenia only ever experience one or two psychotic episodes.[26]

A good prognosis is more likely when a person develops schizophrenia at a later age. This is because they are more likely to have gone through adolescence, completed schooling and developed good interpersonal and social skills and to have actively participated in the workforce. An acute onset with clearly identified precipitating triggers, good social supports and the presence of mood disorder symptoms is also conducive to recovery.[27] Factors that can inhibit recovery are slow onset at an early age with no clearly identifiable triggers, as well as a lack of social supports and social withdrawal.

If symptoms of mania or depression co-exist with schizophrenia, the person may be with schizo-affective disorder or schizophrenia with a strong mood component. A person may be experiencing psychotic symptoms due to a mood disorder not related to schizophrenia.

Mood disorders

The main mood disorders treated in mental health settings are bipolar affective disorder, formerly known as manic depression and depression. The term bipolar affective disorder is believed to better reflect the range and severity of mood swings that a person may experience. Mania is the term used to describe an elevated mood state.

Common features of mania are high spirits, increased energy levels, reduced sleep and irritability, with rapid thoughts and speech. A person with mania may become less inhibited than usual. This may be in relation to personal behaviour, spending or other aspects of the person's life. Someone in the early stages of mania can be terrific fun and great company and really seem to be enjoying themselves. However, the problem lies in the continued mood escalation that can result in irritability, delusions and impaired thinking and judgement causing considerable detrimental consequences for the individual and those close to them. Hallucinations usually occur when the person's mood is elevated to the extent that they become restless and irritable. Voices usually speak to the person directly and are consistent with the person's mood. Due to the grandiose thinking that generally occurs during mania, voices are often experienced within this context.

Kylie's husband approached the local hospital seeking a psychiatric admission for her. The psychiatric registrar and psychologist who assessed her were perplexed as she presented as very bright and engaging. She was immaculately groomed and they commented later on her beautifully manicured nails. There was no evidence of disturbed thinking or perceptual abnormalities. However, she did speak of having difficulty sleeping and also requested hospitalisation for a rest and to feel safe. She was sent home with follow-up in the community. Kylie's husband continued to contact the hospital and staff felt more concerned with what was seen as his demanding behaviour than about her. Kylie moved out of home into a local motel and staff saw her as asserting herself by leaving a domineering husband. She befriended a neighbour who was a prostitute and began working with her. It was not until Kylie's mood escalated to a state where she was sleeping very little and was not able to care for herself that mental health services responded. She was drinking heavily and began experiencing hallucinations and delusions. Finally there seemed no choice but to admit her to hospital as an involuntary patient. This was much to the relief of her husband, who had continued to agitate for mental health involvement.

In Kylie's case, both she and her husband were aware that things were not right in the very early stages of the onset of mania. However, unfortunately this is often not evident to others, mental health workers included, until later stages. A lot of damage can be done if early responses are not put in place. Kylie was terribly embarrassed about her behaviour while manic and this also had implications for her relationship with her husband. When well again, Kylie moved back with her husband who seemed very supportive of her. It is often those closest to the person who will notice slight differences in behaviour that serve as early warning signals.

Trevor's wife Brianna knew his mood was starting to escalate when he began to whistle around the house. He was normally a very quiet and reserved man. To others he seemed bright and cheerful but Brianna knew what was to come if he did not receive appropriate mental health care. This couple were in their fifties and had been used to Trevor being admitted to a psychiatric hospital at such times. However, community treatment now meant they did not have this option and Trevor was to be treated at home. Trevor, like Kylie, experienced an increasingly elevated mood, restlessness and later irritability. He also was eventually hospitalised involuntarily after his wife called in crisis saying that he was threatening her with a knife. This may have been true or it may have been a desperate act on her part to have him hospitalised.

Both Kylie and Trevor had to hit rock bottom before they could get the service responses they and their partners felt were necessary. The difficulty with mania is that others around the person often cannot keep up with them and find the intensity difficult to cope with. The disorganisation that can occur can make it difficult to get the person to follow through on agreed interventions and management plans. It can also result in financial problems, with the person spending a lot of money when manic. Often, the work of mental health workers is to deal with creditors to undo spending that has occurred during a manic episode. Relationship difficulties can also occur due to out of character disinhibited behaviours.

Some people may experience mania only or depression only – this is generally referred to as unipolar – while others will experience depression and mania.

There is a worldwide increase in rates of depression in both developed and developing countries. Studies conducted in Australia, Britain, the United States, Canada, Italy, Sweden, Germany, France and Lebanon have found an increase in rates of depression, as well as earlier ages of onset.[28] Depression affects men, women and to a lesser extent children across all social classes and cultures. Two types of depression are commonly diagnosed. These are endogenous depression, where the person is seen to have a genetic or biological vulnerability to developing depression and reactive depression, whereby depression is seen as resulting from stressful personal and social circumstances. However, others argue that all depression is related to emotional and social factors and is not solely biological or environmental. It is argued that many studies reflect only the classic diagnosis of depression and do not include the great number of men who demonstrate more covert symptoms of depression.[29] The depression that many people suffer, men in particular, takes on a more mild, elusive and chronic form and is not referred to in much of the literature on depression.[30]

Depression in men is often not recognised and as a consequence not diagnosed because it is unmanly, something that affects women not men. Thus men with depression suffer the double stigma of being mentally unwell and not manly. Due to the shame associated with male depression, it is often not acknowledged by the person affected, those close to him and health professionals.[31] This situation has changed in recent years following successful advocacy campaigns by the national depression initiative Beyond Blue.

It has been estimated that between 60 and 80 per cent of people with depression never receive appropriate assistance. This is a personal and social travesty, considering that in most cases depression responds well to treatment. It is estimated that between 80 and 90 per cent of those who receive a combination of counselling and medication for treatment of depression get relief.[32]

Depression is generally used to depict feelings of sadness that we all experience at some time in our lives. In mental health, clinical depression is used to describe intense and prolonged feelings of depression for two weeks or morwe that can also include anxiety and sleep disturbance. This is often characterised by waking early in the morning at around the same time and not being able to get back to sleep, alongside changes in appetite, with either rapid weight loss or weight gain. A person who is experiencing depression will often feel fatigued or irritable and may be forgetful or have difficulty making decisions. Often the person who is clinically depressed has feelings of worthlessness or guilt and possibly thoughts of, or a preoccupation with, death or suicide. This may be associated with obsessive, intrusive unwanted thoughts. Other symptoms of depression are pessimism, frequent crying and agitated behaviour. Some people may not feel real or fully alive; this is generally referred to as 'depersonalisation'. For others, the world takes on a dreamlike quality; this is called 'derealisation'.

Clinical depression may include a preoccupation with health; the person may present with aches and pains; constipation is a common physical complaint with depression. Psychotic symptoms of delusions and hallucinations may also be present in cases of severe depression. Research findings suggest that as many as one-quarter of people with depression experience psychosis.[33] Usually this is voice experiences that are transient, and limited to single words or short sentences. The content of the voices is generally critical and consistent with the person's depressed mood. The voices usually speak to the person directly and may be accusing the person of wrongdoings and commanding them to do certain things to make amends.

Approximately half of all women who have just given birth experience what are generally regarded as symptoms of depression, including difficulty sleeping, irritability, anxiety and lethargy, commonly referred to as the 'baby blues'. It is debatable how much this is depression or simply a natural response to the physical and emotional demands of giving birth and caring for a newborn infant. For most women, these symptoms dissipate but for approximately 10 per cent of women they continue and develop in range and intensity, and those affected find it increasingly difficult to manage. All of the signs and symptoms of depression discussed above can be present in post-natal depression. Psychotic symptoms may be hearing the baby cry or voices questioning the woman's capabilities as a mother.[34]

> Following the birth of her first child, Janet became increasingly depressed. However, she continually said how blessed she was to have such a beautiful baby. On all accounts, the baby seemed to be sleeping and eating well. Janet was having difficulty sleeping and was waking at three o'clock each morning and having difficulty getting back to sleep. She was not getting any support with the care of the baby. Her husband was working long hours and left the care of the baby to her. She did not have any extended family or support from close friends. Janet's depression continued to get worse. She became fearful of leaving the house even to go to the clothesline. She spoke of hearing the baby cry only to find it was fast asleep. She became preoccupied with cleaning the house and scrubbing the kitchen due to the ants that were crawling all over everything, including her. She rang me in an extremely distressed state saying the ants had taken over and that she could not get rid of them. I went to see her to find her scrubbing furiously and having been scratching herself quite severely. I could not see any ants but clearly in Janet's mind they were there. Janet and the baby were hospitalised in a mother and baby unit where she was treated for post-natal depression. Following her discharge, she left her husband and her mood continued to improve.

In Janet's case, the baby was being well cared for. However, this was not so with Belle, who was frightened to feed her baby because she believed the formula was poisoned.

> Belle had lived in Australia for 12 months. She had no family or friends apart from Hans, an older married man who paid for all of her expenses. Hans visited Belle several times a week and was having an extra-marital relationship with her. He was well off and provided Belle with expensive clothing and personal items such as furs and perfume. However, he would not spend money on household furnishing and appliances with only the bare minimum provided. Belle had very limited English language skills. She was extremely socially isolated and totally reliant upon Hans for money and social contact. Hans was angry when Belle became pregnant and he did not want her to keep the baby. Their relationship had deteriorated significantly since the birth as had Belle's mental health. It was only when problems were extreme and the baby was at risk that Hans reluctantly

contacted a male general practitioner for assistance. This general practitioner had not had any previous contact with Hans or Belle.

A person may present with a depressed mood or other problems associated with substance misuse that are affected by alcohol or other drug use issues that are often not disclosed. Depression and anxiety are common when people present with unexplained somatic complaints. It is important that medical explanations are not overlooked and that the person receives a proper medical examination. It is a poor reflection on our health system when those with undetected medical problems are dismissed as hypochondriacal simply because medical staff are not able to detect the problem.

Katherine was 75 years of age and complained of leg and hip pain over an extended period. She was examined on several occasions by her general practitioner, who could not find a physical problem and diagnosed her as having an unexplained somatic complaint. Katherine insisted that the pain was real and that there must be a physical reason for this. Her doctor insisted there was not. The pain continued and no one listened to Katherine's complaints or took them seriously. It was simply 'all in her head'. Eventually Katherine called herself an ambulance and was taken to Accident and Emergency at the local hospital. At the hospital, medical staff also tried to send Katherine home as they could not detect a physical problem. When Katherine vehemently refused, she was reluctantly admitted with orders for further X-rays that discovered that she did indeed have a fractured hip.

When a person presents with sleep problems, it is important to assess whether or not this is a symptom of depression, and in particular check for a pattern of early morning awakening. A medical assessment is required for physical causes, and in particular sleep apnoea. A person may present with symptoms of both anxiety and depression.

Anxiety disorders

Anxiety is a normal part of everyday life. Anxiety is a term used to describe feelings of discomfort, tension and general unease. Different circumstances cause people to become anxious, with varying impacts. Some people experience extreme anxiety if asked to speak in front of a large audience, whereas others will not experience any anxiety at all. It is when feelings of anxiety prevent people from doing what they want to do and they lose the ability to get on with daily life that they are likely to be with having a generalised anxiety disorder or anxiety and depression. Some physical physical health problems and medications can cause anxiety symptoms; however, this does not result in excessive worry.

Many major life events cause anxiety for most people: loss of employment, serious illness, relationship breakdown, major accident or the death of a family member or close friend. Intense feelings of anxiety will generally be experienced around such life events for a limited time, and this will vary from one person to another. This does not deny the ongoing hurt and loss people experience but rather acknowledges that they develop the ability to get on with life in the face of adversity. Anxiety affects a person's thinking, emotions and behaviours and can cause considerable distress. Fear and panic are characteristic of most anxiety disorders.

Agoraphobia is the most common anxiety disorder and accounts for approximately half of those who seek professional help for anxiety, most of whom are women.[35] Agoraphobia is a fear of being in places or situations that may be difficult to leave. This may be crowded or confined spaces. Specific phobias relate to particular objects or situations such as intense fear of heights or spiders.[36]

A person may be with a panic disorder if anxiety attacks occur in situations where there is no apparent trigger.

Obsessive-compulsive disorder is an anxiety disorder that involves constant and unwanted thoughts that can lead to repetitive behaviours and rituals that can severely interfere with everyday life. Increasingly, obsessions involve technology that can lead to addictions and are of particular concern in young people. When the person is spending more time in the virtual world than the real world, and this virtual world takes priority, it is an indication that intervention may be required. This also includes online gambling that can lead to addiction. A significant proportion of women with obsessive compulsive disorder have a history of anorexia or have been previously with bulimia.

> Melanie's husband called the mental health crisis team late one evening because she would not stop picking her nose. Her nose was bleeding but still she would, or could, not stop. When we arrived she had blood down the front of her shirt and was continually shoving her finger in and out of her nose as she paced up and down the room. She seemed oblivious to the bleeding. The only way to stop her was to hold her hand and try to guide it in a different direction. This was not easy to do as she continued to pace in an agitated manner around the room. Unable to calm her down, we decided to call an ambulance as we were concerned about the internal damage to the membranes in her nose. I recall the ambulance drivers were not impressed with the call and did not want to take her but after some persuasion reluctantly agreed to do so. My colleague was covered in this woman's blood and as we headed back to the centre she asked me to pull over while she vomited into the gutter.

Trauma

Most people who use mental health services report adverse experiences during childhood that impact negatively upon their adult lives. It is essential that mental health workers recognise and acknowledge the relationship between childhood abuse and trauma and long-standing mental health issues as an adult. Trauma-informed care and practice is a main intervention and is discussed in Chapter 10 on interventions.

Post-traumatic stress disorder is a type of anxiety disorder that develops after seeing or experiencing a traumatic event that involves the threat of injury or death. Post-traumatic stress can result from extreme trauma such as war, accidents, fires or personal violence. The person can be left with intense feelings of terror, nightmares and flashbacks that can last for many years after the event and may be with an adjustment disorder.

If dissociative symptoms are present with a sudden onset of dramatic or strange somatic symptoms, the person may be with a dissociative (conversion) disorder.

Personality disorder

Mental health service providers generally have difficulty working with people with personality disorder as they do not respond to usual forms of psychiatric treatment.

Behaviours can be extreme and often disturbing, particularly self-harming. People diagnosed with borderline personality disorder (BPD) are frequently hospitalised, which is not helpful, and often not managed well in the community.

> Personality traits become a personality disorder when the pattern of thinking and behaviour is extreme, inflexible and maladaptive. They may cause major disruption to a person's life and are usually associated with significant distress to the self or others.[37]

Personality disorder is not listed as a diagnostic category for eligibility for government-funded focused psychological strategies. However, given the high prevalence of anxiety amongst those with personality disorder, it is likely that a diagnosis of anxiety disorder may lead to a referral for mental health services.

The main features of a diagnosis of personality disorder are instability in relation to mood, self-image, interpersonal relationships and behaviour. Psychosis is not experienced as a result of the personality disorder.[38] It is estimated that 2 per cent of people in the community have a diagnosis of BPD, mostly young women. Approximately 75 per cent of these are women who have a history of sexual abuse in childhood; one study found 90 per cent had experienced severe and sustained childhood sexual abuse and neglect.[39] Self-harm and suicide attempts are a main feature of these women's lives. A main limitation of the diagnosis is that it is gender and culturally neutral with no consideration of social context.

People diagnosed with BPD are often regarded as often showing little understanding or insight concerning their own or others' feelings. Another view, however, is that the person is experiencing such intense feelings that at times they are not able to manage them appropriately.

Deb harmed herself when she was very upset. For her it was a release of intense emotion and brought some relief. Other women describe feelings of emotional numbness with self-harm a reminder that they are still alive.

People diagnosed with BPD can be extremely lonely and alienated as others reject them because they are at a loss as to how to deal with their difficult behaviours that often result in chaos and uncertainty. Some workers are frustrated by treating emergencies that are self-inflicted. Women diagnosed with BPD are often dismissed as attention-seeking and a waste of time and resources that could be spent on 'real' emergencies. This is particularly an issue with admissions in busy accident and emergency departments, and influences service responses that can at times be punitive.

Sharon lived alone in her flat. When I first met her, she told me she didn't really want to see me as I was like all the other mental health workers. She would get used to me and then I would leave. I could visit her if I wanted to but she really didn't care if I did or not. She didn't want to get to know me because I would leave her like the rest. While confronted by what Sharon said, I realised how astute she really was and that she was prepared to say what others only felt. Sharon had been referred to the community mental health centre because she was disturbing neighbours and threatening them. When upset, Sharon would become extremely abusive to both herself and others. In my relationship with Sharon, she would also be extremely verbally abusive. It was as if she was seeing what my limits were and if I would stick around when things got tough. She cut her arms and burnt herself with cigarettes. When Sharon was upset, she would put her belongings out on the nature-strip. It seemed that the fewer things she had in the flat the more manageable her life became. I recall trying to locate her television following a rubbish collection, only to be told that it had been crushed. The cost of replacing household items made living on a pension even more difficult.

Eating disorders

Eating disorders date back many centuries, with cases of self-starvation documented in the Middle Ages. Two main diagnoses are bulimia and anorexia nervosa.[40]

People diagnosed with anorexia have a body weight 15 per cent below that expected for age and height. They will have a distorted body image and an intense fear of gaining weight even though they are considered by others to be underweight. Depression may occur with an eating disorder. A low body weight can result in the loss, or absence of menstrual periods and other physical problems including chronic constipation. Two subtypes of anorexia include those who restrict food intake and do not binge or purge and those who restrict food intake and who also regularly engage in bingeing or purging with self-induced vomiting or misuse of laxatives or diuretics. Anorexia can also be associated with depression, suicide risk and substance abuse.

Bulimia nervosa made its first appearance in the DSM in 1976, with bulimia requiring at least two episodes a week for the preceding three months. It often commences in late adolescence and mostly affects women aged 18 to 40 years. Bulimia is characterised by binge eating, with the uncontrolled consumption of a large amount of food in a short time period. As well, the person will regularly engage in behavious and activities designed to control body weight and shape, such as vomiting, use of laxatives, strict dieting or fasting, or excessive and vigorous exercise, and self-evaluation which is unduly influenced by body weight and shape. Two types of bulimia have been identified, including those who regularly purge through vomiting and/or use of laxatives and those who do not purge but rather fast or exercise excessively. This latter group generally fall within a healthy weight range and therefore have fewer immediate health risks.

The cause of eating disorders includes cultural factors; a thin female form is highly valued in Western society. This is reinforced in the media, fashion and careers such as gymnasts, models, ballerinas who are required to be of what may be considered an unhealthy body weight. Pressures on girls from an early age to put the needs of others before their own can create role conflict around independence. There is no typical family pattern. Individual factors often include high personal expectations and unrealistic goals with the belief that achievement will result in love from family and friends. Outwardly the person may appear intelligent, achieving well at work or studies and be well disciplined, yet inwardly experience low self-esteem and have a strong need for approval from others. Difficulty expressing needs and emotions, especially negative feelings, and social anxiety are common.

Eating disorders are often precipitated by a life crisis or can come after the accumulation of a number of minor stressors. Dieting may be the only area of life where there is any sense of control. Self-starvation can numb the person affected to feelings and emotions due to the preoccupation with food. All feelings are related to food, so other problems disappear or seem more manageable, creating a sense of a safe place to be. Starvation will have physical effects while also impacting upon a person's thinking and mood.

Kelsey was 16 years of age when she was referred to the mental health crisis team following discharge from an eating disorders unit at a general hospital. She had been in hospital for most of the previous two years. When I first met Kelsey, I recall the prominence of her cheek bones and eyes. She was dressed in an oversized tracksuit and always wore loose fitting clothes. Kelsey was an expert on food and knew numerous recipes. She loved to cook and feed the rest of the family but would only eat very small serves of food herself very slowly. Kelsey was very bright academically and good at sport. She was very quiet and seemed to lack self-confidence. It was very difficult to engage her in any conversation apart from discussing food. Her weight was so low it was life threatening but Kelsey continued to believe she was overweight. She would exercise excessively in an endeavour to continue to lose weight. Kelsey had developed anorexia shortly after her family moved overseas for her father's work. She did not want to go and found it difficult to readjust and make new friends. Her mother also found it difficult and the family cut their trip short to return home after one year rather than two years as they had planned.

Organic disorders

Organic disorders have identifiable physical or biological causes. Many organic mental health disorders are characterised by noticeable changes in memory, intellectual functioning and judgement. These include psychotic disorders whereby a person experiences a marked degree of loss of contact with reality. The two main types of organic psychosis are delirium and dementia. Delirium has a rapid onset and will usually dissipate spontaneously or when the physical cause is treated. Strange behaviours or speech are often a signs of a medical condition.

Delirium and dementia can be caused in older people from medication or mild infections. Delirium is characterised by confusion and rapidly changing behaviour. This can affect memory, thought processes, attention, orientation and perception. With organic psychosis and delirium, hallucinations are usually visual, although other types also occur.

Medical conditions that can lead to a person developing an organic psychotic disorder are herpes, syphilis, HIV, and bacterial or viral meningitis. Other medical conditions include endocrine imbalances affecting the thyroid, nutritional deficiencies of niacin and thiamine, vascular abnormalities and temporal lobe epilepsy. Either delirium or psychotic states can develop from use of, and withdrawal from, alcohol and other drugs, including prescribed medications. Head trauma and metabolic disturbances such as electrolyte imbalances, kidney and liver failure and epilepsy can also cause a delirium or psychosis to develop.[41]

Mandy, a nurse in an acute psychiatric unit, was very surprised to discover a patient, Jean, who was the mother of a close friend. She had not seen her in years. Jean was quite confused and disoriented. This was quite a shock for Mandy who then took an active interest in Jean's situation. Mandy immediately contacted her friend, spoke with Jean and reviewed her file notes. Mandy formed the opinion that Jean's problems were of a physical nature. Further assessment revealed this to be the case and with appropriate physical treatment Jean's former mental state returned.

The frightening thing about this true story is that if Mandy had not found and taken an active interest in her, the physical cause of Jean's problems might have remained undetected. How many older people in particular may have an underlying physical illness or condition that is directly impacting upon their mental state, but has not been detected? A study of 658 psychiatric outpatients conducted in the late 1970s found that 9.1 per cent of them had a physical condition that was affecting their mental state. What was disturbing about the findings was that approximately half of these people, and their medical practitioners, were not aware of the existence of the physical condition.[42]

Dementia is caused by chronic and irreversible physical deterioration. While generally associated with the elderly, dementia is not a normal part of the ageing process. Many older people well advanced in years retain full intellectual functioning. Its occurrence is determined by genetic predisposition, family history, and general health and well-being.[43] Delirium may occur in those with previously normal mental functioning or in people with dementia. Dementia is common in older people but quite rare in middle age or young people.

Dementia of the Alzheimer's type affects 6 per cent of people over 65 years in the Australian population. This percentage rises to 11 per cent for those aged over 75 years. It is a condition for which there is no known cure or medical treatment and which results in the gradual deterioration of memory, intellect and the ability for self-care. Its onset is slow and insidious and leads to major personality alteration, markedly affecting the individual's ability to continue to relate to the world around them. In advanced stages, the person affected will not recognise loved ones or even her or his own face in the mirror. It is a condition that presents a social problem of considerable magnitude in countries like Australia with an ageing demography. Dementia is difficult to diagnose and is a major challenge in terms of its management over often quite long periods of time.

Conclusion

General practitioners and psychiatrists, as members of the medical profession, are in effect the gatekeepers of mental health services as they are responsible for defining and determining what constitutes mental health issues. Models of managed care increasingly rely on general practitioners to refer to allied health professionals for focused psychological services. A major challenge for social workers is how to work effectively within a mental health system that allows entry via diagnostic frameworks that have a predominantly biological focus with service provision that privileges medical and psychological interventions. The next chapter focuses on the social dimensions of assessment and diagnosis with a discussion of the contribution of critical social work theory to mental health knowledge and practice.

Reflection

How does diagnosis determine eligibility for mental health services?

What is a social work diagnosis?

What are the advantages and disadvantages of having one or more mental health diagnoses?

What might negative symptoms of schizophrenia be confused with?

A good prognosis is more likely when a person develops schizophrenia at a later age. Why might this be so?

8

Luisa

In this chapter, an assessment of Luisa is presented to illustrate the assessment set out in Chapter 6. The same headings and format are used, and a copy of the intake and assessment form is provided at the end of the book. Personal reflections are shared, as well as a discussion of relevant theory that informed my work with Luisa as a social worker in community mental health. The assessment provides a broad bio-psycho-social assessment that was continually adapted and reviewed as my relationship with Luisa strengthened and we got to know each other better. This took time and it was only after several visits that Luisa confided in me. Luisa and her husband Peter, and I attended the first assessment interview at a local neighbourhood centre. Due to the referral information, it seemed that Luisa might require support with caring for her daughter Antoinette. I therefore contacted a family support worker at Luisa's local neighbourhood centre and asked her to attend the first interview so that we could do a joint assessment and arrange services as quickly as possible for Luisa if this was necessary. We decided to conduct the interview at the neighbourhood centre, rather than at the community mental health centre, to try to foster this link at the outset. The day after this interview, a home visit was conducted and this is where most of the work with the family occurred. As you will see under the mental status examination conducted at the first interview, Luisa said very little. Much of the early information was provided by Peter and staff from the hospital. It took time to establish a good working relationship with Luisa and to establish her trust after all she had been through. Visiting her at home was important for building this relationship.

Presenting situation

Luisa was referred for follow-up after discharge from a week-long psychiatric hospital admission. According to Peter, Luisa had been admitted to hospital because she was no longer capable of physically caring for herself or for their three-year-old daughter, Antoinette. Luisa was not sleeping much and had put on a considerable amount of weight in the months before her admission. Peter had told hospital staff that Luisa had begun ringing up people from the telephone book to talk to, and that she was repeatedly ringing one man and asking him to marry her. He spoke of how this man had contacted him in an attempt to stop the calls, denying having ever met Luisa or encouraged her in any way. Luisa reported hearing voices inside her head that she was finding very disturbing. Peter tried to reason with Luisa and in desperation took her to see a local general practitioner who arranged for her to be admitted to a psychiatric unit at the hospital.

Luisa is a 30-year-old woman of southern European background who stays at home to care for her three-year-old daughter Antoinette during the daytime. She finds it difficult looking after Antoinette, complaining that she is very naughty. Luisa gave examples of Antoinette's misbehaviour as spitting, deliberately throwing glasses of drink on the floor, not eating properly, refusing to be toilet-trained and not going to bed on time at night. Both Luisa and Antoinette went to bed around midnight and slept through until midday. Up until migrating to Australia, Luisa's mother had provided a lot of assistance caring for Antoinette. This was the first time in her life that Luisa had had to look after Antoinette without the support of her mother. As well, it was the first time Luisa had had primary responsibility for cooking and household chores. At the home visit, the house was very sparsely furnished with few personal belongings apart from a computer and textbooks, and the garden was very overgrown. During the interviews it seemed apparent that the family was very much in the early days of resettlement in Australia. They were extremely socially isolated and struggling financially.

Past psychiatric history

Luisa and Peter report no known psychiatric history. This was her first psychiatric hospital admission. On admission, Luisa was described as having blonde hair and dressed in brightly coloured clothing, wearing a miniskirt, low-cut blouse and stilettos. Her mood was elevated and she was seen to be excitable and laughing inappropriately, yet at the same time irritable and angry about being admitted to hospital. After anti-psychotic medication was administered, Luisa's mood soon lowered and she was seen as having becoming depressed. She was diagnosed as having a schizo-affective disorder and was discharged on anti-psychotic medication to be taken twice daily. Luisa expressed concerns about side effects from the medication and wanted to stop taking it. She said it made her feel tired and sleepy and that her mouth felt dry.

Luisa was assessed as in good physical health at the time of admission to hospital and did not have any physical or medical conditions requiring treatment. Luisa has no history of violence, suicide attempts, or deliberate self-harm. She also has no history of substance use and no past forensic involvement.

Family

Luisa and Peter have been married for three years with one child, a three-year-old daughter named Antoinette. Luisa spoke of growing up in a happy home environment, with a great deal of affection towards her brothers and sisters and her mother in particular.

Genogram

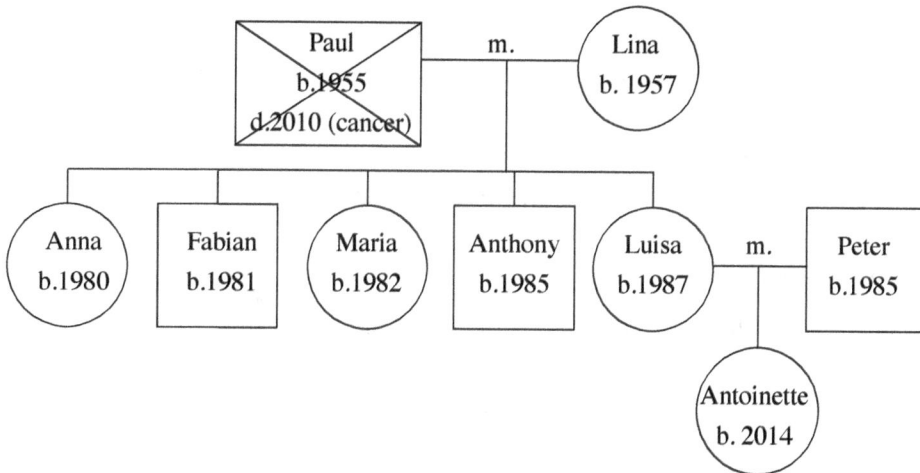

Luisa and Peter report no known family psychiatric history. Luisa's father died of cancer four years ago. Luisa is the youngest of five children and she describes her family as being very close and supportive. In Italy, Luisa and her husband and daughter lived with Luisa's mother whom Luisa is very close to. Before migrating to Australia, Luisa contacts her mother three times a week. Luisa spoke longingly of her family and former life. Luisa worked full-time as a travel consultant, and her mother cared for Antoinette. She would come home of an evening to a meal cooked by her mother, who would also have Antoinette bathed and ready for bed.

Personal

Luisa's pregnancy and labour with Antoinette went well. Luisa described a very happy and satisfying relationship with Peter up until their migration to Australia seven months ago. She felt it had been Peter's decision to migrate and that she had no say in the matter. Luisa was angry with Peter and blamed him for taking her away from her family and home. She was also angry that he had limited her packing; many of her personal effects, including wedding presents, were left behind at his insistence. He had made room, however, for his rather extensive library of textbooks, which Luisa resented him for. Luisa described Peter as becoming increasingly moody and non-communicative since their migration to Australia. He worked long hours and spent much of his time at home on the computer. Luisa described herself as having changed a lot since coming to Australia. Physically she had put on a lot of weight. She was very unhappy with her appearance and Peter had let her know he was not happy about her weight increase either. She now felt she did not have any energy or motivation to perform even simple everyday tasks. Before going to hospital, Peter reports that Luisa had not had a shower or bath for two weeks.

Culture

Luisa and Peter are from Europe. They still strongly adhere to their culture and place considerable importance on the family. They do not know anyone else in Australia apart from Peter's work colleagues and do not socialise at all. Luisa reluctantly migrated to Australia, in an attempt to further her husband's career. She has no family or friends, apart from her husband and daughter, in Australia and is terribly lonely and isolated.

Spiritual background

Luisa and Peter are Roman Catholic. They do not attend church services or participate in church activities.

Education and employment

Luisa achieved well academically at school and got on well with her classmates. She went on to do further studies in tourism before taking on a position as a travel consultant, which she worked at up until her migration to Australia. She has not been in paid employment since coming to Australia.

Accommodation and finances

The family are currently living in a very sparsely furnished rented house. Financially they are struggling as most of their savings have been spent on the move to Australia. Peter is employed in his chosen industry at a lower level than at home, and is working very long hours to support the family.

Social history

Luisa described herself as having a lot of energy in the past and how much she enjoyed working and socialising with family and friends. Luisa and Peter had a very active social life and she loved her job in the travel industry. She was popular among family, friends and colleagues. She was particularly close to her mother, as was Antoinette. In Italy she enjoyed going shopping, keeping up with the latest fashions, going to the cinema and cafés. She had not done any of these things in Australia due to financial difficulties and lack of friends and family.

Pre-morbid personality

Luisa and Peter both described her as bright, energetic and full of fun. Luisa was always happy and busy socialising with her family and friends. She was of an easy temperament and did not often get angry. Peter described Luisa as very orderly, well organised and self-disciplined.

Mental status examination

The mental status examination presented here was conducted at the first interview. There is a sharp contrast in this MSE and the MSE conducted on Luisa's admission to hospital, with both of these also different from how Luisa usually is when well.

General appearance and behaviour

At the first interview Luisa was dressed in a very long oversized black knitted dress. She had shoulder-length black hair. Her speech was quite slow with very little eye contact. Luisa looked mostly down at the floor during the interview.

Speech

Luisa spoke in a soft voice. She gave brief answers to questions put to her but did not speak otherwise. For the majority of the interview Peter spoke on her behalf.

Affect

Luisa's mood was lowered, with a decreased range of emotional reactions. She seemed quite guarded throughout the interview. As most of the discussion was focused around past and present difficulties, her affect was appropriate to the content of the conversation as it was no doubt difficult and embarrassing for her.

Thought

When Luisa did speak she expressed herself clearly and appropriately. There was no evidence of obsessional or delusional ideas. Nor was there was any evidence of suicidal or homicidal ideation.

Perception

Luisa did not show any signs of hallucinations during the interview. She said that the voices she had been hearing before her admission had ceased.

Cognition

Luisa was well oriented to time, place and person. She did not appear to have any problems with attention or concentration. Luisa was able to recall information using both her long-term and short-term memory. She was aware of recent significant events.

Insight and judgement

Luisa seemed very confused about her stay in the hospital and events immediately preceding her admission. Luisa was aware she was not coping with things as well as she would like to and that she had been behaving strangely prior to her admission to hospital. She was fearful of this happening again and being made to return to the hospital. Luisa was accepting of treatment yet was keen to come off the medication as soon as possible.

Formulation of assessment

Luisa is very lonely and socially isolated. She has undergone considerable financial hardship and experienced major stress associated with the family's migration to Australia. This is the first time Luisa, Peter and Antoinette have lived together without any family or other support. It is also the first time that Luisa has had primary responsibility for the care of Antoinette, and for cooking and domestic chores, due to the extended family living arrangements and the support provided by Luisa's mother in Italy.

Luisa was experiencing significant stress and isolation before her hospitalisation. This is her first contact with mental health services and there is no individual or family history of psychiatric problems. Without adequate social support, risk of relapse seems quite high if the situation at home remains the same, particularly Luisa's social isolation and lack of assistance and support in the care of Antoinette.

Immediate management plan

The neighbourhood centre provided short-term family support services of a practical nature focused on parenting issues, household chores, meal preparation and social contact. A family support worker, from the neighbourhood centre visited Luisa three times a week to discuss and plan with her issues around household management as well as parenting concerns with Antoinette. At the same time, Luisa was linked into a parent education program run by the same agency and a social support group.

The social worker from the neighbourhood centre met with Luisa once a week to provide follow-up and coordination of the services provided by this agency. As a mental health worker, I met with Luisa once a week for counselling around issues associated with her migration to Australia and resettlement as well as helping her make sense of recent and ongoing experiences with psychiatric services. Family sessions were also conducted. A main focus of the work with Luisa was to empower her by helping her to rebuild her sense of confidence and self-esteem and assist her in finding suitable directions for the future. It was important that time was spent discussing her recent hospitalisation and events preceding it, as well as future management and the likelihood of her experiencing difficulties of a similar nature in the future. I kept in regular contact with the social worker from the neighbourhood centre, Luisa's psychiatrist and her general practitioner.

The assessment formulation and management plan were very much influenced by my personal reflections on the information gained, and impressions formed, during the assessment interview, and the integration of these with theory. My personal reflections are provided below, followed by a discussion of theory relevant to Luisa's situation.

Personal reflections

I felt a real sense of loneliness and sadness when hearing Luisa's story and had feelings of despair at the end of the first session. I felt that she was going to need short-term intensive support initially. I was sensitive to the stressors associated with international migration and resettlement and the huge strain this had put on Luisa. I wondered about Luisa's level of parenting and domestic skills due to the support provided by Luisa's mother. I was mindful that this was the first time Luisa, Peter and Antoinette have lived together without any family or other support. I was aware that Luisa was experiencing significant stress and isolation before her hospitalisation, that this was Luisa's first contact with psychiatric services and that there was no past individual or family history of psychiatric problems. These factors, combined with Luisa's high level of functioning before this episode, made me hopeful for Luisa's recovery, albeit aware that further assessment and monitoring of her mental state was required.

Linkage with theory

Critical theory provided a critique according to Luisa's status as a woman, a new immigrant, the family's low socio-economic status since migrating to Australia and the lack of power she had over major decisions in her life. It was important to empower Luisa and give her a sense of control over her life once more. Critical theories helped raise questions about the appropriateness of practices in psychiatric hospitals and the diagnoses used due to the lack of recognition and acknowledgment of gender and cultural differences and the demoralisation that can occur in such settings. Structural theory helped provide a critique of both the personal and political dimensions of Luisa's situation. Anti-oppressive theory highlighted issues associated with the stigma of having mental health issues. At all times Luisa was treated with dignity and respect and the main focus of intervention was on her hopes, dreams and aspirations for herself and her family in Australia, while acknowledging the pain and hardship she had experienced in leaving her home and resettling in Australia. Her psychiatric diagnosis and mental state were discussed but they certainly were not the focus of work with her.

The relationship with Luisa was the key to being able to work effectively together. This is consistent with critical theory's critiques of professional distancing and the importance of workers being human and caring. Skills in a structural approach were particularly useful in establishing rapport and connecting with Luisa. I was able to normalise her situation by talking of other people I had seen who had become mentally unwell due to major stressors in their lives and to universalise her situation by establishing links with others who had become mentally unwell following the trauma of migration. We talked about how the conditions of the move, combined with personal characteristics, may lead to an improvement or deterioration in mental health. The crucial factor was how the person adjusts to these changes and the supports available to them. I was also able to normalise the difficulties and frustrations she was having raising a young child and the loneliness and isolation she was experiencing. Connecting her with a group of women in similar circumstances both helped to normalise the difficulties she was experiencing as well as providing opportunities for social contact and the development of friendships. At the same time it was important to individualise her situation as her own unique experience. Critical postmodern theory was useful in drawing attention to the importance of valuing the uniqueness of Luisa's own story.

The main skills were listening and taking the time to hear Luisa's story and validate her thoughts, feelings and experiences. Critical questioning was useful to help get different perspectives on past and present events as well as hopes for the future. The turning point in our relationship came on a home visit when Luisa brought out her photo album to show me. Looking at Luisa's photos and listening to the memories they triggered increased my knowledge and understanding of her. Here in the photographs was Luisa as I had never imagined and this was her self and the life that she wished to regain in Australia.

The interventions may not seem particularly consistent with a feminist approach as ultimately we worked with Luisa to assist her to adequately manage childcare responsibilities and household chores and we did not insist on Peter's involvement. However, consistent with a recovery-oriented approach, we were ultimately guided by how Luisa and Peter had divided labour within the family and what their priorities were. They both agreed that in order to establish Peter's career and support the family financially, in the short-term Luisa needed to focus on care of Antoinette and home duties to allow Peter to do the long hours of work he felt were necessary. Culturally it was expected that Luisa would assume primary care for Antoinette. Thus we listened to Luisa and Peter and respected Luisa's active role in decision-making and supported and affirmed this rather than endeavouring to impose what we as social workers may have seen as more politically correct.

Recovery

Collaborative work across agencies, rather than working solely within one service or referring across services, is central to a recovery-oriented approach. This is evident in arranging the first interview at the neighbourhood centre even though the actual referral had been made to the community mental health centre. This was responding to the possible care issues for Luisa's daughter Antoinette. The referral information informed the way the first interview was conducted. However, decisions were made only with the involvement and consent of Luisa and Peter. Due to Luisa's depressed state on discharge from hospital, we did assume a more interventionist role than may sit comfortably with critical theories. However, this was deemed necessary and ultimately was more empowering for Luisa as she was set up to succeed with the necessary supports at the outset. Ultimately this provided support and relief for Luisa, who was empowered as she gradually resumed full care of Antoinette and took charge of her life. What was most important was monitoring and pacing the amount of support Luisa needed. Too much would ultimately be disempowering as Luisa could feel reliant upon others who she might come to see as more capable than her. This would simply be replacing the functions of Luisa's mother in a way that was not sustainable or positive for the family. Too little support might mean Luisa becoming unwell again and not able to manage. This was a fine balancing act that had its ups and downs and certainly was not a linear progression. There were times when supports needed to be increased once they had been gradually reduced as the family circumstances warranted this. Luisa's story illustrates the importance of being tuned into where she was at and what she required at any given time, rather than working from a predetermined one-size-fits-all model of service delivery.

Social isolation was a major factor leading to Luisa's psychiatric hospital admission. Linking her with the parenting and social groups provided opportunities for mutual support and friendships. At the same time it gave Luisa a break from her daily routine at home and Antoinette had other children her age to play with. As Luisa's confidence and self-esteem increased, she began talking about returning to work in the travel industry. Together we explored different possibilities. Ultimately, Luisa was supported to manage her mental health and other aspects of her life.

Postscript

One year after services first began, Luisa's mood remained stable. She returned very much to the way both Peter and she had described her pre-morbid personality. She became more proficient with caring for Antoinette, cooking and household chores. She thoroughly enjoyed the social group as well as the parenting program. Counselling sessions were helpful in adjusting to life in Australia and addressing issues of loss and grief associated with the migration process. The relationship between Luisa and Peter improved, with a gradual reduction in financial stress. Luisa decided that she wanted to do a bridging course so that her qualifications in travel could be recognised in Australia and she could return to work. She enrolled in a local college with childcare attached for Antoinette. As well Luisa commenced a home business franchise selling cosmetics. Her medication was gradually reduced to a maintenance dose. Luisa remained well and continued to make a new life for herself but she was fearful that she could become unwell again. At the same time she wanted to completely come off her medication, particularly as she wanted to become pregnant again. This was supported by her psychiatrist with close monitoring. This included encouraging Luisa and Peter to contact the community mental health service immediately if things started to deteriorate, so as to initiate early intervention and avoid the possibility of a further hospitalisation.

Conclusion

Luisa's story is an example of recovery-focused practice. An assessment framework, reflective practice and the application of critical theory and skills informed this practice. The assessment interview and intervention planning were respectful of Luisa and Peter's wishes and supported the goals Luisa and her family were striving to achieve in Australia. A focus was on Luisa living well in the presence or absence of signs and symptoms of mental health issues. It was about getting back the things Luisa had lost due to her migration experience and subsequent mental health issues and about moving forward. Connecting Luisa with relevant services and supports was essential to her recovery. This included mental health and community services, social supports and education and employment. Consistent with recovery focused practice this was done in partnership with her family. Both mental health and community services working together rather than simply a referral across services. The next Chapter looks at the importance of consumer and carer partnerships in mental health recovery.

9

Consumer and Carer Partnerships

Consumers and carers are key players in the design and delivery of mental health services due to their personal experience of mental health issues. The deinstitutionalisation of mental health services and closure of stand-alone psychiatric hospitals has witnessed a shift in responsibility for the care of people with mental health issues from the health system to the community sector. The people who are now providing this care are family and friends, with support from workers. Recovery-focused practice therefore necessarily requires the development of effective partnerships between workers, consumers and carers. In this chapter, consumer participation is discussed with consideration of the notion of consumer leadership. The exercise of power by mental health workers over those they are working with is discussed, particularly in relation to acute mental health care and crisis intervention. The concept of cooperative power is explored and the promotion of meaningful and reciprocal relationships with consumers. Issues for families and carers are raised and the importance of families and carers being listened to and their decisions respected with support provided for those who assume a carer role. Social work involvement with consumer and carer-led groups and advocacy campaigns is also discussed.

Consumer and carer participation

In Australia in the past three decades consumers and carers have had a much stronger voice in the design and delivery of mental health services. One of the most promising and exciting developments to date is the notion of co-design, whereby consumers are now taking responsibility for leadership in the design of mental health services into the future. Social workers play an important role in supporting this process and not leaving consumers to do this alone. They must ask consumers how they can best assist. This has been particularly so since the release of the findings of the reconvened Inquiry into the Rights of People with Mental health issues in 1996.[1] The reconvened inquiry saw consumers and carers as central figures in the mental health system yet found that their views were not adequately taken into account in government decisions about the system. They endorsed the importance of consumer and carer advocacy groups as legitimate and important participants in the mental health policy process, independent of non-government service providers. They reported that advocacy groups felt their criticisms of the mental health service were not considered on their merits but rather are perceived as an attack on the government department providing these services. The reconvened inquiry maintained that consumers were being denied the care and treatment they need, due to ineligibility, inaccessibility or unavailability of services.[2]

On 22 March 1996, the then Mental Health Branch of the Victorian government launched the consumer participation policy. According to this policy, mental health services were now obligated to consumer participation initiatives in the management and evaluation of mental health services. Funds were allocated to each Area Mental Health Service for consumer participation for the improvement of service delivery programs. The idea for this policy came from consumers. However, consumers were later to express concerns about the invisibility of consumers' contribution to the policy. According to the policy, a wide-ranging view of partnership was needed at the state, area, individual and family level. No fixed format was provided on how to achieve such partnerships. It was suggested that it must be guided by the needs and goals of the particular consumers and mental health services concerned. Guidelines for consumer participation in mental health services were released in March 1996 to assist in this process.

Consumer participation was acknowledged as crucial for the achievement of suitable outcomes for people with mental health issues. Case management practices within mental health services were to be established, with workers and consumers developing partnerships to the greatest degree possible in a cooperative and collaborative manner. Good practice embraced consumer involvement in joint decision-making with workers about support and treatment.[3] Consumers were now involved in a range of activities at the local, regional and state levels. Areas of involvement were policy, service planning and development, service delivery, training and staff development, social research and service evaluation. At the agency and organisational level, activities included participation on advisory boards, planning committees and the daily operation of mental health organisations. Consumer participation includes self-help groups, consultation, lobbying and advocacy, peer support and co-design of services. Peer support has gained increased importance in recent years as increased numbers of consumers are employed in these roles and provide valuable assistance and depth of understanding from also experiencing mental health issues that may or may not be ongoing. Consumers report on the value of this empathy and understanding and the support provided by peers. At the state level, the Victorian Community Advisory Group provides independent advice to the Minister.[4] Although numerous initiatives for consumer participation were undertaken, these did not include forensic mental health services; consumer participation was '...forgotten within forensic mental health services'.[5] Initiatives in recent years, however, have seen increased consumer participation in this area.

Recovery-focused practice takes consumer participation one step further by advocating consumer leadership.[6] Consumer participation is very different from consumer leadership. This is quite confronting for some mental health workers who take a paternalistic stance and argue that people with mental health issues are not capable of making decisions about their own care, let alone policy and service development decisions. Thus consumers can face institutionalised discrimination from workers as well as the broader community. It relates back to the notion of being let in and being allowed to participate in meaningful ways – discussed in Chapter 3 in relation to community living. The term empowerment is often used by social workers. However, this can also be paternalistic as it suggests that workers are giving power to consumers. Rather, workers need to support and assist consumers in accessing and using their own power.

Identity and power

A major concern of consumers of stand-alone psychiatric hospital services was that they were not treated as individuals when in hospital. People described feelings of loss of identity and a lack of power when what was needed was a reinforcing of the self. Consumers stressed the importance of personal contact with workers. This may seem obvious, yet workers, particularly nursing staff, often get caught up in the administration of the ward and do not spend time developing relationships with people. It also highlights the valuing and devaluing of activities; talking to consumers is sometimes seen by nursing colleagues as slacking off.

The continued practice of locating the nurses' station behind a locked door with windows looking out on to the ward creates a fishbowl effect of us and them. Admittedly, privacy is needed for keeping personal files and private discussions and telephone calls, but much work can actually be done in the ward itself. I recall numerous occasions being on a ward where consumers would knock several times on the door only to be ignored by staff, or the door would be opened and the person dealt with in a terse and abrupt manner. In such instances, the powerlessness of the consumer was evident; they were treated as either insignificant or invisible.

Social workers too are guilty of not allocating appropriate time and resources to spending time with people to get to know them by listening to their stories, acknowledging their experiences and affirming them as individuals. In psychiatric settings, social workers and other allied health staff often have their offices separate from the ward and the majority of their time is spent outside the ward or at meetings. I once encountered a social work student on placement at a psychiatric unit in a general hospital who complained that he did not have enough to do. I asked him how he spent his days. It soon became clear that he spent very little time on the ward. When I suggested spending more time on the ward getting to know the patients better, he was reluctant and clearly did not see this as a valued activity.

Commenting on consumer experiences at Royal Park Psychiatric Hospital, the last stand-alone psychiatric hospital in Victoria, Epstein and Wadsworth describe what they saw as a paradox in the delivery of acute mental health care:

> The same mental health system which was working so hard towards healing patients was... both delivering some damaging effects to patients and also itself suffering symptoms of stress, distress, poor self esteem, depression, anxiety and even fear. The same fears and ways of being human would, we think, eventually resurface in any new building. The answer lies in a shift to a sufficiently respectful and responsive organisational culture for both consumers and staff. Mental health services can take a lead by building in mechanisms which systematically guard against the system's own various tendencies to contradict its own healing purposes.[7]

Although written about a stand-alone psychiatric hospital, these comments are relevant to services in the community and psychiatric units in general hospitals. Respectful relationships and a culture of recovery need to be built into policies and practices in all mental health settings. Otherwise, community care will simply mean replicating past disempowering practices in new services. This is particularly an issue for work on crisis assessment treatment teams and residential settings in the community.

Acute mental health care: crisis intervention[8]

It is virtually impossible for people to refuse services from community assessment and treatment teams if they appear to be mentally ill and are deemed to be in crisis and a danger to self or others. If a person refuses entry, workers simply return with the police. The dilemma is that if a person is in crisis they need to be seen, but having police involvement is an extreme action. This is power over and not power with consumers and carers. I recall numerous crisis situations in mental health where we exerted power over consumers, as in the following example.

A community nurse and I responded to referral from a worker at a community mental health centre in our area. We were to follow up a woman, Elaine, aged in her 30s, with schizophrenia and considered at risk because she was refusing treatment and not attending scheduled appointments. We arrived at the house and as we walked up the driveway a woman who looked to be around 60 years of age had her head out of the front window of the house, shouting at us to go away and leave her and her daughter alone. The nurse and I simply ignored her and continued to proceed to the front door and ring the doorbell. Elaine opened the door and we went inside. She said it was perhaps best if we spoke in her bedroom at the end of the house. Elaine's mood was quite flat and she appeared underweight and was not eating or sleeping well. As we spoke with her in the bedroom, we could now hear her mother calling out, 'Get out of my house.' Again we ignored her and continued our conversation with Elaine. We then heard footsteps hurrying up the passage and the door was flung open; Elaine's mother started swinging a broom at us, shouting for us to leave. It was only then that we quickly took notice and left in a hurry with her chasing us up the passage with the broom. We left and returned not long after with the police.

On reflection, it was quite an extreme response to call the police but one that we were accustomed to, and now normal practice. But it is common practices such as these, incorporated into the culture of mental health organisations, that are the most dangerous. We were adopting practices that were both distressing and damaging rather than sensitive and respectful. If someone did not allow us entry, we simply returned with the police. Sometimes even more extreme measures were taken, as with Maria.

Maria was aged in her early 40s and had a diagnosis of schizophrenia. She lived on her own in a flat and experienced what mental health workers assessed as auditory hallucinations and delusions with religious themes. Maria attended church daily and dressed in the religious robes of a nun. She was having difficulty with side effects from her medication and had stopped taking it. After she stopped her medication, Maria experienced an increase in disturbing and distressing voices and thoughts about people persecuting her. These were particularly directed at her elderly neighbours. She was quite frightened and fearful that people were trying to harm her. Maria agreed to try a new medication we hoped would be more agreeable to her, as well as regular visits from the crisis team. On one such visit, a worker arrived and knocked on Maria's door. Maria did not answer the door. After Maria did not respond, he climbed into her flat through a window.

This worker had good intentions and was genuinely worried about Maria. However, this act was a gross violation of Maria's privacy and even more concerning due to her already fearful state. Following this incident, it was clearly stipulated by management that entry was to be gained from a trusted person. The minister from the local church was contacted and became a liaison support between the crisis team and Maria. This was very helpful in establishing positive working relations, as the minister was also a source of comfort and support for her.

The challenge for workers in crisis situations is how to be both responsive and respectful. Just because a person is in crisis, does not mean they cannot be involved in decisions about what is going to happen to them. In fact, it is usually the opposite. Involvement in such decisions means a greater sense of personal control at a time when this appears to have been lost. It also means the person is going to have a greater commitment to agreed interventions, and take responsibility for her or his own recovery. Careful thought and planning is required for responses to crisis situations. Workers need to collect as much information as possible from referral sources and any existing file notes, before responding, so that they can get a sense of the present situation and past problems and solutions as well as who are key figures that may be able to provide care and assistance. Coercive and disrespectful practices should be avoided.

Cooperative power

An analysis of power is central to recovery-focused practice. It is useful for social workers to reflect on the following questions on a personal level as well as explore these with the people they are working with.

What does power mean to you?
Who has power over you?
Over whom do you have power?
Around whom do you feel powerful?
How do you give away your power?
How do you share power?

People often give power to others in situations where there is a valued relationship or where they are relying on the other person's expertise. A person may comply with someone else because of reward or punishment or simply because they have been persuaded by him or her. In many situations in mental health, social workers exert power over those they are working with.

It is useful to consider the difference between manipulation and influence. In situations of manipulation, people feel tricked and outcomes favour the manipulator often at the expense of another. If a person is manipulating someone, they are inclined to discourage input from others. This results in the presentation of biased information. The manipulator less frequently considers the needs and concerns of the other person and is less committed to making solutions work. Manipulative behaviours tend to stunt relationships with people who often feel tricked or taken advantage of. In situations where a person feels influenced, they are more likely to feel persuaded with outcomes favouring others as well as the influencer. People who are influencing others are inclined to encourage and value input from others with balanced information presented. They will frequently consider needs and concerns of others and be committed to making solutions work.

I attended a home visit one evening with a colleague Marcus. We had received a call from a woman who was concerned about her husband Jason's 'threatening behaviour'. Jason had a diagnosis of bipolar-affective disorder and we had been working with him for a few days prior to receiving this crisis call. His wife had clearly indicated at the outset that she did not want to care for Jason at home and wanted him hospitalised. She was told that this was not possible because Jason was not a danger to himself or others nor did he require the facilities of a hospital. It was assumed his wife would care for him even though she had said she did not want to. This crisis call from her however changed this.

When we arrived at the family home, Jason greeted us and invited us in. Marcus had said that he thought it best if he spoke privately with Jason in the lounge room while I spoke with Jason's wife in the kitchen. This is what we proceeded to do. After quite some time, I noticed it was very quiet in the lounge room and discovered that neither Marcus nor Jason were there. I then discovered that the car Marcus and I had travelled in was also gone. Nobody in the family knew where Marcus or Jason was. Eventually I received a telephone call from Marcus to say that he was at the admissions office of the psychiatric hospital and that he would come and pick me up when he had finished arranging Jason's admission. This had not been discussed with myself as a co-worker, Jason's wife and sons nor Jason himself as it turned out. Marcus seemed quite pleased with himself as he told me how he had asked Jason to go for a drive with him to get something to eat and had instead driven him to the hospital.

Certainly in this situation Jason was manipulated and tricked into going with Marcus. However, Marcus felt quite justified and even proud of what he had done. He argued that according to his assessment Jason needed to be hospitalised and he had facilitated this. He was quite adamant that Jason would not have gone to hospital voluntarily. At the request of both Jason and his family, we did not have any further contact with Jason following this admission.

The challenge for workers in mental health is to develop models of cooperative power with and not over others and to learn from and influence the people they work with and not manipulate them.[9]

Promoting meaningful and reciprocal relationships

Consumer involvement and participation of people who have first-hand knowledge and experience of mental health services is crucial to the redevelopment of services. However, promoting meaningful collaboration is complex. A focus is on ensuring that genuine partnerships are developed between consumers and workers. Consideration needs to be given to how collaboration between consumers, carers and staff can be enhanced. Time needs to be spent reflecting on what the attributes of a collaborating service are, as well as what genuine partnerships between consumers and staff might look like.

In accordance with the consumer participation policy, government funds were allocated to support projects that supported consumer and worker partnerships. One such project was the Lemon Tree Learning Project conducted by the Victorian Mental health issues Awareness Council. The main aim of the project was to sensitise workers in mental health settings to the lived experiences of consumers. This was done through narratives, or storytelling, with consumers telling groups of workers of their experiences and perceptions of mental health staff and services. However, the process of revealing very detailed personal information and the lack of reciprocity or response from workers left members of this project feeling discontented. Consumers involved in this project commented, 'We were annoyed that we so often came away from these experiences [group presentations] as though we had taken all our clothes off in public in a gesture of self-exposure that was not reciprocated.'[10] This adds a further dimension to partnerships. The challenge is to develop meaningful and collaborative relationships that include reciprocity. These consumers raised a very important point that as social workers we often taken for granted. It requires reflection on how we develop working relationships with people and use of self.

Social workers are busy collecting very personal information from people yet reveal very little if anything about themselves. Self-disclosure is usually taught as a skill to be used sparingly and only if direct benefits result in the sharing of this information for the consumer. Social workers are also taught to maintain a professional distance and not to become over involved with those they are working with. As mentioned in Chapter 6, social theorist Thomas Scheff was critical of the emphasis on the professional relationship in social work, with the encouraging of neutrality and emotional distance resulting in social workers being seen as aloof and uncaring.[11] The challenge is how to be responsive and to self disclose in ways that are appropriate and build positive reciprocal working relationships. Social work students at the University of Malaysia are assessed on their ability to demonstrate a 'warm and friendly manner' when working with people and to think about what impression they are making.[12] This serves as a good beginning to developing collaborative relationships.

The challenge for workers is to translate espoused organisational values and policy directions on consumer participation into actual practices. It is important that an appropriate infrastructure is in place to facilitate consumer involvement. Representation by more than one consumer on a committee is advisable so that duties and responsibilities can be shared as well as more varied input. This avoids tokenism by providing acknowledgment that consumers are not a homogeneous group and will contribute different views on any given issue. The committee needs to be clear on what they want to achieve by involving consumers. In addition, consumers need to be adequately briefed about their role and function on the committee. The identification of staff to assist consumers in developing meeting and communication skills and support during and between meetings is important for developing confidence and active participation. Feedback is required for consumers to feel their input is appreciated.[13]

In considering the development of meaningful reciprocal relationships, it is also worth considering some of the limits to effective consumer participation.

Limits to effective consumer participation include

differences between stated organisational values and actual practices
tokenism
inadequate clarity about role/s and function/s
representation
role strain
generalisations
consumers' and workers' relationships in different settings
communication and language (and)
economic factors.

Limiting factors can be differences between stated organisational values and actual practices that lead consumers to believe that the service's response to consumer participation is tokenistic rather than genuine. Even if workers do not believe this to be the case, it is important that workers respond appropriately to consumer concerns and treat them seriously. The involvement of consumers without the infrastructure to support them is negligent. Consumers need to be supported and briefed appropriately about their role and function in the mental health service and participation on committees and meeting processes if relevant.

Appropriate consumer representation is an important consideration, as are the dangers of generalising and treating consumers as if they are a homogeneous group. Role strain may occur, with consumers and workers relating differently in diverse contexts. An example would be where a worker is the case manager of a consumer who is also a member of a staff consumer advisory committee. In this instance, the worker would be privy to much personal information about the consumer that they would not normally have about colleagues. This can create tension if not acknowledged and addressed.

Communication in meetings can be difficult for consumers who may be unfamiliar with meeting processes and language and acronyms used. Shared assumptions and understandings between workers can be excluding and stress-provoking for new participants.

It is important that workers promote an inclusive atmosphere and ensure that written and verbal communications are understood and meeting processes are clear. It is useful to nominate support staff during and between meetings to ensure that adequate briefing and de-briefing is provided. Economic factors for consumer participation need to be considered. For some consumers, attendance at meetings may mean loss of wages or additional costs due to childcare and transport. Workers need to be sensitive to the fact that whereas they are being paid for their time at meetings, consumers generally are not. Often, they are also out of pocket for travel expenses. This tension also needs to be acknowledged and funds used wherever possible to pay consumers for their participation and contributions. It may be necessary to provide transport to and from meetings.

Families and carers

It was estimated that in Australia in 2011 there was a hidden workforce of at least 2.9 million carers ranging from age 10 to ninety, providing care across all disability groups.[14] According to Louise Gilmore, the president of Carers Victoria, myths about carers as 'something like a cross between a guardian angel and motherhood itself' are not only a fantasy but also 'insidious' because it makes carers 'invisible and easy to ignore'.[15] Gilmore states,

> Carers are not necessarily warm, kind, self-effacing, heroines and heroes. Carers are people. Some of us are kind. Some of us are not. Some do it for love. Some do it for duty. Some do it because there are simply no other choices. Many would give anything not to be doing it. Some shoulder the task with resignation, others with grief, with bitterness and even with resentment.[16]

Often with community care, family members are bestowed a new title of 'carer' by mental health workers. This language is powerful in the way it transforms relationships and power dynamics within a family. A husband may become the 'official carer'. However, the 'unofficial carers' are often children. This has huge ramifications in terms of the transfer of power within a family. It is more likely that rather than having a carer in the community many women have themselves been providing primary care for children and other family members. It is these gaps in care provision that need attention, to ensure that these responsibilities are being undertaken appropriately in the woman's absence. At times, children are given responsibility and decision-making powers beyond what would be normal when their mothers are well. At the same time, their own primary carer is not fully available for them.

Human Rights Commissioner Brian Burdekin highlighted the plight of children of parents with mental health issues in 1993 in his inquiry into mental health issues. In 2000, however, little had changed; the situation was still described as 'scandalous' by general practitioners and welfare experts.[17] Some children will confide in trusted adults such as school teachers and get support. Others will go it alone due to the stigma and associated embarrassment of mental health issues. I listened to the stories of two girls aged in their early teens about their lives as carers of their mothers. One had gained a lot of support through her school. The other had not told anyone at her school and preferred they did not know.

Sometimes carers have competing interests and may change their plans without letting workers know, as in the situation of Sally in Chapter 10. Workers thought her husband was at home caring for his wife when in fact he was away interstate on a business trip. Or the competing need may simply be to get some rest, as in the situation of Lily in Chapter 1, who cut her throat while her husband, who was her carer, slept. Interestingly, both of these carers were males who were not used to providing this type and level of care.

Clearly the responsibility of care is being placed on carers and the community sector. However, not all husbands or wives or children want to assume or are capable of assuming this role. As one woman commented, 'Involuntary patients – what about involuntary carers?'[18] There may be times when carers are not able to provide the care required or simply do not want to or are unable to do so. Indicators of likelihood of care being provided are the history of the relationship, the amount and type of care required and personal resources to be able to.

Sometimes a person may reluctantly agree to care. It is not easy to say that really you do not have the time due to work and other commitments, and are unable to care for a close family member. This is particularly so for women because of the social expectation that they will provide care. In some cases, it is an implicit assumption by male medical practitioners and psychiatrists that female family members will provide care without it even being discussed.[19] As in the situation of Rosemary, presented in the next chapter, sometimes the designated carer is not capable of providing the care required due to her or his own mental health issues. In such situations, the difficulties and mental health issues of both parties are compounded.

Regardless of their reasons, family members must be listened to and their decisions respected if they say they are not able to take on the role of carer. Workers expect women to provide the care and often family members do as well. If this is not forthcoming, the result is often family conflict. In extreme cases this can result in violence, as in the situation of Cecelia.

Cecelia's aged mother was with early stages of dementia. Her family followed traditional Chinese cultural beliefs that family members will provide care and support for their parents in their advanced years. Cecelia was the youngest of three sisters. Her mother was living with her oldest sister and brother-in-law and they were finding it increasingly difficult to care for her. This sister called a family meeting. Her brother-in-law told Cecelia that she was to assist in the care of her mother. Cecelia had two young children of her own and was working full-time. She had lived in Australia for many years and adopted a Western lifestyle. Caring for her mother did not fit in with her busy life and it was not something she wanted to commit herself to. She expressed her difficulties in being able to look after her mother but was told she must. She reluctantly agreed to have her mother on weekends with the other two sisters sharing her during the week. This arrangement did not work well and Cecelia was told by her brother-in-law she needed to do more during the week and to reduce her hours of work. When Cecelia refused to do so, he beat her quite severely.

Cecelia's situation reflects how the clash of two different cultures can produce very different messages and expectations. Cecelia's Western individualistic lifestyle was very challenging for older family members who followed more traditional collective ways. Violence is also an issue between carers and the person they are caring for. I once worked with a young man whose older brother threatened to beat him up if he did not listen to me and do as I said. Although I said this really was not necessary or appropriate, I had no control over what his brother did in the name of 'caring'.

Family carers must be heard when they say they are not coping. Workers need to think in more systemic ways and realise that it is often a team of carers that is required and not just one person. Lessons can be learnt in this regard from the LGBTI community, where groups of carers are often involved in looking after each other. Workers need to foster group models of care and learn how to communicate effectively in such situations. Much of my time spent working with a young woman was driving her to different friends and relatives as they took turns in looking after her.

More supports will need to be provided in the home as well as respite. In the situation of Jason and his wife described earlier, she clearly indicated she did not want to provide the care. She could only get respite by calling in crisis and saying he was now dangerous. Whether he was or was not behaving in a threatening manner, this story shows how respite was not provided until the family or the consumer were seen to be in danger and in a desperate situation. Previous requests had fallen on deaf ears. Another young man I worked with, aged in his early twenties, was homeless and asked if I could arrange for a hospital admission so he could sleep on a bed with clean sheets and have a cooked meal. For him, the hospital was seen as a place of asylum where he could have a rest. I advised him that this was not possible any more and that he needed to be mentally unwell and in danger to himself or others to be admitted. He later presented at hospital admissions complaining of disturbing voices telling him to kill himself and gained admission.

There is a real risk of people feigning danger in a desperate attempt to secure a hospital admission, thus reinforcing stereotypes and myths of mental health issues and dangerousness. Other families speak of the difficulties in getting a hospital admission these days; as well, the short length of hospital stay can mean that there is little difference between the person when they are admitted and discharged.

Due to the importance of early intervention, social workers and other mental health professionals must not exclude families. All family members will be affected in some way. As well as dependent children, brothers and sisters can feel frightened, isolated and confused if they are not involved. According to a carer, 'The best possible care in the community will come about when family carers are informed.'[20]

Gary's elder brother Ian spent most of his time alone in his bedroom except when he went to visit his psychiatrist each fortnight. He did not discuss these visits with other family members. Nor did the psychiatrist speak with other family members until a family meeting was arranged after Ian suicided. Gary spoke of incredible feelings of helplessness at not knowing what was happening to his brother. He grieved the loss of Ian, as he knew him before developing schizophrenia, and the loss he felt due to Ian's tragic death. He felt guilty that he had got on with is own life and somehow left Ian behind as his own way of coping.

Carers have raised numerous concerns about the exclusion of family members in relation to treatment and rehabilitation. Often family members are not included in assessment or intervention planning due to issues of confidentiality. Workers must be clear on legal and ethical requirements for professional practice, including confidentiality, yet at the same time develop appropriate interventions that are inclusive and responsive to family needs as well. This includes familiarity with mental health legislation that allows for the provision of information to primary carers, as discussed in Chapter 4.

Carers need to be included as positive team members and be consulted on diagnosis and treatment plans. As one carer poignantly commented, 'Why aren't carers included in the diagnosis and treatment of their loved ones? After all, we care for them on a day-to-day basis.'[22] Carers must be involved as much as possible in the care of their loved ones. Work with carers includes the provision of information and support, and access to a range of respite opportunities and financial assistance.[23] Carers need ongoing information about medication, treatment and management and services. There is often confusion about different agency responsibilities. Work with services includes advocacy for the development and promotion of respite options and support for carers.[24]

Another very real concern is care for carers. There are considerable economic and personal and health costs involved in caring, including lost opportunities. There is increasing concern about the costs of mental health issues being shifted from the government sector to the private sector, and the increased responsibility and financial burden being placed upon family members to provide care, which was previously provided by state mental health services. This is reflected in reductions to not only the number of people with mental health issues on disability pensions but also reductions in the numbers of people receiving carer payments. Barbara Fawcett argues that mental health and community care is an abusive combination for women, due to the demands placed upon them as carers.[25] Increased demands on women as carers is within the context of increased participation of women in paid employment.[26] It has been estimated that people diagnosed with schizophrenia and their carers bear the financial burden of over one-third of all the costs associated with the condition.[27]

Concerns have been raised about general practitioners medicating carers when they experience emotional distress in relation to their role as carer. Women are often blamed for family members' problems. They are criticised for not providing enough nurturing or for being over-involved or too controlling. Often, women cannot win in such situations and it is useful for them to gain the support of others in similar circumstances who recognise and understand the difficulties. Social workers are often asked to be involved with such groups. The role assumed by workers vis-à-vis carer and consumer groups requires careful thought and consideration.

Consumer and carer groups

At a community mental health centre staff meeting, it was announced that a new branch of a carers support group was opening in the area. A request was made for a staff member to be assigned to this group. I volunteered, and was given the name and number of Albert, the convenor of the group. I called Albert and introduced myself and let him know that I would be working with the group and asked to arrange a time to meet. To my surprise at the time, Albert declined this offer and said he would prefer to take my name and number and that they would call me if the group wanted to invite me to speak at any of their meetings. He said that the group was still forming and they did not want workers to be involved at this early stage. Management of the centre had taken it for granted that the group would want our involvement even though they had not requested it.

This experience made me aware of how often as workers we unwittingly take it for granted that consumers and carers will want our involvement. A more humble approach is required where services are offered and negotiated rather than workers assuming they have power over carers and consumers and a right to be involved. This left me in the somewhat difficult position of having to report back to management that the group did not want our involvement at the moment. I could not help but feel I was held personally responsible for this and had failed in this seemingly simple task. To be truly respectful of consumers and carers' wishes, collaborative and reciprocal relationships are required, based on respect and humility on the part of workers. This needs to be promoted and supported by agency management in both policy and practice.

Conclusion

Consumer participation and leadership in mental health services in Australia have come a long way over the past two decades. A conscientious and tenacious approach is necessary to ensure that consumer leadership is supported and enacted in organisational policies and services. This creates a culture that promotes respectful and responsive interactions that are crucial to a person's self esteem and dignity.[28] It entails respect and humility on the part of workers and the development of meaningful collaborative and reciprocal relationships. Multiple points of consumer involvement in mental health services are required, with strategies that facilitate and strengthen partnerships between workers, consumers and carers. It involves power with and not over consumers. Carers are crucial to community care and the redevelopment of mental health services; the most exciting future initiatives for service development are to be led by consumers in co-design. Family and friends must be listened to and supported in their roles as carers. Their views need to be respected, even when they are not able or willing to provide the care required. The notion of individual carers needs to be reconsidered by workers, as often this is simply not feasible and in fact it is a team of carers that is required. In this regard, there is much to be learned from the LGBTI community, where rosters of care are more the norm. Workers must learn how to work appropriately with groups of carers and not only individual carers. Partnerships between consumers, carers and workers will ultimately bring about best outcomes. A well-resourced and coordinated program of community care is needed to reduce the spiralling health costs of mental health issues and to bring about improvements in quality of life for individuals affected by mental health issues and their carers.

Reflection

What is a consumer perspective in mental health?

What is a carer perspective in mental health?

How do consumer and carer perspectives inform your thinking and approach to social and emotional well-being?

What might consumer and carer partnerships look like in practice?

What would you do if the person you are working with does not want you to communicate with a primary carer?

10

Interventions

The aim of social work interventions is to assist people to live well in the presence or absence of mental health issues as well as preventing loss and rebuilding their lives to get back the things they may have lost due to mental health issues. This includes physical, psychological, social and economic losses that may be tangible or missed opportunities. It is by redressing these missed opportunities that social workers assist people with mental health issues to lead fulfilling lives in the community, with access to full community participation. It is also about facilitating the provision of appropriate responses if a person is not able to manage certain aspects of their lives when experiencing mental health issues. This is particularly important for those who are reliant upon the person as a primary carer. A full understanding of discrimination faced by people with mental health issues is essential. Social workers demonstrate hope, and listen to and respect those they are working with and involve them in all decisions about their treatment and care, wherever possible, supporting people to manage their own mental health issues. Central to social work interventions are empowerment, consciousness-raising and personal and social change. This is in conjunction with more targeted interventions to manage disturbing signs and symptoms of mental health issues. Personal change focuses on developing resilience and protective factors focused on the prevention of mental health issues and on early intervention when they do occur. Social change aims to eliminate discrimination due to mental health issues and promote community inclusion. Interventions to manage symptoms are predominantly behavioural, at the same time focusing on the relational aspects of people's lives. A range of recovery-focused interventions used by mental health workers today are presented in this chapter with a focus on the role of social workers. The following chapter is devoted entirely to focused psychological strategies as these evidence-based interventions are prioritised for funding by government.

Community care: everybody's business

Changes to funding arrangements for mental health social work services, alongside the increasing number of mental health social workers who are working in private practice, means that social work as a profession must carefully frame practice for the future in accordance with social work aims and principles. Social workers must not lose sight of their mandate to work to improve the circumstances of the most disadvantaged and oppressed members of society. In mental health, these are people with persistent ongoing mental health issues who are over-represented in the homeless and prison populations – those who may not respond well to the focused psychological services funded by Medicare as a first line of intervention due to overwhelming physiological and safety needs.[1] As mentioned in Chapter 5 on theory, these basic needs identified by Maslow must be met before any therapeutic interventions can be effective. A person must have food and shelter and feel safe before they can engage in cognitive behaviour therapy.

Social workers are skilled and equipped to work well across all of the major psychiatric diagnostic categories. However, managed care funding models could inadvertently focus social work private practice activity in the area of mood and anxiety disorders. Social workers must not lose sight of their mandate to work with and advocate for the most disadvantaged and oppressed members of society.

Recently I expressed concern to a mental health social work colleague that the focus of mental health social work has shifted away from this more disenfranchised group. The reply was affirmation of my observation with a further observation that seemed to support, or at least explain this move: 'It's not glamorous. It's very difficult work with few rewards.' Another mental health social worker commented, 'We've moved on... Look at how far we have come. That work is best left to the nurses.'

These are personal observations – no more and no less and certainly not evidence-based. What they do suggest, however, is the need for evidence-based research that focuses on social work expertise, particularly for the vulnerable and marginalised to contribute to policy and service delivery frameworks. Social workers have a major contribution to make with people with mental health issues regardless of the nature and severity of the mental health issues. This is because of the centrality of the social context and relationships in all of our lives. It is more important than ever before for the social work profession to reassess and reaffirm its contribution and expertise in the field of mental health and not be carried along by the tide created by limited psychological service funding models and the lure of increased professional status.

Social work practice is based upon humanist principles of participation and equality in relationships and the capacity of individuals to freely make reasoned and informed choices. The interaction between the individual and the environment is highlighted in existential perspectives, particularly symbolic interactionism and interpretative interactionism where people are seen as both subjects and objects of their environment.[2] This two-way process of how people act upon, and are affected by, their environment is useful when attempting to understand the complexity of behaviours and problems and the seeking of solutions.

Social work, as the name implies, focuses on the social context. Unfortunately, some social workers lose sight of this, engaging predominantly in individual practices with this is supported by current federal government polices and funding arrangements for managed care. The question of who pays for community-focused interventions is a real one and policies and funds must support the social context of interventions. It is a cause of alarm that the policy and funding shifts that have occurred in the growing area of private mental health social work are focused on a limited range of short-term psychological interventions.[4] Mental health social work is at the crossroads. Government funding arrangements promote individual services yet the dominant paradigm of recovery demands interventions in the social context that address issues of access and equity to rights and entitlements. Social workers must not forsake this main area of practice by being seduced into clinical individual practices that mimic those provided by psychologists without addressing broader social issues. According to a recovery framework, people with mental health issues have the same rights and entitlements as other members of the community and social workers must work to ensure that opportunities are not denied due to discriminatory practices.

Mental health is everybody's business, as people with mental health issues engage actively in the community in education and training and employment; using the same services as all members of the community when they are mentally well and unwell.

Mental health services are now located in community settings. Currently, a range of mental health services are provided by government and non-government agencies, with the latter generally referred to as psycho-social rehabilitation services and an increasing number of private mental health social workers. The discussion of deinstitutionalisation and community care in Chapter 2 details current mental health service delivery frameworks. With the closure of stand-alone psychiatric hospitals, the location of service delivery is clearly in the community. Treatment is to occur in the community unless the best outcome can only be provided in an in-patient setting. An emphasis is on managed care, with private organisations contracting with state governments to provide cost-effective care.

Two main implications of managed care are the difficulty in obtaining a hospital admission, and confidentiality.[3] For those who are hospitalised, stays are short in duration. This is in stark contrast to practices 20 years ago when people were usually hospitalised for lengthy periods and a hospital stay of a month or more was not uncommon. In the past, people complained of difficulties getting out of hospital. Today they are frustrated by difficulties gaining admission and remaining in hospital for an appropriate length of time for treatment to be effective. It can be exasperating for family members who go to considerable lengths to get a family member admitted only to find they are back home again a few days later, with little if any noticeable improvement. The person can, in fact, be worse off due to the trauma experienced as a result of the hospital admission, particularly if involuntary practices were used and they were forcibly restrained by police and security staff. The person may be angry with family members for allowing this to happen to them and not protecting them. This is particularly a problem when family members have initiated contact with mental health services. Problems can, in fact, be far worse, with relationships damaged and increased risk of suicide due to anger, breach of trust and demoralisation. The person may no longer feel they have anyone they trust and can talk to. If this is the case, suicide risk is extremely high and further hospitalisations may only exacerbate this.

People with mental health issues will use mental health services as well as general community services. Interventions occur in accident and emergency services and mental health units in public hospitals, community mental health settings, private mental health clinics, day programs, psycho-social support services, community services, people's homes, cafés, parks and on the streets. During the deinstitutionalisation process, many generic community services, such as neighbourhood houses, were renamed psycho-social rehabilitation support services and are now simply referred to as community support services. New skills were required for effective social work practice with people with mental health issues in these community settings, as staff did not have specialist training or skills in mental health care.

Some staff in these community services argued that, despite them being called psycho-social support services, specialist assessment skills in mental health are unnecessary and best left to workers in clinical mental health services. This approach is inconsistent with a holistic approach to mental health care that requires a thorough knowledge of mental health issues that may be affecting a person regardless of the setting. The distinction between community and clinical is based on the false premise that the services in these two service settings are somehow quite different. The reality is that all services are community-based and must work closely together for optimum results. This disjuncture still persists and must be challenged by social workers for a holistic approach to social and emotional well-being to occur.

Social workers in all settings must be equipped with the knowledge and skills to intervene in appropriate ways on an individual, family, group and community level for the benefit of those they work with.

I asked a social worker in a psycho-social rehabilitation service, who was supervising a social work student, about assessment opportunities available. The supervisor replied with a question: 'What is a social work assessment?' The result of the exchange that followed was a puzzled expression with the reply of 'You seem to be confusing us with the clinic. We don't do that here.'

The question I ask you, the reader, to seriously consider is 'How can social workers reasonably say they are working in the best interests of their clients if they are not using social work assessment skills?' In some instances, these services present as two different worlds not simply in the approach taken by workers but in the service setting. The so-called clinical services replicate the clinical environment with consumers seen in consultation rooms, not unlike a doctor's surgery. On the other hand, psycho-social support services generally feel more like going into someone's home, rather than a mental health organisation, with services provided in a very relaxed environment. Workers in both of these settings must grapple with the question of how they can effectively work together in the best interests of consumers, consistent with a recovery paradigm. All contemporary models of social work practice embody a strengths approach.

Strengths approach

Mental health issues are viewed as transient and not seen as a permanent condition that a person cannot recover from. A strengths approach cautions against seeing mental health issues as a chronic state and, as with physical illnesses, people generally improve over time. The use of the term remission is challenged because of the frequency of misdiagnosis of mental health issues due to altered reality states from other causes apart from mental health issues as discussed in Chapter 1, or transitory symptoms.[4]

Central to a strengths approach is a belief that change is possible. A strengths approach calls on social workers to develop a greater depth of understanding of how people gain fulfilment. It requires a shift in thinking away from pathology towards positive ways in which people attain happiness. A focus is on strengths and positive emotions. Virtue, religion and philosophy are seen as important aspects influencing personal happiness. Seligman has developed strengths-based approaches for working with depression and has identified six core virtues of healthy people. These are

wisdom and knowledge
courage
love and humanity
justice
temperance (and)
spirituality and transcendence.[5]

Mental health services are revising intake and assessment forms and interventions consistent with recovery-focused interventions based on strengths rather than deficit approaches. For many years individual service plans (ISPs) have been used to identify areas of deficit that require intervention. This is a predetermined assessment format that covers main areas of daily living. A strengths approach is more focused on the values that are important to a person, the goals they hope to achieve – both short term and long term – with a management plan developed to assist them to achieve these goals. The Recovery Star presented in Chapter 3 is a simple tool to assist with the identifying areas of priority.

It is argued that people are more motivated to work towards goals they have identified that are consistent with their value base rather than working on areas of deficit identified by a broad assessment tool. In this approach, work is directed towards identifying the values that are important to a person. This may be aided by using cards with values on them that are sorted in piles according to priority. This process in itself can trigger conversations about values in a person's life and hopes and dreams. People will respond differently to the use of tools such as the Recovery Star, values cards and assessment rating scales. What is important is that the tool is suited to the person and not a standardised procedure used with everyone simply because the worker feels comfortable using it or it contributes to useful service statistics. Improved outcomes for the consumer are the primary goal and all activities must be tailored to achieve this. Tools can be helpful but they can also get in the way of relationship building and genuine rapport.

Social and emotional well-being, prevention and promotion

Social and emotional well-being prevention and promotion interventions aim to reduce mental health issues in the community as well as increasing community awareness and understanding of mental health issues. Well-being, prevention programs and campaigns concentrate on positive self-esteem, healthy living and lifestyles. Health promotion campaigns focus on the reduction of stigma and the acceptance of people with mental health issues in the community.

A focus is on providing accurate information and dispelling myths surrounding mental health issues, particularly mental health issues and violence. Often, mental health issues are seen as associated with incompetence or acts of violence, or as a form of amusement. It is only when mental health issues are included in conversations and seen as a normal part of life for many people that the stigma can be addressed. This means workers openly naming and challenge discriminatory practices in both work and social settings. This includes challenging aspects of traditional Western socialisation where men are discouraged from expressing emotions and women are viewed as subordinate to men. Affirmative action campaigns are required to prevent loss and assist people to regain opportunities lost due to mental health issues and identify possible new opportunities.

Working with individuals

Most mental health social work is still with individuals. This includes social work with adults, young adults, adolescents, older adults, school-age children and preschool children. It is well recognised, however, that work in isolation from significant people in the person's life is often futile and generally does not bring about sustained change.

Consumer and carer partnerships are required at all stages of the design and delivery of mental health services. Social workers assist in developing early detection and early intervention plans that identify early warning signs of relapse for those with recurring mental health issues, with a well developed action plan if a person becomes unwell. As mentioned in Chapter 4 on legislation, these action plans are now formalised in the legislation as advance directives. Basic physiological and safety needs must be met at the outset.[6] Physical symptoms need to be treated seriously, rather than assuming psychological causes. This can be particularly an issue for women as they get older; their symptoms may often not be taken seriously by general practitioners who express frustration with this group.

I was recently at a workshop on trauma with a very experienced presenter who asked workers to come on stage and have a consultation in front of the class. A worker spoke of a person she was working with who had experienced, and had ongoing issues with, trauma. When asked what the issues were, the worker replied sleep disturbance, fearfulness, nightmares, panic attacks and diarrhoea. At this point, the presenter stopped her and enquired about the diarrhoeea and whether the person had seen a general practitioner about it. The worker seemed perplexed and replied that it was not necessary as the diarrhoea was a symptom of the trauma. The consultation ended there, with the presenter insisting that the worker arrange for a physical examination to rule out physical causes for the diarrhoea and not to assume it was related to the trauma. The worker didn't necessarily seem convinced or was perhaps embarrassed in front of colleagues. The worrying aspect is that because much of this work is done in private, consumers can be denied proper services due to the lack of knowledge and skills or misplaced beliefs of workers.

Drug-free options and complementary therapies, discussed below, need to be considered as legitimate interventions.[7] In the past, medical assessments were routinely carried out at admissions in psychiatric hospitals. As most people are now cared for in the community, this important aspect of assessment must not be overlooked. This requires close liaison with the person's general practitioner, who is often the case manager or point of referral. Assistance may be required to find a suitable general practitioner.

Safety is paramount in both community and hospital settings. If a person is in an abusive relationship, this must be named, and strategies for working with violence and abuse enacted. Discharge planning needs to take account of potential return to an abusive relationship, with residential services addressing the reality that abuse occurs in these settings and not turning a blind eye to it. Timely and appropriate responses to reports of sexual abuse are necessary, as well as liaison with and referral to specialist services in this area. If a person is assessed as a danger to self or others, this must be a focus of intervention. Once this crisis is resolved, it is then possible to work on other areas.[8] Interventions may also be required in the area of alcohol and other drug use and forensic involvement.

Hope, active consumer participation and quality of life are central features of recovery-focused interventions, as discussed in Chapter 3. Meaningful community participation means that people have opportunities to have physical, psychological, emotional, cultural, social, vocational, environmental and spiritual needs met in the presence or absence of symptoms of mental health issues. It is about having family and friends who care about you, adequate regular income, access to education and training, meaningful employment and appropriate housing.

In setting goals of intervention it is important to gain a sense of a person's aspirations and dreams and lifestyle before they developed mental health issues. It is also necessary to get a sense of the person's personality and social interactions. This is often referred to as a person's pre-morbid personality. It gives an indication of what the person was like before developing mental health issues. Changes will vary over time and according to whether there has been a rapid or gradual onset of symptoms. There may be unresolved issues surrounding loss of former self and lifestyle. Recovery-focused practice aims to prevent loss and get back what people have lost through mental health issues.

Ensuring access to adequate income is necessary for food, clothing and housing. Adequate income is generally gained through employment; many people with mental health issues can and want to work. This needs to be real employment with an appropriate matching process and not endless vocational training programs or enforced work placements. The privatisation of these employment services is extremely worrying and the profits private providers are making for placing people with mental health issues in employment. This should not be an area for profit, and government must take responsibility for closer monitoring of these services, or preferably for providing them, to prevent scams and the demoralisation of people with mental health issues who genuinely want meaningful employment. In a capitalist system, profit motivations and not necessarily the person's social and emotional well-being will always be a priority of private providers. Interventions may be required to find affordable and appropriate housing options that support recovery or prevent housing loss. As mentioned earlier, in Chapter 3, this is particularly important for people with dependent children, as loss of housing can mean loss of care of children. Apart from the emotional trauma and disruption, this results in a reduced income that makes it difficult for a woman to re-establish herself and regain care of her children.

Counselling and psychoanalysis focus on conscious and unconscious processes exploring thoughts, feelings and unresolved intra-psychic and interpersonal conflicts and trauma. A focus is on addressing the needs identified in Erikson's stages of psycho-social development and developmental tasks and in the later stages of Maslow's hierarchy of human needs identified in Chapter 5. Freudian psychoanalysis was a main mental health intervention up until the 1970s. It is used less frequently today due to the time and costs involved.[9]

Gender-sensitive practices are required in assessment, diagnosis and intervention. The ways in which women and men generally express and manage their feelings are very different and also vary across cultures. Unravelling male and female stereotypes and male privilege is important, particularly highlighting issues of power and powerlessness. For women, empowerment begins with recognising and asserting needs to combat oppression, often at the risk of financial security. Feminist counselling and therapy focuses on the expression and acknowledgment of women's emotions as legitimate. Individual work with women contributes to, and informs, work on a broader structural level. This occurs alongside activities to promote and develop self-confidence, with women supporting each other in promoting anti-sexist practices for themselves personally as well as for other women. This often occurs in group settings.

For men, the challenge is to become more emotionally connected and to abandon the trappings of patriarchy that continue to oppress and dominate women and their true selves.[10] Ultimately, the challenge is to recognise as a society that the old paradigm of male worth through dominance no longer fits the complex world of the 21st century and only serves to perpetuate the overt oppression of women and alienation of the inner self for men and boys.[11] Narratives are useful in assisting people to explore issues of socialisation and unresolved issues – both past and present. The skill of re-framing can help people see things from a different perspective and develop new understandings.

Collaborative work across a range of services is required for best service outcomes. This requires cultural sensitivity and respect for gender, cultural, spiritual and sexual differences. This may be negotiating with Centrelink or the Guardianship and Administration Board or referral to general community services, mental health services or specialist services such as centres against sexual assault and services for trans-sexuality and gender dysphoria. It is important that workers are able to work appropriately with people from a range of different cultures. If a person does not speak English, a consideration is whether to refer to a bilingual worker or to use interpreters. Again collaborative work often has the best outcomes and provides access to a wider range of resources and interventions. If a person is of Aboriginal or

Torres Islander descent, Indigenous mental health workers must be contacted for consultation and referral at the earliest opportunity unless the person has specifically requested a non-Indigenous service and worker.

Medication and complementary therapies

Most people who use mental health services are on some type of psychotropic medication used to treat symptoms of mental health issues. Psychotropic medications work best when combined with more therapeutic interventions such as counselling and promotion of self-esteem. In mental health services, medical practitioners prescribe medication; allied health workers are also involved in monitoring and assessing a person's use of this medication and possible side effects. Prescribed medications used to treat distressing voices are called anti-psychotics, neuroleptics or major tranquillisers. When combined with therapeutic interventions, the usual effect of these medications is a reduction of distressing voices. However, these medications are not effective for all people and in some instances can cause voices to worsen.[12] The properties of some of these medications have a sedating effect that can result in feelings of calm and lowered stress levels. It is unclear how much relief is brought about by this calming effect and how much by the effect of the medication on other neurological processes.

People may try numerous medications before they find one that is right for them. Dosages may be too high or too low and side effects may be causing physical, psychological and social problems. Medications can have an impact on libido; this can be a significant issue in couple work. The side effects of major tranquillisers are similar to what are often described as the negative symptoms of schizophrenia, including tiredness and lethargy that impact upon energy levels and motivation. More recent developments with these medications have seen less problematic side effects for some people. However, many people are still struggling with distressing side effects.[13]

Unfortunately, psychoactive medication is often used inappropriately as a means of restraint both in hospital and community contexts. Once a person is medicated, it is very difficult to do any meaningful counselling due to the sedating effect of the medication. This is particularly an issue for allied health workers on community crisis teams and those working in acute in-patient settings, as often the people they are working with are on heavy doses of medication. Medication should not be used to contain difficult behaviours, nor should it be used to make things easier for workers.[14]

At times, allied health professionals choose not to be interested or involved in medical treatments, leaving it to people trained in this area. The problem with this approach, however, is that whether you like it or not most people using mental health services are on strong medications.

Ethan, a psychologist on a mental health crisis team, was required to take medication to people he was visiting and to supervise them taking it. At first, Ethan refused to do so yet after persuasion from management he reluctantly agreed. However, he still claimed to have no knowledge of the medications or interest to find out. One evening Ethan was required to visit Leanne and take her medication to her and supervise her taking it. When he visited, Leanne was not home so he diligently returned the next morning. Leanne was getting ready to go to a friend's birthday party when Ethan arrived with her medication. When she said she didn't need it, Ethan insisted she take it. What Ethan did not know was that Leanne was right when she said she did not need it, as it was sleeping tablets that she had been meant to take the night before. Unfortunately, Leanne missed her friend's party and slept for most of the day.

Since the 1990s, complementary and alternative therapies have increased in popularity and status as legitimate forms of treatment and some schools of medicine now include these therapies in their curriculum. The main complementary and alternative therapies used in mental health are acupuncture, herbal therapy, homeopathy, massage and aromatherapy. Acupuncture is based on the ancient Chinese belief that illness is caused by an imbalance in the yin and yang energies flowing through the body. Very fine small needles are inserted into the skin to redress this imbalance. Western acupuncturists are now using electrically charged probes particularly to treat depression and anxiety.[15] St John's wort is a herbal therapy used to treat mild cases of depression. Valerian is used in cases of anxiety and sleep disturbance and rescue remedy for drug withdrawal.[16] A number of herbal teas such as camomile can also have a calming effect.

Electro-convulsive therapy

While in the past electro-convulsive therapy (ECT)was viewed with scepticism, it has gained increased popularity in recent years. Electro-convulsive therapy is used when a person is not seen to be responding to treatment. It is also used instead of medication if a person is having difficulties with side effects from medications or is not able to tolerate them. ECT is usually used to treat moderate to severe depression but is also increasingly used to treat schizophrenia or schizo-affective disorders. It produces a seizure by administering electrical shock waves to the neurotransmitters of the brain. One of the reasons for greater community acceptance is because it is now administered under anaesthesia, with a neuromuscular blocking agent used to prevent uncontrolled movements caused by the seizure. A person may receive treatment two to three times a week over a course of six to 10 sessions.[17] Marked improvements in symptoms are often observed, but little is known about how ECT works and its longer term effects. Short-term memory loss is associated with the use of ECT but is generally seen to resolve within a few days after the procedure. Regardless of the effects, ECT is a highly invasive procedure that should be used sparingly and only as a treatment of last resort and with the informed consent of the person to whom it is being administered.

Rosemary was a 55-year-old woman who lived alone in a very large house. She was a widow and had two adult children, a son and a daughter. Her father-in-law had lived with her for the past couple of years up until his recent death. Rosemary and her husband had migrated to Australia as refugees. They worked extremely hard in factory jobs to raise their family and make a new life in Australia. Their dream was to have a home of their own that they could be proud of. They built a very large house for their children and grandchildren as well as Rosemary's father-in-law. However, the children decided to move out and establish their own homes. Rosemary's husband died suddenly and she was left in the house with only her father-in-law. He was quite ill and needed constant care from Rosemary. When he died, Rosemary felt terrible guilt that she had not cared for him properly due to her own health problems at the time. She had been urging him to move into supported accommodation where he would be looked after but he did not want to do so.

Rosemary spoke of a life of shattered dreams. She now rattled around her large home alone. She was virtually only living in two rooms of the house. She cried as she waved her arms asking 'What for? What for?' Rosemary had been treated for depression for the previous 12 months and was not responding to any of the medications prescribed for her. Her doctor decided to admit her to hospital and she was administered ECT. Rosemary's mood lifted very quickly and she was very pleased with the results. However, her mood became very depressed again over the next few months. No amount of ECT was going to rid her of her grief and the terrible guilt that burdened her over the death of her father-in-law and the accumulated losses she had suffered.

Working with individuals from a family-centred perspective

Many people with ongoing mental health issues are socially isolated or the responsibility for care is with family, who are often in need of assistance and support. Frequently, family members also feel isolated and confused. Sadly, many family members are angry and disillusioned with the mental health services provided to them. This is illustrated by the following comment by a mother, caring for her daughter, about the psychology and social work services provided to the family: 'They sit in a chair and give theoretical advice and create conflict and intrude and put your daughter against you.'[18] This is not an isolated incident and social workers must closely reassess their work and ensure that practices are useful and affirming for families, who are often desperate for respite and assistance in managing what can often be very disturbing and distressing behaviours.

Everyone has connections with a biological family at some stage in their lives. For some, these relationships are very apparent and easily identified. For others, these family ties may have been severed for any number of reasons. These reasons are many and varied and might include relinquishing a child at birth, death, separation and divorce, family disputes, mental health issues, loss and separation due to war and migration for those who have sought refuge or asylum. For some, the mention of family can arouse feelings of being loved and cared for, while for others it can arouse feelings of hurt, loss and grief. Consumers may feel some pressure being applied to them to reveal personal information about themselves that they may prefer to keep private. It is important that this is acknowledged as important and legitimate and it is up to the person what they choose to disclose and to whom. This may be a lot or it may be very little, depending upon the consumer–worker relationship. Many families comprise people who are not necessarily blood relatives. Terms such as 'kith' and 'kin' are sometimes used to distinguish between blood relatives and other close relationships. Some people include close friends in the definition of who they consider to be family.

In certain cultures, family may refer to immediate members of their own nuclear family, extended family, friends and community. For instance, many Indigenous and Asian cultures embody a broad definition of family, with extended family members and community leaders playing a crucial role in family matters. Level of assimilation and intergration of different cultures will affect the degree to which this applies. A more Western view is focused on the privacy of the immediate nuclear family of parents and children. As a social worker, it is important to know who is considered family in terms of close relationships, as this is where most assistance and support is likely to come from.

Family structures to an outsider can seem very confused and complicated. It has been suggested that the people one includes in main celebrations such as Eid, Christmas, birthdays and so on can give a sense of who might be included in a broad definition of family. Or even who do people share their evening meal with? Who do they mostly choose to spend their leisure time with? It is therefore useful to have approaches and methods to go about unravelling and making sense of our own and others' family situations.

Family and significant others

It has been estimated that approximately one-quarter of women who use mental health services are living with dependent children.[19] There are a number of issues for these women and children if the mother develops mental health issues. Family members and significant others can experience major grief, personal turmoil and family disruption when a close relative experiences mental health issues. Support is needed within these relationships and the provision of information so that changes and adjustments to the impact of the issues can occur. It is crucial that information is provided to families and carers about the service system, organisations that can provide support and how to access these.[20]

It is important for links between the woman and significant people in her life to be fostered and maintained to the greatest extent possible. Case managers need to be sensitive to the needs of family members and carers and seek their involvement in the person's care. Case managers must familiarise themselves with the range of services for support and assistance to family members and carers and actively work with them.[21]

Fortunately today there is increased recognition of the needs of children of parents with mental health issues. A focus of interventions is peer support and providing opportunities for a break from the responsibilities of caring for a parent. Children may experience confusion and difficulty understanding some of the strange behaviours and thoughts a parent is expressing and may be embarrassed and teased by peers about this. They may have mixed emotions, ranging from anxiety and concern to fear and anger, possibly experiencing difficulties with schooling during such times. Particularly during adolescence, children become fearful that some of the changes that are naturally occurring at this stage of development may be signs or symptoms of the onset of mental health issues. For those with a family history of ongoing persistent mental health issues, family education and support is crucial for preventing the onset of mental health issues.

Apart from the specialist mother and baby units, for post-natal depression, children are not admitted with their mothers to hospitals providing psychiatric care. It is usual practice within adult psychiatry for the woman to be admitted to hospital and separated from her children. This practice, however, is not universal and it is possible for women and children to be admitted together in private clinics.[22] Separated women need to be confident that adequate care arrangements have been made for their children if they are hospitalised. The loss of their mother poses a threat to the emotional security of the child and can result in them becoming fearful and confused if they do not have adequate support and information about what is happening.[23] This in turn will impact upon the mental health of the woman who will be concerned about the health and well-being of her children. A constant tension for women when they experience mental health issues is to maintain respectful relationships and parental influence and guidance. Visits of children to in-patient settings need to be carefully planned so that they support mother–child relationships rather than adding to trauma and confusion.

There is a need for specialist in-patient programs for pregnant, psychotic women, particularly those with drug addictions, as well as ongoing parent support programs and supported housing options in the community.[24] It is estimated that as many as one in seven mothers suffer from post-natal depression.[25] This highlights the importance of care and support in the periods immediately before and after the birth. Education that goes beyond the delivery room and regular weigh-ins – to include issues of physical and emotional changes, adaptation to a new family member, changed roles and responsibilities, parenting and self-care – is required. Further funding is required for maternal and child health and early childhood intervention programs focused on preventive health.

Family systems and ecological perspectives

The application of systems and ecological perspectives to social work practice is in identifying the interaction and relationships between people. The idea of reciprocity has particular application in that if change occurs in one party, change is likely to occur in the other as a follow-on effect. The clear delineation of patterns of relationships, boundaries and transactional analysis is useful and is widely used for purposes of identifying relationships, associated expectations and emotional ties.

The systems approach was developed in the late 1960s and early 1970s largely in response to a push for more scientific, measurable indicators of family functioning at that time. It was developed in a pseudo-scientific form and this was reflected in the language used in early works. A lot of this language is now seen as quite distasteful, with terms such as 'dysfunctional' families used. Later developments have seen the incorporation of a strengths approach with a systems perspective; this earlier language has been rejected as being dysfunctional in itself and damaging to the integrity of the family. Nonetheless, apart from some of the early language and negative classifications made, family systems theory does make an important contribution to contemporary social work practice.

A family systems model sets out to describe rather than to explain. It is characterised by the grouping together of different family members into family sub-systems. These include the parental sub-system, the marital sub-system and the sibling sub-system. The worker in systems theory literature is generally referred to as the therapist and joins with the family system. The therapist is usually drawn at the top of the family system, above the parental sub-system but in the course of working with the family will at different times join with other family sub-systems to strengthen their position in an attempt to bring about change within the family.

The worker focuses on transactional patterns within and between the family sub-systems looking particularly at what are referred to as boundaries between the sub-systems that are classified as disengaged, clear or enmeshed. A system toward the extreme disengaged end of the continuum tolerates a wide range of individual variations in its members. Only a high level of individual stress will be responded to by the family. At the enmeshed end, the opposite occurs, with the behaviour of one family member immediately affecting other family members.

Members of enmeshed family systems may have a heightened sense of belonging that discourages autonomy and individual problem solving. Members of families with more disengaged family relationships may function more independently, with reduced feelings of loyalty and belonging, capacity for interdependence, and ability to request support when needed.

The role of the worker is to assess the family sub-systems and boundaries. Work will be done to open up what are seen to be inappropriately rigid boundaries and to tighten loose boundaries, frequently parenting, in an endeavour to improve family relationships and individual functioning.

Genograms and eco maps are useful tools for plotting family and social connections. They are particularly useful for organising a large amount of information about the family system in space and over time. They provide an objective and visual portrayal that can lead to new insights into the complexity of the family system. These can lead to new ways of bringing about change within the family. More recent and promising developments are in attachment based family therapy that focuses specifically on relationships. The focus of change is on relationships and where breakdowns have occurred. No blame is apportioned and problems are not the focus. This is consistent with a strengths approach and can be very powerful when working with suicidal young people discussed further in Chapter 12 on suicide and self-harm.

A community development model for working with families

Theories on social and community development focus on environmental, economic and social concerns relevant to all levels of society with a focus on empowerment at a local level. These theories contribute to a broader understanding of social and cultural issues and perspectives. Community usually refers to people with something in common, for example residents of a local geographic area, or members of a religious or ethnic group. Community development is an area that has been neglected in the mental health literature and service development due to the focus on the clinical. Social workers have a major role to play in community building activities that foster relationships between people to make the community a better place to live for people with mental health issues.

A focus on social capital includes

networks that link people together
trusting relationships
shared expectations of social norms and behaviour
mutuality – working together for the benefit of the group (and)
reciprocity – doing things for others with the expectation that these benefits will be returned.[26]

Community building and social capital models are based on a strengths approach that embraces diversity and opportunities. When it comes to mental health, it is important that community building occurs across the entire community, not only looking at opportunities confined within mental health services. People with a mental health issue want to participate in a range of community activities like everyone else. It is how to develop and maintain this participation and protect relationships during times of mental health issues that can pose the greatest challenge.

Solution-focused therapy

Solution-focused therapy is concerned with future-focused outcomes rather than a preoccupation with the problem or its causation. A basic premise of this approach is that increased knowledge of a problem does not necessarily lead to improved solutions. To the contrary, it is argued that the opposite can occur with a preoccupation on problems taking time and energy away from solutions. This is particularly so when problems are used consciously or subconsciously as a means of gaining attention from others. In such circumstances, the problem itself can serve a useful purpose in rallying others and gaining support, with the person becoming the embodiment of the problem. When the person is seen as the problem, it is extremely difficult to work towards solutions, as their strengths and resourcefulness are overshadowed. A dependency situation may develop, with the person coming to rely upon the advice and support of others who may enjoy helping at the outset but often tire of the demands placed upon them.

Amaya was with schizophrenia and experienced major problems with motivation. How much of this was due to her mental health status and how much to the side effects of her medication was unclear. It was difficult for Amaya to get up in the morning and to organise her day. Assistance was sought from the local mental health service; a social worker arranged morning visits everyday for Amaya for a fortnight to get her out of bed and stay with her while she had breakfast and organised her day. Amaya seemed to enjoy these visits and so did the worker. However, the problem did not improve and Amaya felt after the two weeks she still needed the daily visits – more than ever. The visits were extended for another fortnight – with still no improvement in Amaya's ability to get up in the morning on her own. The social worker began to tire of the visits and seeming lack of progress with Amaya and decided to reduce the visits. Amaya was very unhappy about this and the worker became even more frustrated with her. Amaya was now quite dependent upon the worker and the visits and enjoyed this new routine. Finally the worker decided to refer Amaya to another service and within a fortnight Amaya was found on an early morning visit hanging from a beam in her bedroom.

Amaya was very happy to be looked after by workers but when this support was withdrawn she was no longer able to cope. Amaya's story is a reminder of the concept of learned helplessness and also how social workers and others in the helping professions can often do things for people to make themselves feel good by helping, but in reality they are promoting dependency in the same way that this was promoted in stand-alone psychiatric hospitals. Responsibility for this is often put back on the person for having a dependent personality. This has disastrous effects and is again a reminder of the importance of guarding against practices that promote dependency and impede recovery. Amaya was construed as not capable; the worker became part of the solution. This approach fostered dependency on the worker and it was difficult to focus on Amaya's strengths and resources. Amaya felt she simply could not cope without the support of the worker.

A solution-focused approach would have assisted in identifying problem-saturated approaches that result in discouragement and dependence.[27] The technique of externalising is useful for viewing the person within the problem situation rather than being seen as the problem.

Workers look for exceptions to the problem to discover situations or aspects of a person's life where things are going well. A focus is on what the person is doing to achieve these positive results and look at transferring this approach and skills used to the areas that are problematic. An emphasis on ability and strengths provides an encouraging environment where the worker expresses confidence in the person's ability to problem solve. This may or may not require the provision of additional resources in the short or long term.

Validation of the person's, or family's, experiences by the worker is essential so that they are not seen as underestimating the impact of the problem, or trivialising it. An essential component is validation of emotions. Due acknowledgment of the range of feelings involved is required for a person to be able to move on and work towards a solution. Worker skills in empathy are important at this stage. Even after a worker has used validation skills, the person may still feel at a loss when it comes to finding solutions. At this point, the worker may set a homework task, asking the person to take notice of the things that happen between now and the next visit that they would like to happen more so. At this point, the worker is drawing upon behavioural change techniques by getting the person to notice and record behaviours to reinforce and encourage for the future.

Another well known technique used in solution focused work is the miracle question. The worker asks,

> You go to bed tonight and without you knowing it, a miracle happens. When you wake up in the morning, your problem has been solved. What will you be doing differently?[28]

The miracle question does not require the person to come up with a solution but rather to focus on what it would be like if the problem is resolved. The worker may also ask how the person is feeling. This technique can assist a person or family to develop a solution that leads to this desired state. Bowen stresses the importance of clarity, noting, 'The clearer the vision of the behaviour in action, the more confident the family will feel about being able to achieve that behaviour.'[29] The worker may assist the person or family to identify behaviours that are not helpful and introduce new behaviours and skills. The worker will highlight the transfer of behaviours and skills across different contexts, particularly from those where the problems are not present.

Solution-focused therapy questions the notion of workers empowering individuals or families. Rather, the role of the worker is to assist people to find their own solutions, focusing on strengths and decision-making capabilities. The solutions are those of the individual or family, who are experts in their own lives, not those of the worker. The worker listens and assists by exploring feasibility testing of the solutions under consideration. Strategic questioning focused on the solution implementation plan, availability of resources and likely outcomes can assist in selecting appropriate interventions, alongside solution review and evaluation strategies. The measurement of change is important to gauge the effectiveness of solutions. This includes the recording of desired behaviours that result in positive feelings and outcomes. If old patterns re-emerge, what works is clearly evident and more of this is encouraged. Fundamental to the success of a solution-focused approach is the belief by workers that clients have the capacity to find their own solutions.

Crisis intervention and task-centred models

Similarly to solution-focused therapy, the focus of both crisis intervention and task-centred models is on short-term intervention aimed at the resolution of current problems. Actions and interventions are structured and contracts or agreements are frequently used. The effectiveness is in dealing with presenting problems rather than underlying issues and contributing factors.[30] Social work crisis intervention requires the following steps:

1. Provide immediate assistance.
2. Affirm strengths and resources.
3. Contract for short term service up to six weeks.
4. Encourage hope and positive expectations.

5. Mobilise resources.

6. Provide material resources if required.

7. Develop new perspectives.

8. Refer to longer-term services if required.

9. Review and evaluation.

A woman named Sally, aged in her mid-30s, presented herself to the local hospital requesting a mental health admission. Reasons for requesting admission were feelings of inability to cope with pressures of care for two young children, stress from her full-time work and a lack of support from her husband. She was particularly distressed that he was leaving the following morning on a business trip interstate. As a social worker on a 24-hour crisis team, I assessed Sally with the psychiatric registrar at admissions in the hospital and we decided she did not require hospitalisation as she did not show evidence of mental health issues. We arranged with her husband over the telephone that he would remain home with her the following day and not go interstate as planned and that I would do a home visit the following morning at nine o'clock.

When I arrived at Sally's house, the keys were in the front door. I knocked on the door and there was no answer so I turned the key and let myself in. Inside the house were Sally's two young preschool children. I was told by the four-year-old that his mother had been crying and had swallowed a bottle of tablets. He told me that she was asleep and that he could not wake her. He also told me that he was looking after his younger 16-month-old brother.

Intervention

Step 1. I found Sally lying on her bed in a very deep sleep. I asked the four-year-old if he knew what the tablets were that his mother had taken and he directed me to the empty bottle. I immediately called for an ambulance. He told me that his father had gone away on an aeroplane that morning. I thanked the child for his help and told him that I would now look after him and his brother while his mother was sleeping and tried to get details from him about where his father was. I told the boy that his mother was not well and needed to go to the hospital in an ambulance. I directed him to watch the television and got him something to eat. The toddler was quite settled playing in his cot. I tried to wake Sally by applying cold compresses, moving her into the recovery position and constantly talking to her until the ambulance arrived. The ambulance came within about 15 minutes but it seemed like hours at the time. I also located a telephone directory and called Sally's mother who arrived a couple of hours later. I called the crisis team and informed them of the situation and arranged for the day shift staff to come and assist if required. I then minded the children, cleaned the kitchen and folded the washing while I waited for Sally's mother to arrive.

Step 2. After Sally's return home from hospital, work was done with her to regain power over her situation rather than feeling completely overwhelmed and turning her anger and frustration in on herself. A shift was made from her own sense of individual blame and sense of failure to locating the problems she was experiencing within a broader social framework. Much time was spent on identifying and affirming Sally's individual strengths and resources and generating energy for Sally to take control of her situation.

Step 3. An agreement was reached between Sally, her husband and myself for short-term marriage counselling with a contract for weekly sessions over the next six weeks.

Step 4. Hope and positive expectations were a key feature of all work done with Sally.

Step 5. Support was sought and provided by family and a neighbour, who was a good friend of Sally. Sally generally coped well but, like many women who are constantly attending to the needs of others, found it difficult to accept help. A balance needed to be maintained to provide support needed without infringing upon Sally's independence and sense of pride. Care also needed to be taken not to send double messages to Sally in terms of support required and her own abilities, strengths and resources.

Step 6. Material resources were not necessary, apart from mobilising the ambulance at the time of overdose.

Steps 7. & 8. Through the process of marriage counselling, Sally was able to develop a new perspective by focusing on issues in the relationship with her husband and also within her environment rather than blaming herself as she had done in the past.

Step 9. My initial feelings when I found Sally that morning were of shock and disbelief. There had been no doubt in my mind about sending Sally home from the hospital the previous night. I began to question my own skills of assessment as well as my judgement. What if I had been late for the planned home visit? What if I had postponed the visit due to a need to attend to a crisis call? What could I have done differently the previous night? Four things came to mind:

1. Rather than waiting until the following morning, follow Sally home and conduct a home visit that night to meet her husband in person rather than speaking with him over the telephone.

2. Remove from Sally's house any substances that she might potentially use to overdose with.

3. Collect a more detailed history of past suicide and self-harm attempts and locate Sally's previous file and workers in the mental health system. Contract with Sally not to harm herself before the planned visit the following morning.

4. Mobilise social supports that evening. It had not occurred to me that Sally's husband would leave her and go interstate on his business trip without letting us know. However a more thorough assessment would have revealed severe marital problems and raise doubts as to his willingness and appropriateness to provide the care Sally required.

Violence and abuse

A high percentage of people who use mental health services are survivors of abuse, particularly women. Forms of abuse include physical violence, sexual assault, emotional or psychological abuse, neglect, destruction of property and financial abuse. Cognitive behavioural and social learning approaches are often used in work with violent men in the United States, Britain and Australia.[31] McLellan argues that 'psychological explanations of violence and abuse are being used today in the service of perpetrators'.[32] She cites the example of the diagnosis of post-traumatic stress disorder as a commonly used defence for violent acts, particularly childhood trauma resulting in men being treated leniently by the courts. This creates an environment where increased violence becomes tolerated in the community both in the home and on the streets. The sad irony is the adoption of the language of survivors by perpetrators. Judith Herman has likened the effects of childhood sexual abuse to the effects of war resulting in post-traumatic stress.[33]

Until such time as the violence is targeted 'in its own right, victims of violence will continue to be over-represented as users of mental health services'.[34] This is often due to the sense of entrapment people feel emanating from the shame, low self-esteem, social isolation and fear of living in a violent relationship. It is understandable that those in such relationships develop symptoms of anxiety and depression, substance misuse, personality disorder, eating disorders, psychosis, suicidal behaviour and post-traumatic stress disorder.[35] Some people will present their distress in psychosomatic illnesses such as chronic pelvic pain or irritable bowel disorder.[36] The situation of those with pre-existing mental health issues or disability is exacerbated if the abuser is their carer due to increased dependency needs and difficulties leaving.[37] Community-based group homes and secure hospital wards are frequently closed. Power rests with management with people often vulnerable to abuse from co-residents and carers.[38] Many of the mental health issues presented by adults are second-order effects of abuse in childhood. This includes issues around trust, intimacy, agency and sexuality.[39]

The usefulness of psychiatric diagnoses is questionable as it can create a diversion from tackling the abuse and violence to treating mental health issues. Feminist writers see this as a means of social control, with women's genuine distress being defined by psychiatry as madness.[40]

Herman argues that recovery happens in the context of a supportive relationship and can only occur if a woman

has achieved safety
is provided an opportunity to tell her story to process feelings of grief and anger and
starts reconnecting socially.[41]

For children who live in violent or abusive families, alternative sources of warmth, fun and support are sought from outside of the family. Knowledge and exercise of the law is crucial in collaborative work with lawyers. Useful interventions include cognitive therapy or narrative therapy to transform views survivors have of themselves and events, support groups and advocacy and social action. The provision of appropriate social and emotional support immediately after the assault and later in life reduces the likelihood of long-term adverse psychological and social outcomes.

Loss and grief

Losses are many and varied and might include loss of a significant person, part of self, external objects, developmental loss or lost opportunities. For instance, a person who has developed mental health issues as a teenager may lament the loss of opportunities to develop strong peer relationships, disruption to education, personality changes and lost life opportunities that can result from these. Personal responses occur on emotional, physiological, cognitive and behavioural levels. The grieving process involves feelings of

numbness/blunting or complete disbelief
pining/yearning
disorganisation and despair
reorganisation.

The depth and extent of the grief response will be influenced by the closeness of the relationship, interdependency issues, past experiences of loss and grief and attitudes. The tasks of grieving are

1: to accept the reality of loss
2: to experience the pain of grief
3: to adjust to an environment in which the deceased person/object of loss is missing.

The role of the social worker is to

assist the person to come to terms with the loss
where appropriate, assist the person to accept the pain of grieving, and provide them with time
    to grieve
help the person to understand their emotional reactions
assist the person to identify and express their feelings
expect and allow for individual differences in grieving
provide continuing support as appropriate
enable the person to move to greater independence
refer on if necessary.

In addition, social workers might be involved in community education to foster the development of more constructive community attitudes towards dealing with loss and grief.

Jeff was referred by his general practitioner for loss and grief counselling. Jeff was 65 years of age and his wife had recently died suddenly of a heart attack. He was in a state of shock and disbelief. His wife had always done everything around the house, cooking, cleaning and so on. Jeff felt totally lost without her. He was recently retired and had been planning for the past few years how the two of them would spend their retirement years together. Jeff had been prescribed Valium by his general practitioner to help him relax. Jeff and his doctor were concerned that he had become addicted to this medication. Jeff was ashamed at taking it although it did seem to help him feel calmer. The social work intervention with Jeff followed the eight steps detailed above with a referral to a mutual support group for people who had experienced a significant loss. The individual counselling, group sessions and development of practical skills resulted in Jeff coming to terms with the loss of his wife and moving to greater independence without Valium.

Concerns have been expressed by the possible pathologisation of grief in the DSM. Workers do, however, need to be able to recognise when assistance with grief is required and this will generally be if it prevents the person from performing their usual responsibilities and this is having negative consequences. Workers need to recognise and balance when additional support is required and this will vary according to the nature of the loss, the circumstances of the loss, relationships, responsibilities, social supports available and personality.

Trauma-informed care and practice

Trauma-informed care is premised on a human rights approach and public health model. This includes acknowledging the relationship between the psychobiology of trauma and social determinants of health and well-being. In Australia, work towards a national strategic direction commenced in the mid-2000s with research by the Mental Health Coordinating Council, the peak body for over 200 mental health services in New South Wales, on access and equity to mental health services by women survivors of interpersonal abuse revealing that these women had poor access to services.[42] Mental health workers were found to have inadequate knowledge and skills in recognising the relationship between trauma, psycho-social difficulties and the development of mental health issues. Complex trauma was often not recognised or was misdiagnosed, and workers were not able to adequately respond to the needs of trauma survivors. Service responses were fragmented with inadequate referral, coordination and follow up. It was argued that appropriate responses required a collaborative approach that included consumers, carers, policy makers and service providers across different service systems, including primary healthcare, child protection, sexual assault, violence and abuse, substance abuse and mental health services. Continuing education on knowledgeable and skills in trauma is essential including an understanding of vulnerabilities and triggers experienced by trauma survivors. This is a priority given that the general experience of services by women survivors has been one of feeling unsafe, not validated and disempowered. This system failure to provide adequate services has resulted in women not using services, an exacerbation of physical and mental health issues and heightened suicide risk.

Trauma-informed care and practice, using a recovery paradigm, is based on the premise that recovery is not possible until the woman is physically and emotionally safe. This includes safety from the perpetrator of the violence and abuse as well as safety within services. A model of recovery through trauma-informed care endeavours to provide sanctuary and healing. The aim is to eliminate re-victimisation or lack of service provision by using a systemic whole of service approach based on the premise of 'no wrong door'.

Trauma-informed care and practice services

are open to outside parties, advocacy and clinical consultants
are inclusive of the survivor's perspective
value consumers in all aspects of care: power sharing
presume that all users of mental health services may have been exposed to abuse, violence, neglect or other traumatic experiences

ask questions about current abuse, listen and provide choices. Workers ask what happened to you not what is wrong with you

address the current risk and develop a safety plan focusing on physical and psychological safety first

focus on what is happening to the person rather than on diagnosis

avoid all shaming/humiliation

recognise that coercive practices re-traumatise people and create further trauma

recognise high rates of mental health issues related to trauma exposure

recognise that mental health services are often traumatising – both overtly and covertly

recognise that some mental health staff are uninformed about trauma – do not recognise it or respond appropriately

respond empathically, be objective and use supportive language

offer individually flexible plans or approaches that are responsive to culture, promote dignity and respect, hope and optimism

provide early intervention that is thoughtful and considers trauma in relation to those seen to have complicated issues that are not responsive to treatment approaches

provide awareness/training on re-traumatising practices

provide training and supervision in assessment and treatment of people with trauma histories.[43]

Well integrated psychological/therapeutic services that recognise the role and centrality of trauma in a person's life are most effective. These services use a holistic approach focusing on individual needs and not on diagnosis. Successful interventions result in wide-ranging benefits that include improvements in daily living and an associated decrease in symptoms of mental health, substance abuse and trauma. Positive effects are achieved in housing, education and employment and overall quality of life. Women report higher levels of satisfaction with trauma-informed recovery and support services and service providers report more effective service provision with fewer adverse incidents and increased staff morale.

Group work and interdisciplinary collaboration

The early focus of group work in the 1960s was on leisure activities and camps for youth. This was in response to the emerging social problem of juvenile delinquency at the time. This followed developments in group work in the United Kingdom and the United States. In the United States, group work was recognised as a method with its own professional association and body of knowledge in the 1950s and 1960s.

Recovery-focused practice supports group-intake processes alongside individual and family casework practices. This is so that, as much as possible, people in similar situations are brought together to share the connections they perceive between the similar contradictions they experienced as individuals. This strategy provides support by normalising problems and experiences and providing for a collective response to institutionalised problems. This process facilitates the development of knowledge about a particular area or group of people that can be responded to collectively that might remain invisible if dealt with individually.

Social workers use group work as a method of social work to assist people to improve their social functioning through meaningful group experiences. The focus may be on individual, family, group or community problems. Groups provide a medium for mutual support as well as enabling personal, group, organisational and social change.

Types of groups include

1. therapeutic and counselling (individual therapy, personal growth and change, and psychodrama)
2. educational (living with mental health issues, parent education, assertiveness training, life and social skills, formal education)
3. social support and recreational activities (activity groups, camping programs)
4. organisational maintenance and development (teams, staff meetings, case conferences, residential house meetings)
5. problem solving and self directed (rehabilitation and recovery)
6. collective or social action (linking personal issues and problems to social actions – for example, Beyond Blue campaigns for depression).

The focus of social psychology is on the effects of relationships within and between groups and the development and maintenance of associated identities, roles and expectations. This is of particular importance when working with organisations and social collectives.[44] The importance and power of information and how this is processed is stressed in communication theory. Sometimes groups will focus on a specific intervention technique such as mindfulness, narrative approaches, or focus on a particular aspect of intervention like stress management or relaxation, incorporating a variety of different approaches.[45] These groups might be directed at a particular age group or focus on a specific diagnosis such as schizophrenia or depression, or on a particular style of intervention. For instance, a narrative group work approach, mindfulness and cognitive therapy, discussed in the next chapter, have been found to be useful for people with anxiety and depression. The group provides support for people so that they learn they are not alone in their struggle. Dominant social beliefs about anxiety and depression are explored or deconstructed with the development of alternative stories that are re-affirming. A focus is on self acceptance, self appreciation and nurturing of the self.[4746]

Many people who attend such groups report the social benefits as well as increased ability to manage disturbing symptoms of mental health issues. However, in the community these groups are scarce and provided in an ad hoc manner.[47] Planning and financial support is required for the development of comprehensive and accessible groups targeted specifically at mental health issues, as well as support for people to fully participate in groups in the community.[48] Some people with mental health issues simply do not want to be attending groups with others with problems but rather want to join groups according to shared interests. The group may be time away from problems rather than focusing on them. Cost is a key factor. For instance, exercise is proven to be successful for the treatment of depression yet private gymnasium memberships are often not affordable for many.

Advantages of group work are skills acquisition whereby skills developed in created groups can be transferred to the many natural groups that are part of our daily lives. Groups are a powerful provider of mutual support and problem solving. Through role modelling, reinforcement and feedback, groups enable attitudes, feelings and behaviours to be changed. In a group, every member is a potential helper, and the roles of social worker and client are less differentiated. As a group can be democratic and self-determining, it can give more power to the consumer. Group work is particularly suitable for people such as those who find the intensity or intimacy of one-to-one relationships very difficult. It can also be a more economical use of social worker time and effort.

Some potential difficulties of group work can arise from maintaining confidentiality and following group rules. It can sometimes be very traumatic if these are not respected. The complexity of planning, organising and implementing a group is not always recognised or adequately resourced. Resources might include childcare, equipment, funds, transport and so on. Some people's individual needs are too great, impacting upon sharing time and competition between members in the group. The group may be a negative experience for some people. There is also the possibility of labelling and stigma resulting from membership of a mental health group. It is important to carefully match people with potentially suitable groups to meet their particular needs and personality. Too much diversity in group membership and expectations can problematic.

Groups may be consumer-led or worker-led, or have shared leadership, and may be time-limited or open-ended. As a function or process, this leadership role focuses on the exercise of influence or power to assist the group perform tasks, achieve goals and maintain positive working relationships. The most appropriate type of group leadership needs to be determined according to the aim and purpose of the group:

1. autocratic: leader makes decisions and gives orders to group members
2. democratic: leader helps and encourages group members to interact. decisions are made after proper group discussion
3. laissez-faire: leader participates very little.

Interestingly, studies have found that that the autocratic approach is as effective as the democratic approach in task achievement and productivity. However, the autocratic approach produces much more dependence and resentment. The democratic approach is much more acceptable, satisfying and creative for group members. The laissez-faire approach is less productive; group members spend a lot of time discussing their tasks. It is important to note, however, that a democratic leadership style is not always preferable. The style of leadership that works best depends on the particular situation and the function of the group. For instance, if an urgent decision needs to be made, the autocratic style of leadership may be most suitable. If a group is committed to a decision and very capable of getting on with tasks without much interference, a laissez-faire style might be most appropriate.

Feminist social workers advocate for shared leadership whereby workers and consumers form collaborative partnerships based on mutual respect. Recovery-focused practice advocates for consumer leadership, with social workers supporting consumers in leadership roles wherever possible. Shared leadership is a particularly useful framework for two reasons:

1. to locate the particular group model being used
2. to look at the movement that occurs in the balance of control during a group's life and whether leadership is controlled by workers, members or shared.

Therapy groups are led by workers with members controlling self-help groups. Developmental factors, including groups for young children, may require a leader-directed group. Many groups in social work start as leader-directed, particularly in situations where workers are involved in the establishment of a new group. As the group develops and members take on more responsibility, there can be a shift to shared management. If the goal is for the members to assume responsibility for the group, the shift would then occur from shared management to member management.

Much of the literature on leadership does not take into account the effects of gender, or else it draws on male-led groups. Most of our models of leaders have been males, especially high-profile leaders in politics until recent times. We therefore have a particular image of leaders based on male characteristics. Studies have shown that female leaders are seen differently to male leaders even if their behaviours are the same. This is due to perceived role and status incongruence:

1. Role incongruence: according to this view, women ought not to be leaders but are. There is a conflict between competence and femininity. The behaviour of female leaders is closely scrutinised, more so than their male counterparts, with female leaders often experiencing isolation.
2. Status incongruence: women generally have lower status than men in society but as leaders have higher status. This often leads to confusion in the group and can result in leaderless groups. The group can act as if there is no leader because people want to keep gender-clear; gender status equates with more input and power.

Conflict is an issue that is always likely to occur in groups at some stage, to a greater or lesser extent. Group workers, especially beginners, may feel concern because of a sense of loss of control. When conflict does occur, it is the role of the group leader to identify what the conflict is about, identify different viewpoints, re-establish and reassesses ground rules and the goal of the group. This helps the group to refocus, and is particularly effective for task-focused groups such as multidisciplinary teams.

Work groups in mental health are interdisciplinary in recognition of the need for teamwork so that people can benefit from the knowledge and skills of different professions. These teams predominantly comprise psychiatrists, general practitioners, nurses, psychologists, social workers, occupational therapists and consumers and carers. Strategies that build positive working relations across disciplines and with family members are shared goals, effective leadership, role clarity and clear communication.

Advocacy and social action

Advocacy is the art of persuasion and is a core skill of recovery-focused practice premised on the belief that people working together can make a difference. Due to the level of social disadvantage and stigma associated with mental health issues, advocacy for rights and entitlements and anti-discrimination for active community participation are important for improvements to occur in the lives of people with mental health issues.[49]

An advocate is a person who represents the cause of another. This notion of representation of another is a difficult aspect of advocacy from a critical theoretical perspective as the social worker is arguing and representing the interests of the consumer. This could promote dependency and position the social worker in a superior position to the consumer. From a critical theoretical perspective, a broader definition of 'representation' includes interpreting or displaying the value of consumers to powerful groups in society. According to this view, advocacy means,

1. a service arguing consumers' views and needs
2. a set of skills and techniques for doing so (and)
3. the interpretation of powerless people to powerful groups.

Advocacy is generally conducted on two levels, addressing both individual needs and broader structural change. Social work advocacy includes helping people to connect with needed resources, to negotiate problematic situations and to change social arrangements where the current arrangements cause hardship or are abusive. Central to recovery-focused advocacy are rights to adequate income, education, decent housing, humane treatment and participation in society on equal terms. Social workers are responsible for looking beyond the individual to see if there are others experiencing the same difficulties. Case advocacy is appropriate if only the individual is affected, cause advocacy is used if many people are affected.

Advocacy aims to reduce the imbalance in power between service providers and consumers. Social workers help people to gain the personal power to achieve their aims in life. This is achieved by creating structures for consumer cooperation to advocate for needs. Effective social work must include advocacy. This requires a political perspective and an understanding of how the consumer's situation is connected to issues of power according to class, race, age, gender, mental health, disability and sexuality.

Social work practice embodies empowerment, consciousness raising and social change particularly around issues of stigma and discrimination. Often, advocacy requires courage as it is not easy to be disliked, particularly when fighting for basic human rights. Advocacy involves the provision of information for consciousness raising. Different perspectives are provided using a structural analysis that looks at political, economic and social factors that challenge the view of personal inadequacy. Advocacy is often used to challenge accepted organisational practices. It is questionable how much advocacy government and other organisations will tolerate before they respond in negative ways by withdrawing funding or other support. This is an important consideration in a context of privatisation and service contracts. As mentioned previously, advocacy is not a service funded by government for social workers in private practice.

Three different types of advocacy social workers might be involved in are

self-advocacy
citizen advocacy
legal advocacy.

Self-advocacy is when an individual or group of people speak or act on behalf of themselves pursuing their own needs and interests. In mental health, this includes groups advocating on behalf of themselves as consumers of mental health services and/or carers. Self-advocacy is consistent with a strengths approach, as client strengths and resources are recognised and social workers are involved in linking people to share resources. Social workers may assume a silent role as a support person and must ensure that they do not intervene unless invited to do so by the consumer. This means sitting comfortably with silence as a consumer takes time to collect their thoughts and not assume this is an invitation to intervene on their behalf. Some consumer advocacy groups become service providers; consumers may then complain about their practices. When consumer advocacy groups are absorbed into organisations and bureaucracies, they may become seen as part of the problem. The most effective forms of self-advocacy are those where consumers act collectively, combining both legal and non-legal activity. Social workers are often involved in facilitating the establishment and ongoing support of self-help advocacy groups.

Citizen advocacy occurs in partnership between the consumer and the advocate. The advocate will represent the consumer's interests as if they are their own. Sometimes social workers assume if the consumer has been refused a service it is of little use for them to become involved. Often, however, services refused to a consumer are easily obtained when requested by a social worker. Unfortunately, many organisations treat social workers much better than they do their clients. In other instances, social workers will have to argue strongly for rights and entitlements. A dilemma arises if the worker starts to identify with the organisation they are acting against on behalf of the client.

Legal advocacy involves representation of clients before courts and tribunals. This often involves complex rules of conduct and codes of language and behaviour. In recent years, there has been a proliferation of alternative dispute resolution processes, predominantly mediation. A main issue is whether or not a person can adequately participate in a fair mediation process with an equal balance of power. It is here that advocates have a major role to play to ensure that people with mental health issues are treated fairly and with due process and representation if required.

A potential danger of advocacy is the conscious or unconscious exploitation of consumers. For every advocacy campaign, social workers need to ask themselves, 'Is advocacy cynical manipulation by middle-class workers or a genuine attempt at partnerships?' Social workers need to apply the self principle by actively pursuing opportunities to influence colleagues, community members, government and professional associations.

Advocacy campaigns by consumers and carers, social workers, civil libertarians and social justice lawyers can assist in reducing oppressive aspects of mental health legislation and practices by focusing on rights and entitlements. Long-standing advocacy campaigns continue for the discontinuation of the oppressive practice of mixed-gender psychiatric wards due to issues of safety and the past histories of sexual abuse of many women who use mental health services. A further area for social work advocacy is for additional funding for services that specialise in sexual abuse and mental health given the high proportion of women who use mental health services who are survivors of sexual abuse.

Social workers in collaboration with consumers, health promotion units and other relevant services conduct prevention and mental health promotion activities. Those who are passionate about their cause usually lead the best social action campaigns. These are often people who have experienced mental health issues personally or through family and friends.[50]

In advocacy and social action campaigns, it is important to bear in mind the principle of least contest. This is based on the assumption of shared interests rather than competing interests and use of the least force necessary to achieve desired goals. This occurs in the following order:

private talk
group representation
campaigns
protests
negative publicity.

It is important that social workers use conciliatory approaches prior to moving on to more adversarial interventions that damage relationships. This is particularly important when ongoing relationships are involved. Social workers must be mindful of the negative consequences of more threatening types of social action and assist people to make informed decisions considering best and worst possible outcomes. This is done with respect for clients' decisions and self-determination. Effective advocacy requires skills in assertiveness and conflict management presented in the next chapter under communication skills.

Critical social work intervention skills

Competent mental health workers have self-awareness and respectful communication skills. They can work with diverse cultures and accommodate different views on the causes and treatment of mental health issues, in the knowledge that access to mental health services is generally determined by having a psychiatric diagnosis listed in the ICD or DSM. Social workers understand discrimination and ways to reduce and eliminate it, supporting family-based inclusive interventions in collaboration with consumer and carer services and organisations.

Core social work interviewing skills, mentioned earlier in Chapter 7, are also used for intervention. These skills include demystifying the social work contact, creating a safe place, believing, clear contracting, skilled observation, listening, body language, eye contact, empathic statements, paraphrasing, and open, closed and critical questioning. These skills will be applied selectively depending upon the intervention required. For instance, if a person is highly paranoid, it may be appropriate to engage in less direct eye contact and avoid more intrusive interventions such as questioning.

Engaging the person in an effective working relationship is paramount. This occurs by consciously putting the person at ease, and displaying respect, genuineness and honesty. Skills in listening, attending and exploration using minimal encouragers, open and closed questions and silence assist the person to tell her or his story. Information is provided as needed with a tentative assessment made about the situation with an agreement to work together.

Structural social work interventions focus on power relations and discrimination at both the personal and structural level. These include consciousness raising, normalising, universalising, individualising, re-contextualising, reframing, empowerment, advocacy, assertiveness and conflict management. Self-awareness, combined with political awareness, is required for effective social work practice. Self-awareness includes knowledge of ways we deal with power and powerlessness in our own daily lives and in our professional work.[51] Self-knowledge and the valuing of difference are central to engaging in recovery-focused practices. Recovery-focused practice challenges notions of professional distance focusing more so on power sharing and egalitarian relationships based on shared values.[52] Political awareness requires critical reflection and analysis of dominant discourses on mental health. Disempowering aspects of these discourses are to be questioned and challenged with the development of new discourses that are respectful and empowering.[53] With the advent of the recovery movement in mental health, dominant medical model discourses in the DSM and ICD that guide assessment, diagnosis and intervention have been questioned and challenged on a number of levels including not taking adequate account of gender, culture and spirituality. Disempowering negative stereotypes of lifelong illness have also been questioned, resisted and challenged. This has resulted in new policies, structures and guidelines for recovery-focused practice.[54]

The sharing of information with consumers about dominant oppressive discourses enables consciousness raising. This can result in normalising people's situations; feelings, thoughts and behaviours are seen as understandable given their circumstances. This can reduce feelings of guilt and hopelessness, with people no longer blaming themselves for their situation or feeling embarrassed about particular behaviours when experiencing mental health issues. Universalising creates linkages between people with similar experiences; individualising respects the uniqueness of the person's own circumstances. Re-contextualising is looking at different contexts where feelings, thoughts and behaviours currently rejected would be acceptable and linking people with these. Reframing is used to assist people to consider other possibilities and to think more positively. This is not to deny the person's views but rather to look at things from a broader and less personal perspective.[55] Empowerment recognises people's resourcefulness, with workers sharing resources and information to support them in making informed decisions.

Conclusion

Social work interventions in mental health focus on empowerment. An analysis and understanding of power and powerlessness is essential for effective practices to bring about both personal and social change. Power with and not over consumers and carers and significant others is required. A holistic approach to intervention addresses biological, psychological, emotional, social, cultural, spiritual and environmental aspects and is respectful of gender, age, sexuality and socio-economic status. Social workers develop collaborative relationships with consumers and develop interventions that are respectful of consumers' hopes and dreams and support recovery-focused trauma-informed care and practice.

Main interventions used in mental health today focus on individuals, families, groups and communities. Ultimately, interventions are required that improve a person's mental health functioning and overall quality of life, assisting them prevent and mange loss when this does occur, to get back the things lost due to mental health issues and to move forwards. This can only be achieved through the development, and ongoing nurturing, of professional working relationships based on mutual respect and consumer choice, celebrating difference and redressing the discrimination faced by people with mental health issues. Effective partnerships between social workers, consumer and carers and other mental health service providers are essential for this to be achieved.

Reflection

Identify the mental health services available in your local area. Describe this service network and the range of services and interventions available.

How can you access these services?

How much choice is there?

Would you be confident that this mental health system would work well for you if you needed to use it yourself? Provide reasons.

What are the main interventions used by social workers in mental health?

Who do you include in intervention planning and implementation? Who is best to decide on the most appropriate intervention/s?

11

Focused Psychological Strategies

Increasingly, social workers are being required to provide evidence that their interventions are proven to be effective with service funding models designed to fund evidence-based practices and not others. This has resulted in major shifts in how social work services are designed and delivered in recent years. Mental health social workers in Australia provide services in private practices under a range of programs. These include Employee Assistance, Access to Allied Psychological Services (ATAPS) Department of Veteran's Affairs, Victims of Crime, Work Cover, Family Court, Transport Accident Commission and Medicare (Better Access) Program. Under Medicare (Better Access)[1] social workers are eligible to claim only for the delivery of focused psychological strategies (FPS).

In August 2010 the General Practice Mental Health Standards Collaboration (GPMHSC) revised and updated the requirements for the delivery of FPS. Representatives on the GPMHSC are the Royal Australian College of General Practitioners, the Australian College of Rural and Remote Medicine, the Royal Australian and New Zealand College of Psychiatrists, the Australian Psychological Society and the Mental Health Council of Australia. The GPMHSC is a key national body for the development of standards in mental health in Australia.

According to the GPMHSC,

> Focused psychological strategies (FPS) are specific mental healthcare management strategies, derived from evidence based psychological therapies that have been shown to integrate the best research evidence of clinical effectiveness with general practice clinical expertise.[2]

Focused psychological strategies are often used in conjunction with other approaches due to the complexity of the problems consumers present with and in recognition of the relational aspects of these. Often, people present with mental health issues that are related to family and relationship breakdown, issues of attachment and loss, and grief and trauma.

Medicare rebates differ across and within different occupational groups for the same services.[3] To be eligible for referral to a social worker for FPS, the person must not be a hospital in-patient and be assessed as having a chronic condition with complex care needs managed by a medical practitioner. In the case of aged care facilities, the medical practitioner must have contributed to a multidisciplinary care plan.

Most referrals to allied health professionals, including social workers, for mental health services are made by general practitioners. Referrals for FPS are currently made in the context of a psychiatrist assessment and management plan or GP mental health treatment plan. This three-step mental health process of assessment, care planning and review was introduced by the Australian federal government on 1 July 2002 for effective management of mental health issues by general practitioners.

Focused psychological strategies

FPS include mental health care treatment strategies, derived from the evidence-based psychological therapies of cognitive behaviour therapy (CBT) and interpersonal therapy. The FPS approved for use by Accredited Mental Health Social Workers (AMHSW) under the Better Outcomes and Better Access initiatives are

- psycho-education (including motivational interviewing)
- cognitive behaviour therapy, including
- behavioural interventions
- behaviour modification
- exposure techniques
- activity scheduling
- cognitive interventions
- cognitive therapy
- relaxation strategies
- progressive muscle relaxation
- controlled breathing
- skills training
- problem solving skills training
- anger management
- communication training
- social skills training
- stress management
- parent management training
- interpersonal therapy (especially for depression)
- narrative therapy (only for clients of Aboriginal and Torres Strait islander descent).

The most common focused psychological strategies used by mental health social workers are interpersonal therapy and cognitive behavioural therapy, followed by psycho-education, relaxation strategies, skills training and narrative therapy.[4]

The Royal Australian College of General Practitioners (RAGPS) provides a description of focused psychological strategies that provides information on what the strategies involve and their application. This definition is relied upon by social workers and other allied health professionals as general practitioners are the main referral source for these services. Programs for general practitioners to improve access and outcomes in mental health also provide definitions and procedures for implementing all of the focused psychological strategies.[5]

Developments in FPS in Australia follow earlier initiatives in Britain under Improving Access to Psychological Therapies (IAPT). Research findings indicate that since the introduction of IAPT there has been improved access to counselling and psychological therapies for those suffering from anxiety and depression. In Britain what are referred to as the third-wave CBT treatments, mindfulness-based CBT and meditation, have recently been added to the IAPT-approved list. This is considered to have improved services for people from culturally and linguistically diverse backgrounds due to the relevance of these approaches in many regions around the world. Further work is being done on looking at the culturally responsiveness of these approved therapies and any adaptations that may be required. This includes service location, language, belief systems, presenting problems and service expectations.[6]

1. Psycho-education

Psycho-education strategies aim to promote an increased understanding of mental health issues. Evidence-based research demonstrates that the more people understand about their mental health issues and treatment the more likely they are to follow treatment plans and have improved outcomes.[7] This includes information on the natural history of the mental health issue, symptoms and effective treatments. All self-help programs include psycho-education.

Psycho-education involves explaining the mental health issue to the person and answering any questions. Information is provided at an appropriate level and typically would include education about how common the mental health issue is, symptomatology, any possible complications or other problems, causation, what may happen in the longer term, what treatments work and the pros and cons of those treatments. It may also be useful to supplement this with printed information or websites that the person can take away with them, read and refer to as needed.[8]

Motivational interviewing

Motivational interviewing was first used for treatment of problem drinking.[9] It is particularly useful for those who are ambivalent or reluctant to change. This is particularly so when the problem behaviour is pleasurable or addictive. Motivational interviewing requires an empathic approach that elicits reasons for change from the person and exploring these in a supportive manner. The aim is to highlight how current behaviours are impacting negatively upon desired goals and quality of life and to enhance motivation for change.

Studies have shown that this approach is far more effective in bringing about behaviour change than arguing about the harmful effects of the behaviour. This is considered to be ineffective resulting in resistance and less likelihood of change. The more a person is confronted about a problem, the more likely they will continue with it.[10]

Motivational interviewing involves the following five steps:

1. express empathy
2. develop discrepancy
3. avoid arguments
4. roll with resistance (and)
5. support self-efficacy.[11]

When adopting this approach, it is assumed that the person is ambivalent or reluctant to change. Prochaska and DiClemente's[12] six-stage change model for change, also commonly used in alcohol and other drug settings, is used as a guide for understanding personal change processes. These six stages are

1. pre-contemplation
2. contemplation
3. determination
4. action
5. maintenance (and)
6. exit.

Main skills used in motivational interviewing are

open-ended questions
reflective listening
affirmation
summarising (and)
eliciting self-motivating statements.[13]

The worker starts with open ended questions such as 'What's brought you here?' 'What's been the problem?' This is followed by reflective listening to check you fully understand what the person is telling you and to encourage further discussion. Affirmations demonstrate understanding and appreciation of the person's situation with statements such as 'I appreciate how difficult it is for you to talk about this.' Summary statements are a further check that you have understood what the person has said as well as linking information and highlighting ambivalence such as 'It sounds like you want to...but then again maybe you don't because...' The goal of self-motivational statements is for the person to develop these in appropriate language and arguments rather than the worker providing them. This might be along the lines of 'This is serious because...' 'If I don't do something...' 'I'm going to change things by...'[14]

It is important to ascertain how change-ready the person is. This is done through exploration of the advantages and disadvantages of the problematic behaviour, with the worker providing feedback on discrepancies between current and desired behaviours, with the aim of eliciting feedback and enhancing motivation. Miller and Rollnick recommend that an assessment summary statement include

detailed description of the risks and problems that have emerged
the person's own reactions to the feedback and any self-motivational statements that have been made (and)
an opportunity for the person to correct, or add to, the summary.[15]

This is followed by intervention planning that continues to strengthen the person's commitment and motivation to change with the negotiation of specific tasks for this to be achieved. This includes a process for review and evaluation.

2. Cognitive behaviour therapy

In Britain in 2006, CBT was offered as a panacea to alleviate misery, with the claim that crippling depression and chronic anxiety were the biggest causes of misery in Britain at that time. CBT was considered to be not only short term and cost effective, it also increased productivity with any health costs offset by reduced disability payments, due to increased workforce participation by those with mental health issues treated with CBT.

CBT is not without its critics with the focus on thinking and behaviour considered narrow in scope due to the exclusion of broader social contextual factors. Thought processes and belief systems when seen within their proper context may not be seen as faulty and in need of correction. Ethical issues arise from the use of directive therapies aimed at changing cognitive processes, quite forcibly in some instances. David Pilgrim questions the reduction of the notion of happiness to social conformity that values rationality, and human capital in the form of workforce participation. Pilgrim's insightful critique of the evolution of CBT provides two narratives; one medical and the other psychological.

According to the medical narrative, behaviour therapy developed in the twentieth century as a form of psychological medicine that directly challenged both a bio-medical approach and psychoanalysis. This was the beginning of what came to be known as behavioural psychiatry with behavioural approaches evident in medical hypnotism and most notably the work of the Russian scientist Ivan Pavlov (1849–1936) on conditioned learning. Pavlov demonstrated initially how dogs, and then humans, could be conditioned to respond in a certain way to a particular stimulus. American psychiatrist, Aaron Beck (1921–) is considered to be the pioneer of CBT focusing on the influence of thoughts, emotions and beliefs on behaviour. He has gone on to further develop his CBT inventories, ranking scales and interventions with a different formulation for each psychiatric disorder.

Psychological approaches developed in three waves. The first wave was behaviour therapy as developed by Pavlov, and behaviour modification developed by American psychologist B.F. Skinner (1904–1990). Skinner's operant conditioning and schedules of reinforcement, focused on the reinforcement of desired behaviours and gained popularity in applied psychology in the 1950s. The second wave is what has come to be known as CBT, with thoughts and feelings included in addition to behaviours. A focus was on interpersonal negotiation by changing maladaptive ways of thinking and behaving. This approach was considered to be scientific with psychiatric diagnoses accepted uncritically. Psychologists joined psychiatrists as experts in the treatment of mental health issues. A new version of CBT, rational emotive therapy, was developed in the 1950s by American psychologist Albert Ellis (1913–2007) focusing on activating events, beliefs, emotions and consequences. His later work on happiness is also part of the third wave that saw a further inclusion of Eastern philosophies, in particular 'mindfulness' approaches used in Zen Buddhism, combined with systems theory and cognitive science. This has resulted in a range of interventions including dialectical behaviour therapy (DBT) incorporating mindfulness, acceptance and commitment therapy (ACT) multimodal therapy (MMT) and many more.

CBT is the second most common focused psychological strategy used by accredited mental health social workers in Australia and is often used in conjunction with other therapies and interventions. This is generally decided with the consumer, according to what is likely to be most helpful. CBT is particularly effective for the treatment of anxiety, depression, bipolar affective disorder, schizophrenia, post-traumatic stress disorder, eating disorders, phobias and pain management.[16] However, CBT is not suitable for all people. It can be an effective way for assisting consumers to develop and maintain meta-cognitive awareness to assist in challenging unhelpful cognitions such as managing flashbacks or intrusive thoughts and memories often present in post-traumatic stress disorder.

Cognitive and behavioural techniques are combined to target symptoms with a focus on self-management strategies and changes in thinking. The strategies the person has learnt should aid future problem solving and the management of symptoms should they re-occur. CBT is a time-limited intervention with clear goals and strategies. A randomised control study by Andrews found CBT to be as effective as drug therapy.[17] Sustained long-term benefits have also been reported.[18]

Behavioural interventions

Behaviour modification

Behaviour modification techniques are often used in mental health to assist in alleviating distressing symptoms of mental health issues. In mental health services, behaviour modification is often used in conjunction with other interventions such as individual or family counselling. Behaviour modification is primarily concerned with changes in behaviour. It is heavily influenced by systems theory[19] as well as learning theory and theories on conflict management. A focus is on decreasing problematic behaviours and increasing and reinforcing positive behaviours. This often includes an educational component as new skills are learnt. A detailed behavioural or task analysis is conducted that involves careful observation and recording of the behaviour to be altered. This includes examination of the setting where the behaviour occurs and factors that support the continuation of the behaviour or facilitate change. This is followed by the development of a systematic program that alters the environment that triggers the unwanted behaviour, develops new behaviours to replace the unwanted ones with strategies designed to reinforce these. Techniques for maintaining these new behaviours and generalising them to other settings are developed alongside strategies for relapse prevention.

Systematic desensitisation is a cognitive behavioural technique often used to alleviate fear and anxiety. With this technique, the person is gradually exposed to the cause of distress until a level of intensity and exposure is reached that provides the person with mastery over the situation. A number of behaviour modification techniques are used to manage distressing voices and intrusive thoughts. These include focused activity, socialisation, recognition of early warning signs, relaxation and stress management, physical activity, earplugs and headphones. Although voice experiences are highly individual it is likely that one or a combination of these techniques will bring some relief.[20]

Relief from disturbing voices can be gained by focused activity. This will vary from person to person, and might be music, painting, craft or reading. Television is not a preferred activity, particularly for lengthy periods, as it can often trigger hallucinations and delusions. The more interesting and personally rewarding the activity, the greater the focus of energy and attention is likely to be, thereby lessening the impact of the voices. As mentioned in Chapter 3, employment can result in a reduction of hallucinations. Socialising with others in a supportive environment provides a focus on other things and activities away from the voices. Voices will often stop when a person is speaking to someone. This may be face to face or over the telephone. If alone, singing or humming a tune can sometimes reduce disturbing voices.

Behaviour modification can assist with learning to recognise a particular mood or frame of mind that precedes the onset of voices; strategies to prevent the voices from occurring are developed with the person. Others close to the person may also recognise these signs and intervene. Some people find self-monitoring helpful and keep a record of the time, location, duration and content of voice experiences. Some people report a reduction in voice experiences simply by recording them in this manner. For others, the recording provides valuable information about patterns of voice experiences and potential triggers. A number of stress management and relaxation techniques may also help in the reduction of disturbing voices.

Often, the voices reflect the negative and critical thoughts a person has. Reducing or stopping the voices by using one, or a combination, of the above techniques can lead to improvements in self-esteem. Likewise, certain techniques aimed at improving self-esteem can reduce voice experiences. This may be repeating positive self-talk and self-affirmations with those of family and friends also included. Some people write these down so that they can focus on reading them when disturbing voices occur. Others might make a recording that is listened to at such times. These positive affirmations may be read, or listened to, at other times of the day when voices are not heard as a means of confidence building. Some people find talking to voices helpful. This may be telling them to 'stop' or 'go away'. However, a pre-occupation with trying to stop the voices can make them worse; it is often best to focus on something else rather than become preoccupied with them.

Exposure techniques

Exposure techniques are particularly useful for dealing with all anxiety disorders and phobias, including agoraphobia and obsessive compulsive disorder, with long-lasting benefits.[21] These are often used in conjunction with other techniques such as cognitive therapy (discussed below).[22] Evidence-based research has demonstrated positive treatment outcomes for generalised anxiety disorder by using exposure techniques with problem solving and relaxation strategies.[23] Exposure to painful memories and the situations triggering these has been proven to be successful for the treatment of post-traumatic stress disorder. However, this must be voluntary and no pressure should be put on the person to do so.

Graded exposure is the most frequently used behavioural technique, with the person gradually exposed to the feared object or situation with the aim of reducing or eliminating the fear generated. The first step is to identify a person's fears and then develop a hierarchy with them of the least to most feared situations. Anxiety-provoking situations are approached in graded steps so that the person is able to maintain control without becoming overwhelmed. The person is encouraged to remain in the anxiety-provoking situation until the anxiety decreases and the fear subsides.

Exposure techniques often include systematic desensitisation that incorporates controlled breathing and other relaxation techniques. Cognitive coping statements or positive self-talk are also used. The person is taught to use the relaxation techniques on exposure to the anxiety-provoking situation and to use these until the fear reduces.

It is important that a good rationale is provided for the use of exposure techniques, given that the person is likely to become extremely anxious at the prospect of engaging in the feared activity. As well as explaining the rationale, it is important to clearly explain the process and how the gradual increase in exposure and repetition will assist in overcoming the fear and anxiety. This five-step process includes

Step 1: providing a good rationale to increase the likelihood of compliance

Step 2: developing a goal and an exposure hierarchy in collaboration with the person acknowledging complexities

Step 3: together with the person, design approximately 10 specific and detailed tasks or activities to form the basis of an exposure plan in a logical and ascending order (1 to 10) ensuring the range of activities is of appropriate intensity

Step 4: encouraging exposure by asking the person to commence with one of the easier tasks or activities and remain engaged until the anxiety level is halved, repeating this several times per week

Step 5: reviewing progress weekly acknowledging efforts and providing positive reinforcement. Use the rationale as a constant reference point to increase motivation to move through the steps in the hierarchy.

Brenda was frightened to leave her home and relied upon her partner and children to do the shopping and engage in activities outside of the home. She was extremely anxious and fearful at the thought of leaving her home. A graded exposure hierarchy was developed with her (see Figure 11.1). Goal: to walk to the Community Health Centre for a social work appointment.

Once Brenda achieved this goal, a further goal and exposure hierarchies were developed for Brenda to go to the shops and use public transport. In addition to exposure techniques, cognitive therapy was used as well as interventions focused on poverty alleviation, family relationships and social networks.

Repetition is important even after fears have subsided. Monitoring of the exposure hierarchy is required to ensure it is appropriate and achievable with modifications made as required. Some people may initially find it easier to do the task with a friend or family member

Activity	Level of anxiety
Step outside back door	1 (mild)
Step outside front door	2
Take three steps down path	3
Take six steps down path	4
Walk to letter box	5
Walk on footpath to end of property	6
Walk to end of neighbour's property	7
Walk to corner of the street	8
Walk to corner of street and cross road	9
Walk to Community Health Centre (in same street)	10 (extreme)

Figure 11.1: Brenda's exposure hierarchy

Time	Activity	Rating (1–5) (P) pleasure (A) achievement
0700	get up	
0800	have shower	
0900	make breakfast	
1000	clean house	
1100	do washing	
1200		
1300	walk to shops	
1400		
1500	meet friend for coffee	
1600		
1700		
1800		
1900	read book	
2000	go to bed	

Figure 11.2: Sample daily activity schedule

or worker rather than alone. A diary can be useful for recording anxiety levels, achievements and difficulties encountered.

Activity scheduling

Activity scheduling involves time management to plan a daily routine that includes both pleasant activities as well as those that provide a sense of purpose and satisfaction (see Figure 11.2).

This is a particularly useful technique for people recovering from depression who are finding it difficult to perform basic daily tasks and who have lost interest in usual pleasurable activities.[24] A focus is on increasing enjoyable activities and encouraging the person to participate in these so as to improve quality of life and prevent further episodes of depression. An emphasis is on how to motivate and reinforce the person to remain actively engaged in performing daily living tasks, pleasurable activities and physical exercise. The aim is to assist mood improvement by working with the person to increase these activities in an organised and structured manner. As with exposure techniques, it is important to provide a rationale as to why it is important for the person to actively engage in these activities; explain how the less they do the worse they will feel rather than aiding recovery.

Activity scheduling involves

Step 1: providing a rationale for increased activity and the importance of maintaining a balance between daily living tasks, pleasurable activities, exercise and rest

Step 2: asking the person to write down current activities and to rate these from 1 (no pleasure/ sense of achievement) to 5 (extreme pleasure/sense of achievement)

Step 3: asking the person to list daily activities currently neglected and at least 10 things they used to enjoy but no longer do or new activities they would like to do

Step 4: arranging the activities identified in 3 in a hierarchy from easiest to hardest with complex tasks broken down into smaller more manageable components if necessary

Step 5: developing a planner with the person to organise these activities in a structured manner commencing slowly with easiest tasks

Step 6: asking the person to rate the activity according to pleasure (P) and achievement (A) on completion

Step 7: asking the person to record other activities they engage in on the planner and to also rate these according to pleasure (P) and achievement (A) on completion

Step 8: reviewing the schedule with the person in terms of what did and did not go well, providing encouragement to continue until they resume normal functioning and no longer require the planner.

It is worth noting that some people like to continue with the planner as part of their normal daily routine to provide a sense of structure, not unlike a business diary. However, this planner is a reminder of the importance of life–work balance.

Daily activity schedules form part of a weekly planner. It is useful to have pro formas available to assist with organisation, recording and discussions of progress. Encourage the person to set aside a regular time for planning each day to develop a sense of routine. Some people will to do this at night and others in the morning with night-time preferable for those who are having difficulty sleeping. It may be necessary to build this planning time into the activity schedule. However, it is important that the schedule allows for flexibility to allow for changes and rescheduling as needed with the emphasis on quality of life.

Cognitive interventions

Cognitive therapy
Cognitive therapy is based on the belief that past experiences determine how current situations are perceived; influencing thoughts, feelings and actions. Cognitive therapy is a structured

time limited directive approach that is used to treat depression, generalised anxiety, phobias, panic disorder and pain management.[25] Cognitive therapy interventions used by some mental health social workers frequently incorporate mindfulness and meditation practices. These interventions include cognitive processing therapy (CPT) and acceptance and commitment therapy (ACT). Studies have shown cognitive therapy to be an effective treatment in sustaining positive long-term outcomes and preventing relapse.[26] Cognitive therapy focuses on changes to a person's thinking, whereas behavioural techniques are directly targeted at symptoms or problematic behaviours.

Ellis has developed a useful model to make plain the interplay between thoughts and actions:

A – activating event
B – belief or reaction to event
C – emotional consequences.

Worker intervention:
– challenge negative or irrational ideas
– new emotion.[27]

Commonly referred to as the ABC model, it is the belief or reaction to an event, that is often more significant than the event itself in terms of emotional response. A person's beliefs (B) and self-talk strongly influence emotional responses (C) to events (A). With help from a therapist, the person learns to challenge negative thoughts replacing these with more rational ones resulting in a changed emotional response.

Cognitive therapy is often used with other behavioural techniques. These other interventions will be chosen in response to the problems presented. For instance, cognitive therapy and exposure techniques may be used concurrently when working with anxiety. The following process is a useful guide for cognitive therapy:

Step 1. Explain the ABC model.
Step 2. Identify and elicit negative automatic thoughts (NAT) and problematic beliefs.
Step 3. Test NAT by generating and assessing the evidence for and against.
Step 4. Challenge NAT and problematic beliefs.
Step 5. Generate more rational and realistic counter-statements.[28]

The worker explains the rationale behind cognitive therapy using the ABC model. The term negative automated thoughts (NAT) is often used in cognitive therapy. These thoughts may occur consciously or unconsciously and are often the main focus of cognitive therapy due to the powerful influence of these beliefs on emotions and actions and interpretations of events.

Record sheets (see Figure 11.3 overleaf) are sometimes used to monitor thoughts in relation to events between sessions.[29]

Together the worker and client explore these thoughts; the worker asks for more detail about the situation and what the person was thinking at the time. A focus is on attention

Date	Emotions	Situation	Automatic thoughts
	What do you feel?	What are you doing	What are your thoughts?
	How bad is it (0–100)?		How much do you believe them (0–100)?

Figure 11.3: Thought record sheet

Evidence for	Evidence against
What do you actually know about this?	Have you possibly forgotten, or not acknowledged, something that may be relevant?

Figure 11.4: Evidence record sheet

regulation and control, acknowledging distorted cognitive processing that often focuses on negative aspects rather than neutral or positive interpretations. Part of this process is considering evidence for and against these thoughts. Recording sheets (see Figure 11.4) are also used to assist with this.[30]

The worker teaches the person how to challenge their thoughts and to look at other possible interpretations. A main focus is on how rational or irrational the person's thoughts appear to be. Cognitive analysis, challenging and restructuring requires the identification of negative thoughts, emotions and behaviours.

Common erroneous thinking patterns arise from

seeing things in extremes (black or white, all or none)
over-generalisation (conclusions drawn on the basis of one or more isolated events)
selective abstraction (a particular detail is taken out of context)
discounting or disqualifying the positive (rejecting successful experiences)
jumping to conclusions (not supported by facts)
magnification or minimisation (too much or too little importance assigned to an event)
personalisation (unwarranted self-blame).[31]

By asking questions about the event and suggesting alternative explanations, the worker assists the person to identify how realistic these thoughts are. These questions might include

What's a more reasonable and helpful way of looking at this situation?
What could you tell yourself next time you have this thought?
What would a different person say about the thought?
What advice would you give someone else with this thought?[32]

These questions are written down for the person to take home and consider when confronted with new situations between sessions to assist them to self-talk. It is useful to ask the person to self evaluate how much they believe the thought after you have been through this exploration process. Ask the person to do a second ranking of emotions and beliefs, again out of 100, and compare this with the original scores given. This can be an effective measure of changes in thinking.

The identification of communication and interpretative patterns across a range of interactions can lead to increased self-knowledge. This process assists in heightening self awareness when engaged in similar interactions in the future. Self-instructional training involves replacing negative thoughts by self-talk which is positive and assists the person to develop useful responses to situations they find difficult.

Cognitive behaviour therapy and depression
Depression may be a one-off occurrence but for the majority of those affected it is recurring. Risks factors that increase the likelihood of depression recurring are

genetic vulnerability
early onset
long and severe duration
residual symptoms
past history of dysthymia or previous episodes of depression
multiple diagnoses
early discontinuation of antidepressants
unresolved loss and grief
psycho-social stressors
negative thinking patterns (and)
low self-efficacy.[33]

Wilson, Duszynski and Mant's[34] five-year follow-up study of general practitioner patients experiencing depression found that 77.5 per cent of patients experienced a further episode of depression. A recommendation of this study was that a long-term approach to management and care is required. This follows an earlier recommendation by Andrews that depression be managed as a chronic condition.[35]

Management of persistent and ongoing mental health issues involves consumer-centred planned care based upon a comprehensive assessment that focuses on long-term improved health outcomes. This includes a multidisciplinary teamwork approach to recovery-focused interventions utilising community resources to live well in the presence or absence of signs and symptoms of depression and relapse prevention. This includes identifying problems and issues to be addressed, strategies to be adopted, multidisciplinary team approach and long-term management plans (see Figure 11.5 overleaf).

The more involved the person is in the development and implementation of their management plan, the increased likelihood of positive outcomes. Self-management focuses on

managing symptoms of depression that impact upon daily functioning
reducing negative impacts by following treatment plans
engaging in a healthy lifestyle that promotes health.[36]

Treatment guidelines for general practitioners recommend maintaining treatment until the person's condition stabilises. The recommended timeframe is one year for a first episode

Severity of depression	Focused psychological strategies
Mild depression	*Psycho-education:* *– information on depression and anxiety and relapse prevention* *Lifestyle changes:* *– sleep* *– nutrition* *– exercise* *– stress management* *– relaxation techniques* *– social support* *– enjoyable activities* *– activity scheduling* *Problem-solving approaches:* *– bio-psychosocial assessment* *– develop a plan to manage early symptoms of depression* *– mood diary* *– setting goals* *– monitoring progress* *Interpersonal therapy:* *– hopelessness* *– relationship issues* *– goals* *– education/employment* *– finances/housing* *– loss and grief* *– self-esteem* *– anger and guilt* *– suicidal thoughts* *Brief CBT:* *— helpful thinking or cognitive strategies (thought monitoring, analysis and challenging).*
Moderate depression	*Anti-depressants may be introduced in addition to the FPS used for mild depression.*
Moderate depression with substance use or physical condition	*Concurrent treatment of the substance abuse and physical condition is required in addition to the FPS for mild depression and medication.*
Severe depression	*Anti-depressants are a first line of intervention in cases of severe depression. Once there is a response FPS will be introduced.*
Psychotic depression or severe depression with suicide risk	*Refer to specialist mental health services. Medication and FPS used for mild depression.*

Figure 11.5: Depression and focused psychological strategies[37]

and three years for those with a history of recurring depression.[38] There is evidence that CBT prevents relapse.[39] Segal's research has found improved outcomes from the integration of mindfulness approaches with cognitive behaviour therapy for those with three or more episodes of depression.[40]

Relapse prevention is a crucial component of any depression management plan and includes recognition of early warning signs. This is often by someone close to the person who may be the first to recognise these signs. It may be something quite subtle related to grooming or behaviour. Contracting when the person is well is important so that permission is granted as part of a relapse prevention management plan for a designated person to instigate a referral for early intervention so that relapse can be prevented and high-stress situations avoided. This is aided by the person having an Advance Directive in place. Early intervention, medication compliance and FPS lead to improved outcomes.

It is important to identify both risk and protective factors to prevent a further episode of depression from occurring. Cognitive, psychological and social interventions, combined with medication when required, are important for optimum treatment outcomes. Problem-solving skills are particularly useful for relapse prevention planning and managing early symptoms of depression. A relapse prevention and management plan includes

identifying early warning signs such as tearfulness, difficulty sleeping, increased irritability, loss of interest in usual activities and rapid gain or loss in weight

identifying times of high stress and devise strategies to manage them

an emergency plan in times of relapse; this might include making an emergency appointment with a mental health professional or general practitioner as soon as signs of relapse are detected, monitoring and challenging negative thought patterns, self affirmation, taking time out, seeking social support from family and friends.[41]

Given the limited number of FPS social workers are funded to provide, it is essential that collaboration with general practitioners occurs for optimum health outcomes in the longer term. General practitioners undertake an initial assessment and then refer to allied health professionals including social workers. For referrals to occur, it is essential that general practitioners are aware of the knowledge and skills of social workers in mental health assessment and intervention. Social workers need to promote and market their services to general practitioner networks and build relationships with local practices. The marketing of services is a new area for many social workers now employed in private practice, who previously have worked in public systems or the not for profit sector. It is still relatively new territory for the professional body, the AASW. Successful practices generally have a clearly defined target population and clearly identified services and intervention strategies as part of their advertising and marketing.

3. Relaxation strategies

Relaxation strategies are useful for treating a range of mental health issues, including phobias and panic attacks. These are most effective as a component of a broader intervention plan rather than alone.[42] Mental health social workers use a range of relaxation strategies with their clients as well as stress management techniques including body/breath work, guided imagery, progressive muscle and isometric relaxation and controlled breathing in conjunction with other interventions. A number of mental health social workers also use clinical hypnosis for relaxation and stress management and have done further training in this area. Mindfulness techniques and meditation are also used for stress reduction.[43] Massage and aromatherapy can also produce relaxed states and lessen the negative impacts of stress.[44] Physical exercise such as walking, jogging, swimming, gardening, team sport or exercise class can be effective in bringing about improvements in mental health, including reducing disturbing voices.

It is best to teach and practise these techniques at times when the person is in a calm state. Stress management and relaxation require a balance of time alone as well as time with other people, and proper rest, diet and exercise. Relaxation therapy is used to avert a build-up of stress and reduce anxiety by producing a relaxed state. This is achieved by the voluntary release of tension and reduction in arousal of the central nervous system. Over-arousal can trigger hyperventilation; controlled breathing techniques prevent this. Anxiety also results in increased muscle tension and it is important for the person to be aware of when and where in the body this occurs. Progressive muscle relaxation strategies whereby the person is taught to tense and relax certain muscles through out the body can alleviate and prevent the build up of stress. Isometric relaxation is a brief intervention focused on a particular muscle group only to be implemented in an anxiety provoking situation. Guided imagery provides a script for peaceful surroundings enabling relaxation.

The two main recognised focused psychological strategies for relaxation are progressive muscle relaxation and controlled breathing. Skills in relaxation strategies are easily learnt and can assist the person to gain control over symptoms of anxiety. However, for those who fear losing control and possibly panicking when in a relaxed state, progressive muscle relaxation is preferred.

Progressive muscle relaxation
Progressive muscle relaxation, combined with guided imagery to develop pleasant images, can reduce stress. Consciously relaxing muscles by tightening and stretching them as well as relaxing muscles where stress and tension build up the most, particularly in the neck and shoulders and face can also help a person to feel more calm and relaxed. As with all interventions, it is important to provide a rationale as to the benefits of the particular approach recommended and to set time aside to answer any questions or address concerns with more detailed information provided if necessary. Assist the person to relax by providing a comfortable environment to help them to clear the mind of any worries or thoughts. Calming phrases or words said in a soothing tone can assist, such as 'Relax', 'Let your thought go.' Assist the person to slow down by controlling breathing intervals, saying in a soothing tone, 'Breathe in (pause) breathe out...' Repeat this and then get the person to guide this themselves possibly counting out the breaths in and out. Guided imagery may be used to create images of tension being released from the body with each breath out.

While the person continues to breathe slowly, ask them to close their hands in a fist and hold this for 10 seconds and then relax instantly letting the muscles go limp. Contrast this with the tightness of the clenched fist. It is important to monitor that the person is not experiencing any pain whatsoever. If deemed appropriate, continue to instruct the person to tense and relax the muscles in the following order:

Lower arms – bend your hand down at the wrist, as though you were trying to touch the underside of your arm, then relax.

Upper arms – tighten your biceps by bending your arm at the elbow, then relax.

Shoulders – lift your shoulders up as if trying to touch your ears with them, then relax.

Neck – stretch your neck gently to the left, then forward, then to the right, then to the back in a slow rolling motion, then relax.

Forehead and scalp – raise your eyebrows, then relax.

Eyes – screw up your eyes, then relax.

Jaw – clench your teeth (just to tighten the muscles) then relax.

Tongue – press your tongue against the roof of your mouth, then relax.

Chest – breathe in deeply to inflate your lungs, then breath out and relax.

Stomach – push your tummy out to tighten the muscle, then relax.

Upper back – pull your shoulders forward with your arms at your side, then relax.

Lower back – while sitting, lean your head and upper back forward, rolling your back into a smooth arc thus tensing the lower back, then relax.

Buttocks – tighten your buttocks, then relax.

Thighs – while sitting, push your feet firmly into the floor, then relax.

Calves – lift your toes off the ground towards your shins, then relax.

Feet – gently curl your toes down so that they are pressing into the floor, then relax.

As the person progresses through the muscle relaxation, continually remind her or him to clear away any thoughts or worries and to maintain the relaxed state in each muscle. When finished, ask the person to remain still and experience the relaxed state and to slowly open the eyes when ready. Ask the person to practise this strategy at home on their own in a quiet setting and provide a recording to use if this is preferred. Greatest benefits are achieved if this is done for 15 to 20 minutes daily at a regular time, possibly built into an activity schedule.

Controlled breathing

Anxiety causes increased breathing rates resulting in over-breathing, more commonly known as hyperventilation. Over-breathing results in decreased levels of carbon dioxide in the blood, causing breathlessness or light-headedness – symptoms commonly experienced in panic attacks. This can be rectified by techniques such as breathing into a paper bag whereby the exhaled carbon dioxide is breathed back into the lungs. This, however, is not a socially appropriate intervention nor does it address the factors that have triggered the anxiety. A more effective measure that can be used in all settings is controlled breathing. By helping to control early symptoms of hyperventilation, future episodes are prevented, with a lessening of other symptoms associated with panic attacks such as sweating and fearfulness. It is recommended that the following exercise be practised for five minutes four times per day as well as at the first signs of panic or anxiety:

Hold your breath and count to six (do not take a deep breath).

When you get to six, breathe out and say the word relax to yourself in a calm, soothing manner.

Breathe in and out slowly through your nose in a six-second cycle. Breathe in for three seconds and out for three seconds. This will produce a breathing rate of 10 breaths per minute. Say the word relax to yourself every time you breathe out.

At the end of each minute (after 10 breaths) hold your breath again for six seconds and then continue breathing using the six-second cycle.

Continue breathing in this way until all the symptoms of over breathing have gone. It is important for you to practise this exercise so that it becomes easy to use any time you feel anxious. It is helpful to time it using the second hand of a watch or a mobile phone.

Mindfulness

In Chapter 1 on reality states, the terms depersonalisation and derealisation were introduced. Depersonalisation was described as a state of where the person is detached from what is going on around them with derealisation resulting in a loss of sense of reality. These can both be used as defence mechanisms during times of extreme distress. Daydreaming is an example of depersonalisation that we all engage in and as discussed earlier this can assist in alleviating boredom and also foster creativity and problem-solving. However, if a person becomes too detached from themselves and their environment in ways that interfere with daily living, this can become problematic. Mindfulness is the opposite of depersonalisation as it is focused on 'being in the present'. It is a technique that can be used to stop or interrupt automatic responses where a person tunes out of their environment, with their thoughts focused elsewhere, when this is not a helpful response. For people experiencing emotional difficulties or mental health issues, detachment from their environment can be characterised by negative thoughts that involve over-thinking situations, a preoccupation with themselves or a focus on the past or the future. Mindfulness is a skill to direct the person back to the present and to not be distracted by these often unpleasant and distracting thoughts. Mindfulness comprises five core features: (1) observing (2) describing (3) full participation (4) a non-judgemental approach and (5) focusing on one thing at a time.[45]

Observing involves focusing on directly experiencing the environment through the senses rather than cognitively. The aim is have a sensory experience rather than an analytic thinking type response. Analytic thinking can be a more automatic response so the person is required to deliberatively shift from this cognitive mode to a sensory mode. It is a gentle approach based on interest and curiosity while observing thoughts, feelings and the sensory responses of sight, touch, sound, taste and smell.

Describing comes from the fine detail in these observations and being able to put into words what is being experienced.

Full participation requires consideration of the entire experience that comes from complete care and attention with a focus on being present in the here and now.

A non-judgemental approach involves suspending judgement or trying to control or avoid the situation but rather accepting things for what they are. In doing so the person avoids evaluating experiences as good or bad or right or wrong but rather is open to immersing themselves in the full experience. Accepting this entire experience is considered to be the most difficult aspect of mindfulness, as people generally try and exert control over situations and do not allow the time for such an immersive and open experience. Time and practise is required to develop this particular skill.

Focusing on one thing at a time and noticing minute changes is important when observing and there is a high likelihood that distracting thoughts will arise during these observations. Noticing these diverting thoughts that are causing the person to drift away from their observations and sensory experience is key to diverting attention back to being present.

Mindfulness is a skill that requires full commitment and takes time, effort and practice to learn. It often also includes a component on meditation or other techniques.

4. Skills training

Skills training includes various combinations of cognitive and behavioural strategies tailored to a particular condition or problem situation. The aim is to assist the person to develop the skills needed to achieve desired outcomes.

Problem-solving skills and training

Problem solving involves developing a series of systematic steps with the person to gain an increased sense of control over the situation. It has broad application to a wide range of problems of varying magnitude. Problems may involve issues of loss, major choices, relationship problems, work or study difficulties, low income, inadequate housing and/or stigma of mental health issues. Problem solving is a useful life skill for us all and has been found to be particularly useful with people recovering from anxiety and depression and adjustment disorders.[46]

It is important that the person's problems are clearly defined and realistic goals developed. The person is then taught the seven steps of problem solving so that they are able to apply these themselves to other difficult situations in the future. These seven steps include

Step 1: define the problem
Step 2: brainstorm all possible solutions
Step 3: evaluate the advantages and disadvantages of all possible solutions
Step 4: choose the solution or combination of strategies that meet most needs
Step 5: develop an implementation plan
Step 6: implement the plan (and)
Step 7: review and evaluate.

Careful listening is required using skills in empathy so that both the emotional and practical aspects of the problem are acknowledged. Skilled questioning is necessary to ascertain the parameters of the problem and develop a full understanding of how the person is affected. Once all of the problems have been identified, one problem is chosen to start working on. This may be the easiest problem to solve, or it may be the most pressing one. What is important is that only one problem is worked on at a time. This may seem unrealistic given the multitude of problems many people who seek social work services present with. It is, however, a useful technique for managing problems and working out a plan to deal with them. The other problems on the list are not forgotten but rather prioritised in order of importance. Solving one problem at a time will often result in improvements in other areas, with natural attrition reducing the number of problems listed.

Brainstorming is a useful approach for generating possible solutions as it encourages lateral and spontaneous thinking by listing all possible solutions no matter how absurd they might seem. Each solution is then evaluated in terms of how well it addresses the problem situation, and linkages are made between those that are complementary. The solution or combined solutions that meet most needs and are easily implemented are chosen. This requires an assessment of the resources required to implement the chosen plan and whether or not this is feasible. The commitment of all parties involved in the plan is required for effective implementation. A time for review and evaluation of the plan is important to evaluate suitability and appropriateness and make any changes that may be required. Acknowledgment of the efforts involved in problem solving is important as well as rewarding positive outcomes to encourage the person to commit to the agreed plan and use this approach for future problem solving.

Anger management

Anger management involves additional problem-solving techniques, to identify the build-up of anger and ways of responding to it. The aim is to assist the person to have a better understanding of how emotions influence behaviours and impact on relationships and overall mental health and well-being. Cognitive behaviour therapy is the main intervention used for anger management and is proven to be successful.[47]

The person is taught both cognitive and behavioural skills to recognise and respond appropriately to early signs of conflict. Skills in problem solving, communication, stress management and relaxation are often used in anger management. Stress inoculation training (SIT) initially developed for the treatment of anxiety, has been adapted for anger management and is frequently used.[48] This involves cognitive preparation, and learning and applying new skills. Coping skills are taught, and opportunities are provided to practise these using role plays or simulated learning environments. An emphasis is on the relationship between thoughts, emotions and behaviours, and the person is taught how to regulate these to prevent inappropriate responses.

Cognitive preparation involves educating the person about emotional responses and how these impact on relationships and well-being. The person is asked to identify and record anger response patterns over a week. This includes emotional, physiological, and behavioural responses. Recording these responses may in fact change behaviours as the person becomes more conscious of them. This recording will also show possible changes in response according to level of conflict. Cognitive therapy is useful for examining thought patterns and challenging usual responses focusing on appropriateness and other possible interpretations. This can assist in reducing levels of emotional arousal and how to modify expectations and interpretations of events. Often, angry responses develop within the context of high expectations of self and others that may or may not be appropriate.

Anger management skills are taught and learnt over a series of sessions and often include cognitive therapy, conflict scoping and analysis, problem solving, communication, stress management and relaxation skills. The person is taught to recognise patterns in anger responses identified in the weekly recording and to modify preconceived expectations of people and events. Anger regulation is taught by applying problem solving skills using context specific self affirmations to increase the person's level of confidence and sense of control. Skills in communication are taught, as people with anger problems often need to be taught or reminded of the importance of the skills of listening and assertiveness discussed later in this chapter.

The person is then asked to do a further weekly recording of anger response patterns monitoring levels of emotional arousal, use of skills and outcomes. Self instruction techniques are used to manage unresolved conflict and anger, to prevent the person becoming preoccupied and increasingly distressed.

The application of Novaco's[49] model of anger management is recommended for anger regulation as adapted below:

Preparing for the provocation
Use self-affirming statements. Be mindful of the time and place and medium for communication as well as who needs to be present for the likelihood of best outcomes.

Impact and confrontation
Continue to use self-affirming statements. Remain in control. Focus on what needs to be done and not the person and keep things in perspective. Look for the positives and avoid jumping to negative conclusions.

Coping with physical arousal
Be mindful of physiological responses, including changes to breathing and consciously regulate this using controlled breathing techniques. Likewise be mindful of the tightening of particular muscles and use techniques in muscle relaxation.

Coping with cognitive arousal
Use problem-solving techniques to slow things down and partialise the problem to make it more manageable, continuing to use skills for impact and communication.

Subsequent reflection
– Conflict unresolved
If the conflict remains unresolved, use strategies to assist the person to move on and see the situation in perspective and not taking things personally.
– Conflict resolved
Self-reflection and acknowledgement of differences in approach and attitude. Self-affirmation of skills and strategies used to resolve the conflict.

Application of anger management skills is practised over a number of sessions before the person engages in a real-life situation. This is done gradually so that the person has the opportunity to learn and apply new skills in a safe environment with a steady increase in the complexity of conflict scenarios. This is done initially by the person imagining how they might respond to a particular situation, later progressing to role play scenarios with the person practising skills in a simulated learning environment. Increasingly, these scenarios are practised face to face and in online environments. A gradual progression is made to practising real-life scenarios prior to implementing these.

Communication training

Communication training involves both verbal and non-verbal skills and congruency between these. The aim is to teach people how to communicate their thoughts in constructive ways. This will range from making simple requests to discussing complex issues. Skills in anger management are also incorporated in this approach for communication skills in conflict situations. Evidence-based research has found communication skills training useful in the areas of disability, substance misuse and working with families and carers.[50] A focus is on how messages are given and received with appropriate communications not always getting the desired or anticipated result. For instance, a message may have been delivered in a very thoughtful manner but received as hostile by the other person. It is important to reflect on why this might have occurred, considering the quality of the relationship with this person, past communications, the medium of communication – electronic or face to face, as well as an assessment of the communication skills of the other person. Part of the communication training is identifying the communications skills of others and responding in appropriate ways but at the same time not taking responsibility for the shortcomings of others' communication skills or inappropriate behaviours. The notion of problem ownership is important here. An emphasis is on keeping messages simple, clear and positive using appropriate tone of voice and body language. A recommended process adapted from *The Management of Mental Disorders* is

Make clear and simple statements.

Use short statements or questions.

Only make one request or question at a time.

Be specific.

Display emotion appropriate to the situation avoiding strong emotional responses.

Provide positive specific feedback as appropriate to express appreciation and reinforce positive behaviours. Sincerity is important so that people do not feel they are being manipulated.

When providing positive feedback,

Look the person in the eye.

State the behaviour that was appreciated – do this as close to the event as possible.

Tell the person how you feel.

Acknowledge both minor and major accomplishments in terms of process and outcomes. Avoid back-handed compliments such as 'I liked the way you did...but...'

Shills for making a request of someone include

Make eye contact with the person.
Make a specific request as to what you want the person to do.
Say how you feel, expressing appreciation for their efforts.

It is important to avoid nagging, put-downs, criticism or demands, as these will reduce the likelihood of the person doing what you have asked and interfere with relationships and cause resentment.

Useful statements are

'I would really appreciate it if you would..
'It would make a big difference to me if you would help me with the..
'If you could.. I would really feel a lot more relaxed.'

Reflect on both process and outcomes, being mindful that a request delivered in an appropriate manner may not be responded to for a variety of reasons. These may include availability, assessment of reasonableness of the request, distracted by other problems or issues, or overly focused on self and not considerate of others. Reconsideration will be required according to this assessment as to how best to proceed.

It is important to teach the person to express both positive and negative feelings to avoid the build-up of stress and possible resentment that may result in angry outbursts later on. The person may avoid expressing negative feelings due to fear of a negative response from the other person. The timing and manner in which these feelings are expressed is important.

Skills for expressing negative feelings are

Make eye contact with the person.
State what the person did that upset you – be specific.
Tell the person how you felt – use 'I' statements (see skills training on assertiveness).
Suggest how this could be prevented in the future.

A useful statement is

'I feel quite upset about... I would really appreciate it if you would...'[51]

Listening skills are particularly important to convey that you are listening, interested and trying to fully understand what the other person is saying. This is often referred to as the quality of your presence with others. Skills for being a good listener are

Look at the person and maintain eye contact without staring.
Show interest using appropriate body language, tone of voice and minimal encouragers.
Pay full attention by minimising distractions.

Ask questions to seek clarification.

Make reflective statements of content to show you have heard the person and to encourage them to continue.

Make empathic statements to convey that you care about the other person's feelings.

Social skills training

Evidence-based research has found that social skills training is effective in the treatment of schizophrenia, depression, social phobias and child behaviour difficulties.[52] Social skills training further develops those skills learnt in communication training. This includes skills in individual and group conversations such as how to approach people and start, maintain and end a conversation. Skills in cooperative behaviours include sharing and taking turns focusing on developing relationships. Assertive behaviours and responding to unpleasant reactions or rejection are also taught. These skills are taught and practised in a similar manner to the process described earlier under anger management. Considerable time is spent on learning and rehearsing these skills. Evaluation and review of the application of these new skills in the person's social setting provides feedback and reinforcement and is an essential feature of all skills training programs.

Assertiveness training

Conflict is a normal part of everyday life. People respond differently to situations of stress and conflict in one of three ways: fight, flight or assertive behaviours. The first two responses are primitive urges; assertive behaviours are a learnt response. Assertiveness and listening are the keys to effective communication.[53] As well as listening skills, assertive behaviours require engaging in respectful dialogue and taking time out if necessary. The manner in which decision making and problem solving occurs will influence whether relationships are harmed or enhanced. A weekly record, similar to that described earlier under anger management, is useful for identifying usual patterns of communication and categorising these as fight, flight or assertive. If the person's usual style of communication is assertive, a different intervention may be more appropriate.

Fight or flight behaviours are often spontaneous reactions to primitive urges; assertive responses require a more reasoned approach. Fight or aggressive responses include refusing to listen, manipulation and sulking, shouting, screaming and physical violence. The main messages of fight behaviours are 'I'm right, therefore you're wrong', and 'I'm okay but you're not.' The main intentions are to blame, punish and threaten. Aggressive behaviours result in loss of respect from others, severely damaging relationships. Aggressive people often get what they want but at the expense of developing and maintaining close interpersonal relationships.

Flight or passive behaviours send messages that the other person's needs are more important or that it is easier to let others make decisions. In an abusive relationship, they may be told they are incompetent, weak, unintelligent and unable to decide for themselves. This belief may become internalised resulting in internalised oppression. Ongoing passive behaviours can result in low self-esteem, depression, anxiety, anger and somatic complaints. The person can also be seen as weak and lose the respect of others.

Assertive or flow behaviours include discussing the issue, listening to others, taking time out and articulating perspective and needs. Main messages of assertive behaviours are 'There must be a way to solve this' and 'I'm okay and you're okay.' The main intentions are to respect others and to make sure everyone is satisfied with the solution. Assertive statements are often referred to as 'I' statements. Assertive responses are respectful and start with 'I', rather than 'you' associated with more aggressive and accusatory interactions. Body language and tone of voice are particularly important as well as the content of what is actually said.

It is important to remain calm while responding in a way that is appropriate to the seriousness of the situation. For instance, it may not be appropriate to appear relaxed and cheerful if the person you are talking with is extremely agitated. You do not want to give the impression that you fail to appreciate the importance of what is happening. Timing and venue are important. A simple assertive response starts with 'When' and then describes the offending behaviour. 'When... I feel...' or 'I would like...'[54]

Assertiveness skills may be taught in individual and group sessions. Opportunities for feedback are provided in group sessions from the worker and other group members, with wider role play opportunities. Practice is important to reinforce new skills; it is not unusual for those who have been passive to sometimes confuse assertive behaviours with aggression. It is also important to prepare the person for others possibly feeling threatened initially by these new behaviours. However, in the longer term, improvements will be made in self-esteem, relationships and happiness.

As with all skills training, it is important to provide a rationale for learning skills in assertiveness. The worker explains how assertiveness can be useful particularly in situations where individual needs are not being met or other people are often left feeling insulted or resentful of the person's behaviour. Assertiveness is presented as an alternative whereby thoughts, feelings and needs are communicated honestly and directly in an appropriate manner. Explain how assertiveness is standing up for your rights without infringing upon the rights of others. It results in an increased sense of control and personal agency, and others are less likely to take advantage. Choices as to how best to respond are made depending upon the situation. A passive response may be quite appropriate in certain circumstances if a person is unwell or it is a special occasion. The important thing is that the person is in control of the situation, having made a conscious decision that is respectful. It is useful to remind the person that even though they may behave assertively, the desired response may not occur, particularly if the other person is trying to manipulate them.

It is important to locate the person's behaviour within its proper social context and ask how they developed this particular style of communication.

Useful questions include

How were you taught to manage conflict as a child?

What were the dominant messages?

How did you get what you wanted? Do you still do this?

What problems have resulted from this style of communication?

The person must make the decision to change current behaviours. The worker can assist with this decision by sharing the potential benefits of assertive behaviours; a cost–benefit analysis highlights how the gains outweigh the losses from non-assertive behaviours. Once the decision to change has been made, ask the person to list difficult situations where assertiveness skills might be useful and set goals for all of these. Organise this list from least to most difficult situation and start with the easiest one. It is useful to explain some of the myths that prevent people from being assertive. These myths include expecting that those close to you should know what you want without having to tell them, others' needs are more important than yours, anxiety is a sign of weakness, it is not possible to say no if someone close requests a favour and it is necessary to follow gender stereotypes.

The Bill of Assertive Rights serves as a useful reminder of personal rights. Ask the person to repeat these each day, especially those that are the most difficult.

Bill of Assertive Rights[57]

I have the right to be the judge of what I do and what I think.

I have the right to offer no reasons and excuses for my behaviour.

I have the right to refuse to be responsible for finding solutions to other people's problems.

I have the right to change my mind.

I have the right to make mistakes.

I have the right to say 'I don't know.'

I have the right to make my own decisions.

I have the right to say 'I don't understand.'

I have the right to say 'I don't care.'

I have the right to say 'No' without feeling guilty.

Refer to the Bill of Assertive Rights when discussing difficult situations to identify the rights that apply. If assertive statements do not get the desired response, and the situation becomes increasingly difficult, a number of assertive techniques can assist as protective skills.[55]

Running record

Running record involves repeating the same response over and over again even though different reasons or arguments may be put. Usually repeating the same statement two or three times is enough. Of course you may change your mind but, if you do not, this technique usually works.

Selective ignoring

Selective ignoring is not responding to inappropriate comments and requests and responding only to those considered appropriate. This may be done by responding to only certain parts of the conversation or by telling the person that you are not going to discuss certain things.

Disarming anger

It is stressful and futile to have a reasoned conversation with a person when they are angry. If it is a conversation you believe needs to be had, tell the person you would like to discuss this when you are both calm. Arranging a time to meet may be helpful.

Separating important issues

Sometimes people will try and manipulate others by combining issues that are not related. It is important to respond in a clear manner identifying that these reasons do not sit together saying, 'It's not that I…but rather it is because…' Running record can also be useful.

Dealing with guilt and apologies

Feelings of guilt can arise if a person is told they are not meeting others' expectations of them. This is often a perfect stereotype that is not practicable and can result in the person feeling inadequate and eroding confidence. The person may suffer with low self-esteem and continually apologise to others. Setting realistic and achievable goals is important, with apologies only given when genuinely appropriate. When apologising, make it clear what the apology is for and that it is not for groundless accusations.

Agreement

Appearing to agree with the other person by using phrases such as 'You may be right', 'That sounds probable' can be an effective way of easily stopping criticism.[56]

Stress management

The first task for stress management is identification of the stressful situation or event, and assessing whether it can be changed or is ongoing and needs to be adapted to. Stress is a natural daily experience that can heighten awareness and increase energy levels. However, too much stress, and/or an inability to cope adequately with stress levels, can result in problems with anxiety and depression and lead to relapse of disturbing psychotic symptoms such as hearing voices and paranoia common in schizophrenia. Stress management is a crucial intervention for recovery and relapse prevention.

Daniel's solicitor referred him to the community mental health centre. Daniel, who had a diagnosis of schizophrenia, had for some time been accusing the solicitor of improprieties that initially he had simply brushed aside and saw as humorous. However, he believed that Daniel was becomingly increasingly agitated and the intensity of the accusations had increased. The most recent accusation by Daniel was that his solicitor had been breaking into his house and putting footprints in the butter. He also accused him of moving things about his house, such as putting shoes in a different order. I contacted Daniel, who had had past contact with staff at the community mental health centre. Initially he was suspicious about the call as he saw it as a further intrusion by the solicitor, who he believed was plotting against him. However, he did finally agree to see me.

Daniel spoke of the footprints in the butter and many other things the solicitor had done. He also spoke of his fears of further things the solicitor might do. He was extremely frightened that the solicitor might try and burn his house down. These fears were very real to Daniel and were extremely distressing. Further exploration revealed the increased control the solicitor had assumed in Daniel's life since the death of his mother a year earlier. The solicitor was appointed the administrator of Daniel's mother's estate and controlled the money Daniel received. It seemed that this real control and intrusion into Daniel's finances by the solicitor had assumed larger proportions in Daniel's mind. However, the issues of power and control were very real. A combination of anti-psychotic medication and counselling focused on Daniel regaining greater control of his life, particularly of his finances. This resulted in a lessening of Daniel's fears about his solicitor and accusations, reducing his anxiety and stress levels.

Stress management focuses on the areas that are seen as too difficult to cope with that are interfering with daily living (see Figure 11.6).

These may be difficulties associated with a major life change or increased demands keeping in mind that stress is generated by both pleasant and unpleasant situations. The aim of stress management skills training is to assist the person to better manage the new lifestyle demands placed on them. The aim is to address the cause of the stress as well as developing coping strategies to manage the physical and emotional symptoms. These include negative thinking and feelings of low self-worth, heart palpitations, sweating and difficulty breathing.

Time management involves assisting the person to prioritise, organise and implement

Stress management activity	Skill development
time management	prioritise organise (and) implement tasks in a timely manner.
problem solving	define the problem brainstorm all possible solutions evaluate the advantages and disadvantages of all possible solutions choose the solution or combination of strategies that meet most needs develop an implementation plan implement the plan (and) review and evaluation.
relaxation	progressive muscle relaxation isometric relaxation guided imagery (and) controlled breathing.
behaviour modification	exposure techniques (and) activity scheduling.
cognitive therapy	A – activating event B – belief or reaction to event C – emotional consequences Worker intervention: challenge negative or irrational ideas new emotion

Figure 11.6: Stress management activities and skill development

tasks in a timely manner. First a list is prepared of the tasks that need to be completed with these then arranged in order of priority. ABC can be used to assign tasks according to priority, A – immediate, B – important and C – can wait, with the tasks then completed in this order. Tasks are organised within an adequate time frame, with the clustering of those that sit well together. The establishment of feasible goals is important for effective implementation as well as encouragement and rewards for positive reinforcement when goals are met. It may be necessary to break goals down into smaller more achievable steps.

Problem solving skills (see above) are taught to assist the person to develop new and more structured approaches.

Relaxation (see above) is an important component of stress management as the person is taught how to recognise the build-up of stress and to use strategies to reduce arousal by releasing tensions to reduce the physical symptoms of stress.

Behaviour modification (see above) involves the recognition of difficult situations and problematic behaviours and developing new skills to cope with these.

Cognitive therapy (see above) is used to identify and challenge negative thought patterns and explore other possible interpretations using cognitive restructuring techniques.

Parent management training

Parent management training involves teaching parents appropriate skills to raise their children. It is based on social learning theory with behaviours learnt through socialisation and modelled by significant figures in the person's life and operant conditioning with behaviours shaped according to responses from others. A dilemma arises when the person does not have positive parenting role models to use as a reference point or if social attitudes are different due to changed views and attitudes or cultural norms and values. For instance, in the 1950s and 60s corporal punishment was accepted and promoted in the home and at school. Today, however, parents are more responsive to the expressed needs of children and physical punishment is admonished. The parent figure may believe what they are doing is correct because that is how they were raised but this may not be acceptable by contemporary social standards. Training is provided for most things today. However, when it comes to parenting, one of the most important jobs a person can ever do, there is no formal training. Training is provided on how to give birth and care during pregnancy and then it is up to the parents how they raise their child unless the state intervenes due to child abuse and neglect. It is a major oversight to not teach all new parents parent management skills. It cannot be assumed that this will be handed down from previous generations and that these skills are appropriate to today's standards and cultural norms.

The aim of parent management training is to teach parents to understand the basic needs of children and to develop realistic expectations of their behaviour. Behaviour modification strategies are used to reinforce positive behaviours and manage difficult ones. Parent management training may focus on improving parenting skills in general and parent–child relationships and social skills development or they may be targeted at treating specific problems. These may be associated with the diagnoses of anxiety, depression, attention deficit hyperactivity disorder, oppositional defiant disorder, conduct disorders, sleep disorders or behaviours such as enuresis or encopresis.[57]

Parent management training involves

psycho-education

improving communication skills

setting appropriate expectations and rules

developing appropriate and consistent patterns when applying consequences for violating rules

acknowledging and rewarding positive behaviour

promoting positive interactions between parents and children

practice, evaluating outcomes, modifying strategies when required

parents working together.[58]

Psycho-education

Parents may require education on what is considered to be within the so-called normal range of development and typical behaviours at different stages. Information is provided on appropriate expectation and rules and how to enforce these distinguishing between natural and logical consequences of behaviours. Parents are taught to identify and monitor difficult or inappropriate behaviours in an endeavour to understand the context of problem behaviours and in particular events that immediately precede the behaviour and how to respond appropriately.

Another ABC model is commonly used in psycho-education for parent management training:

Antecedent – when, where and who was present?

Behaviour – type, intensity and duration

Consequences – outcomes including parental responses.[59]

Information is provided on the effectiveness of current parenting approaches and is a useful ongoing strategy to monitor parent–child interactions. Information is also provided on the goals of behaviour. Children's behaviours have a purpose, with the fundamental goals of being secure, finding a place of significance to belong, or to protect one's sense of identity. When children feel discouraged and threatened, they may replace these fundamental goals with other goals. They may convince themselves that the only way of getting what they want is to behave in ways that others find difficult. It is the way that others and, in particular, parents respond to these behaviours that will influence whether or not these behaviours persist. The four goals of difficult behaviour are attention seeking, gaining power, display of inadequacy or revenge with the child's difficult behaviour assessed according to these categories (see Figure 11.7).

Attention-seeking behaviours cause annoyance and are best managed by ignoring them and acknowledging and rewarding positive behaviours and contributions. Power struggles evoke a stronger emotional response of anger and are best managed by withdrawing from the

Goal of difficult behaviour	Appropriate response
gaining attention	ignore
gaining power	withdraw
display of inadequacy	provide encouragement
revenge	do not retaliate

Figure 11.7: Goal of difficult behaviour and appropriate response

conflict situation and looking at other ways to engage that include encouragement and positive reinforcement of cooperative behaviours. Appearing-inadequate behaviours cause extreme frustration and are best managed by encouragement and reinforcement of efforts to engage in positive and assertive behaviours. If a child is seeking revenge or has engaged in retaliation, an even stronger emotional response occurs and it is important that the parent adopts a conciliatory approach and does not retaliate, as this will escalate the difficult behaviour.[60]

If considered on a continuum, these behaviours are listed from the easiest to most difficult to manage. Attention-seeking behaviours can result in a brief feeling of sense of significance particularly when a child is receiving lots of attention. By gaining power through negative behaviours, a child may feel secure. When displaying apparent inadequacy, a child may feel they belong if others look after them. A child may seek to maintain his or her sense of identity by seeking revenge and inflicting hurt and provoking hostility.

Improving communication skills
This includes effective listening and planning quality time to spend together. Communication needs to be geared to the child's level of understanding, with appropriate negotiation.

Setting appropriate rules and expectations
The worker assists the parents to negotiate a list of appropriate rules and behaviours for the children to follow. These rules can be used as a guide to assess current behaviours.

Developing and applying consistent and appropriate consequences
A distinction is made between natural and logical consequences. The child learns from natural consequences that follow from actions such as getting cold from refusing to wear warm clothes. Logical consequences are developed to match the particular behaviour such as being allowed to watch television once homework has been completed. This is important for discipline and needs to be consistently applied. This is based on operant conditioning whereby positive behaviours are rewarded with negative behaviours dealt with in logical ways such as losing privileges. It is important that the consequences logically relate to the behaviour. At times it may be more appropriate to ignore difficult or inappropriate behaviours, particularly if these are attention-seeking, and look for positive ways to engage the child.

Acknowledging and rewarding positive behaviour
Parents are encouraged to use positive reinforcement to acknowledge and reward positive behaviours to reinforce these and increase the child's levels of self-esteem and confidence.

Praise is specific and related to a particular activity rather than general statements such as 'Good boy' or 'Good girl'. In some instances such as bed-wetting charts and stickers work well with a sticker for each dry night and a reward for one week of dry nights.

Promoting positive interactions between parents and children
Parents are encouraged to take an active interest in their children's activities and to include children in parent activities as appropriate. Planned quality time each day with children in activities of their choosing will lead to improved levels of confidence and self-esteem and family relationships.

Practice, evaluating outcomes, modifying strategies when required
Group sessions are useful for teaching, practising evaluating and modifying parenting skills. Parents learn from each other with guidance from a worker or co-workers. Modelling and role-playing of new skills allows for feedback and reflection and further skill development prior to implementation. It is important to advise parents that behaviours often get worse before they improve, as children often rebel against new ways of doing things, so they do not become discouraged and stop using these new skills. In a group situation parents support each other in this process. New strategies or consequences are developed if necessary.

Parents working together
Difficult behaviour in children is often symptomatic of parents not working together. Part of the psycho-educational component is to educate parents on the importance of working together to support each other and to provide consistent messages to the children on what is acceptable and unacceptable behaviour. Parents need to be agreed on approaches to discipline and support each other when consequences are applied. Getting parents to work together often has the unintended consequence of improving the marital relationship with this having positive outcomes for family interactions.

5. Interpersonal therapy (especially for depression)

Interpersonal therapy is a focused psychological strategy used especially for depression with evidence-based research finding it is particularly successful for the treatment of acute major and moderate depression.[61] It is based on the theory that interpersonal relationships play a major role in the development and continuation of depression. It is also considered particularly effective in conflict situations with significant others and adjustments to major life changes such as major life transition, career or social role. Interpersonal therapy was originally developed for use over a series of 12 to 16 sessions with people with non-psychotic depression.[62] It is not recommended for use with those who are psychotic, have substance abuse problems or are suicidal.[63] The aim is to identify interpersonal difficulties related to the person's depression. These will be varied and might include issues of grief and loss, interpersonal conflict, role difficulties and social isolation.

Interpersonal therapy is generally a component part of a broader social work practice context with a focus on the importance of relationships. Strength-based models and evidence-based approaches are used that build upon individual and family strengths and recognise spiritual, physical, psychological and emotional well-being. The goals of interpersonal therapy are developed by identifying areas of dissatisfaction and the specific impacts of symptoms of mental health issues on goals and functioning with adaptation plans and skills developed to manage these. Journals are often used for recording. Interpersonal therapy is frequently supported by couples/families/systems therapies and interventions that include a family strengths approach addressing parenting strategies, couple therapy, and relationship therapeutic work.

6. Narrative therapy

As mentioned at the beginning of the chapter, narrative therapy is recognised as a Medicare-funded intervention only for clients of Aboriginal and Torres Strait Islander descent. This is in recognition of the importance of storytelling within Indigenous cultures. In recent years short-term intervention models of narrative therapy have developed focusing only on certain themes or aspects of a person's life.

Techniques for narrative therapy include: in-depth interviewing, autobiographies, correspondence, records and diaries. A focus is on significant events and experiences in a person's life, checking for irregularities and contradictions in the person's story by using other sources of relevant information, including perspectives of other family members, professionals and the media. An emic approach uses thick descriptions and looks for cultural meaning in the person's life. These cultural meanings are particular to individual circumstances.[64]

The worker encourages the person to

1. tell the story in its natural or chronological order of events;
2. deconstruct: analysis of the person's story according to other perspectives including different views of what happened at the time and possible reasons for this, as well as retrospective analysis based upon the person's biological, psychological, social and cultural context;
3. establish the validity of the above sources and the priority placed on different perspectives;
4. look for negative evidence that questions aspects of the story that may have been taken for granted; and
5. reconstruct: re-write and edit the person's story in light of 1 to 4 to develop 'preferred alternative accounts of their experiences and identities'.[65]

Language, both spoken and unspoken, is of crucial importance as it is the main medium of communication in a narrative approach. Going public with one's memories, even to a single listener, can have a profound effect on the person's sense of self, which is so reliant upon memories. Memories give rise to a number of questions that may or may not be shared openly. These might include What were my alternatives? Where did I go wrong? How did all this start? Could I have done things differently? Dominant social discourses are explored that impact upon meanings and interpretations.

People tend to speak through their actions, routines, daily work, habits and commitments to others. They do not usually speak about their thoughts and feelings, preferring them to remain private. Emotions are intrinsically interwoven throughout people's stories and often include blame, guilt and self-doubt as a result of loss, trauma or grief. A focus is on how the person acknowledges and articulates his or her emotions and the manner in which these emotions reflect the personal experience of events. Due to the subjective nature of narrative therapy, the worker needs to be intensively involved with the client. The worker's own personal world of emotions and the relationship developed with the consumer becomes an integral part of the therapy.

In Matthew's story, detailed descriptions and cultural meanings focused on the importance of Aboriginal culture and family. It was important to be sensitive to the psychological impact that Matthew's memories had, and the associated meanings given to the interaction between Matthew and myself. While Matthew remembered events that he had experienced personally, many of his memories were second-hand knowledge of things that had happened to other people. It was particularly at these points that the memories of other family members and elders familiar with the person, event or place being described, were sought in an attempt to see the similarities and differences in interpretation. It also was an indication of whether Matthew's account was one generally accepted, or very much his own individual view and interpretation of events.[66] There were many events in Matthew's life that aroused intense emotions.

This was particularly so when he related his story of being removed from his family by social workers and placed in state care. Matthew's memories also triggered off vivid and at times disturbing repetitive dreams of his past life. I listened to him tell these tragic stories and felt like joining with his tears. The following week he cried as he told me the same story again, as if I had not heard it the previous week. I listened attentively, realising his personal need at that moment to tell the story again. The following week he was ready to move on.

The goal is to explore new possibilities by externalising the problem with listening and empathic skills central to this approach alongside strategic questioning. Not one story is explored but many different interpretations, challenging the notion of the true or the right story but rather different views and meanings that often change over time. A comparison of past and more recent experiences, highlighting successes forms part of the discussion. Preferred stories are developed and shared, 'highlighting examples of survival, self care and protest. This can be seen not just as rewriting the family's story, but as the emergence of new identities for family members.'[67] The sharing of new stories with significant others is important for highlighting change, and workers often have a role in facilitating this. This may include recording and sharing information in ways that are deemed personally, culturally and age appropriate.

Conclusion

Mental health social workers in Australia are now eligible to claim rebates for FPS under the Medicare Better Access Program. These services have been approved by government due to the evidence-based research that supports the efficacy of these interventions in improving mental health and well-being outcomes. These services include psycho-education, cognitive behaviour therapy, relaxation strategies, skills training and interpersonal therapy. These FPS are provided by a range of health and allied health professionals including general practitioners, psychologists, nurses and occupational therapists. The challenge for social workers is to provide these services in a manner consistent with the regulatory requirements for eligibility for Medicare rebates while at the same time remaining focused on social work interventions that address the broader political, economic and social aspects that impact on people's lives and issues of human rights and social justice.

Reflection

How do current funding arrangements influence social work practice in mental health?

How can social workers best use focused psychological strategies in their work with families and individuals?

What practice contexts are best suited to focused psychological strategies?

How can social workers combine FPS and social work interventions focused on broader structural issues to achieve best outcomes?

12

Suicide and Self-harm

Social workers need to be competent to assess the risk of suicide and self-harm and respond appropriately in ways that are affirming, recognising and responding to the biological, psychological, emotional, social, cultural, environmental and spiritual context within which the suicide risk has arisen. In this chapter, the incidence of suicide in the general population is discussed, followed by consideration of suicide and mental health issues. Areas of assessment discussed are protective and precipitating factors and warning signs as well as useful interview questions for assessing suicide risk and self-harm. Recovery-focused social work interventions discussed include a suicide prevention plan, involvement of families and carers and other significant people in the person's life who may be of assistance, continuity of care, suicide prevention and health promotion.

Suicide

Suicide is a major public health problem worldwide; approximately 900,000 suicides annually accounted for more deaths each year than from armed global conflicts or from the road toll.[1] In Australia in 2015, this figure was just over 3,000; males accounted for just over three-quarters of these deaths by suicide.[2] This was on average 8.3 deaths by suicide in Australia per day.[3]

The main source of information on rates of suicide in Australia is mortality data from the Australian Bureau of Statistics (ABS). A main component of the reporting of suicide data by the ABS is information provided by coroners. This suicide data is classified and recorded on the National Coroners Information System (NCIS) and in accordance with the ABS data coding rules from the International Classification of Diseases (ICD). However, the accuracy of suicide reporting continues to be hindered by the lack of a national central register and variations in definitions and recording by government state and territory agencies. These recording systems influence how suicide rates are reported. Reported rates before 1997 have been criticised as being under-representative of the actual numbers of death by suicide due to delays in coroners determining cause of death. Changes in reporting since this time, most recently in 2010, provide greater scope for the adjustment of figures, resulting in more accurate reporting.[4]

Actual numbers of suicides are generally thought to be higher than the number of registered suicides due to uncertainty surrounding the true intentions of some deaths. The recording of some accidental deaths may in fact be death by suicide. For a death to be classified as a suicide, it must be established by coronial inquiry that the death was not by natural causes and that it resulted from a deliberate act by the deceased to end his or her life.[5] Where doubt exists, coroners will be reluctant to give a verdict of suicide due to the social stigma and the emotional and socio-economic impacts on families.[6] For every suicide there are another 30 attempted suicides.[7]

According to the ABS figures, in Australia in 2015 the main age groups for death by suicide were older males aged 85 years and over and 45–49-year-old women.[8] The next highest group was middle aged men 40–54 years old. Hanging, followed by poisoning by drugs, were the main cause of death for both males and females. Groups identified as at a higher risk of suicide are those who have a previous suicide attempt, people who have with a disgnosed mental disorder immediately following release from hospital or a reduction in services and those with substance abuse issues.[9] Since 1980 there has not been one age group for females that has consistently shown higher rates of suicide for an extended period.

Suicide is the third cause of death globally for 15–34-year-olds.[10] Suicide is a rare occurrence for children under 15 years of age.[11]

There is disparity in views on what is occurring and reported in different states and territories of Australia. Marion Sycamor, the chair of a Northern Territory all-party parliamentary committee inquiry into youth suicide, is reported as saying,

> Young women are hanging themselves, overdosing and attempting suicide and there is nobody to talk to. Suicide has always been regarded as a men's problem but clearly that is no longer the case. Young women are taking their lives in greater numbers and we have more and more children growing up in violent situations.[12]

In Australia, the ratio of male to female suicides doubled from 2:1 to over 4:1 in the 40-year period from 1960 to 2000, dropping to 3:1 by 2009.[13] While men are more likely to suicide, women attempt suicide in greater numbers and have a greater propensity for self-harm.[14] For the one-year period from 2008 to mid 2009, 26,935 (117.9 per 100,000) hospital admissions in Australia were due to self-harm. This includes those who had attempted suicide. Just under two-thirds of these hospitalisations were females, with highest representation amongst those in their mid to late teens.[15] For both males and females, 75 per cent of all hospitalisations due to self-harm were in the 15–44 age group. It is important to remember that there was an alarming increase in suicide rates within this age group from the mid 1960s to mid 1970s; suicide rates for Australian males aged 15–24 at that time were the fourth highest amongst Western countries. A correlation was found between suicide rates and substance abuse in this age group. Findings of the 1997 National Survey of Mental Health and Wellbeing indicated that substance abuse, particularly alcohol abuse, was highest amongst males aged 18–24 years.[16] The use of alcohol or drugs, such as marijuana, amphetamines or heroin, was found to be closely connected with suicide.[17] It is important that suicide prevention campaigns targeted at this age group continue so as to further improve outcomes, alongside new initiatives for older males and middle-aged women. While older males and females have lower numbers of hospitalisations as a result of self-harm than younger people, their average length of admission is longer.[18] This data suggests life-stage adjustment, including loss and grief, may be a significant factor for both male and female suicide and self-harm.

The suicide rate of Aboriginal and Torres Strait Islander peoples in twice as high as the non-Indigenous population.[19] Similar trends were recorded for incarcerated populations and it was noted that Aboriginal and Torres Strait Islander people are over-represented in this group. The Kimberley region in Australia has one of the highest suicide rates in the world. In early 2010 the suicide rate in the Kimberley region was 182 times higher for Aboriginal people than the general population. Suicide rates for young Aboriginal and Torres Strait Islander youth are 10 times higher than non-Indigenous youth. A main driver for Aboriginal suicide is disempowerment due to generational trauma and social marginalisation resulting in overwhelming rage that the person cannot fight or flee from.[20]

Suicide rates for first-generation immigrant groups are similar to those for their country of origin, with little variation for women and slightly higher rates of suicide for Australian-born males.[21] Suicide rates are twice as high for single people than for those who are married. Young males who are gay or bisexual, or have been sexually abused, have higher rates of suicide, as do both male and female prisoners; suicide rates in the immediate period after release from prison are particularly disturbing.[22]

It is difficult to accurately conduct international comparisons of suicide rates due to different procedures for classifying, counting and reporting deaths.[23] Suicide trends in Australia are similar to those in other Western countries including the United States and Canada. These rates are much higher than those in the UK and lower than New Zealand figures. Females in Asian countries have higher reported rates of suicide than males.[24]

Suicide and mental health issues

Mental health issues pose a major risk factor for suicide. It is estimated that 'up to 90 per cent of people who suicide may have been experiencing a mental health issue at the time of their death'.[25] People who are with mental health issues have a higher incidence of suicide when compared with the general population. Suicide is the major cause of premature death of people with a mental health issue. It has been estimated that more than 10 per cent of people with mental health issues will attempt to kill themselves within the first 10 years of being diagnosed.[26] Most of those who do suicide will have experienced significant depression. Depression may occur as a result of the mental health issue itself, significant change or loss, realisation of the severity of the mental health issue or occasionally due to the side effects of medication.

The likelihood of death by suicide has been found to be 12 times higher for people with schizophrenia than for members of the general population.[27] In 2002, 84 per cent of the deaths of people with schizophrenia were a result of suicide. These figures reflect a disturbing trend of increasing suicide rates for people with schizophrenia. An alarming 40 per cent increase has been recorded over the past 40 years.[28] A study of the costs of mental health issues conducted in 2002 found that schizophrenia-related suicide has resulted in 'spiralling social and economic costs directly linked to a growing number of people with schizophrenia living on the edge of effective treatment and care'.[29] This study revealed significant gaps in the care people with schizophrenia were receiving in the community. This increase in suicides corresponds with the deinstitutionalisation of mental health services and increased programs· of community care. One-third of people with schizophrenia in the study were being treated with older anti-psychotic medications that caused significant distressing side effects. Approximately two-thirds were not receiving any supportive counselling; less than one in five attended community programs.

Fifteen years on, little has changed. The reasons for attempted suicide and self-harm are varied. Attempted suicide might occur in a state of fear, anger or confusion or in response to hallucinations or in an effort to stop disturbing symptoms. For some, the distress caused by mental health issues can be so overwhelming that suicide is viewed as a means of ending the pain. This includes the mental torment and the pain of loneliness and social isolation with these described as the most painful consequences of mental health issues.[30] For others, it is an attempt to get help and to be taken seriously, and in some cases it may be an early sign of the onset of mental health issues.

Suicidal intention is generally assessed according to level of severity. Extreme caution must be taken here as all levels are serious and must be responded to. The use of the term severity is problematic as it suggests that some are low risk and others high. This may be so in terms of likely imminent suicide but all thoughts of death must be taken seriously. In order of severity the levels of suicide intention are

1. sub-intentional death
2. suicidal ideation
3. threatened suicide
4. attempted suicide (and)
5. completed suicide.[31]

Sub-intentional death is when people engage in risky behaviours that may result in them being killed. Suicidal ideation is when a person is thinking about suicide yet does not appear to have any plans to enact it. The level of risk is generally assessed as much lower than for a person who is threatening suicide and has clear plans and is intent on carrying these out. However this can easily escalate and must not be ignored. This is particularly so if the person experiences a crisis, that is often unanticipated, and is under the influence of substances at that time. Attempted suicide is when a person sees no way out and cannot stand the emotional pain any longer. The intensity of this state means that it is hard to maintain and often brief, but if support is not available an attempt is likely. However, thoughts of suicide may well persist. A completed suicide is when a person makes a conscious decision to end his or her life and completes this. Often, however, an attempted suicide has the same level of risk because even though the person has survived the intention was to die.[32] A further attempt is likely if change for the better does not occur.

The risk of suicide increases with the number of what are called para-suicide attempts. Para-suicide is regarded as a deliberate non-fatal act of self-harm. An example of a para-suicide would be a deliberate non-lethal overdose. What is significant is that it is a cry for help and should not be seen as a not-so-serious attempt. Often the system response to para-suicides is punitive; medical staff may be angry and frustrated, particularly when they are in a busy emergency department. They resent time spent pumping the stomach of someone who has deliberately overdosed or stitching up the wrists of someone who has deliberately cut themselves when they have health emergencies waiting that are not self-inflicted. I remember a doctor in an emergency department telling me that the stomach pump he was about to give someone who had overdosed, would ensure that the person would not return for more. People complain of being given stitches with inadequate anathaesia. Regardless of intent, all suicidal and self-harm thoughts and actions are a cry for help that could result in death and must be treated seriously. Even if workers predict 'low risk', or 'no risk' of suicide, this does not mean the person will not make a suicide attempt. If the person's situation worsens, the level of risk is likely to increase.

Self-harm is frequently associated with childhood trauma, particularly childhood sexual abuse.[33] Issues of self-harm and suicide are complex and a number of reasons have been identified to explain why people harm themselves. These include depression, to reduce feelings of anxiety and tension, to regain control, and to communicate distress and anger. Some people have described feeling a rush of energy when they harm themselves. One woman commented, 'My adrenalin was going. When I saw the blood I felt better. Watching all the blood flow away is like watching all the dirt flow away.'[34] Following self-harm, some people have described feeling more in control, relieved, calm and relaxed whereas others become tearful, frightened and guilty.[35]

Risk factors and risk assessment

The combination of substance abuse and previous suicide or para-suicide attempts present as high-risk factors for suicide. More men than women abuse substances but women who abuse alcohol are a much greater suicide risk than their male counterparts.[36] Furthermore, a correlation has been found between suicide, use of alcohol and other drugs and violence. Howard Bath, former Children's Commissioner for the Northern Territory, is reported as saying,

> Aboriginal women are being hospitalised for assault at eighty times the rate of other women. It beggars belief. Exposure to violence greatly increases the risk of a person taking their own life. The proportion of Indigenous girls committing suicide in the territory is now the highest in the Western world.[37]

Sometimes people leave clues that they are going to suicide or let someone know of their plans. This may be a person who is close to them or possibly a complete stranger. Others will show no warning signs at all. Assessing suicidal intent is not easy and it is useful to be mindful of high-risk populations and settings. These include people in any form of custody – and in particular Aboriginal and Torres Strait Islanders – and people who are depressed or who experience psychosis, and particularly those with schizophrenia. The highest risk of suicide among people with schizophrenia occurs within the first two years of onset of symptoms. For many people there is generally a significant delay between the initial onset of symptoms and treatment.[38] Times of greatest risk are around admission and post-discharge from hospital or community mental health services.[39] Compared with men, women have been found to pose a greater risk of suicide during an in-patient stay or shortly after discharge. It is quite possible that the trauma and humiliation surrounding, and during, the hospital admission has contributed to this in terms of demoralisation and perceived betrayal of trust by loved ones who may heave been involved by calling mental health crisis services, who in turn have called the police or who have called and assisted the police themselves. For those new to mental health services, they are not likely to realise the brutality of the service response if a person is not cooperative. Thus family members and carers can experience terrible guilt by calling in such services, yet are at a loss as to that else they could have done. This trauma can worsen a person's suicidal intent and must not be ignored. Developments in trauma-informed care and practice, discussed in Chapter 10, provide hope for mental health service development into the future that does not traumatise people.

This is no criticism of health professionals, who do their best under extremely difficult circumstances. It is symptomatic of an often brutal system that relies upon coercion for the provision of in-patient mental health care. As described earlier, this is a system that cannot, or refuses to, provide compassionate responses to those with a mental health issue and deemed at risk of suicide. This raises the question as to what compassionate means. Some may say it is compassionate to breach confidentiality and call in ambulance and police to forcibly escort a person to hospital if they refuse to cooperate. This type of response has never sat easily in my mind – especially when people complain of being kept in police cells, use of handcuffs and other means of restraint, including capsicum spray. In extreme cases, the person has actually died in custody. This cannot be in anyone's mind mental health care. It is better named for what it is and that is protective custody. Given the earlier discussion reporting on the risk of suicide increasing post hospital discharge, this is a short-term solution that is potentially worsening the situation for many people. A much greater focus is required on having a risk plan yet at the same time enabling supportive relationships in the community that are likely to be within the family – but may not be. In some situations, the extreme distress is coming from the family, such as in cases of incest. However, other family members, apart from the abuser, may have a close relationship with the person who is suicidal yet may or may not be able to provide the protection required. Social workers must prioritise mobilising supportive relationships and support services rather than coercive services. Social factors such as poor housing, unstable employment and lack of supportive networks increase suicide risk for those with a mental health issue.[40]

A major time of risk for those with depression is when they start to show signs of improvement. However, many workers continue to claim ignorance of this, which I find astounding given that this is the time of highest risk. Social workers need to know and act on this so that they can inform family members and other support people so they can respond appropriately. It is possible that workers do not share this information as it is often at the point of discharge from mental health services. It is easier to comfort a family by saying, 'No one was to know. They seemed so much better. Who would have thought?' when in fact they really did know of the increased risk and, if not, should have known. An impression of ignorance by workers can also be used as protection from possible reprisals, perhaps litigation due to negligence, from family members. The community expects and should demand better than this from mental health service providers.

This raises questions regarding the education of workers. It is of ongoing concern that some universities do not have attendance requirements for social work students who are doing face to face courses and where they do exist it is often for the mandatory attendance requirements of distance programs. So it is understandable that some social workers simply do not know vital information, as they have got through their studies without proper due diligence and have not filled these gaps on the job or in ongoing professional development. This situation cannot continue and must be addressed. Social workers argue that they are trained in accordance with the Australian Association of Social Workers education standards for professional qualifying degrees yet often cannot prove attendance at all, or beyond 20 days per year, for degrees delivered on-campus. This situation degrades the quality of services provided by these graduates and is ultimately detrimental to the profession. However, the greatest travesty is that workers are not equipped to assist consumers and families appropriately when it comes to complex situations that involve suicide and self-harm. They may think they already have this knowledge due to personal experience. This is also problematic as consumers expect from social workers a professional knowledge and skill base beyond personal experience. This may be acceptable if a person is working as a peer support worker rather than as a social worker. However, peer support workers are likely to be trained in suicide and self-harm.

Suicide can occur at any time of the day or night; it is a myth that suicide is most likely to occur at night. Most suicide attempts occur in the late afternoon or early evening. It is thought that this is due to people's ambivalence about dying and the greater likelihood of them being discovered at such times.[41]

Risks are politically, socially and culturally determined in accordance with the interests of dominant groups in the community. In practice, risk is generally focused on undesirable outcomes, although its original meaning is 'balancing probabilities'.[42] The emphasis on risk allows for the allocation of blame when things go wrong. This can result in workers adopting defensive practices that avoid risk taking by consumers. Practices that support risk taking can be difficult to implement and follow through unless adequate resources are available. The availability of resources, or lack of them, will necessarily influence how risk is assessed and managed.

Since the 1990s, levels of risk, and danger to self and to others in particular, have increasingly become the criteria for eligibility for mental health services as opposed to level of mental disturbance.[43] Levels of dangerousness and lack of social supports, as opposed to level of disturbance, are key factors in decisions to admit a person to hospital.[44] Deinstitutionalisation and community care have seen a greater focus on issues of public safety with an emphasis on control and protection. With widespread concern about the shortfalls of community care, risk assessments tend to be focused on levels of danger to others rather than on suicide or deprivation of liberties. There is a community perception that people with mental health issues health issues, particularly those who experience psychosis, are dangerous, but this is not the case. In reality, the majority of people with a mental health issue are not dangerous to others but are at greater risk of harming themselves. Help and support are needed rather than fear and increased measures of control.[45] What is quite clear is that people with mental health issues have a greater risk of suicide, or attempted suicide, than the general population.[46]

Risk factors to consider when assessing suicide risk are

1. degree of hopelessness
2. planning for suicide
3. past suicide attempts
4. mood and affect – especially depression
5. social context
6. cultural context
7. relationships – quality
8. recent losses
9. mental status
10. willingness to accept assistance.[47]

Apart from levels of dangerousness, risk assessments often do not include areas of particular concern to social workers such as disempowering practices in mental health settings. It is important that suicide and self-harm are viewed within the context in which they have occurred with attention focused on contributing factors; in particular, what has been happening in this person's life recently and personal impacts.

Numerous studies have shown that although much of the work in mental health is focused on risk assessment, workers in mental health generally are not particularly good at assessing high levels of risk. The accuracy of such assessments is dubious at best. Studies have focused on psychiatrists, nurses and psychologists in inpatient settings, with scant attention to social workers. The few studies conducted on social workers show that they lack clarity in assessing risk and lack confidence in applying a social rather than medical perspective.[48] According to Langan, social workers 'need to develop confidence in the specific contribution they make in approaching risk assessment from a social rather than from a medical perspective'.[49] The challenge for social workers is to draw greater attention to contextual social, political and economic factors that impact upon a person's health and well-being. The primary focus on medication and ensuring a person's compliance needs to be questioned by social workers. A social perspective needs to be developed to see the person within her or his cultural, social, environmental, spiritual, psychological, emotional and interpersonal context. This involves a wider ambit of general health and community services as well as mental health services.

Social workers have been found to be far more accurate in predicting those who will not be violent as opposed to those who will be violent. Interestingly, women and violence is often underestimated, but predictions of violence from men and people from ethnic minority groups are overestimated.[50] Violence needs to be assessed within its proper social context, looking at issues around provocation rather than focusing solely on one party in the conflict.[51] Of far greater importance in predicting violence are issues around alcohol and other drug misuse.[52] Substance abuse by single, young adult males poses a greater risk of violence than mental health issues.[53]

Protective and precipitating factors

The presence or absence of 'protective' and 'precipitating' factors will influence the level of suicide risk.[54] Unfortunately, people with mental health issues generally rate low on the protective factors and high on the precipitating factors. Protective factors against suicide include having friends and family who care about at least one significant person to talk to in times of difficulties, employment, housing and adequate finances. For people with an ongoing mental health issue such as schizophrenia, particularly at a young age, some of these factors are often missing. As mentioned in Chapter 3, loneliness and isolation are common features of those with mental health issues.[55] People with mental health issues also experience high rates of unemployment.[56] Mental health issues can cause a person to become, or remain, homeless and subsequently not to have economic and social supports they can rely upon.[57]

Social support is important in reducing suicide risk. This is not easy to achieve and requires the ability to live independently and create and maintain a supportive social network while coping with a mental health issue and the associated stigma and discrimination that go with it due to discriminatory attitudes and behaviours in the general community. Studies on social attachment and social capital consider suicide as representing individuals who are not well integrated and supported in the community.[58] This makes it extremely difficult to carry out programs of community care, particularly if a person is experiencing a suicidal crisis because, sad as it may seem, they simply may not have anyone who cares enough to assist. Workers cannot assume this to be the case as many people do have strong supports especially from family. However, the reality is that many people are going it alone and for some the burden is too much to bear. The prevalence of mental disorders is greatest for those living alone.[59] However, even when high levels of family support are available, the person may still decide to kill themselves, as in their own mind this is the best option.

Precipitating factors are often associated with change and loss. Changes and losses produce stress and require personal coping and adaptation or removal if the situation is unsafe. However, if removal occurs, there must be direct benefits for the person and it must be a better place than the one they are leaving or being removed from. The reality is that this is often not the case and this is particularly the situation of many young people put in group homes in out-of-home care. It is possible that these young people may be developing mental health issues, and group homes do not have the supportive and nurturing environment required to prevent mental health issues from developing further, supporting and sustaining relationships and preventing loss. When a person is with a mental health issue, considerable lifestyle changes are required to remain well. Often multiple changes or losses occur, making it difficult for a person to cope. Previous coping strategies in situations of crisis will often give a good idea of a person's abilities, resources and supports. However, the loss of a major support may precipitate a suicidal crisis. Even changes that are planned for and seemingly happy occasions, such as moving house or the birth of a child provoke stress due to changes required. Commonly experienced changes occur in relationships, living situation and conditions, school, work, finances, health and personal well-being.[60] The intensity and severity of these changes and the impact they have on people's quality of life will influence how they cope. If a person feels trapped by these changes and can find no way out, suicide may seem the only solution.

Losses are also varied. Many people with mental health issues have multiple and accumulated losses and this needs to be taken into account in a social work assessment as well as the impact of such losses on a person's self-esteem. Some of these losses will be usual losses experienced by people during their lives and others will be directly associated with having mental health issues. Usual losses include loss, or perceived loss, of a relationship or a loved one, unemployment and employment opportunities, physical health, mobility and independence. Additional losses associated with mental health issues are the loss of family and friends due to their inability to understand or cope with what may seem strange and unusual behaviours or depressive mood. The loss of supportive family and friends can be devastating for those who have difficulties forming new relationships due to mental health issues. Lost opportunities are a particular problem for people with mental health issues due to the stigma and discrimination.

Warning signs

Warning signs of suicide include previous suicide attempts, feelings of hopelessness and helplessness, shame, verbal or written threats or hints of suicide, depression and a sudden improvement. There may be noticeable changes in behaviour such as the person getting her or his affairs in order and giving away possessions or saying goodbye to loved ones. It is usual to see more than one warning sign to appear.[61] The one most commonly misunderstood by workers and the general community is a sudden improvement after depression. It takes time to recover from depression, and sudden improvement is not usual. For those who appear to have suddenly improved and are in a peaceful state, it may mean that she or he has decided to suicide. They may also have more energy to actually carry out a suicide plan. At such times, workers and carers often reduce support just when it is needed most.

A social work assessment of suicide risk must include thought processes, intent, severity and degree of planning.[62] Sometimes workers are uncomfortable asking people direct questions about suicide in case they give them the idea to do so. However, this is not the case. Rather, asking a person directly about suicide gives them an opportunity to communicate openly about it.[63]

Useful interview questions (in addition to those in Chapter 7) include

1. Have you been thinking about killing yourself?
If yes,
2. How often do you think about this?
3. Have you made any plans to actually do this?
If yes,
4. What are they?
5. How likely is it that you will actually do this?
6. Have you tried to kill yourself before?
If yes,
7. What happened?
8. Have family or friends or people you care about attempted suicide?
If yes,
9. What happened?
10. Have you tried to harm yourself in any way before?
If yes,
11. What happened?
12. What has caused you to feel this way?
13. Is this situation improving?
14. What might help you to feel better about things?
15. What losses have you experienced lately (include anniversaries of significant losses)?
16. What plans do you have for the future?
17. Who cares about you and supports you?
18. Do you think that you really will suicide?

If a person does have plans to suicide, a worker needs to consider the plan according to how lethal and how accessible the method of suicide is. This includes considering the viability of the plan and the amount of time that has gone into it. The likelihood of a person being discovered in the act is also important, and whether or not they have taken precautions to avoid being discovered.[64] Workers can sometimes relax if these imminent signs are not evident and not take thoughts of suicide seriously – dismissing them as fleeting ideas that many people have from time to time. This is a dangerous view because, as mentioned earlier in this chapter, all thoughts of suicide must be taken seriously and responded to, keeping in mind that this person is already seeking services. Some people will have heightened vulnerability due to an extremely sensitive nature that absorbs difficulties which others might ignore. The increased focus on resilience in recent years is important but for many people the realities of their lives, and the sensitivity of their nature, mean that problems are simply too great to bear even when support is provided.

Interventions

Recovery-focused interventions aim to prevent further losses and get back as much as possible what people have lost due to mental health issues (see Chapter 12). This can safeguard against self-harm and attempted suicide. In cases where this does occur, workers need to provide support and assistance and respond to the level of emotional distress the person is experiencing by letting them know they are not alone in their struggle to cope.[65] Social workers need to model humane responses, and challenge inappropriate and punitive practices that are pervasive in involuntary mental health service models which are often the primary response for suicide intervention.

The first step to intervening in a suicidal crisis is to stay with the person until the suicidal crisis resolves and to establish good rapport with the person and to assist in accessing appropriate supports.[66] A close working relationship is required between the person, carers and workers to ensure the safety of the person as much as possible. Part of working with a person who is suicidal is to acknowledge and minimise risk. However, it is also to acknowledge and learn to understand that risk is a part of working with someone who is suicidal and is something that needs to be acknowledged and worked with. Ultimately, risk will always be present and strategies are required to try and minimise it as well as to show the person concerned and those close to them how to live with it.

Some people will have persistent thoughts of suicide over many years. The challenge is not to underestimate possible intent when such thoughts are pervasive. Again, by focusing on relationships and quality of life, the focus moves beyond the act of suicide and it is here that most gains can be made. Attachment-based family therapy is consistent with a recovery approach and is focused on strengthening attachments to support a person not only during a suicidal crisis but during other times of difficulty. It is knowing that someone loves and cares about you and is there for you. Problems need to be identified and clarified with an assessment of lethality, level of distress, judgement and impulse control. Effective listening skills are essential. Careful use of empathic statements acknowledging feelings and emotional content is required due to the intensity of emotions. These emotions will often include both despair and anger that has been internalised. Tapping into this anger and endeavouring to externalise it, using strategies such as normalisation and consciousness raising, can assist with this. Getting a person to identify and sit with their sense of despair can be the turning point in terms of them wanting something better for themselves, and not necessarily death. Statements reflecting content rather than feelings can help a person regain self-control and composure. This is particularly important towards the end of the interview. Possible solutions are explored with critical questioning around suicide as the only way out.

Accessing supports within the person's network is crucial, as it is these people who will ultimately provide greatest assistance and support during and following a suicidal crisis. It is important that assistance is provided to these people on strategies and approaches that will assist most, including listening and a non-judgemental approach. This includes elimination of any methods that make the person feel guilty or ashamed for their suicidal thoughts or actions. Shame and suicide are closely connected, and shame should never be used as an intervention strategy, particularly with suicidal young people whose fragile psyche is still developing. Re-integrative shaming is an approach that is used in justice settings to endeavour to get a person to acknowledge wrong doing and to re-integrate into the values of the community. This is used particularly with Australian Aboriginal and New Zealand Maori communities. Social workers should never use shaming practices such as these, and should challenge their use. What is needed are approaches that validate the self, family and community, and foster securing attachments, supports and role models. It is affirmation and nurturing of the self and relationships and opportunities that are required most. Strategies that affirm a person's sense of self and support a positive reputation are essential for recovery. Practices that deliberately shame a person are not consistent with a recovery approach and have no place in healthcare. Shaming can lead to suicide and these practices are questionable in justice settings where there is an over-representation of people with mental health issues.

Aboriginal communities have developed preferred models of suicide prevention and intervention modelled on community care. This involves someone, often an aunty in the community, being on suicide or crisis call, coming and staying with the person during a suicidal crisis and being available to talk with them about the issues and difficulties they are experiencing. The aunty will take the person to members of their family or community who can continue to stay with them and be there to listen and help provide perspective as to other possibilities. This is an intensive model of community care and support that mental health services have much to learn from. It is similar to the mental health crisis services model. However, it is a model that deliberately avoids use of emergency and police services and in-patient models of care, which is what makes it uniquely different. Ultimately, the person feels reassured that others do care for them and that there are other alternatives.

A contract is often agreed to in writing or verbally, whereby the person agrees not to harm him- or her-self for a specified period of time. This is often until the next appointment with a worker. In some cultures, however, it is inappropriate to ask for a signed contract, particularly if there is a history of fear and persecution by authorities. If a person has a plan to suicide and remains in the community, the means by which the person planned to suicide are removed where possible, with close supervision provided generally by a team of carers, with worker support. If the person is not considered safe in the community, a voluntary or involuntary hospital admission needs very much to be considered as a last resort, keeping in mind that people also suicide in in-patient settings and there are higher rates post discharge. A traumatic hospital admission can increase suicide risk due to heightened levels of distress, hopelessness and anger.

Families and carers

I learnt the hard way of the importance of time spent with family and carers planning the care arrangements. These include sharing assessment information as to the lethality of the person's suicidal thoughts and details of who the carer is to contact if the risk increases or if the situation changes and care can no longer be provided.

In a suicidal crisis, it is best that the carer is not left unsupported to care for extended periods of time. It is often best if care of the suicidal person is shared among family and/ or friends if possible as often it is too much for one person as in the case of Lily's husband, discussed in Chapter 1, who simply fell asleep from exhaustion. In one instance, we worked with a man of Vietnamese background who was suicidal. He had several friends, all of whom stayed with him, everyone sleeping on the floor in the lounge room. Each time we visited, the lounge room was full of people – some awake and others sleeping. They were keeping a close eye on him day and night but this was not too obvious. It seemed as if they were all enjoying catching up with him and each other, sharing stories, laughing and joking, eating meals, watching movies, sleeping and simply being together. On another occasion, we drove a young woman who was experiencing a suicidal crisis to different family members' homes each day to ease the burden of caring for her during an acute suicidal crisis.

As mentioned previously, confidentiality is often misunderstood, resulting in carers being excluded from intervention planning. In a suicidal crisis this has disastrous implications and the withholding of such information is negligent. This is particularly so now that most care is provided by carers in the community. Information must be conveyed to those who can assist, in particular the primary carer, and the law requires workers to do so. This carries the message that the worker is treating what the person is saying seriously and that other people also care.

Carers can provide support by asking at regular intervals how the person is feeling, showing concern and providing opportunities for the person to talk about the circumstances leading up to the suicidal crisis and his or her needs and concerns and expectations. It also provides an opportunity to talk about times when the person is feeling most vulnerable and to identify triggers for suicidal thoughts. Plans should be made with the person, carer and workers about how to deal with such thoughts. This often involves the use of positive self-affirmations. Encouragement by carers for the person to attend appointments with workers and groups and follow agreed intervention plans also assists with recovery. Support of carers and ongoing assessment of their ability to continue to provide the care required is crucial in a suicidal crisis.

A key aspect is relationships and for the person to have someone, or a number of people, they can genuinely discuss difficult issues with and confide in. Attachment based family therapy, discussed in Chapter 10 on interventions is a promising approach for working with suicidal young people that focuses primarily on attachments with a primary care giver, often the mother, rather than problems. Where supportive attachments are not able to be provided within the family due to health or other reasons, it is important to look further into the young person's networks, such as school, sporting clubs and other areas of a young person's life, where they may have developed supportive attachments with adults who genuinely care about their welfare. People outside the family often provide perspective as they are not as emotionally involved and can also be a useful adjunct to family support when this is available.

Relationships and attachments in a person's life are the key to improved quality of life and a wish to live. Workers can support this but cannot assume, or replace, these primary and crucial roles in a person's social network. Individual counselling alone, using focused psychological strategies, is not likely to bring about sustained improvements in the long term. Families and significant others must be involved.

Also mentioned previously is the fact that, rather than having carers, most people with mental health issues are actually caring for others. In 2000 it was estimated that approximately one million Australians under 21 years of age had a parent with mental health issues.[67] These children have been identified as having a higher suicide risk yet their plight continues to be ignored.[68]

Continuous, coordinated and integrated care

High levels of attempted and completed suicides amongst people with mental health issues indicate that improvements are required in the development and delivery of both mental health and community services. It is important that those services that are effective are supported and replicated.

Continuous care is extremely importsnt for people with mental health issues. Before the closure of stand-alone psychiatric hospitals, people in the community with a mental health issue such as schizophrenia could expect to have a mental health worker allocated to care for them indefinitely. An increased demand for community mental health services, alongside economic rationalist policies, has resulted in pressures to provide short-term services, increase case loads and discharge consumers who were deemed to be well. Previously, the focus of community mental health services was to assist people to remain well. However, now if a person is well they must be discharged. This has huge implications for mental health service delivery because discharge from a mental health service may precipitate a suicidal crisis. As mentioned earlier, the other factor that is often not well understood is that people often suicide after their mood has improved. Families, friends and workers often comment on what a shock it was because the person seemed to be a lot better. It is often after improvements occur that services are terminated, particularly crisis services. Services should be vigilant at such times and not be withdrawn prematurely.

A crisis team worked with Mark during a suicidal crisis. When workers deemed that the crisis was resolved, services were terminated. However, Mark kept calling the service in crisis. His calls were now seen as attention seeking and a behaviour management plan was put in place to manage his calls. He incinerated himself in his shed in the period immediately following his discharge from the crisis service.

Mark's story and that of Maya in Chapter 10 are a stark reminder of the importance of continuous and coordinated care and how today mental health workers are not able to provide this in the same ways they were able to in the past. Careful discharge planning is needed that is mindful of this and assists people with this transition with a gradual reduction of services. This includes coordination and liaison with the person's general practitioner and those who are able to provide ongoing care. People with schizophrenia and treated by general practitioners have been found to have better treatment outcomes than those treated at community mental health centres.[69] General practitioners do not discharge their patients in the same way hospitals and community mental health centres do and are generally more accessible. However, the trend toward super clinics with less personalised service threatens this doctor–patient relationship.

It is important that plans are made for early intervention if the person shows signs of becoming unwell again or is suicidal. Early intervention programs are important for early diagnosis and treatment. Often a carer is the first person to recognise early warning signs and will initiate this contact. Carers are in effect performing a case management role and play a key role in accessing and coordinating services. However, if people do not have carers or workers, they are left to coordinate their own care. In practice, this often means that people who may need mental health services the most do not access them. Generally, if behaviours are disturbing others, and workers are notified, there is a greater likelihood of crisis interventions at such times.

Continuous, coordinated and integrated care requires collaboration between consumers, carers and workers across a range of services. General practitioners are particularly important given the key role they play. Services must be responsive to mental health issues and substance misuse and abuse issues, and address the complex interplay between the two, rather than the current trend to see them as requiring quite separate services. As mentioned in Chapter 3, talk about mental health issues and suicide is not encouraged in Aboriginal communities; suicide is treated as the result of family trouble, alcohol or accident.[70] It is essential that Indigenous workers are contacted and referrals made to specialist Aboriginal health and mental health services. The Victorian Aboriginal Health Centre has a number of mental health admission hospital beds allocated for Aboriginal people, with the beds managed by the Aboriginal Health Service. The use of isolation in prisons and hospitals, especially for Aboriginal people and Torres Strait Islanders, requires urgent review. A focus must be on the necessary care required during a suicidal crisis and afterwards, rather than the focus being solely on removal of means of suicide. Isolation can markedly increase levels of distress, anger and despair and ultimately heighten suicide risk. Increased preparation for the discharge of people with mental health issues from both hospitals and prisons is needed, with adequate supports provided to assist with adjustment back into the community.

Suicide prevention and health promotion

The aims of preventive mental health and suicide programs in the community are threefold. These are to promote positive mental health and well-being, provide community services to those at most risk of developing mental health issues in the community and to heighten community awareness of suicide and mental health issues to eliminate stigma and discrimination.[71]

People with mental health issues must be able to participate as active and worthwhile members of society and must be afforded opportunities for education, employment and recreation in a supportive environment. For this to happen, community education programs on suicide and mental health are needed as well as additional resources for carers, general practitioners, mental health service providers and general community services.

Alongside policies aimed at suicide prevention are those focused on mental health and well-being. The National Depression Initiative, conducted by an independent body, Beyond Blue, was established to increase community understanding of depression and to support research into the prevention and management of depression.[72] Since the 1990s, suicide has emerged as a major area of public health policy in Australia. The National Youth Suicide Prevention Strategy 1995–1999 was followed by a further commitment to a National Suicide Prevention strategy. While the focus remained on youth suicide, the ambit of the strategy has been expanded to include other groups identified as high risk, including older people with mental health issues or substance abuse problems, those living in rural communities, Aboriginal people and Torres Strait Islanders, and prisoners.[73] Even with these additional resources, suicide rates have continued to increase, indicating that those claiming to be the leaders in suicide prevention strategies do not in reality have the answer. This is an area where co-design and principles of trauma-informed care and practice have considerable potential and is an area that must be prioritised.

Stigma can make recovery from mental health issues harder due to prejudice and discrimination. This can erode a person's confidence and self-esteem and result in them not mixing with people for fear they may be ridiculed or misunderstood. This can lead to loneliness and isolation and perpetuation of the symptoms of mental health issues and suicidal thoughts. The effects of stigma can be as distressing as the mental health issues itself.[74]

Responsible media reporting of suicide and mental health issues is important to reduce stigma and disadvantage. In 2000 a national mental health and media group was established in Australia to portray mental health issues and suicide in a responsible manner and to reduce the harm, stigma and copycat behaviours that can occur following media reporting of suicide. This group was formed in recognition of the impact of the negative and inaccurate stereotypes in the media, particularly surrounding mental health issues and violence and the effect that suicide reporting can have on vulnerable people.[75] The sensationalism of suicide in the Australian media is prevented by guidelines from the Media, Entertainment and Arts Alliance and the Australian Communications and Media Authority; reporting on individual cases of suicide is disallowed unless deemed to be in the wider public interest. Some argue for more public reporting of suicide figures to heighten the extent of this problem in the community. To increase community awareness and sensitivity about a major social problem that is usually not discussed or reported in the media, the White Wreath Association was established by family and friends of people who have been with mental health issues and suicided. This is a good example of how support of the media in publicising issues appropriately, and the use of technologies can enhance public awareness and encourage discussion and debate as well as provide comfort for grieving loved ones left behind in the knowledge that they may be able to assist others.

Co-design can also be valuable in reconsidering how to best go about media reporting of suicide, given that most people will continue to communicate about suicide on social media in ways that do not conform with these media guidelines. This needs to be acknowledged and incorporated in media and suicide reporting guidelines and prevention strategies. The ultimate goal is to have everyday informed conversations about suicide rather than approaches that lead to silence and awkwardness which leave people to cope on their own or rely on sources of variable quality on the Internet. Some of these Internet sites encourage suicide and many are linked with pornography. To leave people to use the Internet as their primary source of information on suicide is simply negligent.

Conclusion

Suicide and self-harm are a cry for help and social workers need to be skilled to respond appropriately. Since the deinstitutionalisation of mental health services and the closure of stand-alone psychiatric hospitals, there has been an increase in suicide among people with mental health issues, particularly those with schizophrenia. Social workers require an awareness of the risk factors for suicide, particularly substance abuse, social isolation, gender, age, sexuality, violence, sexual abuse and lethality. For those with mental health issue, additional risk factors include depression and sudden improvement, and discharge from hospital, community mental health services or prison. It is important that social workers recognise and respond appropriately to the warning signs of suicide. These include persistent suicidal ideation, previous suicide plans and attempts and previous deliberate self-harm. Interventions require collaboration between workers, consumers, carers and a range of community services for the provision of continuous, coordinated and integrated care. It is important that social work interventions go beyond risk assessment and crisis intervention to address the contextual factors that have contributed to the person's distressed state, with all ideas of suicide treated seriously regardless of intent and lethality. Social workers must adopt trauma-informed care practices and are cautioned against involuntary interventions that can cause further distress and trauma. A priority is on relationships and attachments and activating them within the person's environment. This is so that a person has people within their family or wider network who they can turn to in times of major difficulties. A key aspect of the worker role is to support and enhance these relationships and not endeavour to replace them. Health prevention and promotion, and advocacy campaigns, can heighten community awareness about mental health issues and suicide so that people can get much needed support during and after a suicidal crisis. The most promising intervention in this area is models of crisis intervention used in Aboriginal communities, and attachment-based family therapy. It is interesting that sometimes the best service models evolve from those who are forced to rely on their own community rather than government-provided services due to the inadequacies of the service system. This has also been witnessed in communities of care developed in the LGBTI community discussed in Chapter 9.

Reflection

What are the risk factors for suicide?

What are the high risk population groups for suicide?

What are the reasons a person may want to take her or his own life?

What are the warning signs for suicide?

What are appropriate responses to someone who is showing signs of suicide?

Is it appropriate for a social worker to assist a person to die? Is this assisted suicide?

Do you think the national suicide toll should be reported in the media in the same way as the road toll?

13

Alcohol and Other Drugs

A drug is any substance that, when taken into the body, changes the way that the body functions. Legal drugs and substances include alcohol and tobacco, prescription medications, anabolic steroids, petrol and some fluorocarbons.[1] The term illegal or illicit drugs refers to cannabis, marijuana, hashish, cocaine and heroin. Other illicit drugs sometimes referred to as 'club drugs' include LSD, ecstasy and phencyclidine (PCP) mescaline and other hallucinogens.[2] Drugs are generally divided into the three groupings of stimulants, depressants and hallucinogens. Stimulants include LSD, caffeine and nicotine. Alcohol is the main depressant. Hallucinogens include PCP, LSD, heroin, cannabis, mescaline, peyote and amphetamines. Some stimulants such as LSD and depressants such as alcohol can also be hallucinogens. In this chapter, the use, misuse and abuse of alcohol and other drugs is explored including reasons for misuse and abuse. This is followed by consideration of substance use and mental health issues. Substances focused on are cannabis and alcohol as they are the main mind-altering drugs used in the community generally, and by those with mental health issues. It is noted, however, that methamphetamine use, and the use of other synthetic drugs, many of which are new and not known to health practitioners and authorities, are increasingly problematic in bizarre and aggressive presentations of people at emergency departments who are often brought in involuntarily by the police. It is most common for multiple substances to have been used, and medical staff are faced with the task of deciding if it is a drug-induced state alone or also a mental health issue. Issues for assessment and intervention are discussed with a focus on integrated integrated mental health and alcohol and other drug services and early psychosis prevention and intervention.

Use of alcohol and other drugs

Alcohol and tobacco are the most commonly used substances in the general community and among people with severe mental health issues.[3] Cannabis is the next most common substance used and is often used in conjunction with alcohol.[4] However, among younger age groups, cannabis use is often found to be higher than alcohol.[5] Use of cannabis has decreased slightly over recent years but it is still the most widely used illicit drug in Australia. Misuse of cannabis and other drugs has been found to be more prevalent in urban areas in comparison with rural areas. This contrasts with alcohol use, where little variation is found in rates of use between urban and rural areas.[7] Seventeen per cent of males aged 20 to 29 years drink at what is considered risky or high-risk levels at least weekly.[8] The mean age of commencement of use of alcohol and other drugs has remained the same for the past decade. This is 17 years of age for alcohol, 18 years for cannabis and around 20 to 22 years for other illicit drugs.[9]

Alcohol use by teenage girls aged 14 to 19 years and young men aged 20 to 29 years is of particular concern, and increased usage has been reported in recent years. For teenage girls, greatest harm results from binge drinking, which is often combined with use of illegal drugs. Harm includes injury, accidents and assaults. It is estimated that 11 per cent of teenage girls in Australia drink at risky levels weekly and 22 per cent have used illicit drugs. The younger a woman is when she starts drinking alcohol at risky levels, the greater the likelihood that she will have problems with alcohol later on.[10]

Use of ecstasy has increased in use since the mid-1980s. A study of ecstasy use in the United States found that 90 per cent of people who used ecstasy had also used other drugs in the previous 12 months. Over half of those surveyed had used up to four other illicit drugs in that period.[11]

Misuse of prescription drugs is an increasing problem, particularly among teenagers and young women.[12] The term misuse is used to describe problematic substance use that has not developed into an addiction, as seen in substance abuse. Misuse of substances is more likely to be seen in younger people who have not been using substances for lengthy periods. In terms of early intervention, substance misuse in young people is a priority area to prevent substance abuse developing.

Substance abuse, or addiction, is seen to be the continued use of a substance with knowledge that the substance has harmful consequences.[15] A person who is dependent upon alcohol or other drugs uses the substance with a sense of compulsion that may result in neglect of responsibilities and harm. Substance misuse is more likely to be seen in younger people who have not had prolonged use of a substance to develop an addition. Signs of substance misuse must be taken seriously for early intervention to prevent addictions from destroying their adult life and that of others dependent upon them.

For every person who has an alcohol or other drug problem, another four people are affected and their quality of life will also improve with the person's recovery.[16] In the United States, it is estimated that approximately 10 per cent of children live with at least one substance-abusing or substance-dependent parent.[17] This is twice as likely to be the father rather than the mother, with alcohol the main substance used.

Reasons for use of alcohol and other drugs

Different substances have varied effects that may change according to the setting the substance is taken in and the mood of the person at the time. The choice of substance may be due to the desired effect. For instance, some drugs such as alcohol can relieve a sense of inner coldness and emptiness and the person may become more sociable and less inhibited. Opiates such as heroin have a tranquillising effect; cocaine increases energy levels and alertness.[18] Often

248

the person does not know what they are taking, or the dosage or strength, due the lack of regulation that comes with illegal substances.

People use alcohol and other drugs for a variety of reasons. They might find it helps them to relax for social and recreational purposes. For some, it may provide temporary relief from daily problems. The reported reasons of most individuals with schizophrenia for using alcohol, amphetamines, cannabis, cocaine and other drugs are the same as the general population. These are to alleviate boredom, to provide stimulation, socialisation, relief from anxiety, depression and tension, sleep problems and distancing from life's problems. These reasons are broadly classified into the three categories of social, coping and recreational motives for substance use.[19] Individuals with mental health issues who use substances for recreational or coping reasons have been found to have greatest problems with substance misuse.[20] Social use of cannabis and alcohol has not been found to lead to misuse, but there are a number of costs associated with illicit drug use:

There is generally a decline in other activities as time is taken for drug use.

Financial difficulties can result from the costs associated with drug use and this can have a flow on effect in terms of spending in other areas, such as food and accommodation.

Housing and rehabilitation opportunities may not be available due to issues around ongoing substance use.

There is also an increased risk of criminal activities, particularly fraud and burglary among those who use illicit drugs.[21]

Substance use and mental health issues

Individuals who abuse alcohol and other drugs experience greater difficulties with symptoms, treatment, social functioning and outcomes.[22] Those with psychosis who use substances are also reported as having more intense and prolonged psychotic symptoms. They also have a higher rate of presentation to emergency services as well as hospital admissions. This is in the context of inadequate service provision within the community for these people.[23]

Drugs that are most commonly used by those with mental health issues are those that are most readily available, generally tobacco, alcohol and cannabis.[24] Secular trends and the availability of certain drugs need to be taken into account. For instance, in 1992, Mueser reported higher use of cocaine than cannabis in the city of Philadelphia among those with a mental health issue. This was at a time when Philadelphia was reported to have been experiencing a cocaine epidemic.[25] Thus market availability will have a strong determining effect upon which substances individuals use. Some argue that Australia is experiencing a methamphetamine epidemic. While there has certainly been increased use, and this is problematic in emergency hospitals and in in-patient psychiatric units, alcohol and cannabis are still the main substances used by people with mental health issues.

Rates of cannabis use have been found to be significantly higher for those with mental health issues, particularly psychotic disorders such as schizophrenia and severe major affective disorders, than people in the general population. The use of other drugs such as cocaine, amphetamines, hallucinogens and stimulants is also reported to be higher for those with mental health issues than the general population.[26] The 2003 Australian Treatment Outcomes Study found that a large number of people seeking treatment for heroin addiction also had mental health issues.[27] Just under half of those surveyed were with post-traumatic stress disorder and a quarter with depression. Over one-third had attempted suicide, with 13 per cent having made an attempt in the previous 12 months.

For the most part, the focus has been primarily on substance use and schizophrenia and mood disorders to a lesser extent.[28] Substance abuse is the main mental diagnosis for men, accounting for 33 per cent of male mental health issues. This is in comparison to affective disorders representing 39 per cent of female mental health issues. However, closer study of the interconnection between the two is warranted. It is asserted that affective disorders in men are masked by excessive alcohol use.[29] A high rate of alcohol and other drug abuse among people with schizophrenia is increasingly being recognised. It has been asserted that people with schizophrenia have increased vulnerability to abuse alcohol and drugs. People with a dual diagnosis of schizophrenia and alcohol or other drug abuse have been found to relapse sooner than those who do not use substances.

Late adolescence is when behaviours such as smoking, drinking and illicit drug use tend to cluster. Most adolescents who casually experiment with cannabis do not develop mental health issues.[30] However, heavy cannabis use has acute effects on memory and attention, and can impair judgement and motor skills.[31]

There is a high correlation between substance misbuse and first onset of psychosis.[32] It may be that the substance misuse occurs before the onset of the psychosis or afterwards in an attempt to alleviate distressing negative symptoms or disturbing effects of anti-psychotic medications. There is a lack of consensus in the research literature as to whether or not substance misuse causes psychosis. However, the literature supports the view that certain drugs, such as stimulants, can precipitate the onset of psychosis in those who are biologically susceptible.[33] It has also been found that prolonged substance use can result in psychosis for those who are not considered vulnerable to psychosis.[34] It is interesting to note, however, that in Australia, although there has been an increase in the prevalence of drugs in the community in recent years, there has been no associated increase in the incidence of psychosis.[35]

It has been found that a significant number of people who are with schizophrenia have had at least one diagnosis of drug-induced psychosis before being with schizophrenia. This is an issue of concern as it may mean that treatment of the schizophrenia is delayed. Delays in treatment have been found to lead to a poorer prognosis and to impede recovery. Those who have abused substances are often younger than those who have not when they have their first psychotic episode. At the same time, the early onset of symptoms may lead to use of alcohol and other drugs at an earlier age.[36]

Cannabis

Cannabis has been widely used around the world, for social and therapeutic reasons, for thousands of years.[37] Cannabis is the general name used for marijuana and hashish, commonly referred to as 'pot', 'weed' or 'grass'. It is a plant derivative and is generally smoked or, to a lesser extent, eaten. The physiological affects of cannabis are the slowing down of thought processes and responses of the central nervous system. It can also cause hallucinations. Only in the past decade has understanding developed about how cannabis actually works and the regions of the brain that are affected.[38]

Over 400 distinct chemical compounds have been found to be present in the cannabis plant. Approximately 30 of these structurally related compounds are considered to be psychoactive. The cannabinoid, tetrahydrocannabinol (THC) is the most prevalent and potent compound found in dried cannabis leaves. It has therefore become the main focus of studies examining the psychoactive component of cannabis. It is generally agreed that the 'high' people experience from cannabis use is due to THC and related compounds; however there is no conclusive evidence available to support this.[39] Patterns of use of cannabis suggest that it does not have the addictive properties of other commonly abused drugs such as cocaine, opiates, amphetamines, tobacco and alcohol. Studies in the USA have found that use of cannabis is usually sporadic, or intense over a brief period. Despite it being illegal, cannabis is readily available yet progression to intense daily use is not common in the USA.[40]

The majority of people who use cannabis do not experience any obvious detrimental effects. However, regular and prolonged use of cannabis can lead to short-term psychological effects of increased anxiety, confusion, paranoia, hallucinations of several hours' duration, poor concentration and memory, learning difficulties and occasionally psychosis.[41] Heavy use of cannabis can result in a drug-induced psychosis characterised by hallucinations which are often visual, delusions, confusion and loss of memory. Neurologists assert that psychotic disorders involve disturbances in the dopamine neurotransmitter system in the brain. Drugs such as THC increase dopamine release and can result in psychotic symptoms.[42] Neuroleptic drugs, used in the treatment of psychosis, reduce dopamine levels and generally reduce psychotic symptoms.[43]

A strong association between cannabis use and psychosis has been found but this relationship is not definitive. Very little is known about cannabis and psychosis. It is a point of contention as to whether mental health issues lead to cannabis use or vice versa.[44] In the past, a considerable focus has been on causal relationships between substance abuse and mental health issues. It has generally been found that substance abuse precedes the onset of psychotic symptoms.[45]

One causal explanation is that cannabis use precipitates the onset of schizophrenia in people who are genetically vulnerable to developing schizophrenia. This is seen to be due to a combination of predisposing personality features, family history of psychosis and psycho-social stressors. Although this argument is plausible, there is very little evidence to support the view that genetic vulnerability increases the risk of psychosis in cannabis users. This is in the context of the number of individuals with early onset acute psychoses declining, or remaining stable, since the 1970s, while cannabis use among young adults has increased in Australia and the USA.[46] However, stage models of schizophrenia see most cases of schizophrenia ending with the development of psychotic symptoms rather than beginning with them. The focus is on the process that generally begins in an insidious manner characterised by social withdrawal rather than the onset of psychotic symptoms.[47]

A further causal explanation is that schizophrenia causes individuals to use substances in an effort to relieve the unpleasant negative symptoms of depression and blunted affect associated with schizophrenia, or to lessen the impact of the side effects of traditional anti-psychotic medication.[48] Rather than relief, though, most people experience an increase in symptoms of depression, anxiety, and lethargy. This is coupled with an increase in positive symptoms of delusions and hallucinations.[49] Depressed males have been found to experience higher levels than females of paranoia, following heavy use of cannabis, although females are seen to have increased irritability.[50]

There are some indications that mild, as opposed to heavy, use of cannabis and other drugs can have some positive effects. Mild users can experience less depression and anxiety than heavy users or non-users, and have fewer hospitalisations. However, this is generally at the cost of increased suspiciousness.[51] Todd found an increase in paranoia among depressed males with a dual diagnosis of cannabis dependence and depression.[52] Cannabis use was associated with higher levels of depression and poorer social functioning in comparison with depressed males who were not using cannabis. The more recent the use of cannabis, the higher the levels of paranoia found.

A shift in thinking has occurred since the 1990s away from causal relationships to thinking in terms of co-morbidity.[53] Cannabis use generally precedes the onset of psychosis. Heavy use of cannabis can exacerbate psychotic symptoms for those with a pre-existing psychotic condition and interfere with the therapeutic effects of neuroleptic drugs used to treat psychotic symptoms. It can also lead to reduced compliance with treatment and increased hospitalisations.[54] The use of multiple substances, particularly concomitant use of alcohol and cannabis, is common among individuals with schizophrenia.[55] Alcohol, cocaine, amphetamines or other psychostimulants or hallucinogens can produce acute paranoid psychosis.[56] Therefore it is difficult to determine the relationship of other variables such as possible use of other substances or a genetic predisposition to use cannabis and develop schizophrenia.[57]

The vulnerability-stress-coping model of schizophrenia presented in Chapter 5 is a useful framework for considering the relationship between schizophrenia and use of substances. A strong correlation has been found between depression and alcohol abuse.[58]

Alcohol

There is some evidence to suggest that alcohol and amphetamines have a greater effect on the development of psychosis than cannabis.[59] Alcohol abuse has been found to be a stronger predictor of psychotic symptoms than cannabis.[60] However, as mentioned above, cannabis is frequently used with alcohol. Individuals in the general population and those with mental health issues are more likely to have problems with alcohol abuse if it is used for coping rather than for recreational or social purposes.[61] Alcohol is generally regarded as far more harmful than any of the illicit drugs such as cannabis, cocaine and heroin. Many prescription drugs, over the counter medications and natural remedies have a negative interaction with alcohol.[62] This is complicated by the fact that alcohol use is far more prevalent due to its legal status and thus may cause greater problems because more people use it.[63]

Most people who drink socially do not experience any detrimental effects from alcohol. However, for those who drink for coping reasons, problems are likely to arise. Real asserts that for many men excessive drinking is an attempt to self-medicate the pain emanating from covert depression.[64] Real argues that addictive behaviours in males, including substance abuse, mask depression in men.[65] Both addictive and recreational drinkers have been found to feel positive mood-enhancing effects from alcohol. The difference between recreational and coping drinkers is that recreational drinkers generally feel a greater sense of self-worth. Research findings indicate that depressed individuals may experience the effects of alcohol to a greater extent than those who are not depressed. Those who are depressed will also have higher expectations that the substance, whether it be alcohol or illicit drugs, will make them feel better.[66] For those who are alcohol-dependent, drinking is frequently a means of temporary relief from emotional distress and pain, and feelings of worthlessness. The relief is transitory as the person either returns to the same distressed starting point or feels even worse. The cycle continues as the person seeks temporary relief from alcohol time and time again.[67]

It is argued that men in particular use alcohol or drugs as a means of treating covert depressive symptoms, but it is also asserted that alcohol in general, and prolonged use in particular, causes depression. This is similar to the arguments above concerning the causal relationship between cannabis and psychosis. What is apparent with alcohol and other drug use and depression is that increased amounts of the substance are needed over time, and decreased relief is experienced.[68]

Assessment

Workers are faced with a number of challenges when working with individuals with mental health issues who are also heavy users of alcohol and other drugs. This is due to the interaction of these substances with prescribed medications, and the effect on affective, cognitive and perceptual processes. Heavy use means increased likelihood of hallucinations, delusions, paranoia and depression, and poorer prognosis in terms of recovery. This is complicated by the social nature of most substances, the illegal status of many and general community perceptions that alcohol and cannabis are relatively harmless drugs.[69]

Differences in perceived use of substances have been found among workers, according to whether they come from mental health or alcohol and other drug services. A study in the United Kingdom found that workers from mental health services believed the people they worked with used substances primarily for pleasure, secondly for socialisation with coping reasons last. Habit or dependency were regarded as reasons for use among a minority of individuals. This was in contrast to the views of alcohol and other drug workers, who saw coping as the main reason for use of substances, habit second and dependency last. Socialisation was the main reason for perceived use for a minority of clients.[70] It is possible that if mental health workers see pleasure as the main reason for substance use, given the increased prevalence and social acceptance of alcohol and cannabis use in the general community, it is less likely to be included as part of the person's intervention plan. As a result, substance use may receive too much or too little attention by health professionals.

Routine screening for use of drugs and alcohol is required at the intake assessment when the person is first seen by a service with subsequent screening done at regular intervals. Opportunities for intervention are often missed due to variable screening for substance use, particularly use of alcohol.[71] Often, the person tries to hide their drug use or underestimate the types, amounts and frequency of substances used. If drug use is admitted, the person may often be excluded from service provision or receive minimal intervention. Specialist services in alcohol and other drugs and mental health have arisen since the mid-1990s but the integration of services across the fields of mental health and alcohol and other drugs is often poor; health professionals tend to focus on either the substance use or mental health issues, depending upon the focus of their service.

Service delivery is characterised by a lack of communication between agencies. Much of the time spent in communication between agencies is focused on determining whose responsibility it is to see the person. This is generally determined by whether mental health issues or substance abuse is assessed as the primary diagnosis. Today, mental health workers are meant to provide a holistic approach that is responsive to both mental health and substance use issues. However, mental health workers are not adequately trained to work with mental health and alcohol and other drugs problems concurrently, resulting in inappropriate assessments and intervention plans. Likewise, workers in alcohol and other drug settings are not adequately equipped to deal with the mental health issues their clients are presenting with.[72]

Intervention

As in the discussion of suicide in the previous chapter, people are often reluctant to openly talk with workers about alcohol and other drug problems. Thus problems can be avoided by pretending they do not exist or are private. Those who do recognise they have a problem may find it difficult to ask for or accept help. If people believe that workers are genuinely concerned about them, and have the competencies to assist, they are more likely to engage in meaningful discussion.

Unravelling male stereotypes and male privilege is important in treating covert depression in males, making the depression overt so that the inner pain can be explored and worked with. Addictive defences need to be confronted and stopped so that the underlying depression, or often trauma, can be dealt with.[73] These addictive behaviours are more readily identified if they involve substance abuse or Internet addiction. However, those who have people as the focus of their addiction or actions, particularly violence, are more likely to be misdiagnosed as having a personality disorder. They become entangled in the forensic rather than the mental health service system.[74] As mentioned in the previous chapter, drug and alcohol misuse is of far greater importance in predicting violence than mental health issues.[75]

In the past, negative attitudes and low expectations have hindered recovery. These include the view that a person must 'hit rock bottom' and that 'nothing can be done unless the person wants to stop'.[76] Individual blame was attributed, with the person's use of alcohol and other drugs seen as 'personal misconduct, moral weakness or even sin'.[77] The reality is that with alcohol and other drug problems, and likewise with mental and physical health issues, early interventions have greatest likelihood of success. These include individual, family, group work and health prevention and promotion. The reframing of negative stereotypes that blame the individual can lead to improved outcomes as the impacts of broader political, economic and social factors are considered.

Family members can be assisted by seeing that the person is unwell and in need of assistance. This can promote a sense of caring, rather than hostility and rejection. Skills in assertiveness and conflict resolution discussed earlier in Chapter 11 are useful in letting the person know of the day-to-day consequences of his or her behaviour. Talking about hopes and dreams, in a manner that is open and honest and not blaming or accusatory, reassessing, and setting new goals for the future can assist in recovery. Maintaining a healthy lifestyle and atmosphere in the home gives the person an opportunity to participate in ways that are pleasurable and meaningful. However, it is important to be aware of ongoing tensions and resentment and the lack of willingness or reluctance of some family members to participate due to negative past experiences of feeling hurt and let down, often on multiple occasions spanning many years.

Social workers can assist family members to identify behaviours that do not assist recovery. These include punishment, threats and bribes and hiding or throwing away bottles of alcohol or drugs. Emotional appeals can add to feelings of guilt and increase rather than decrease alcohol or other drug use. Talking or arguing with the person when they are affected, and drinking or taking drugs with them, is also not helpful. Removing or lessening responsibilities and making excuses can shield people from accepting the real consequences of their behaviours.[78]

It is strongly recommended that an integrated approach is taken with mental health and alcohol and other drug use for those with mental health issues. Research findings indicate that integrated services are far more effective than traditional approaches to service delivery whereby services for mental health and alcohol and other drug services are provided separately.[79] Methods of treatment vary across the integrated services. However, a number of common themes for successful treatment outcomes emerge:

The same clinicians provide treatment for both the mental health issues and substance use simultaneously.

Assertive outreach is used.

Stage-wise interventions are used to match treatment to the individual's level of motivation;

Multiple options are provided at each stage of recovery.

A long-term optimistic approach is taken to treatment.

Motivation to change and quit use of substances is a major treatment consideration. Interventions generally focus on issues around motivation, and integrating techniques used for substance abuse with those used in mental health. Active treatment and relapse prevention are important components of intervention. Interventions include the use of twelve-step models such as those used by Alcoholics Anonymous, social skills training, supportive counselling, harm minimisation and psycho-educational models. Over the past three decades, harm minimisation has been the focus of drugs policy in Australia. The 1985 National Drug Strategy introduced harm minimisation as a way of addressing the harmful consequences of alcohol and other drug use.[80] The focus is on reducing the harm caused by alcohol and other drug use for the individual and others affected by this behaviour.

Harm-reduction activities include providing clean syringes and safe disposal to people who inject drugs; selling low alcohol content beer at sporting events, and education. Alongside harm reduction are interventions aimed at reducing supply and demand. Supply reduction includes restricting the sale of alcohol to people aged over 18 and border control for the importation of illegal drugs such as amphetamines, heroin, cocaine, marijuana and ecstasy. Demand reduction involves information and education about the harmful effects of alcohol and other drugs targeted at young people as a preventive measure. Treatment programs are provided for people with an alcohol or other drug dependency.

It has been suggested that preventive interventions focusing on the risks associated with substance use may be beneficial to those who are not using substances. This is particularly so for those who have been assessed as having a high risk of developing psychosis due to personality, family history of psychosis and environmental factors.[81] The delivery of brief interventions focused on enhancing motivation and providing information can be effective in the reduction of alcohol consumption. The lower the dependence on the substance is, the greater the likelihood of a positive outcome.[82]

Assertive outreach programs are required to engage individuals in their familiar environment. This is important for gaining an understanding of the person's social context and the development of appropriate interventions that support positive mental health and reductions in harmful use of substances. Assertive outreach programs have been found to be successful in reducing the severity of symptoms and number of hospitalisations experienced by individuals with persistent mental health issues.[83]

Due to the strong relationship between severity of symptoms and alcohol and other drug use for coping, interventions focused on alternative ways of dealing with stressful situations are necessary to increase the individual's coping repertoire and thereby reduce dependence upon drugs. It is crucial that addictive behaviours are addressed and openly confronted so that underlying issues can be addressed. Specific strategies need to be developed for dealing with sleep problems and the negative symptoms of depression, anxiety and lethargy, particularly associated with schizophrenia and depression. Behavioural techniques are useful in dealing with addictive behaviours.[84] Self-evaluation of use of cannabis and alcohol, or other substance use, is important for the person to re-examine beliefs as to the perceived benefits of use. Evaluation of the evidence supporting these beliefs may assist in motivating the person to reduce, or stop the substance use.[85]

The high correlation between cannabis use and recreation needs to be acknowledged, as many people with mental health issues use cannabis to alleviate the boredom they experience. Due to the early age of initial substance use, other recreation and leisure activities may be less developed or non-existent. The ability to access and participate in leisure activities may also be restricted due to associated costs and limited finances. Motivating interest and skill enhancement in affordable social and leisure activities to alleviate boredom is necessary. It may be that these activities are scheduled at the same time that would usually be spent using substances. Perceived short-term benefits are positive engagement in an activity with the long-term benefit of an activity the person is interested in pursuing.

The stigma of mental health issues needs to be addressed as well as promoting a vision of recovery. Often cannabis use, and membership of a cannabis-using peer group, provides a new and preferred identity to that of being viewed and treated by society as 'mad' or 'crazy'. The development of a positive identity beyond that of psychiatric patient, or drug user, is important for a sense of hope for the future. Setting personal recovery goals, beyond avoiding hospitalisation, is important in assisting a person to reshape her or his future.[86]

Early psychosis prevention and intervention

A main focus of government policy in Australia, Britain, the United States and Canada is on early psychosis prevention and intervention. Early intervention programs for psychosis are developing around the world in recognition of the need for an early response to psychosis for optimum potential for recovery.[87] These services are designed for young people with a first diagnosis of psychosis and aim to increase community and government awareness of psychosis in young people, advocating for services to prevent and respond appropriately to early signs and symptoms of psychosis in young people.

Delays in receiving appropriate treatment can lead to serious health risks and have a marked impact on quality of life. The person can be at greater risk of behaving in inappropriate and unpredictable ways, abusing substances, self-harm and suicide. Changes in the person's behaviour may have a detrimental effect on housing, education, employment and finances, and relationships with family members and friends. The damage that is done in this period is sometimes irreparable. The longer the delays in treatment – the more difficult the symptoms are to treat, with a poorer recovery and increased likelihood of relapse of symptoms.

Conclusion

Alcohol and cannabis are the main substances of choice for those with mental health issues as well as members of the general community. Reasons for use of alcohol and other drugs are usually for social, coping or recreational purposes. Those who use alcohol and other drugs for coping have a greater likelihood of developing problems with substance dependence and abuse. People with mental health issues who abuse alcohol and other drugs tend to experience increased difficulties with symptoms of mental health issues. Services which provide assessments and interventions that focus concurrently on a person's mental health issues as well as alcohol and other drug use are far more effective than the separate provision of mental health and alcohol and other drug services. Early psychosis prevention and intervention services have particularly favourable outcomes.

Reflection

What are the main reasons people use alcohol and other drugs?

When does use of alcohol and other drugs become problematic?

What issues need to be taken into consideration when assessing someone who has concurrent mental health and substance use issues?

What interventions are likely to be most effective when working with someone concurrent mental health and substance use issues?

14

Women Prisoners

Since the deinstitutionalisation of mental health services, there has been an increase in the criminalisation of women with mental health issues.[1] Deinstitutionalisation and community care are applauded by government and policy makers for moving people with mental health issues out of institutions and into the community. While it is proven that women with mental health issues benefit tremendously from programs of community care and this is conducive to recovery, the funding of these programs is often not sufficient to be of benefit to those in greatest need. The policy of community care has in practice resulted in abuse and incarceration for many women who are unable to survive in the community and who are desperately in need of mental health care. Deinstitutionalisation for these women is re-institutionalisation in another kind of institution in a different sector. It has been asserted that 'the spectre of institutionalisation common in previous days, may very well be reinventing itself in today's prisons'.[2] However, the increased numbers of women in prison do not match those in the old institutions, so in this sense for many women community care has potentially resulted in successful outcomes. A paradigm shift has seen mental health become law and order. Women with mental health issues who are experiencing homelessness or inadequate housing, social isolation, unemployment, malnutrition and alcohol and other drug use and who are survivors of violence and abuse are increasingly ending up in the prison system. Prisons have been described as increasingly becoming the default placement for people with mental issues.[3] Issues of care and control are paramount as control and community safety takes precedence in sentencing and prison management systems. This serves to promulgate the myth of mental health issues and dangerousness and the need for community protection.[4] In this chapter, the situation of women prisoners is discussed with reference to types of offences women are being imprisoned for and length of sentences. Mental health issues for women prisoners are identified with consideration of social contextual factors. The impact of the prison environment on a woman's mental health is discussed and implications for program development and service delivery.

Women prisoners

Women prisoners today are likely to have been convicted of far more serious offences than in the past. However, these offences are predominantly non-violent with no association found between violent offending behaviours and mental health issues.[5] The type of offences for which women are imprisoned has changed in recent years. Prostitution and drinking offences have been replaced by drug trafficking and property related crimes. Crimes against property are often conducted in an effort to obtain money for drugs. Women have been increasingly arrested for burglary, motor vehicle theft, fraud, robbery and assault. Although women are predominantly serving short sentences, they are serving longer sentences than in the past because drug trafficking and property crimes carry higher minimum sentences than prostitution and drinking offences.[6] Truth in sentencing has also resulted in women serving longer sentences. A number of studies have reported on the increase in the number of women in prison and the growing overall prison population in England, the United States, Canada and Australia. Rutherford observes that in England 'women represent the fastest growing sector of the spiralling expansion which characterises the prison system as a whole'.[7] Of particular concern is an increase in the number of younger women in the prison system in recent years. The increase in the number of women prisoners is in the context of increased government cuts to education, welfare and health services, and an increase in privatisation of health and welfare services.

Increasingly, Aboriginal women are being imprisoned for breaches of parole.[8] Reasons for breaches are often due to associating with people that they are ordered not to have contact with. It is not easy to start a new life without adequate housing and income support, family and friends and not being able to regain care of dependent children. This is particularly so given the stigma and discrimination experienced by Aboriginal people and particularly those women with mental health issues. Presented with few options, many women return to abusive relationships and lifestyles.[9] They are often disinclined to seek protection from police due to fears of retribution and few viable alternatives. Often, women who do take the courage to call the police are in turn charged with an offence themselves, particularly in situations where they have defended themselves against abuse. This is particularly a concern for Aboriginal and Torres Strait Islander women.[10] The private nature of the context in which the abuse often occurs makes it difficult to substantiate complaints.

A significant number of incarcerated women are from culturally and linguistically diverse backgrounds, including those arrested, mostly for drug offences, on tourist visas. Women deemed illegal immigrants are imprisoned in immigration detention centres. A number of these women have pre-existing mental health issues. Many develop mental health issues while in detention. In some cases, Australian citizens with mental health issues have been wrongfully detained as illegal immigrants. Due to psychosis associated with mental health issues some women have provided authorities with incorrect names and addresses. When no record has been found, they have been deemed 'illegal'. In the past, police would have been likely to call mental health services for assistance, but with the 'war against terror' immigration detention has been used.

Mental health

Women prisoners have been found to have comparatively higher rates of diagnosed mental health issues than women in the community. Diagnoses include schizophrenia, depression, substance abuse and antisocial personality disorder. They also have higher rates of post-traumatic stress disorder and a greater incidence of childhood sexual and physical abuse and violence. Women prisoners who have ongoing mental health issues are unsafe and vulnerable to sexual assault and other forms of violence. Abuse within prison can cause a woman to become psychotic or exacerbate pre-existing mental health issues.

Numerous studies have found extremely high rates of mental health issues within female prison populations.[11] The view of female prisoners as being mentally unstable has seen major prisons for women, at Holloway in England and Cornton Vale in Scotland, transformed into secure hospitals. This model of care was problematic, with many women prisoners resenting being treated as mentally unwell.[12] Fifty-seven per cent of women in New South Wales prisons have been with a mental health issue.[13]

Female and male prisoners have very different mental health needs; many mental health issues of female prisoners are linked to the survival of violence and abuse.[14] Similar gender patterns in psychiatric diagnoses have been observed across Britain, the United States of America, Canada and Australia. Women in the community have been found to be more frequently diagnosed as depressed, whereas men are more likely to be diagnosed as having an alcohol or drug problem or personality disorder. When women in the community are with personality disorder, it is most likely to be a diagnosis of histrionic or dependent personality disorder, whereas for women in prison it is generally antisocial personality disorder.[15] In her study of women in Oregon's prison system, Birecree found one-quarter of the women studied had a diagnosis of antisocial personality disorder.[16] In the past, women in prison were found to have lower rates of psychotic disorders than those in the community and to have higher rates of substance use, depressive disorders, personality disorder and post-traumatic stress disorder.[17] However, there is an increase in recent years of women with schizophrenia and other psychotic disorders in the prison system. Often these women are incarcerated in crisis support units.

Since the deinstitutionalisation of mental health services, an increasing number of women with schizophrenia are in prison. Previously, women with schizophrenia were not as evident in the prison system, as they were the main client group of psychiatric hospitals and community mental health services. This situation has now changed due to the decline in mental health services available. The stress of incarceration and the lack of appropriate mental health care and support mean that the women are increasingly likely to become psychotic and to be placed in high security. It is not uncommon for women with schizophrenia to be transferred to a crisis support unit because they are deemed 'difficult to manage'. The further trauma and abuse experienced by these women has disastrous effects on their mental health, and places them at risk of abuse from other prisoners and prison staff.

Women in prison have been found to have high rates of depressive disorders when compared with women in the community.[18] Women on remand are particularly prone to depression, with some women remaining on remand for up to two years. These women experience deterioration in both their physical and mental health during this time.[19]

A strong association has been found between a diagnosis of personality disorder and a reported history of childhood sexual abuse.[20] An Australian study described women with personality disorder as the '...most neglected women in receiving care and treatment in the mental health system'.[21] Women diagnosed as having a personality disorder end up in the court system due to a lack of adequate services provided by mental health services in the community.

There is a lack of reliable information on the number of women prisoners with drug and alcohol addiction. It has been estimated that as many as 80 per cent of all women prisoners have a history of drug addiction.[22] The high rate of prescription drugs used by women prisoners is concerning. Studies in prisons and in the community have found that when men and women present with similar symptoms of anxiety and depression, women are far more likely than men to be prescribed tranquillisers.[23] As discussed in Chapter 13, treatment of mental health issues is often complicated by self-medication with alcohol and other drugs. In the short term, alcohol and other drugs have been found to alleviate symptoms of chronic anxiety, restlessness, insomnia and nightmares. However, repeated and excessive use can lead to dependency and exacerbation of the initial presenting symptoms. Women in prison who are denied access to alcohol and other drugs may suffer the effects of substance withdrawal as well as resurgence of the underlying symptoms. It is important that detoxification is properly conducted under medical supervision and addresses underlying issues that led to the substance abuse, rather than treating it in isolation.[24] Checks for illegal drugs have a major impact on the entire prison system whether women are using drugs or not. This includes strip searches, random urine checks and limits on personal possessions.

Self-harm and attempted suicide are regarded as a feature of women's lives in prison. Unofficial reports of self-harm and attempted suicide are high.[25] Alder identified self-harm by incarcerated women as an attempt to regain internal control and power within an institution that has removed this from them. Self-harm was viewed as a response to the feelings of anger, hostility and impotence that can arise from incarceration.[26] Other contributing factors include general overcrowding and poor conditions, lack of contact with family, drug usage and drug withdrawal, violence and abuse. All of this occurs within the context of generally inadequate health, welfare and counselling services available to women prisoners.[27] The response from some officers to self-harm within the prison system is often harsh and unsympathetic. Women are punished rather than assisted. These women are often viewed as attention-seeking or endeavouring to get a hospital transfer.[28]

Social context

As mentioned in Chapter 3, a significant number of people with mental health issues are homeless or have inappropriate housing. Women in these circumstances are placed in situations where there is an increased risk of abuse. Increased mobility or no forwarding address often means that women are not eligible or able to access income security, mental health or other services in the community. These women are left to struggle to survive physically, emotionally and mentally in situations where they are increasingly disenfranchised. Attempts to self-medicate with alcohol and other drugs and behaviours arising from their circumstances, combined with a lack of support from mental health and community services, have led to an increase in the criminalisation and imprisonment of women with mental health issues. Many incarcerated women are trapped in a cycle of poverty, violence and victimisation from which it is difficult to escape. The increase in the number of women in prison on drug-related charges has been attributed to the 'war on drugs'. However, Sisters Inside, a community organisation that was set up in 1992 to advocate for improvements in the lives of women prisoners in Queensland, see this as 'a war on the most dispossessed, especially women'.[29] They also note an increase in the 'feminisation and criminalisation of poverty'.[30] Consideration of the personal and social costs of the imprisonment of women is crucial.

A significant proportion of women are homeless on admission to prison. When a woman is imprisoned, she generally loses her home, resulting in her losing custody of her children.[31] Loss of home contents, including furnishings and major appliances, is often associated with loss of housing. It has been estimated that 'over 80 per cent of young people are living in unsafe violent environments when their mother is in prison'.[32] A high proportion of children, approximately half, will end up placed in care, and some of these placements will be inappropriate.[33] These children can end up being quite isolated, and this may be exacerbated if their mother chooses not to, or is unable to, return to her local community.

Due to the high proportion of women who are mothers with sole care of dependent children, imprisonment necessarily has major adverse implications for these children and society.[34] These children experience the trauma of family breakdown due, in most instances, to the removal of the primary caregiver and often the separation of siblings. This trauma is ongoing from the time of a mother's arrest, during her imprisonment and in the immediate period following her release. Impacts will vary according to the age and developmental level of the child, gender and position in the family.[35] Young children may develop fantasies that hold them responsible for what has happened, while older children, particularly adolescent females, may have increased care responsibilities for younger siblings if they remain together. While they may appear on the outside to be strong and coping, many children experience shock and disbelief and sorrow at the loss of their mother and a sense of abandonment. They also feel confused, fearful and anxious. Often, these feelings are not communicated to others due to fear of lack of understanding, the intensity of emotions and the double stigma of having a mother who has mental health issues who is also in prison. Children whose mothers are in prison can experience difficulty concentrating and managing school work, particularly at higher levels of secondary school. This can lead to emotional and behavioural difficulties. These children have an increased risk of truanting and expulsion from school, use of alcohol and other drugs and attempted suicide or self-harm and are at risk of developing mental health issues.[36]

The maintenance of relationships with children and other significant people in a woman's life is crucial for her mental health, sense of hope and reintegration back into the community. This includes frequent visits and telephone contact.[37] However, many children have little contact with their mothers when they are in prison. Some have no contact at all. This is particularly the case for women serving long sentences. This relationship between a mother and child may be lost and not re-established when a woman is released especially with adolescent children. This can result in increased vulnerability of abuse for these young people who are often without support.

Release from prison and reconnecting with family is generally a very traumatic time. As mentioned in Chapter 11, discharge from mental health services is a time of increased risk of suicide with this also the situation of women after release from prison. As well, there is an increased risk of death as a result of unintended drug overdose or abuse from a violent partner.[38]

Many incarcerated women have been institutionalised as children, have problems with alcohol and other drug dependency and are survivors of physical and sexual abuse. It is therefore difficult to distinguish between victim and offender due to the high levels of abuse and victimisation experienced by these women. The majority of women in prison have low levels of education and work skills. The problems experienced by these women are chronic and long-standing. The higher rates in which women return to prison in comparison with males suggests that women face even greater barriers to reintegration into the community.[39]

Prison environment

Mental health services in the community aim to provide services in the least restrictive environment. However, mental health services in a prison environment are provided in the *most* restrictive environment. Sisters Inside argue that the provision of mental health services in prisons is problematic. They assert that

> The reflex of corrections to develop mental health services in prisons is only serving to exacerbate the trend to increasingly criminalise women with mental and cognitive disabilities. Developing such services in prisons at a time when they are increasingly non-existent in the community is resulting in more women receiving sentences because there will be a presumption that there is an ability to access services in prison that are not available in community settings. Prisons are not and cannot be treatment centres.[40]

This also applies to the development of therapeutic communities in prisons to address high levels of dependency on alcohol and other drugs among women prisoners. The development of these services in prisons is occurring alongside the reduction of alcohol and other drug services in the community. The ability to create a therapeutic community in a prison environment is highly dubious. Yet of most concern is the increased likelihood that women will be given a custodial sentence due to the location of services available.

The prison environment is often not conducive to positive mother and child interaction. Strip searches of women prisoners, and in some states their visitors, regularly occur; women tell family and friends not to visit them as they do not want them to suffer the humiliation of stripping. Often, mothers do not have the opportunity to say goodbye to children or explain what has happened and reasons why they are in prison and not there to care for them. Time-limited prison visits in communal areas or with staff present are not conducive to discussing private information and dealing with intense emotions.

Women prisoners have complained of being treated like children, and this is reinforced by prison officers calling them 'girls'. A woman's experience of prison is 'closely related to submissive behaviours towards prison officers and dismissive behaviours in response'.[41]

The practice of strip searching in prison is further victimisation and assault for women who are survivors of sexual abuse and violence.[42] In Queensland 89 per cent of women prisoners have been sexually abused.[43] Strip searching has been described as 'an unjustified assault on women prisoners by the state and thus breaching their human rights'.[44] As mentioned earlier in Chapter 3, there is also a high incidence of sexual assault found among women who use mental health services in the community. The practice of placing women in isolation removes all privacy, as women can be viewed at all times by both male and female prison officers, including when they are going to the toilet and having a shower. If a woman is already experiencing paranoia, the use of isolation could have disastrous effects on her mental health. The use of isolation as a punishment for women who have harmed themselves also has devastating psychological effects and reinforces feelings of low self-worth and poor self-esteem.

Often women who are considered at risk of harm to self or others are classified as maximum security prisoners and are moved to crisis support units in male prisons or to prison hospitals. Most of these women are with mental health issues; Aboriginal women prisoners are disproportionately classified as maximum security.[45] It has been asserted that a prison process that 'converts "disadvantage" or "needs" into "risk" only penalises women for their disadvantage'.[46] In crisis support units, women experience increased isolation; with predominantly male prison officers in a male prison environment. Here women are at increased risk of sexual harassment and rape by both prisoners and staff. This is particularly disturbing when considering that in Queensland seventeen-year-old female adolescents may be placed in crisis support units in male prisons. Sexual assault and rape is often not reported, as women fear a more punitive response and increased isolation.[47]

Women also complain of more limited access to facilities in male prisons.[48] Prison industries are mostly stereotypical 'female' occupations including sewing, word processing and pottery. However, government and private businesses are increasingly seeing opportunities for a cheap labour source. Women have complained of the exploitative practices of poor pay and work conditions and no recourse to complain without being punished.[49]

There is a lack of exercise and active recreation for women prisoners, particularly in comparison with that provided for male prisoners. Restrictions placed on female use of facilities that males have access to at all other times is unjust.[50] Women with poor self-esteem, and those who lack sporting skills and abilities, may be reluctant to try new skills for fear of ridicule or embarrassment. The provision of fewer programs for women has been attributed to their low numbers compared with male prisoners. However, this is more to do with the fact that the prison systems in Australia, the United States of America and Britain were 'developed by males for males'.[51] The position of male privilege, and its protection, is a central feature of the criminal justice system.[52]

The over-prescribing of prescription drugs to women prisoners is an issue of concern in the same way that it is for women who use mental health services in the community. Medication is used as a means of control and restraint, to alleviate symptoms of withdrawal from alcohol and other drugs, to alleviate anxiety and for sleep disturbance. This is particularly concerning given the high number of deaths post-release from drug overdoses.[53]

Language problems, deportation status and culture shock make the imprisonment of women from culturally and linguistically diverse backgrounds particularly difficult.[54] Cultural differences and a lack of family support increase levels of stress and vulnerability to mental health issues among these women. Women are often discriminated against if they do not follow Christian beliefs, with little if any respect of non-Christian ceremonies and practices. Diet may be guided according to beliefs and culture. However, food provided in prisons is predominantly Western.

Program development and service delivery

Alternatives to litigation need to be considered at the time or arrest. Mental health and community services must be considered as first options for women with mental health issues. Early detection is important, with education provided to police so that they can refer appropriately for mental health assistance. For those who are convicted, alternatives to prison need to be creatively explored at the time of sentencing. Many of the women currently in prisons do not need to be there for reasons of public protection. Service provision in the community for women with personality disorder, particularly antisocial personality disorder, needs to improve so that women diagnosed as such do not continue to be over-represented in the prison system. Increased mental health support is required in the community for people with mental health issues to prevent prisons becoming the new psychiatric institutions. It is clear that the supportive interventions required for recovery from mental health issues cannot be provided in a prison system. Recovery-focused practices require a positive therapeutic environment located in the community.

The most successful interventions for women with personality disorder are those that are affirming and encouraging with minimal use of aversion or punishment.[55] Ongoing relationships are important when working with women with personality disorder to enable the development of a trusting relationship.[56] The importance of this relationship is stressed in Derk's study in the Netherlands.[57] In a review of eight prison psychiatric hospitals, including both males and females, a number of variations in ideology, security and approach to treatment were found. However, the one thing that remained constant across all settings was the importance of the development of relationships. Derks concluded, 'all of the hospitals have the same starting point: success or failure of treatment depends on the ability of the therapeutic staff to assist a patient in building a human relationship both with professionals and non-professionals'.[58] While staff in forensic hospitals endeavour to provide a therapeutic environment in secure settings, women are returned to the same prison environment that led to the hospital transfer in the first place. Clearly a prison environment is not suitable for effective care of women with personality disorder.

Advocacy for justice for young people and education for a shift from punitive responses is required, with an emphasis on mental health promotion and prevention. This includes women with pre-existing mental health issues with or without alcohol and other drug problems, those vulnerable to developing mental health issues and women survivors of sexual abuse. Social workers can encourage and support women to complain to the Human Rights and Equal Opportunity Commission and the Anti-Discrimination Commission about human rights violations. However, it is important that the safety of women prisoners is not further jeopardised by such actions. Workers must be mindful of the personal consequences of information sought from and disclosed by women prisoners.

Mental health services are required for women who need them in prison. However, women must not be incarcerated because adequate mental health services, housing, alcohol and other drug services and other necessary supports are not available in the community. Given all of the issues faced by women prisoners Negy observes that '...incarceration would appear to require a level of adaptability that only a person with extraordinary personal and interpersonal skills would possess'.[59] Women with a wider and more flexible range of coping skills have been found to cope more readily with imprisonment. Recovery from mental health issues and management strategies to avoid relapse are a high priority yet difficult to achieve in prison.

In prison, the emphasis is on containment rather than rehabilitation. Where health services are provided, the correctional environment of the prison system impacts upon the development and delivery of such services. Short sentences, security and changes in security levels for individual women and the daily prison routine may reduce the effectiveness of service delivery. The prison day is short, with most women locked in their cells for 12 hours each night. During the day, the women are required to participate in other prison programs such as industry and education. As a result, the delivery of health programs in the prison and the development of trusting working relationships with the women is difficult. Issues for continuity of care are also problematic.

For those in prison, the practice of routinely strip searching women and family needs to be stopped. The maintenance of a reasonable quality of life and hope are crucial. Attention to issues of safety and privacy is particularly important due to the high levels of past abuse many of these women have suffered, combined with their current mental and emotional state. The possible risk of further abuse, harassment or intimidation needs to be minimised. Strategies other than medication are necessary to address the additional stress women experience in prison.

Due to the high levels of alcohol and other drug problems and sexual abuse among women in prison, strong links need to be developed with specialist services in these areas. It is difficult to address past sexual abuse in prison as it is opening up wounds and then leaving the woman to manage on her own in the prison environment. This must be handled sensitively, with adequate emotional support provided.[60] Unfortunately, the privatisation of prisons has seen a reduction in such services and a lack of contractual arrangements with specialist service providers in these areas. Funding limitations and decisions surrounding who pays for services complicates this. This is also the situation where governments have retained management of prisons. Plans for the provision of alcohol and other drug services in prisons should in no way be a substitute for services in the community.

Staffing needs to be addressed, with adequate numbers of female prison staff. Specific training is required for male and female staff to sensitise them to issues faced by women prisoners with mental health issues, as well as specific skills and knowledge of physical and/ or intellectual disability and sensory impairment.

The re-establishment of a woman in the community, with adequate leave programs, is important to assist her transition post-release. Due to the high rates of homelessness of women before imprisonment, it is crucial that accommodation needs of these women are addressed when leaving prison. As mentioned in Chapter 3, accommodation needs to be proper, secure, safe housing, not boarding houses.[61] Carnaby observed, 'The most basic requirement for a satisfactory starting point in cementing or re-establishing bonds with children is safe and secure accommodation.'[62] The importance of ensuring that adequate housing and community supports are available for women on release from prison is crucial for their resettlement back into the community. A lack of adequate housing can result in women being unable to regain custody of their children.

Sisters Inside is an example of women working alongside each other to expose and redress human rights violations committed against women and their families in the prison system and to address the gaps in services available to them.[63] The organisational structure is consistent with recovery principles of consumer leadership. The committee of management comprises women who have been in prison, those currently incarcerated and other interested women in the community.

Conclusion

The increasing number of women prisoners with mental health issues in recent years requires the urgent attention of government and policy makers. The connections between poverty, violence, victimisation and recidivism need to be carefully considered so that wherever possible non-custodial solutions can be applied. This is particularly important considering the social and emotional costs of incarcerating women, who in the main have committed non-violent crimes and are the sole carers of dependent children. The over-representation in prisons of women with mental health issues highlights the lack of appropriate services in the community. Women-sensitive practices are required that demonstrate respect and compassion while promoting recovery and the maintenance of connections with significant people in the woman's life, particularly children. Advocacy is required for pathways that divert women with mental health issues away from the criminal justice system and for the development of appropriate service for these women within the community.

Reflection

What are the main issues faced by women prisoners?

What additional problems do women with mental health issues face within the prison system?

What are the main mental health issues of women prisoners?

What interventions are best suited to improving the lives of women with mental health issues who are in contact with the criminal justice system?

How can social workers prevent women with mental health issues from entering the criminal justice system?

15

Disaster Planning

Social work is uniquely placed in disaster and emergency planning due to a holistic focus on the person in their environment and an ability to respond to complex needs, particularly of those worse affected in disaster situations. This ability to respond to complex needs 'whatever the presenting issue, is something almost unique to social work'.[1] It is argued in this chapter that social workers have a key role to play in all stages of disaster and emergency planning and this role changes according to community needs at the time. This social work role is particularly important given that all disasters have the greatest impact on the most vulnerable and marginalised members of the community, including those with mental health issues.[2] Effective social work interventions have the potential to minimise the impacts of natural hazards, and facilitate well coordinated, timely and innovative relief and reconstruction efforts.

The focus of this chapter is on disaster planning for natural hazards. However, this planning is also relevant for management of emergencies resulting from terrorism, warfare and other acts of human destruction. A discussion of natural hazards and disaster vulnerability is followed by policy considerations for disaster and emergency planning in the local and international context. This is followed by a case study of the bushfire disaster experience in the state of Victoria on Black Saturday, 7 February 2009. The roles of social workers during different stages of disaster planning are highlighted.

Natural hazards and disaster vulnerability

Hazards are inevitable, disasters are not. Worldwide natural hazards are part of life; bushfires are part of the Australian landscape. It is likely that these hazards will increase in number and intensity if scientific predictions of more severe instances in the future are correct. Natural hazards occur in all states and territories in Australia. Tropical cyclones and floods are more prominent in the northern states of Queensland and the Northern Territory; the southern states and Australian Capital Territory are more prone to bushfire. In recent years, there has been an increase in the frequency and intensity of natural disasters in all states and territories in Australia, particularly floods and bushfires. Scientific research indicates that more severe natural disasters are likely in the future, with more extreme weather and large-scale single events such as severe cyclones, storms and floods.

A disaster, or actualised hazard, is an emergency that does not match the society's resources to recover. Thus disaster risk is created by the interaction of hazard and vulnerability.

Vulnerability is determined by physical, political, economic, social, cultural, environmental, spiritual, psychological and attitudinal factors. While natural hazards can occur anywhere, it is the least developed countries that are generally most affected, due to higher levels of vulnerability. Differences in context mean that it is not possible to generalise between disasters, as the impacts are profoundly discriminatory.[3] Diverse groups have varied levels of vulnerability in disaster situations. The level and nature of the impact is influenced by pre-existing social structures and social conditions and how gender is configured therein. While men and women experience vulnerabilities, impacts on women are higher due to unequal economic and social status and roles in child bearing and care giving in the home.[4] Systemic discrimination increases vulnerability to poverty and social exclusion.[5] Social vulnerability mapping identifies population groups at greatest risk in a disaster.

Pre-existing resources are a reliable indicator of vulnerability or resilience. The resources essential for survival and recovery are unevenly distributed within all societies, resulting in different impacts from equally hazardous situations; the most marginalised members are amongst the hardest hit. These are female- and adolescent-headed households, children, older people, those with mental health issues and disabilities, and Indigenous people.[6] Members of these groups have increased vulnerability to poverty and social exclusion. Female-headed households are over-represented amongst the most economically and socially disadvantaged households in Australia.[7] Those with mental health issues and disabilities also experience significant poverty. Recent arrivals, institutionalised populations and those who are homeless are particularly vulnerable in disaster situations. These are also people at greatest risk of social exclusion.[8] Special consideration is required for pregnant women and women with infants and uterine prolapse, as well as those with urinary incontinence, HIV/AIDS and trans-gendered people.[9] Reports on vulnerable populations and fatalities in past bushfires in Australia identify older people as a particularly vulnerable group and those with pre-existing impairments and difficulties.[10]

Disaster reduction policies

The aim of disaster reduction policies worldwide is twofold: to reduce levels of risk while ensuring that vulnerability to hazards is not increased as a result of development and growth activities. For instance, any Australian bushfire policy must be cognisant of the inherent risks of living on a dry continent prone to extreme and unpredictable weather that can and will precipitate bushfire hazards. These risks are increased when housing development occurs on the urban bush land fringe, which is the preferred location for some people, regardless of the threat of bushfires. The period immediately following a disaster provides opportunities for change as regulators endeavour to improve disaster planning for the future.

Australia's bushfire policies have been debated following every bushfire; Black Saturday was no exception. Shifts in policy development and implementation have been slow and debates have been polarised between environmentalists wanting to protect the natural landscape and those advocating bushfire land management approaches. Increasingly, ecologists and foresters have debated management of the landscape and in particular the practice of controlled burning; some residents have been concerned about degradation of the natural landscape and health effects of smoke inhalation from fires. This is also at a time of increasing worldwide concern for the environment and calls to reduce deforestation and protect biodiversity.

The period immediately before Black Saturday witnessed a reduction of controlled burning in Victoria alongside an increase in national parks and reserves. This was in response to environmental concerns about broad acreage burn-offs, the economic costs of this resource intensive activity, planning difficulties due to implementation requiring ideal weather conditions, and management concerns particularly in mountainous areas. Large areas of Victoria are too wet and damp during the winter months for prescribed burning. A more strategic approach was developed, focused on controlled burning of ridge tops or land adjoining valuable community assets and infrastructure rather than broad acreage clearing. Research on the effectiveness of controlled broad acreage burning has found that this approach is not effective in controlling fire fronts in extreme weather conditions, primarily due to the speed of the fires.[11]

In 2003, the Council of Australian Governments endorsed in principle the adoption of a range of new measures for disaster mitigation and preparedness representing a significant policy shift from one previously focused on disaster response. Each state and territory of Australia has a welfare disaster plan where the lead agency is the human services department or equivalent. State emergency recovery arrangements govern the manner in which recovery is handled at the state, regional and local levels. In an endeavour to be able to respond to major emergencies, the Victorian government developed an emergency management structure integrating health and human services. A priority of the Department of Human Services Emergency Management Strategic Plan 2005–2007 was to develop the capacity to improve state emergency management in association with the whole-of-government emergency management and counter terrorism arrangements in preparation for the Melbourne Commonwealth Games in March 2006.[12]

Policy mapping, like social vulnerability mapping, can assist in identifying potential problem areas and policy responses. Disaster policy mapping in Australia highlights a focus on physical aspects of rebuilding and environment protection. The emergency management approach adopted by all levels of government in Australia involves the four interdependent stages of preparing/disaster mitigation, preventing, responding and reconstruction. Disaster mitigation has been identified as a key component. The focus is on a national process for risk assessment and evidence-based cost-effective disaster mitigation with little consideration of vulnerable population groups.

International context of disaster planning

The model of disaster recovery adopted in Australia is similar to the four-stage international disaster planning model used by the World Bank and the United Nations.[13] These four stages include

Stage 1: preparedness

Stage 2: relief

Stage 3: recovery (and)

Stage 4: reconstruction.

Preparedness (prevention/mitigation)

A main role of social workers in disaster preparation is the identification of vulnerable groups and the development of capabilities and strategies to lessen the impact of hazards on them. Disaster management worldwide primarily deals with scientific and technological aspects of disaster planning.[14] Technical components focus on the ability to resist or minimise the impact of the disaster, particularly on infrastructure. Levels of vulnerability to disaster and perceptions of risk are main issues for disaster preparation and reduction.[15] The strategic components of disaster reduction are

1. understanding the nature of hazards
2. identifying vulnerabilities and capacities
3. assessing and analysing disaster risk.[16]

The risk of a disaster can be minimised by developing an increased understanding of the nature of hazards by studying past and present experiences of hazards from a local perspective within a global context. While it is not possible to generalise from one disaster to another, trends emerge in patterns of vulnerabilities and capacities to respond.[17] Vulnerabilities and capacities are embedded in the physical, political, cultural, economic, environmental and spiritual context. A readily available disaster risk assessment and analysis system, that includes detailed and accurate information on both hazard and vulnerability, is a prerequisite for a successful disaster management strategy.[18] Ongoing risk assessment assists in minimising impacts and hastening recovery by developing reliance upon individual capabilities and institutional and community capacities. Social work tools such as eco-maps are useful for mapping social vulnerability risks in a region and can provide extremely useful baseline data for disaster planning.

Regardless of the magnitude of a disaster, there is a general failure worldwide to collect data and information for recovery planning that includes data on the diverse groups and subgroups within the community.[19] Rao and Kelleher recommend collecting gender-disaggregated data on policy reform, advocacy, capacity building, analytic frameworks, program development and monitoring systems to assist in strategic planning. Without such data to inform disaster recovery, efforts and outcomes will be inequitable.[20] This can result in inappropriate interventions affecting livelihood, education and the social structure of the community that often changes following a disaster. A disaster has the potential to significantly alter the gender make-up of a community, resulting in further social impacts. Hurricane Mitch in the United States saw the number of female-headed households increase twofold in some of the hardest-hit areas with a substantial increase in male migration.[21] Reliable baseline gender-disaggregated data is required to develop relief efforts that assist women and men equally, as well as addressing the needs of less powerful or more vulnerable members of the community. Data for assessing community capacities and vulnerabilities includes

community: history, demographic trends, social networks, household structure, local power structures, local community languages, control over key economic assets;

employment: work patterns and skills, working conditions for men and women in major industries and occupations, migrant workers and sole providers, poverty and unemployment rates, networks, associations and cooperatives, division of labour;

disaster-vulnerable groups: people with mental health issues and other disabilities, vulnerable home workers, pregnant women, female-headed households, Indigenous and older people; community vulnerability profile information is often best provided by those working with these groups.[22]

Relief

Social workers play an important role in crisis intervention during relief efforts in the coordination of practical assistance with housing, finances, clothes and other forms of material aid. This coordination is particularly important in the early stages to meet people's basic needs and provide assistance to locate missing persons. Relief efforts have invariably been impeded by delayed responses in the provision of material resources. This is primarily due to the complex community organisation required.[23] The result is local communities often left frustrated and in dire need of help while the organisation of the relief effort is mounted.

Social workers are mindful of the possibility of second-order vulnerabilities and are skilled in developing preventative strategies and approaches to mitigate these. In disaster rescue operations, personnel are generally men, making women and girls particularly vulnerable to sexual abuse, as witnessed in the case of the 2004 Bangladesh floods and cyclone. Trans-gendered people can also experience abuse and discrimination in relief efforts.[24] Increased sexual abuse and physical violence has been evident in international disaster relief efforts in camps and emergency shelters that are overcrowded and lack privacy.[25] Those most vulnerable to sexual abuse in shelters are those experiencing multiple disadvantages, often struggling before the disaster. This was the case in Sri Lanka following the 2004 tsunami, where more wealthy women were able to afford private arrangements or stay with relatives, while those who were poor or marginalised remained in relief camps.

An increase in unpaid care work by women following a disaster can disadvantage them financially due to lost income as well as socially, as it is afforded lower status than paid work and takes time away from rebuilding activities for female-headed households.[26] The focus of men's activities generally occurs outside the family and can remove them from their communities. This includes seeking additional employment, temporary or permanent relocation and in some instances leaving the family.[27] Disaster preparedness and relief is also a responsibility of industries in disaster-prone areas. Income support for workers who have been impacted by a disaster can enhance morale and promote longer-term recovery. Flexible work options, counselling, on-site childcare, respite care for caregivers and other services provided by employers can assist workers and their families to recover after a disaster.

In disaster relief efforts worldwide, payments to female household heads is the preferred means of income distribution; research on post-disaster recovery indicates that payment to males is more likely to result in spending on alcohol and gambling.[28]

Recovery

According to Emergency Management Australia, 'Recovery activities are defined as those assisting persons and communities affected by emergencies to return to a proper and effective level of functioning.'[29] Recovery is considered in terms of resilience as well as personal growth and transformation; spirituality is also recognised as an important aspect of recovery for many people. In their study of survivors of the 1999 Taiwan earthquake, Jang and LaMendola found that cultural beliefs and spirituality had a significant effect on post-traumatic growth. During recovery, social workers have a significant role to play in counselling, service brokerage, case management and professional supervision. Natural disasters have extensive psychological and social impacts. Survivors have to cope with the loss of family and friends, economic losses, a drastically changed environment and, for many, homelessness. Common distress reactions in survivors of disasters relate to the unexpectedness, scope and intensity, and impact upon the community. These symptoms of distress generally reduce over time except in situations where impacts of the disaster are ongoing, such as inadequate housing, displacement or family breakdown. Problem-focused cognitive interventions are generally regarded as more effective following a disaster than approaches designed to regulate emotional states.[30]

Gender differences have been noted in psychological distress after disaster.[31] Men have been observed to have increased levels of risky behaviours, outward aggression, alcohol consumption and gambling. This is in contrast to women, who are more likely to internalise their distress and suffer symptoms of anxiety and depression, sleep disturbance and migraines.[32] There is also an increase in relationship violence and child abuse following disasters. In the aftermath of the 2010 Canterbury earthquake in New Zealand, there was a reported 53 per cent increase in domestic violence call-outs. Perceptions of the impact of disasters can also vary according to gender. Again, women tend to focus on more psychological aspects such as fear and uncertainty, while men focus more on economic factors. Gender differences in coping were observed in a study of post-disaster distress among survivors of the 1995 Dinar, Turkey, earthquake.[33] Women reported higher levels of distress than men, different coping styles and more negative life events following the disaster. A recommendation of this study was to offer women coping strategies and preparedness skills to increase their sense of control and agency. It was also considered important to provide mental health outreach services for women to have opportunities to process their memories of events. It is possible, however, that men's socialisation and often more negative coping styles are also indicators of their need for mental health outreach services. A study of relief efforts in Sri Lanka after the 2004 tsunami that killed over 32,000 people and displaced over 860,000 people found that psychological services were more likely to bypass men and boys due to the social expectation of 'men and boys to be strong and cope with the physical and mental stresses and trauma'.[34] The provision of counselling in psychological recovery following Hurricane Mitch in the United States has been criticised for a lack of attention to gender and vulnerable groups.[35]

Reconstruction

Community development, capacity building and longer-term program management are important social work activities during reconstruction, alongside program evaluation, research and policy development to improve future disaster planning. Counselling and case management are particularly important during this stage for those with multiple and second-order vulnerabilities. The social work role will change according to local contextual needs. Jang and LaMendola argue that 'Respect for cultural differences may require that social workers primarily act as community organizers or developers, not clinicians, focusing on coordination and development of material resources.'[36]

A highly regulated approach, with minimal local community consultation and participation, is commonplace in disaster management worldwide.[37] Consultation with local populations and with women in particular is generally limited. This is mainly attributed to the size of the task and sense of urgency to rebuild communities as quickly as possible. Changes have been made mostly following complaints from community members.

National, state and local priorities often differ. Government plans for rebuilding primarily focus on public infrastructure and efforts that are not necessarily in accordance with rebuilding priorities of members of the local community, who tend to prioritise housing. Investment strategies that focus on physical aspects of reconstruction are likely to generate employment for men, while those focused on social reconstruction programs are likely to employ more women in paid or unpaid capacities. Investment is required in recovery projects in the areas of education, health, social and human services.[38]

Long-term economic recovery requires that women and men have access to reconstruction jobs, investment funds and income-generating projects; careful monitoring of employment creation schemes is required. Following Hurricane Mitch, national government was criticised by local government and non-government organisations for an over-emphasis on the reconstruction plans and lack of support for projects for marginalised groups in the community such as low-income female-headed households.[39]

Men and women have different priorities during reconstruction and are generally engaged in diverse activities. However, gender roles and responsibilities can change significantly during and after a disaster and can result in positive social change. Collaborative on-the-ground efforts involving men and women performing non-traditional tasks create opportunities for changing gender roles. These new relationships can be translated into policies supporting gender-sensitive projects at local, state and national levels for reconstruction planning and implementation. Aspects of some economic and social reconstruction projects have transformed power relationships in households by facilitating the empowerment of women.[40] Opportunities for growth and change, however, are often overlooked in the disaster planning literature, the tendency being to focus more so on resilience.[41]

The following case study of the Black Saturday bushfires highlights vulnerable populations identified by conducting a thematic analysis of the transcripts of the Victorian Bushfires Royal Commission Hearings. Community profile information from the Australian Bureau of Statistics (ABS) for the Murrindindi Shire, that includes the townships of Marysville and Kinglake, is presented in accordance with the recommendations for data collection by the World Bank to assist in planning for disaster-vulnerable groups. Important roles of social workers are highlighted at each stage of the disaster management process.

Black Saturday bushfires

On 7 February 2009, severe bushfires directly impacted 51 townships in the Australian state of Victoria, with a loss of life of 173 people and 2,900 homes destroyed as well as many schools, kindergartens, businesses and community facilities. This was the hottest day on record for Melbourne, with temperatures recorded at 46.4 degrees Celsius and strong northerly winds fuelling the flames at 100 kilometres per hour. The fires have been described as the most extreme in Australia's history and the worst peacetime disaster. The weather conditions were unprecedented in terms of sustained high temperatures and wind speeds, low humidity, bushfires in other regions and years of drought. Emergency services and the systems in place had no experience with a fire of such magnitude as that on Black Saturday.

Bushfires have ravaged the Australian landscape for millions of years before human habitation and, for many thousands of years, Aborigines used fire for land and resource management. Australia's biodiversity has been directly influenced by bushfire survival; this is particularly evident in the prevalence of the eucalypt forest species across the Australian landscape. Loss of life and property is not new, with the past century witnessing numerous fires. These include the 1939 Black Friday bushfires in eastern Australia killing 71 people, the Tasmanian fires in 1967 with 62 fatalities and the Ash Wednesday fires in South Australia and Victoria in 1983 with 71 lives lost. The 2002–2003 Australian Capital Territory and Victorian fires saw four people lose their lives, with over 500 homes destroyed. The pattern of bushfires is the same each year – a hot dry summer with extreme temperatures and gusting winds. Many Australians have built in bushfire-prone areas due to an appreciation of the bush and rustic lifestyle as well as affordability offered on the bushland fringe of major cities. The townships of Marysville, Kinglake and Strathewen, on the bushland fringe of the Melbourne metropolitan area were worst hit by the Black Saturday fires.

Preparedness

The Emergency Management Australia (EMA) approach to disaster preparedness focuses on

plans and arrangements put in place before a disaster occurs;
risk assessment to determine likelihood and severity of emergency event;

business continuity for the continuation of essential business services; and disaster mitigation to address the potential impacts of an emergency.[42]

Risk assessment is to determine risk management priorities according to the likelihood of a hazardous event and its severity. It is targeted at people involved in emergency management looking at potential hazard risks, rather than risks particular to vulnerable populations in disaster planning.[43]

National emergency planning prior to Black Saturday identified 'special needs' groups whose needs may not be met by general evacuation planning stipulating that 'planning must take the social implications of special needs groups into account'.[44] Groups identified included people with disabilities, people from non-English speaking backgrounds, children and young people. Problems with communication, mobility and culture were identified as critical aspects of planning. The welfare of pets and other animals was also identified under planning for special needs.

Reports on vulnerable populations in past bushfires in Australia identify older people as a particularly vulnerable group and those with pre-existing impairments and difficulties.[45] Of the 173 people who died on Black Saturday, 113 were in houses. It is estimated that in over one-third of those houses people probably did not intend to stay and fight the fire, or if they did they had no capacity to protect themselves. These were people who were 'over 75 years of age; people with disabilities; children, and in some cases women with a number of children; and also visitors to houses that weren't their own who were caught there'.[46] On Day 27 of the Victorian Bushfire Royal Commission, Commissioner Pascoe observed, 'I think it would appear that, despite some recent acknowledgement of community diversity and vulnerable groups, the policy is based on a conception of capable, rational adults facing a bushfire.'[47]

Relief

The Victorian bushfire response was managed by the Department of Sustainability and Environment and the Country Fire Authority (CFA) co-located at the Melbourne Incident and Emergency Control Centre with reliance upon divisional coordination. These two agencies were co-located centrally as well as in regional and local areas. However, they maintained separate functions, with each agency having its own fire mapping system and website. The Victorian Bushfire Royal Commissioners heard that, according to the Emergency Management Manual Victoria, it was the responsibility of Victoria Police to issue fire warnings. However, in practice, Victoria police leave it to the fire agencies as experts to issue and deliver warnings to the public. Standard emergency warning systems communicated by the Australian Broadcasting Corporation are used throughout Australia. The Royal Commissioners heard of problems experienced because these messages were out of date, verbose and used language that was difficult to interpret.[48]

A general practitioner from Marysville told the Commissioners that he tried to raise the alarm one and a half hours before the fires hit. He reported speaking with officers from the Department of Sustainability who did not seem to be particularly concerned. Two hours earlier, after observing smoke in the area, he had telephoned the Victorian Bushfire Information line. After waiting for 20 minutes to have his call attended to, he spoke to an operator who had to look up the location of Marysville and then told him that there was a fire at the old Murrindindi Mill and also provided information about a local bridge. There was no further information provided about the fires, nor was there any pre-recorded message with bushfire updates while he was waiting for the operator to take his call.[49] He was in the minority of those whose calls were answered on Black Saturday. Figures presented to the Royal Commission from Telstra, the national telecommunications authority responsible for answering emergency calls, indicated that more than 70 per cent of calls (7,824) were abandoned.[50]

Communication was continually raised as an issue; many people in the fire zones were totally isolated after losing power supplies, telephone and computer connections.[51] This was also a problem for staff at local incident control centres (ICC) who had difficulty communicating alerts to ICCs responsible for fires in their area. During the Royal Commission Hearings, emergency organisations, particularly the CFA, were highly praised for their tireless and heroic efforts, yet at the same time criticism was made of bureaucratic approaches with rules and regulations that were not responsive to local needs.[52] An ICC staff member in Kangaroo Ground, a neighbouring town to Kinglake and Strathewen, raised concerns about the fire in Kilmore entering the area. Distribution was refused by officers in charge as the centre did not have jurisdiction. The ICC officer informed the Commissioners, 'It was a pretty constant response that it was not our area and it was not appropriate to put out an awareness message.'[53] Eventually, an alert was put out later in the day after a failure to get through to the Kilmore ICC responsible for fire warnings in the area. A consistent theme throughout the Commission hearings and media reporting was people not leaving early as intended due to not receiving warnings in a timely manner.

A property owner whose house was under threat from the fire reported to the Commission how relieved he was early the next morning to see a CFA fire truck approaching his property only to find out that it was an interstate fire relief crew that was lost, without a map or briefing instructions. The fire chief is reported by this local resident as commenting that 'the first casualty in this fire has been communication'.[54] Relief efforts to get food, water and fuel into the fire-affected areas were slow; a CFA captain reported to the Bushfire Royal Commission,

I had difficulty understanding why we couldn't get assistance on the Saturday but it was totally beyond my comprehension why no-one turned up on the (Sunday)…no-one came to help us.[55]

Recovery

The Victorian Bushfire Appeal fund was established on 8 February 2009 by the Victorian government in partnership with the Commonwealth government and Australian Red Cross. In just over two months, $389 million was donated to the fund. Distribution of the funds was overseen by an independent advisory committee, with funds allocated to individual and community recovery projects.

On 10 February 2009, then Premier of Victoria John Brumby announced the establishment of the Victorian Bushfire Reconstruction and Recovery Authority (VBRRA) with 'responsibility for coordinating activities of all local, state and commonwealth government agencies and the many community organisations involved aimed at helping communities to recover and rebuild'.[56] A key goal of the VBRRA was to ensure active community consultation and participation, providing people affected by the bushfires with real choices.

The State Emergency Recovery Plan established the management arrangements of the various government and non-government agencies involved; the Victorian Department of Human Services (DHS) was appointed as the coordinating agency for recovery. The recovery efforts coordinated by DHS, following Black Saturday focused on

social, health and community effects
economic effects
effects on the built environment.[57]

Social workers employed by DHS played a key role in relief and recovery efforts following the Black Saturday bushfires.[58] They were joined by social workers in local agencies and private practice working for the Victorian Bushfire Case Management Service, who provided support and assistance with accessing a range of assistance, including accommodation, financial, health, counselling, education, employment and legal advice.[59] Community centres were established in the fire-affected areas to provide personal, psychological, emotional and financial assistance. Telephone counselling services were provided to those affected by the bushfires, as well as targeted mental health services for those with pre-existing mental health issues by workers with expertise in mental health and loss trauma and grief. Social workers were seconded from the Department of Defence to provide counselling and supervision services due to their expertise in post-traumatic stress.

On 23 February 2009, details of the Commonwealth's Bushfire Mental Health Response package were announced. This provided an extension of funding, under the Medicare (Better Access) program, for the delivery of focused psychological strategies (FPS) to those affected by the bushfires. Accredited mental health social workers registered with Medicare provided FPS alongside psychologists and other eligible providers. Accredited mental health social workers also provided services as critical incident counsellors as well as delivering a train the trainer program to local community organisations on skills for psychological recovery.[60] These programs are well developed. However, they do not address broader social contextual issues included in social work interventions. Social workers must look at ways of not only taking up opportunities to provide FPS but also to provide comprehensive social work responses. These will vary according to a person's stage of recovery; many people reported that it was 12 months on that they really felt a need for counselling services. It is important that services are provided in the long-term acknowledging people's changing needs throughout disaster relief and reconstruction efforts.

The national income security organisation, Centrelink, a major employer of social workers, plays a lead role in disaster relief efforts both in Australia and internationally. Eighty social workers and other emergency response staff from Centrelink were deployed to assist those affected by the bushfires with emergency relief payments and ongoing access to financial entitlements. Payments were made to the person nominated on the claim form as the household head. This was not in accordance with recommendations from previous disaster planning research for payments to be made to women and has been criticised by some welfare groups.

Research findings have identified an increase in family violence after Black Saturday. The relationship between payment arrangements, financial hardship and increased family violence requires closer scrutiny.

Reconstruction

The importance of local community participation in disaster planning was mentioned throughout the Royal Commission Hearings; a fire expert commented,

> My belief is that community empowerment is the most important way we can deal with the situation, rather than having a community that is reliant totally on organizations, government departments or other instrumentalities for providing them the decisions, or making the decisions on their behalf.[61]

The Australian Bureau of Statistics Census collects most of the gender-disaggregated data recommended for data collection by the World Bank for disaster planning, especially for the identification of vulnerable groups. This is presented below for the Murrindindi Shire that includes the townships of Marysville and Kinglake for consideration in reconstruction and future disaster mitigation planning.

Community

The Shire of Murrindindi is located on the city fringe in the foothills of Melbourne and includes national parks, state forests and farming land. It is a high-risk area for bushfires over the summer months. Access is mostly by private vehicles on winding bitumen roads and dirt tracks. According to the most recent ABS data from 2006, the population of the Murrindindi shire was 13,672; this comprised 51 per cent males and 49 per cent females. The median age of the population was 37 years – slightly higher than the national average with 31 per cent of the population aged over 55 compared with the national average of 24 per cent.

Of the 3,651 families in the shire, 42 per cent were couples with children, 45 per cent were couples without children, 12 per cent were one-parent families and 1 per cent were from other family structures. Members of this largest population group of couples without children were likely to have young children by 2009. Updating this information through other sources such as the immunization registry will provide more details on this vulnerable group in a disaster. Four times as many lone-parent families were headed by women than by men. Where the parent was 34 years of age or under, all of these families had a female head (n=171).

The ancestry of the population is predominantly Anglo-Saxon, with the main groups being English, Irish and Scottish. Following Australia as the main country of birth were the United

Kingdom, New Zealand and Germany. There is a small Indigenous population comprising 54 males and 47 females. Main languages spoken at home following English were German, Italian, Dutch, Arabic and Macedonian. All of the Spanish speakers were women (n=12). All those (n=19) who spoke English 'not well or not at all' were also women. There is no ABS data on non-verbal languages such as Auslan.

The main religious groups in the shire for both males and females were Anglican, Catholic and Uniting Church. The main gender difference was for followers of Islam, with eight males and no females. Four females and no males followed Hinduism. While these numbers are small, it is important that relief and recovery services are respectful of religious differences and practices and provide an environment where people can still practise their faith. This is particularly important for coping and resilience in a disaster.

A key asset in a bushfire emergency is a vehicle as well as internet access for disaster warning updates. Sixty-two per cent of dwellings had two or more vehicles, with 34 per cent having one and 4 per cent without a vehicle. Both men and women were heavily reliant upon cars as a main means of transportation. If the Victorian bushfire policy of 'stay and defend or go' had been implemented, it is likely that many families would have evacuated women and children, with men staying to defend property, as has been the case in other disasters. This would have left many of those staying to defend properties without transport. Only just over half of the properties (54 per cent) had internet access. This was mostly dial-up rather than broadband access. It would also be useful to have further census data on mobile telephone access and use as a means of communication.

Employment
Unemployment rates for the Shire were 4.2 per cent – 1 per cent lower than the national average. Men had higher levels of employment than women, particularly in full-time employment, with women mostly working part-time. Main occupations for men were technicians and trades, labourers, machinery operators and drivers; women were mostly employed in professional, clerical, administrative, community and personal care positions. Data collected on education and skills shows men mostly qualified in engineering and related technologies: architecture, building and agriculture and environmental related studies. Women were mostly qualified in health, education, society and culture. Average weekly incomes were lower than those for Australia by approximately 20 per cent. While women were more highly qualified than men, they had lower levels of participation in paid work, particularly full-time employment, and received less pay. The average weekly gross income for men was more than twice that for women, with men having three times higher representation in the top income brackets. Only a small number of men (1.2 per cent) and women (1.5 per cent) worked from home.

Organisational networks are reflected in the main occupational groups, these being highly gendered in traditional stereotypical occupations. The division of labour in the home reveals women carrying most of the load for unpaid domestic work and unpaid assistance to a person with a disability. Men and women aged 45 to 64 years provided most assistance to those with a disability. Unpaid childcare for own child/children was fairly evenly spread across both genders, with women recording only slightly higher than men. Care of other children, however, was in the main performed by women. Women (15 per cent) recorded marginally higher than men (13 per cent) for voluntary work for an organisation or group, with the great majority of these volunteers aged over 34 years. It is interesting that men and women's voluntary work participation rates were similar, as this is traditionally seen as an area dominated by women. Closer examination reveals gender patterns and trends in volunteering, with men, particularly those employed in trades, having a strong presence as volunteers in sporting clubs.

Disaster-vulnerable groups

The ABS has developed a variable 'core activity need for assistance' to measure the number of people who because of a disability, long-term health condition (lasting six months or more) or older age require help or assistance in one of three core activities of self-care, mobility and communication. Due to the episodic nature of their condition, most people with mental health issues would not meet this definition of disability or long-term mental health condition. This is an issue that must be addressed in consultation with local mental health service providers so that these people are considered in terms of vulnerability and need for assistance. In the shire of Murrindindi, 4 per cent of the population met the ABS criteria, with slightly more women than men. Twice as many women as men requiring assistance were aged 75 and over, reflecting general population life expectancy trends. Details on the nature of the vulnerabilities and assistance required is essential for disaster planning. Media reports on the Black Saturday fires made little mention of different population groups, focusing rather on efforts to contain the fires and save community assets as well as reporting numbers of casualties.

A main consideration in the aftermath of the Black Saturday bushfires was whether or not locals should be left to decide whether to follow the CFA policy of 'stay and defend or go' or whether emergency evacuation plans should be instigated, particularly for members of disaster-vulnerable groups. In preparation for the fire season following Black Saturday, a focus was on physical and mental preparation, with an emphasis on planning for children and others who are vulnerable. Residents who planned to stay and defend their properties were strongly advised to make a bushfire survival plan that details how vulnerable people will be removed safely in bushfire situations.[62]

Conclusion

Social workers have an important role to play in disaster management due to the fact that the most vulnerable members of a community are worst hit in disaster situations. Social workers have performed important roles and functions in all stages of Black Saturday disaster planning as both public and private providers of mental health and community services. Social workers used a range of skills and approaches including direct practice, community development, community education, program management and policy development, and expertise in mental health, loss, trauma and grief, and violence and abuse. Mental health counselling services have predominantly been provided by accredited mental health social workers under the Medicare (Better Access) program for the provision of focused psychological strategies. New alliances have developed across different agencies at all levels of government, non government organisations and professional associations; including the Australian Psychological Association and the Australian Association of Social Workers for disaster planning following Black Saturday. Opportunities have arisen for social workers to engage with these new structures and organisations. These include the National Disaster Resilience Program, the National Workplan to reduce Bushfire Arson in Australia, the Bushfire Reconstruction Authority and the Victorian Bushfire Case Management Service. Social workers are called upon to embrace and create opportunities at all stages of disaster planning to build community capacity to minimise disaster impacts on the most vulnerable members of the community who are worst affected in disaster situations.

Reflection

What population groups are worst affected in disaster situations?

What are common problems to be addressed in disaster situations?

What are the main contributions of social workers at the different stages disaster planning?

What are the most effective mental health interventions for disaster recovery?

Postscript

Mental Health Social Work (2017) is the third iteration of *Mental Health Social Work* (2012) and *Mental Health Practice* (2008) I have revised this latest edition while on sabbatical at RMIT Europe in Barcelona. Dedicated time away focusing on this book has been a privilege of which I am extremely grateful. Time away from other distractions, and placed in an unfamiliar environment, has helped with the expression and shaping of the views presented in a manner that is more forthright than in the earlier editions.

When writing the first edition, *Mental Health Practice*, a decade ago, I was at pains to be diplomatic and not offend. While I am not now trying to offend, I am naming things as I see them that in some ways is more provocative and in accordance with anti-oppressive and anti-discriminatory social work theory. This is particularly so with my criticisms of current crisis services and hospital-based services in emergency departments and in-patient psychiatric units.

Having worked in paid and unpaid positions in stand-alone and general hospitals, crisis and community services, and researched and taught in this area for nearly three decades, I have observed changes for the better and for the worse. In this book I am naming these areas that are most problematic – especially for those who are suicidal – in the hope that students and workers in social work and human services, will listen and prioritise co-design in their work with consumers to bring about humane responses consistent with a recovery model and trauma-informed care. This requires innovative, creative and lateral thinking, and collaboration across a range of human services and design industries. Hopefully, if the consumer is truly the client being designed for, new and innovative spaces will be developed beyond the standard ward design with the fishbowl of workers in the middle that has been carried over from the stand-alone psychiatric hospitals. This design is not conducive to effective service delivery and especially the enactment of recovery principles. Spaces people inhabit are crucial in terms of possibilities within them. A key consideration is how these spaces are configured beyond elimination of hanging points and other potential risks and the control of difficult behaviours. The challenge is how to design services, and spaces to support people, that are caring and compassionate and promote healing and recovery and ultimately uphold principles of social justice and human rights.

The current emphasis of assessment and service delivery in the community is welcomed if service models are appropriate and can adequately support consumers and their families, friends and carers in times of need. Where in-patient services are deemed necessary, the avoidance of accident and emergency departments is a priority so as to facilitate admission of a person directly to the ward. This will eliminate much of the distress and use of restraint currently observed in emergency departments. The fact that people are being restrained, medically and mechanically, and often placed in resuscitation beds, is evidence that emergency departments are not designed to cope with people with mental health issues. To think they would just fit in to an existing busy accident and emergency setting with high levels of physical and emotional distress and stimulation is strange and bizarre. As Hoult observed, in the introduction of community crisis teams, these people for the most part do not need hospital services. It is in this aspect that government, policy makers and services have truly lost a grasp on reality.

This situation needs to change for the better. This is an exciting time with great potential for change through co-design and trauma-informed care and practice. In my view, it is now that there is most potential for real change to occur beyond the early attempts at deinstitutionalisation. The answers are not known and need to be discovered and hopefully you the reader will play some role in progressing this.

The previous edition, *Mental Health Social Work* (2012), was written at one of the most difficult times in my life. At the time, I thought it would be relatively straightforward but it was extremely hard and no doubt very frustrating for my publisher, Stephen Matthews, as deadlines were missed and the standard of writing was variable. I am very appreciative of Stephen's support and patience with my writing during this period and over the years.

At that time, I had struggled with chronic pain for close on a year and decided to have back surgery at the end of 2011. This meant that I needed to have one month's bed rest and a slow and painful recovery process. It meant that I was reliant upon family members as carers and am grateful for their support. However, with all of the focus on my physical recovery, I was not prepared to also have to battle depression. After three months looking after me physically, this was almost too much to bear for my now somewhat tired and reluctant family member carers. My experience highlighted how frightening it is for family members to lose the person as they knew them and not only to have to cope without them but also look after them as well. One of my children simply said in despair, 'You've changed, Mum.' Physical care is very different to mental health care.

My biggest challenge for recovery was and still is holding on to what I have, rather than trying to get things back. I have had to recognise my own human frailty and seek assistance and that was not easy to do. I knew the importance of early intervention and set about preventing as much as possible a further decline in my mental state. I am sincerely grateful to my counsellor at the time. His patience and kindness and use of listening skills and critical questioning were very helpful for my recovery. My physiotherapist was also extremely kind and empathic, reminding me I was still post-operative, almost giving me permission for perhaps not recovering as fast as others might have expected. Likewise, my surgeon was very understanding and supportive. My general practitioner referred me for a Mental Health Care Plan under the Medicare (Better Access) Program. For that, I am grateful. However, I was surprised when he asked me quite personal questions and typed the answers straight onto the computer in a very brusque and businesslike manner. When I told him I was taking St John's wort and if that didn't work I would decide whether or not to take antidepressants, he looked at me quite sternly and said, 'I will decide,' while recording on the form, 'no current medication'. I kept quiet as I didn't want to jeopardise getting my Mental Health Care Plan. So much for managed care and consumer leadership, I thought. I was surprised when the Mental Status Examination consisted of a ticked box for each category to indicate 'normal' or 'other' without any explanatory notes. I doubted his interpretation of normal' was the same as mine. The costs of treatment were substantial and I was appreciative that I had well paid employment and private health cover. However, I am mindful that this is not the situation for many people who would struggle to pay for these services.

I have decided to share this with you, the reader, to illustrate that none of us are immune from the strange and unfamiliar, and at times frightening, world of mental health issues. I do not take anything for granted and am a strong believer that mental health issues can affect anyone at any time and if we somehow believe we are immune, we are clearly mistaken. Having this understanding will hopefully eliminate the divide of us and them – the othering process – that is so detrimental to humane and compassionate service responses. Working together as equals in terms of strengths, vulnerabilities and resources, we can make a real difference. This egalitarian, collaborative environment is conducive to creativity and innovation to re-envision mental health services into the future.

Appendix
Assessment Form

Date of assessment:

Time of assessment start:

1. Personal details

Name:

Address:

Phone no.:

Date of birth:

Sex:

Religious / spiritual beliefs:

Cultural background:

Interpreter required: Yes No

Preferred language:

2. Next of kin

Name:

Address:

Relationship to person referred:

Phone no.:

Interpreter required: Yes No

Preferred language:

3. Nominated person

Name:

Address:

Relationship to person referred:

Phone no.:

Interpreter required: Yes No

Preferred language:

4. Referral source

Name:

Address:

Relationship to person referred:

Phone no.:

Interpreter required: Yes No

Preferred language:

Date of referral:

5. Reasons for referral

6. Carers / workers and agencies involved

Name:

Address:

Phone no.:

Case manager (if applicable):

Name:

Name and address of agency:

Phone no.:

Other people / workers involved (if applicable):

Name:

Address:

Phone no.:

General Practitioner (if applicable):

Name:

Address:

Phone no.:

7. Presenting situation

Reason for referral / problems and symptoms / precipitating factors / perpetuating factors / onset / cause / duration / current behaviours / eating and sleeping patterns / attempted solutions / responses / social stressors / strengths / resources

8. Personal history

A. Psychiatric history

Diagnoses / interventions / hospital admissions and mental health and other service involvement / allergies / adverse effects

B. Medical history

Diagnoses / treatments / hospital admissions / allergies / adverse effects

C. Violence / suicide attempts / self-harm history

D. Drug and alcohol history

Substances / issues / problems / interventions

E. Forensic history

police involvement / charges / court appearances / sentences / current status

F. Developmental history (include details of who provides this information)

pregnancy and birth / developmental milestones and tasks / childhood illnesses

G. Pre-morbid personality

dominant personality traits / impulse control / anger management / strengths

9. Family history

A. Genogram

B. Family Psychiatric and Medical History

C. Family Dynamics

Relationships / attachments / culture / religious/spiritual beliefs

10. Social history

A. Cultural background

dominant beliefs and practices / special requirements / migration resettlement

B. Spiritual background

dominant beliefs and practices / special requirements

C. Education and employment

Schooling / further education / training /employment / vocational rehabilitation

D. Accommodation and finances

Housing / income / related issues

E. Social

Friendships / relationships / sexual history / recreation and leisure interests

11. Mental status examination

A. General appearance and behaviour

Physical characteristics / dress / grooming / hygiene / demeanour / manner / posture / motor activity / gait / level of cooperation and engagement during the interview

B. Speech

Rate / quality / volume / tone / content / flow

C. Affect

Quality / range / appropriateness / congruency with verbal content

D. Thought

Stream / form / content / possession / delusions

E. Perception

Hallucinations (auditory, visual, tactile, smell, taste) / illusions / phobias

F. Cognition

Consciousness / orientation / attention / concentration /memory (short and long term)

G. Insight and judgement

Recognition of difficulties / attribution / decision-making ability / acceptance of assistance

12. Physical examination

Date performed:

Vital signs and general findings

P=   BP=   Temp=   RR=

Cardiovascularsystem:

Respiratory system:

Gastrointestinal system:

Nervous system:

Central –

Peripheral –

Abnormal involuntary movements –

13. Formulation

Brief summary / risk summary / provisional diagnosis

Factors	Biological	Psychological	Social
Predisposing:			
Precipitating:			
Perpetuating:			
Protective:			

14. Immediate management plan

Interventions / intensity / setting / legal status under Mental Health Act / supports / agencies and carers involved / further assessments required

Time of assessment finish:

Duration of assessment interview:

Level of engagement during interview:

Assessed by:

Name:

Signature:

Designation:

Date:

Useful Web Resources

Aboriginal and Torres Strait Islander health and wellbeing, http://www.hc-sc.gc.ca/fniahspnia/promotion/mental/index-eng.php; http:// www.mhfa.com.au/Guidelines.shtmlhttp:// www.indigenouspsychservices.com.au/viewStory/Cutural+Competency+Test; http:// www.healthinfonet.ecu.edu.au/key-resources/programs-projects?pid=145

ACT Health and Community Care, www.health.act.gov.au

American Psychiatric Association, Diagnostic and Statistical Manual of Mental Disorders, http://www.psych.org

ARAFEMI, Association of Relatives and Friends of the Mentally Ill, http://arafemi.org.au

Attorney General's Department – Australian legal system, http://www.law.gov.au

Australian Association of Social Workers, Medicare and mental health http://www.aasw.asn.au/whatwedo/medicare-mental-health

Australian Association of Social Workers, mental health practice standards, http://www.aasw.asn.au

Australian Bureau of Statistics www.abs.gov.au

Australian Domestic and Family Violence Clearinghouse, www.austdvclearinghouse.unsw.edu.au

Australian Domestic and Family Violence Clearinghouse, Australian Law Online, http://www.law.gov.au

Australian Institute of Criminology, www.aic.gov.au

Australian Institute of Health and Welfare, www.aihw.gov.au

Australian Institute for Suicide Research and Prevention, http://www.griffith.edu.au/health/australian-institute-suicide-research-prevention

Australian legal sources, www.weblaw.edu.au

Australian Psychological Society, Medicare services provided by psychologists, http://www.psychology.org.au/medicare

Better Outcomes Program, http://www.mentalhealth.gov.au/budget/infosheets.htm

Beyond Blue: drug use and mental health – youth, www.youthbeyondblue.com

BOMHCi and other Commonwealth initiatives, www.health.gov.au

Carers Australia, www.carersaustralia.com.au

Carers Victoria, http://www.carersvictoria.org.au/facts

Definitions and implementation plans for FPS for GPs, http://www.gpcare.org

Department of Health and Ageing, Australian government, http://www.health.gov.au/internet/main/publishing.nsf

Department of Health and Ageing, GP programs to improve access and outcomes in mental health, Australian Government, http://www.gpcare.org

Department of Veteran Affairs, mental health and services for veterans as well as family members and carers, www.dva.gov.au

Drug Information Clearing House: mental health and alcohol and other drugs, http://www.druginfo.adf.org

Health Department contacts for state-based data: Forensicare: http://www.forensicare.vic.gov.au/; ACT Health and Community Care www.health.act.gov.au; NSW Health www.health.nsw.gov.au; NT Department of Health and Community Services www.nt.gov.au; Queensland Health www.health.qld.gov.au; SA Department of Health www.health.sa.gov.au; Tasmania Health and Human Services www.dhhs.tas.gov.au; Victoria Department of Human Services www.dhs.vic.gov.au; WA Department of Health www.health.wa.gov.au

Health Insite: mental health issues and drug addiction, http://www.healthinsite.gov.au

Law Handbook 2009, http://www.lawhandbook.org.au

Legislation, http://www.austlii.edu.au

Mental health services in Victoria: VICSERV website, http://www.vicserv.org.au

Mental Health Legal Centre: http://www.communitylaw.org

MIND Australia, http://www.rfv.org.au

Mindframe, Recovery, www.mindframe-media.info/nmmhg.html

New Zealand Mental Health Commission, www.info@mhc.govt.nz

New Zealand Mental Health Commission, Recovery Competencies for New ZealandMental Health Workers, www.info@mhc.govt.nz

NSW Government Health: Mental Health and Drug and Alcohol Office, http://www.health.nsw.gov.au/mhdao

NSW Health www.health.nsw.gov.au

NT Department of Health and Community Services www.nt.gov.au

Odyssey House: drug use and mental health,www.odyssey.org.au

Orygen Youth Health; Early Psychosis Prevention and Intervention Centre (EPPIC) http://www.eppic.org.au

Privacy and confidentiality, http://www.healthinsite.gov.au/topics/Privacy_and_Confidentiality

Queensland Health, www.health.qld.gov.au

Research Centre for Injury Studies, www.nisu.flinders.edu.au

SA Department of Health, www.health.sa.gov.au

SANE Australia, http://www.sane.org

SANE: drugs and mental health issues, www.sane.org

Sisters Inside: http://www.sistersinside.com.au/

Tasmania Health and Human Services, www.dhhs.tas.gov.au

Turning Point Alcohol and Drug Centre, www.turningpoint.org.au

Victoria Department of Health: mental health drugs and regions, http://www.health.vic.gov.au/divisions/mhdr

Victoria Department of Human Services, www.dhs.vic.gov.au

WA Department of Health, www.health.wa.gov.au

World Health Organisation, International Classification of Diseases, http://www.who.int/classifications/icd/en/index.html

World Health Organisation, wellbeing, http://www.who.int

Young Carers, information, contacts and support for young carers, parents, and primary teachers, www.youngcarers.net.au

References

Aaronson, B. (1969) 'Hypnosis, Depth Perception and Psychedelic Experience', in Tait, C. (ed.) (1969).

Abramowitz, J.S. (1997) 'Effectiveness of psychological and pharmacological treatments for obsessive–compulsive disorder: A quantitative review', *Journal of Consulting and Clinical Psychology*, 65:44–52.

Access Economics (2002) *Schizophrenia Costs: An Analysis of Schizophrenia and Related Suicide in Australia*, SANE Australia, Melbourne.

— 2003 *Bi-Polar Disorder Costs: An Analysis of Bi-Polar Disorder Related Suicide in Australia*, SANE Australia, Melbourne.

Acoca, L. (1998) 'Defusing the Time Bomb: Understanding and Meeting the Growing Health Care Needs of Women in America', *Crime and Delinquency*, vol. 44, no. 1.

Adams, I. & Martin, B. (1996) 'Cannabis: Pharmacology and Toxicology in Animals and Humans', *Addiction*, 91:1585–1614.

Adams, R,. Dominelli, L. & Payne, M. (eds) (1998) *Social Work: Themes, Issues and Critical Debates*, Macmillan Press, London.

Addington, J. (1999) 'Early Intervention Strategies for Co–morbid Cannabis Use and Psychosis', Inaugural International Cannabis and Psychosis Conference Final Papers, Melbourne.

Alasuutati, P. (1995) *Researching Culture: Qualitative Methods and Cultural Studies*, Sage Publications, California.

Alberti, R. & Emmons, M. (1998) *Your Perfect Right. A Guide to Assertive Living*, Impact Publishers, California.

Alcohol and Other Drugs Council of Australia (2003) 'High Levels of Depression, Post Traumatic Stress Disorder and Multiple illness: The guiding vision of the mental health service system in the 1990s', *Psychosocial Rehabilitation* Journal, vol. 16, no. 4, 11–23.

— (1994) 'Characteristics of people with Psychiatric Disabilities that are Predictive of Entry into the Rehabilitation Process and Successful Employment', *Psychosocial Rehabilitation Journal*, vol. 17, no. 3, 3–13.

— Treatment Episodes the Norm, media release, AODCA, ACT, at http://www.adca.org.au accessed 10/6/05.

— (2005) Drug Household Survey Results: Tobacco Encouraging but Alcohol Use Concerning, media release, AODCA, ACT, at http://www.adca.org.au accessed 10/6/05.

— (2005) Minimising the Harm, Maximizing the Impact, media release, AODCA, ACT at http://www.adca.org.au accessed 10/6/05.

Alder, C. (1997) 'Theories of Female Delinquency', in Borowski, A. & Connor, I. (1997) 43–59.

Allen, P. (2011) Psychological Treatment of Obsessive Compulsive Disorder (OCD) Using Cognitive Behaviour Therapy (CBT) at http://www.ocd.net.au

Allen-Kelly, K. (2009) 'From the Chief Executive Officer', *Australian Association of Social Workers National Bulletin: Social work in emergency response and community recovery*, 19(1):9–32.

American Psychiatric Association (1994) *Diagnostic and Statistical Manual of Mental Disorders*, fourth edition revised, Washington, DC.

Andrews G. (2001) 'Should depression be managed as a chronic disease', *British Medical Journal*, 322:419–21.

Andrews, G., Crino, R., Hunt, C., Lampe, L. & Page, A. (1994) *The Treatment of Anxiety Disorders*, Cambridge University Press, Melbourne.

Andrews, G. (1993) 'The essential psychotherapies', *British Journal of Psychiatry*, 162:447–51.

Anthony, W. (1993) 'Recovery from mental Appignanesi, L. (ed.) (1989) *Postmodernism*, Free Association Books, London.

Appleby, M., King, R. & Johnson, B. *Suicide Awareness Training Manual*, Rose Education, NSW.

Ariyabandu, M.M. (2006) 'Gender Issues in Recovery from the December 2004 Indian Ocean Tsunami: The Case of Sri Lanka', *Earthquake Spectra* 22, S759.

Armstrong, K., Chatrand, V. & Baldry, E.

(2005) Submission to the Anti-Discrimination Commissioner for an Inquiry into the Discrimination by Women Within the Criminal Justice System in New South Wales, Beyond Bars Alliance, NSW.

Australian Association of Social Workers (AASW) (1996a) *Social Work in Victoria's Mental Health Services*, AASW, Victoria.

— (1996b) *Mental Health Interest Group, Social Work in Mental Health*, AASW, NSW.

— (1999) *Practice Standards for Social Work and Mental Health*, AASW, Barton, ACT.

— (2007) Submission by the Australian Association of Social Workers to the Inquiry by the Senate Community Affairs Committee into Mental health Services in Australia, AASW, Barton, ACT.

— (2008) *Practice Standards for Mental Health Social Workers*, AASW, Barton, ACT.

— (2010a) *Code of Ethics*, AASW, Barton, ACT.

— (2010b) *Requirements for accreditation to practise as a Mental Health Social Worker*, AASW, Barton, ACT.

— (2011) *Accredited Mental Health Social Worker Continuing Professional Development Policy*, AASW, Barton, ACT.

Australian Bureau of Statistics (2000a) *Australian Social Trends 1999: Health – Health Status: Mental Health*, AGPS, Canberra.

— (2000b) *Australian Social Trends 2000*; Health – Mortality and Morbidity: Suicide, AGPS, Canberra.

— (2002a) 'Health Special: Suicide', *Year Book Australia*, Health Special Article, AGPS, Canberra.

— (2002b) *Measuring Australia's Progress: Social Attachment*, AGPS, Canberra.

— (2003) 'Health: Mental Health', *Year Book Australia*, AGPS, Canberra.

— (2006) Census data: Murrundindi Local Government Area, Australian Government, Canberra.

— (2011) Causes of Death, Australia 2009, at http://www.abs.gov.au/AUSSTATS/abs@.nsf/DetailsPage/3303.02009?OpenDocument

— (2016) Causes of death, Australia 2015, Australian Government, Canberra.

Australian Centre for Post–traumatic Mental Health (2009) *Skills for Psychological Recovery; Field Operations Guide*, The University of Melbourne, Parkville.

Australian Health Ministers (1991) *Mental Health: Statement of Rights and Responsibilities*, Report of the Mental Health Consumers Outcomes Taskforce, AGPS, Canberra.

— (1992) *National Mental Health Policy*, AGPS, Canberra.

Australian Institute for Suicide Research and Prevention (2012) home page, Griffith University, Queensland at http://www.griffith.edu.aulhealth/australian-institute-suicide-research-prevention

Australian Psychological Society (APS) (2007) *Better Access to Mental Health Care Initiative*, APS, Melbourne.

Bailey, R. & Brake, M. (eds) (1975) *Radical Social Work*, Edward Arnold, London.

Bainbridge, L. (1999) 'Mental Health Practice and Education', in Pease, B. & Fook, J. (1999)

Baker, E. & Tually, S. (2009) 'Women, Health and Housing Assistance: Implications in an emrging era of housing provision', *Australian Journal of Social Issues*, 43(1) 123–138.

Barkley, R.A., Edwards, G., Laneri, M., Flatcher, K., & Metevia, L. (2001) 'The efficacy of problem-solving communication training alone, behaviour management training alone, and their combination for parent–adolescent conflict in teenagers with ADHD and ODD', *Journal of Consulting & Clinical Psychology*, 69(6) 926–941.

Barlow, D.H., Lawton Esler, J. & Vitali, A.E. (1998) 'Psychosocial Treatments for Panic Disorders, Phobias, and Generalized Anxiety Disorder', in Nathan, P.E. & Gorman, J.M. (eds) (1998).

Barlow, D.H. (ed.) *Clinical handbook of psychological disorders: A step-by-step treatment manual*, third edition, Guilford Press, New York.

Barry, P. (2003) *Mental Health and Mental health issues*, Lippincott, Philadelphia.

Bateman, J. & Henderson, C. (2010) *Reframing responses: Stage 2: Supporting women survivors of child abuse*, Mental Health Coordinating Council, Lilyfield, New South Wales.

Beck, A.T. (1976) *Cognitive therapy and the emotional disorders*, International Universities Press, New York.

— (2011) 'Cognitive Therapy: Current Status and Future Directions', *Annual Review of Medicine*, 62, 397–409.

Beck, R. & Fernandez, E. (1998) 'Cognitive-behavioural therapy in the treatment of anger: a meta–analysis', *Cognitive Therapy and Research*, 22(1) 63–4.

Becker, E.E. & Leber, W.R. (eds) (1995)

Handbook of Depression, Guilford Press, New York.

Begg, C. (1993) Chaos or Reason: Community Safety in the Twenty-First Century, Conference Proceedings, 251.

Belknap, J. (1996) 'Access to Programs and Health Care for Incarcerated Women', Division of Criminal Justice, Cincinnati.

Birecree, E., Bloom, J., Leverette, M. & Williams, M. (1994) 'Diagnostic Efforts Regarding Women in Oregon's Prison System: A Preliminary Report', *International Journal of Offender Therapy and Comparative Criminology*, 38:217–230.

Bland, R., Renouf, N. & Tullgren (2009) *Social Work Practice in Mental Health*, Allen & Unwin, NSW.

Bleuler, E. (1950) *Dementia Praecox or the Group of Schizophrenias*, International Universities Press, New York.

Bolton, R. (1998) *People Skills*, Prentice-Hall, Sydney.

Borowski, A. & Connor, I. (1997) *Juvenile Crime, Justice and Corrections*, Addison-Wesley Longman, South Melbourne.

Boyd, M.A. (2001) *Psychiatric Nursing: Contemporary Practice*, second edition, Lippincott, Philadelphia.

Bradshaw, S. (2004) *Socio-economic impacts of natural disasters: a gender analysis*, United Nations, Santiago, Chile.

Bradshaw, S., Linneker, B. & Zunniga, R. (2001) 'Social Roles and Spatial Relations of NGOs and Civil Society: Participation and Effectiveness in Central America Post Hurricane Mitch', *The Nicaraguan Academic Journal*, at http://ssri,Hawaii.edu

Brammer, L. (2003) *The Helping Relationship and Skills*, eighth edition, Allyn & Bacon, Boston.

Brandes, I. (2003) 'Burning Questions: Australia's bushfire policy', *Australian Review of Public Affairs*, The University of Sydney, NSW.

Braverman, P. & Gruskin, S. (2003) 'Poverty, equity, human rights and health', *Bulletin World Health Organisation*, 81:539–545.

Brewer, W., van Ammers, E., Francey, S., Velakoulis, D., Yung, A., McGorry, P., Copolov, D., Singh, B. & Pantelis, C. (1999) 'Cannabis Use in Never Medicated High-Risk and First Episode Psychosis Patients: Relationship to Cognition', Inaugural International Cannabis and Psychosis Conference Final Papers, Melbourne.

Bromet, E., Dew, A. & Eaton, W. (1995) 'Epidemiology of Psychosis with Special Reference to Schizophrenia', in Tsuang, M., Tohen, M. & Zahner, G. (eds).

Brown, R. (2005) 'Australian Indigenous Mental Health', *Australian and New Zealand Journal of Mental Health Nursing*, vol. 10, no. 1, 33–41.

Bryson, G., Lysaker, P. & Bell, M. (2002) 'Quality of Life Benefits of Paid Work Activity in Schizophrenia', *Schizophrenia Bulletin*, Washington, vol. 28, issue 2, 249–258.

Burdekin, B. (1993) *Human Rights and Mental health issues: Report of the National Inquiry into the Human Rights of People with a mental health issue*, vols.1 and 2, AGPS, Canberra.

Burris, S. (2006) 'Stigma and the law', *Lancet*, 367:529–31.

Burstow, B. (1992) *Radical Feminist Therapy*, Sage, Newbury Park.

Campbell, P. & Lindow, V. (1997) *Changing Practice: Mental Health Nursing and User Empowerment*, Royal College of Nursing and MIND Publications, London.

Caplan G. (1961) *An Approach to Community Mental Health*, Grune & Stratton, New York.

Carers of the Mentally Ill, 1996 State Conference booklet.

Carers Victoria, 2002–2003 *Annual Report*, Melbourne.

Carnaby, H. (1998) *Road to Nowhere: A Report of Women's Housing and Support Needs When Leaving Prison in Victoria*, Flat Out Inc., Collingwood.

Carpenito, L. (2000) *Nursing Diagnosis: Application to Clinical Practice*, Lippincott, Williams & Wilkins.

Cavallaro, T., Foley, P., Saunders, J. & Bowman, K. (2005) *People with a disability in vocational education and training*, Adelaide: National Centre for Vocational Education Research (NCVER).

Centre for Clinical Interventions (2016) What is mindfulness? Western Australia: Department of Health http://www.cci.health.wa.gov.au

Coalition of Australian Governments (2006) *National action plan on mental health 2006–2011*, Commonwealth Department of Health & Ageing, Canberra.

Collins, M. & Mowbray, C. (2005) 'Higher education ad psychiatric disabilities: National survey of campus disability services', *American Journal of Orthopsychiatry*, vol. 75, 304–315.

Commonwealth Attorney General's Department (2009) *National Workplan to reduce Arson in Australia*, at http://www.ema.gov.au

Commonwealth Department of Health and Ageing (2005) *Alcohol Handbook*, at http://www.7health.gov.au/pubs/drug, p. 1, accessed 10/6/05.

Commonwealth Department of Health and Family Services (1997) *National Standards for Mental Health Services*, AGPS, Canberra.

Commonwealth of Australia (2005) *Evacuation Planning*, Australian Emergency Manual Series Manual No. 11, ACT: Attorney General's Department, Emergency Management Australia.

— (2007a) *Guidelines for Emergency Management in Culturally and Linguistically Diverse Communities*, Australian Emergency Manual Series Manual No. 44, ACT: Attorney General's Department, Emergency Management Australia.

— (2007b) *Keeping Our Mob Safe: A National Emergency Management Strategy for Remote Indigenous Communities*, Attorney General's Department, Emergency Management Australia, ACT.

Comptom, B. & Gallaway, B. (1999) *Social Work Processes*, Brookes Cole, Pacific Grove.

Condon, M. (ed.) *Women's Health: An Integrated Approach to Wellness and Illness*, Prentice Hall, New Jersey.

Conflict Resolution Network (1993) *Conflict Resolution Trainer's Manual*, Chatswood, NSW.

Conger, J. (1979) *Adolescence*, Harper & Row, New York.

Connor, H. (1997) 'Women's Mental Health and Mental health issues in Custody: Exploring the Gap Between the Correctional System as it is Presented and the Correctional System as it is Experienced', *Psychiatry, Psychology and the Law*, 4(1) 45–53.

Copolov, D., Bradbury, R., Dong, P., Dean, B. & Lim, A., 'The Interaction Between Cannabis and Dopamine in the Brain: Possible Mechanisms Related to Psychosis', Inaugural International Cannabis and Psychosis Conference Final Papers, Melbourne.

Coppock, V. & Hopton, J. *Critical Perspectives on Mental Health*, Routledge, London.

Corrigan P. & Leonard, P. (1978) *Critical Texts in Social Work and the Welfare State: Social Work Practice Under Capitalism A Marxist Approach*, Macmillan Press, London.

Corrigan, P., River, L., London, R. Wasowski, K., Campion, J. (2000) 'Stigmatizing Attributions About Mental health issues', *Journal of Community Psychology*, vol. 28, 91–102.

Cox, M. (1994) *Good Practices in Women's Mental Health*, Healthsharing Women, Melbourne.

Craighead, W.E., Miklowitz, D.J., Vajk, D J., & Frank, E. (1998) 'Psychosocial Treatments for Bipolar Disorder', in Nathan, P.E. & Gorman, J.M. (eds) (1998).

Creative Spirits (2016) Aboriginal suicide rates, at https://www.creativespirits.info/aboriginalculture/people/aboriginal-suicide-rates

Cunningham, J., Cass, A. & Arnold, P. (2005) 'Bridging the Treatment Gap for Indigenous Australians', *The Medical Journal of Australia*, vol. 182, no. 10, 505–506

Curry, C., Phillips, L., Yuen, H.P., Adlard, S. & McGorry, P. (1999) 'Cannabis Use as a Risk Factor for the Development of Psychotic Symptoms: A Prospective Study', Inaugural International Cannabis and Psychosis Conference Final Papers, Melbourne.

Cusworth, F. (2003) 'Our Isabella', *The Age Good Weekend*, 19 April 2003.

Dalrymple, J. & Burke, B. (1995) *Anti-Oppressive Practice: Social Care and the Law*, Open University Press, USA.

D'Arcy, M. (1993) 'Offending Patterns of Women in Prison', in Begg, C. (1993).

Davidson, L., Stayner, D., Nickou, C., Styron, T.H., Rowe, M. & Chinman, M. (2004) 'Simply To Be Let In', *Ausinetter*, issue 20, no. 1, 12–15.

Deegan, P. (1996). Recovery as a Journey of the Heart, Psychiatric Rehabilitation Journal, Vol. 19, Issue 3.

Deikman, A. (1973) 'Deautomation and the Mystic Experience', in Ornstein, R. (ed.).

Delaney, P. & Schrader, E. (2000) *Gender and Post-Disaster Reconstruction: The Case of Hurricane Mitch in Honduras and Nicaragua*, Decision Review Draft, LCSPG/LAC Gender Team: World Bank, Washington, DC.

Denton, B. (1993) 'Psychiatric Morbidity and Substance Dependence Among Women Prisoners: An Australian Study', *Psychiatry, Psychology and the Law*, 2(2) 173–77.

Denton, B. (1995) 'Drug Dependence and Psychiatric Morbidity in Sentenced and Unsentenced Prisoners: An Australian Study', a paper delivered at the Fifth World Conference on Prison Health Care, 6–11 June, The Sheraton Hotel and Towers, Brisbane.

Denzin, N.K. (1997) *Interpretive Ethnography: Ethnographic Practices for the 21st Century*, Sage Publications, California.

Denzin, N.K. (1983) 'Interpretive Interactionism', in Morgan C. (1983).

Department of Health and Ageing (2009) Continued Professional Development Requirements for Providers of Focused Psychological Strategies Services Under the Better Access to Psychiatrists, Psychologists and General Practitioners Through the Medicare (Better Access) Initiative, ACT: Commonwealth Government of Australia, at http://www.health.gov.au/internet/mbsonline

— (2011a) What is personality disorder? Australian government, at http://www.health.gov.au/internet/main/publishing.nsf

— (2011b) GP Programs to Improve Access and Outcomes in Mental Health, Australian Government, at http://www.gpcare.org maintained by World Health Organisation Collaborating Centre, St Vincents Hospital Sydney.

— (2011c) 2010–2011 *Operational Guidelines for the Access to Allied Psychological Services Component of the Better Outcomes in Mental Health Care Program*, Commonwealth Government of Australia, Canberra.

Department of Health and Community Services (1994) *Community Treatment Orders: Guidelines and Information*, Psychiatric Services Division, Victoria.

Department of Human Services (1996) *Victoria's Mental Health Service Youth Suicide Prevention Information Kit*, Victorian Government, Melbourne.

— (1997) *Cannabis and Psychosis Fact Sheet*, Victorian Government.

— (2005) *Strengthening Emergency Management Capability and Capacity 2005–07*, Victorian Government, Melbourne.

— (2009) *After the Bushfires: Victoria's Psychosocial Recovery Framework*, Victorian Government, Melbourne.

— (2010) *Emergency Management*, at http://www.dhs.vic.gov.au/emergency

Derks, F., Blankstein, J. & Hendrickx, J. (1993) 'Treatment and Security: The Dual Nature of Forensic Psychiatry', *International Journal of Law and Psychiatry*, 16, 217–40.

Deu, N. & Roberts, L. (eds) (1995) Dangerous, Disordered and Doubly Deviant, selected papers from the Hospital Advisory Group Annual Conference, Issues in Criminology and Legal Psychology 27:10–22.

Deveson, A. (1991) *Tell Me I'm Here*, Penguin Books, Ringwood.

Diamond, R. (1985) 'Drugs and the Quality of Life: The Patient's Point of View', *Journal of Clinical Psychiatry*, vol. 46, no. 5, 29–35.

Dimitrijevics, A. (2008) *Mainstreaming Gender into Disaster Recovery and Reconstruction*, World Bank, Washington, DC.

Dixon, L., Haas, G., Weiden, P.J., Sweeney, J. & Frances, A.J. (1991) 'Drug Abuse in Schizophrenic Patients: Clinical Correlates and Reasons for Use', *American Journal of Psychiatry*, 148, 224–230.

Dominelli, L. (1998) 'Anti–oppressive Practice in Context', in Adams, R,. Dominelli, L. & Payne, M. (eds).

Dominelli, L. & McLeod, E. (1989) *Feminist Social Work*, Macmillan Press, London.

Done, D.J. & Thomas, J.A. (2001) 'Training in communication skills for informal carers of people suffering from dementia: A cluster randomized clinical trial comparing a therapist led workshop and booklet', *International Journal of Geriatric Psychiatry*, 16(8) 816–821.

Donnelly, N. & Hall, W. (1994) *Patterns of Cannabis Use in Australia*, National Drug Strategy Monograph Series No. 27, AGPS, Canberra.

Drake, R., Mercer-McFadden, C., Mueser, K., McHugo, G., & Bond, G. (1998) 'A Review of Integrated Mental Health and Substance Abuse Treatments for Patients with Dual Disorders', *Schizophrenia Bulletin*, 24, 443–455.

Drake, R.E. & Mueser, K.T. (eds) (1996) *Dual Diagnosis of Major Mental health issues and Substance Abuse Disorder II: Recent Research and Clinical Implications: New Direction in Mental Health Services*, Jossey-Bass, San Francisco.

Easteal, P. (1992) 'Women and Crime: Imprisonment Issues', *Trends and Issues in Crime and Criminal Justice*, vol. 35, Australian Institute of Criminology, Canberra.

Elkin, I., Shea, M.T., Watkins, J.T., Imber, S.D., Sotsky, S.M., Collins, J.F, Glass, D.R., Pilkonis, P.A. Klerman, G.L., Weissman, M.M., Rounsaville, B.J. & Chevron, E.S. (1984) *Interpersonal Psychotherapy of Depression*, Basic Books, New York.

Elliot, B. (2000) *Promoting Family Change*, Allen & Unwin, NSW.

Elliot, T. & Frank, R. (1990) 'Social and Interpersonal Reactions to Depression and Disability', *Rehabilitation Psychology*, 35, 135–47.

Elliot-Farrelly, T. (2004) 'Australian Aboriginal Suicide: The Need for An Aboriginal Suicidology?' *Australian e–Journal for the Advancement of Mental Health*, vol. 3, no.3, 1–8.

Ellis, A. (1999) *How to make yourself and remarkably less disturbed*, California, Impact.

— (2004) 'Why emotional emotive behaviour therapy is the most comprehensive and effective form of behavior therapy', *Journal of Rational-Emotive and Cognitive-Behaviour Therapy*, 22, 2, 85–92.

Ellis, A., & Harper, R.A. (1975) *A New Guide to Rational Living*, Wilshire Book Co., California.

Emergency Management Australia (2010) About the Bushfire Mitigation Program, at http://www.ema.gov.au

Emmons, K.M. & Rollnick, S. (2001) 'Motivational interviewing in health care settings. Opportunities and limitations', *American Journal of Preventive Medicine*, 20(1) 68–74.

Engel, G. (1977) 'The need for a new medical model, a challenge for biomedicine'. *Science*, 196, 129–136.

Ensink, B. (1992) *Confusing Realities: A Study on Child Sexual Abuse and Psychiatric Symptoms*, Free University Press, Amsterdam.

Epstein, M., & Wadsworth, Y. (1996) *Understanding and Involvement: Consumer Evaluation of an Acute Psychiatric Hospital; A Project Unfolds*, Victorian Mental health issues Awareness Council, Brunswick, Victoria.

Erikson, E.H. (1980) *Identity and Life Cycle*, W.W. Norton, New York.

Estroff S.E. & Zimmer C. (1994) 'Social Networks, Social Support and Violence Among Persons with Severe, Persistent Mental health issues', in Monahan, J. & Steadman, H.J. (eds).

Ethnic Heath Initiative (2011) Promoting a Better Understanding of BME Psychological health and Wellbeing, at www.bmehealth.org

Fabian, E. (1989) 'Work and the Quality of Life', *Psychosocial Rehabilitation Journal*, vol. 12, no. 4, 39–49.

Falloon, I. (1992) 'Early Intervention for First Episodes of Schizophrenia: A Preliminary Exploration', *Psychiatry*, 55, 4–15.

Farraday, A. (1975) *The Dream Game*, Temple Smith, London.

Fava, G.A., Bartolucci, G., Rafanelli, C. & Mangelli, L. (2001) 'Cognitive-behavioural management of patients with bipolar disorder who relapsed while on lithium prophylaxis', *Journal of Clinical Psychiatry*, 62(7) 556–9.

Fawcett, B. (1996) 'Women, Mental Health and Community Care: an Abusive Combination?', in Fawcett, B., Featherstone, B., Hearn, J. & Toft, C. (1996).

Fawcett, B., Featherstone, B., Hearn, J. & Toft, C. (1996) *Violence and Gender Relations*, Sage, London.

Feeney, E. (2004) 'Substance Abuse and Dependence', in Condon, M. (ed.) Fergus, L. & Keel, M. (2005) 'Adult victim/ survivors of childhood sexual assault', *ACSSA Wrap*, no. 1, November, 1–6. Australian Institute of Family Studies,

Fitzroy Legal Service (1988) *Women and Imprisonment in Victoria: A Report*, Melbourne.

Fook, J. (1993) *Radical Casework*, Allen & Unwin, St Leonards.

— (1999) 'Critical Reflectivity in Education and Practice', in Pease, B. & Fook, J. (1999).

Foucault, M. (1965) *Madness and Civilisation*, Tavistock, London.

— (1972) *The Archaeology of Knowledge*, Tavistock, London.

Frame, J. (1997) *The Lagoon and other Stories*, Bloomsbury, London.

Freud, S. (1966) *The Psychopathology of Everyday Life*, Ernest Benn, London.

Gallagher B.J. (1980) *The Sociology of Mental health issues*, second edition, Prentice-Hall, USA.

Galper, J. (1975) *The Politics of Social Services*, Prentice-Hall, New Jersey.

Geldard, D. & Geldard, K. (2005) *Basic Personal Counselling*, fifth edition, Pearson Education, NSW.

Gerrand, V. (1993) *The Patient Majority: Mental Health Policy and Services for Women*, Centre for Applied Social Research, Deakin University.

Gibbs, A. (2010) 'Coping with compulsion: Women's views of being on a Community Treatment Order', *Australian Social Work*, 63:2, 223–233.

Gillies, L.A. (2001) 'Interpersonal psychotherapy for depression and other disorders', in Barlow, D.H. (ed.) 309–331.

Gilmore, L. (2003) 'Everyone Has the Potential to be a Carer', in *Carers Victoria Annual Report*, Melbourne.

Glicken, M. (2004) *Using the Strengths Perspective in Social Work Practice*, Pearson Education, Boston.

Goffman, E. (1974) *Stigma*, Jason Aronson, New York.

— (1961) *Asylums*, Anchor Books, New York.

— (1961) *Asylums*, Pelican, Harmondsworth.

— (1968) *Asylums*, Penguin Books, Harmondsworth, Middlesex, England.

Gottesman, I. (1991) *Schizophrenia Genesis:*

The Origins of Madness, Freeman & Co., New York.

Graham, H & Maslin, J. (1999) 'Cannabis Use Amongst the Severely Mentally Ill and Those Who Experience Psychotic Symptoms in an Inner City Area of the UK', Inaugural International Cannabis and Psychosis Conference Final Papers, Melbourne.

Granello, D. & Wheaton, J. (2001) 'Attitudes of Undergraduate Students Towards Persons with Physical Disabilities and Mental health issues', *Journal of Applied Rehabilitation Counselling*, Manassas, Fall, vol. 32, no. 3, 9–17.

Greyner, B., Solowij, N. & Barlow, K. (1999) 'Cannabis Use is Associated with Greater Psychotic Symptoms and Increased Potential Risk of Aggression', Inaugural International Cannabis and Psychosis Conference Final Papers, Melbourne.

Grinstein, A. (1968) *On Sigmund Freud's Dreams*, Wayne State University Press, Detroit.

Grobb G. (1966) *The State and the Mentally Ill*, University of North Carolina Press, North Carolina.

Gunnell, D.J. & Frankel, S. (1994) 'Prevention of suicide: Aspirations and evidence', *British Medical Journal*, 308, 1227–33.

Hachey, R., Boyer, G. & Mercier, C. (2001) 'Perceived and Valued Roles of Adults with Severe Mental health issues', *Canadian Journal of Occupational Therapy*, Ottawa, vol. 68, issue 2, 112–121.

Haddock, G. & Slade, P. (eds) (1996) *Cognitive-Behavioural Interventions with Psychotic Disorders*, Routledge, London.

Hafner, H. & Janzarik, W. (eds) (1987) *Search for the Causes of Schizophrenia*, Springer, Berlin.

Haley, J. (1971) *Changing Families: A Family Therapy Reader*, Grune & Stratton, New York.

Hall, R., Popkin, M. & Faillace, L. (1978) 'Physical Illness Presenting as a Psychiatric Disease', *Archives of General Psychiatry*, vol. 35.

Hall, W. & Degenhardt, L. (1999) 'Cannabis Use and Psychosis', Inaugural International Cannabis and Psychosis Conference Final Papers, Melbourne.

Hall, W., Teeson, M., Lynskey, M. & Degenhardt, L. (1998) 'The Prevalence in the Past Year of Substance Use and ICD–10 Substance Use Disorders in Australian Adults: Findings from the National Survey of Mental Health and Wellbeing', *NDARC Technical Report* No. 63, National Drug and Alcohol Research Centre, Sydney.

Hambrecht, M. (1999) 'Cannabis, Vulnerability and the Onset of Schizophrenia: An Epidemiological Perspective', Inaugural International Cannabis and Psychosis Conference Final Papers, Melbourne.

Hambrecht, M. & Hafner, H. (1996) 'Substance Abuse and the Onset of Schizophrenia', *Biological Psychiatry*, 39: 1–9.

Hambrecht, M. (1999) 'Cannabis, Vulnerability and the Onset of Schizophrenia: An Epidemiological Perspective', Inaugural International Cannabis and Psychosis Conference Final Papers, Melbourne.

Hampton, B. (1993) *No Escape: Prisons, Therapy and Politics*, UNSW Press, Sydney.

Harding, C., Brooks, G., Asolaga, T. & Breier, A. (1987) 'The Vermont Longitudinal Study of Persons with Severe Mental health issues', *American Journal of Psychiatry*, 144, 718–726.

Harris, E C. & Barraclough B. (1977) 'Suicide as an Outcome for Mental Disorders', *British Journal of Psychiatry*, 170, 205–28.

Harrison, J., Elnour, A. & Pointer, S. (2009) A review of suicide statistics in Australia. Cat. no. INJCAT 121, Canberra, AIHW, Canberra, at http://www.aihw.gov.au/publication

Hassed, C., Sierpina, V. & Kreitzer, M. (2008) 'The health enhancement program at Monash University Medical School', *Explore: The Journal of Science and Healing*, vol. 4, no. 6, 394–7.

Haynes, K. & Tibbits, B.A. (2008) *Trends in Australian bushfire fatalities over the past 100 years*, Centre for Risk and Community Safety, Melbourne.

Healey, B. & Brophy, L. (2002) 'Law, Psychiatry and Social Work', in Swain, P. (ed.) (2002).

Healy, K. & Hillman, W. (2008) 'Young families migrating to non-metropolitan areas: Are they at increased risk of social exclusion?', *Australian Journal of Social Issues*, 43(3) 479–497.

Health Services Division (2000) *Youth Suicide in Australia*, Commonwealth Department of Health and Aged Care, Canberra.

Heimler, E. (1969) *Mental health issues and Social Work*, Penguin Books, England.

Henderson, C. and Bateman, J. (2006) *Reframing responses: Improving service provision to women survivors of childhood sexual abuse who experience mental health problems*, Mental Health Coordinating Council; Lilyfield, New South Wales.

Henry, G. (1985) *Ministerial Review of Community Health Services in Victoria*, AGPS, Canberra.

Herrman, H., Mills, J., Doidge, G., McGorry, P. & Singh, B. (1994) 'The Use of Psychiatric Services Before Imprisonment: A Survey and Case Register Linkage of Sentenced Prisoners in Melbourne', *Psychological Medicine*, 24, 63–8, Cambridge University Press.

Hess, L. (1992) Working Within a Multicultural Setting, paper presented at the Australian Association of Social Workers, Victorian Branch State Conference, Melbourne.

Hiday, V.A. (1995) 'The social context of mental health issues and violence', *Journal of Health and Social Behaviour*, vol. 36, 122–37.

Hollon, S.D., Shelton, R.C., & Loosen, P.T. (1991) 'Cognitive therapy and pharmacotherapy for depression', *Journal of Consulting and Clinical Psychology*, 59, 88–99.

Horowitz, M. & Palmer, C. (1973) *Moksha: Writings on Psychedelics and the Visionary Experience*, Stonehill Publishing Company, New York.

Horwood, B. (1996) 'A history of social work in mental health services', *Negentropia* (Newsletter of the AMHSW) Melbourne.

Hoult J. (1983) *Psychiatric Hospital versus Community Treatment*, Department of Health NSW, Sydney.

Hughes, M. & Heycox (2010) *Older People, Ageing and Social Work: Knowledge for Practice*, Allen & Unwin, NSW.

Human Rights and Equal Opportunity Commission (1993) *Human Rights and Mental health issues*, AGPS, Canberra.

—(1995) *Human Rights and Mental health issues*, Report of the Reconvened Inquiry into the Human Rights of People with Mental health issues (Victoria) AGPS, Canberra.

Hunter, E. & Harvey, D. (2002) 'Indigenous Suicide in Australia, New Zealand, Canada and the United States', *Emergency Medicine Australasia*, vol. 14, no. 1, 14–23.

Huxley, A. 'Drugs that Shape Men's Minds', in Horowitz, M. & Palmer, C. (1973).

Ife (1996) *Rethinking Social Work: Towards Critical Practice*, Longman, Sydney.

James, W. (1973) 'The Scope of Psychology', in Ornstein, R. (ed.).

Jameson, J. (1984) 'Postmodernisn or the Cultural Logic of Late Capitalism', *New Left Review*, no. 146, 53–92.

Jamison, K.R. (2006) 'The many stigmas of mental health issues', *Lancet*, vol. 367, 533–34.

Jang, L. & LaMendola, W. (2007) 'Social Work in Natural Disasters: The Case of Spirituality and Post-traumatic Growth', *Advances in Social Work*, 8(2):306–315.

Jeffs, S. (1993) *Poems from the Madhouse*, Spinifex Press, North Melbourne.

Johnson, K. (1998) *Deinstitutionalising Women*, Cambridge University Press, UK.

Jordan, K., Schlenger, W., Fairbank, J. & Caddell, J. (1996) 'Prevalence of Psychiatric Disorders Among Incarcerated Women', *Archives of General Psychiatry*, 53, 513–19.

Kanowski, L., Kitchener, B. & Jorm, A. (eds) (2008) *Aboriginal and Torres Strait Islander Mental Health First Aid Manual*, ORYGEN Research Centre and University of Melbourne, Parkville.

Karanci, N.A., Alkan, N., Aksit, B., Sucuoglu, H. & Balta, E. (1999) 'Gender Differences in Psychological Distress, Coping, Social Support, and Related Variables following the 1995 Dinar (Turkey) Earthquake', *North American Journal of Psychology*, 1(2):189–204.

Kavanagh, D. (1999) 'Development and Evaluation of Interventions and Service Initiatives for Substance Abuse in Psychosis', Inaugural International Cannabis and Psychosis Conference Final Papers, Melbourne.

Keating, P. (2004) Keynote Address, Jesuit Social Services Annual Dinner, Melbourne Town Hall, Melbourne.

Kendall, P.C. & Hollon S.D. (eds) (1979) *Cognitive-Behavioural Interventions. Theory, Research, and Procedures*, Academic Press. New York.

Kenny, M. Fiske, L and Ife, J. (2002) 'Refugees, Asylum Seekers and the Law', in Swain P. (ed.) (2002).

Kevasham, M., David, A., Steingard, S. and Lisham, W. (1992) 'Musical Hallucinations: A Review and Synthesis', *Neuropsychiatry, Neuropsychology and Behavioural Neurology*, vol. 5, no. 3.

King, R., Appleby, M. & Brown, C. (1995) *Suicide Awareness for Aboriginal Communities*, Rose Education, NSW.

Klerman, G.L., Weissman, M.M., Rounsaville, B.J., & Chevron, E.S. (1984) *Interpersonal Psychotherapy of Depression*, Basic Books, New York.

Knapp, M., McDaid, D., Mossialos, E. & Thornicroft, G. (2007) *Mental health policy and practice across Europe*, McGraw Hill International.

Kocher, P. (1972) *Master of Middle Earth: The*

Achievement of J.R.R. Tolkien, Thames & Hudson, London.

Kopelowicz, A. & Liberman, R.P. (1998) 'Psychosocial Treatments for Schizophrenia', in P.E. Nathan & J.M. Gorman (eds) (1998).

Kosky, R., Eshkevari, H. & Carr, V. (1991) *Mental Health and Illness*, Heinemann, Sydney.

Krausz, M., Haasen, C., Mass, R., Wagner, H., Peter, H. & Freyberger, H. (1996) 'Harmful Use of Psychotropic Substances by Schizophrenics: Coincidence, Patterns of Use and Motivation', *European Addiction Research*, 2, 11–16.

Kreig, A. (2006) 'Aboriginal Incarceration: Health and Social Impacts', *Medical Journal of Australia*, vol. 184, no. 10, 534–536.

Kulkarni, J., Kopolov, D. and Keks, N. (1991) 'Biological Investigations', in Kosky, R., Eshkevari, H. and Carr, V. (1991).

Laing, R.D. (1965) *The Divided Self*, Penguin, Harmondsworth.

— (1967) *The Politics of Experience and the Bird of Paradise*. Penguin, Great Britain.

— (1961) *Self and Others*, Penguin, Harmondsworth.

Ladouceur, R., Dugas, M. J., Freeston, M. H., Leger, E., Gagnon, E., & Thibodeau, N. (2000) 'Efficacy of a cognitive–behavioural treatment for generalised anxiety disorder: Evaluation in a controlled clinical trial', *Journal of Consulting and Clinical Psychology*, 68, 957–964.

Lampe, L. (1996) 'A Management Approach to Anxiety', *Australian Family Physician*, 25(10) 1561–1567.

Langan, J. (2001) 'Assessing Risk in Mental Health', in Parsloe, P. (ed.) (2001).

Lavie, P. (1996) *The Enchanted World of Sleep*, Yale University Press, New Haven.

Lawrence, F. (2011) *Dual Disability: Prevalence, Assessment, Management and Systemic Issues in Victoria*, Victorian Disability Service, Melbourne.

Leber, W.R., Docherty, J.P., Fiester, S.J. & Parloff, M.B. (1989) 'National Institute of Mental Health Treatment of Depression Collaborative Research Program: General effectiveness of treatments', *Archives of General Psychiatry*, 46, 971–982.

Leeder, S. (2003) 'Achieving equity in the Australian healthcare system', *Medical Journal of Australia*, vol. 179, 475–8.

Lehman, A., Myers, C., Corty, E. & Thompson, J. (1994) 'Prevalence and Patterns of Dual Diagnosis Among Psychiatric In–patients', *Comprehensive Psychiatry*, vol. 35, no. 2, 106–112.

Lehmann, J. (1975) *Virginia Woolf and her World*, Thames & Hudson, London.

Leibling, H., Chipcase, H. & Velangi, R. (1995) 'Why Do Women Self Harm at Ashworth Maximum Security Hospital?' in Deu, N. & Roberts, L. (eds) (1995).

Leonard, P. (1993) 'Knowledge/Power and Postmodernism: Implications for the Practice of a Critical Social Work Education', extended version of a paper given at the Annual Conference of the Canadian Association of Schools of Social Work, Ottawa.

Lewinsohn, P.M. & Gotlib, I.H. (1995) 'Behavioral theory and treatment of depression', in Becker, E.E. & Leber, W.R. (eds) (1995) 352–375.

Lindsay, R. (2002) Recognising Spirituality: *The Interface Between Faith and Social Work*, University of Western Australia Press, Crawley.

Linszen, D., Dingemans, P. & Lenior, M. (1994) 'Cannabis Use and the Course of Recent Onset Schizophrenic Disorders', *Archives of General Psychiatry*, 51:273–279.

Loebel, A.D., Lieberman, J.A. & Alvir, J.M. (1992) 'Duration of Psychosis and Outcome in First Episode Schizophrenia', *American Journal of Psychiatry*, 159, 1183–88.

London School of Economics (2006) *The depression report: A new deal for depression and anxiety disorders*, LSE Mental Health Policy Group, London.

Luce, G. (1973) 'Biological Rythyms', in Ornstein, R. (ed.).

Lyons, M. & Ziviani, J. (1995) 'Stereotypes, Stigma and Mental health issues: Learning form Fieldwork Experiences', *American Journal of Occupational Therapy*, 49, 1002– 1008.

Lyotard, J.F. (1989) 'Defining the Postmodern' in Appignanesi, L. (ed.) (1989)

Mackay, J. (1999) *Extraordinary Popular Delusions and the Madness of Crowds*, Templeton Foundation Press, Philadelphia.

MacKeith, J. & Burns, S. (2013) The Recovery Star: User Guide (Third Edition), Mental Health Providers Forum, London.

— (2013) The Recovery Star: Organisation Guide (Third Edition), Mental Health Providers Forum, London.

Mackie, K. & Sorom, A. (1999) 'Cannabinoid Receptor Function and Regulation: A Brief Review', Inaugural International Cannabis and Psychosis Conference Final Papers, Melbourne.

Maden, T., Swinton, M. & Gunn, J. (1994) 'Psychiatric Disorder in Women Serving a Prison Sentence', *British Journal of Psychiatry*, 164, 44–54.

Maidment, J. & Egan, R. (2004) *Practice Skills in Social Work and Welfare: More than Just Common Sense*, Allen & Unwin, NSW.

Mammen, G. (2006) *After Abuse*, ACER Press, Camberwell.

Marchant, H. & Wearing, B. (eds) (1986) *Gender Reclaimed: Women in Social Work*, Hale & Iremonger, NSW.

Martin, J. (1990) Mental Health Care for People with Acute Psychiatric Problems: Hospital or Community Treatment, Master of Social Work Thesis, University of Melbourne, Parkville unpublished.

— (1999) *In-Patient Mental Health Program for Women: An Issues Paper*, Victorian Institute of Forensic Mental Health, Melbourne.

— (2003) *An Ordinary Life in China, Malaysia and Australia*, Gininderra Press, ACT.

— (2007) *Conflict Management and Mediation*, Ginninderra Press, ACT.

— (2010a) 'Stigma and student mental health', Higher Education, *Journal of Higher Education Research and Development*, 29(3):259–274.

— (2010b) Continuing Professional Development and Mental Health Social Work, unpublished report commissioned by the Australian Association of Social Workers, ACT.

Martin, J. & Oswin, F. (2010) 'Stigma and Student Mental Health in Higher Education', *Advances in Social Work*, 11(1): 44–66.

Martin, J., McKay, E. & Thomas, T. (2005) 'Recovery from Mental health issues: Lifestyle and Employment Options', The Mental Health Services Conference of Australia and New Zealand, Gold Coast Convention Centre, Broadbeach, Queensland (September 1–3).

Maslow, A. (1998) *Toward a Psychology of Being*, third edition, J. Wiley & Sons, New York.

Mathers, C. & Loncar, D. (2006) 'Projections of global mortality and burden of disease from 2002 to 2030', *PLoS Medicine*, vol. 3, no. 11, 442, in Mayer R.E. (2001).

Mayer, R.E. (2001) *Multimedia Learning*, Cambridge Press, New York.

McClellan, D., Farabee, D. & Crouch, B. (1997) 'Early Victimization, Drug Use, and Criminality: A Comparison of Male and Female Prisoners', *Criminal Justice and Behaviour*, vol. 24, no. 4, 455–476.

Mcleod, S. (2008) Simply Psychology: Cognitive Behavioural Therapy, retrieved 8 December 2011 from http://www.simplypsychology.org/cognitivetherapy.html

McDermott, F. (2003) 'Group work in the Mental Health Field', *Australian Social Work*, vol. 56, no. 4, 352–363.

Mcgivern, D., Pellerito, S. & Mowbray, C. (2003) 'Barriers to higher education for individuals with psychiatric disabilities', *Psychiatric Rehabilitation Journal*, vol. 26, 217–231.

McGorry, P. (2001) 'Feasibility and Effectiveness of Early Intervention in Psychotic Disorders: the EPPIC Model', in Meadows, G. & Singh, B. (eds) (2001).

McGorry, P., Edwards, J. & Mihalopoulos, C. (1996) 'An Evolving System of Early Detection and Optimal Management', *Schizophrenia Bulletin*, 22, 305–326.

McGuiness, M. & Wadsworth, Y. (1992) *Understanding, Anytime: A Consumer Evaluation of an Acute Psychiatric Hospital*, second edition, Victorian Mental health issues Awareness Council, Brunswick, Victoria.

McIvor, R. (1998) 'The Community Treatment Order: Clinical and Ethical Issues', Australian and New Zealand Journal of Psychiatry, 32, 223–228.

McLean, P. & Andrews, J. (1999) *The learning support needs of students with psychiatric disabilities in Australian post-secondary institutions*, National Centre for Vocational Education Research (NCVER) Adelaide. 321

McLellan, B. (2004) 'Embedded with the Perpetrators', *Women Against Violence* (16):47–53.

Meadows, G. & Singh, B. (eds) (2001) *Mental Health in Australia*, Oxford University Press, South Melbourne.

Measey, M. L., Li, S.Q., Parker, R. & Wang, Z. (2006) 'Suicide in the Northern Territory, 1981–2002', *MJA*, 185, 315–319.

Mechanic D. (1989) *Mental Health and Social Policy*, third edition, Prentice-Hall, New Jersey.

Mental Health Act 1969 of New Zealand, commenced 1 April 1970; see section VII Offences 110, at http://www.austlii.edu.au

Mental Health (Compulsory Assessment and Treatment) Act 1992 (reprint as at 17 November 2003)(5).

Mental Health Coordinating Council and Adults Surviving Child Abuse (2013) Trauma

Informed Care and Practice: A national strategic direction. Paper presented at VICSERV Conference 2013 by C. Henderson available at: http://mhcc.org.au/media/34556/ch-a_national_strategic_direction-ticp-forum-presentation.pdf)

Mental Health Council of Australia & the Brain and Mind Research Institute (2005) Not for service – Experiences of injustice and despair in mental health care in Australia, in association with the Human Rights and Equal Opportunity Commission, at www.mhca.org.au

Mental Health First Aid Australia (2007). Psychosis: First Aid Guidelines for Asian Countries. Mental Health First Aid, Melbourne.

— (2012). Psychosis First Aid Guidelines, Mental Health First Aid, Melbourne.

Mental Health Legal Centre Inc. (Victoria) National Suicide Taskforce, AGPS, Canberra, at http://www.vicnet.net.au/–mhlc

Milburn, C. (2000) 'Call to Aid Children of the Mentally Ill', The Age, Tuesday 29 August, at http/home.vicnet.net.au–nnaami

Miller, W., Benefield, R., & Tonigan, S. (1993) 'Enhancing motivation for change in problem drinking: a controlled comparison of two therapist styles', Journal of Consulting and Clinical Psychology, 61, 4550–61.

Miller, W.R. & Rollnick, S. (1991) Motivational interviewing: Preparing people for change, Guilford Press, New York.

Mims (2003) Suicide and Mental health issues, at www. mydr.com.au

Mindframe (2003) Reporting Suicide and Mental health issues, at www.mindframe-media.info/nmmhg.html

— (2011) Reporting Suicide and Mental health issues, at http://www.mindframe-media.info/site/ index.cfm?display=84350

— (2016.) Facts and Stats about suicide, at: http://www.mindframe-media.info/for-media/reporting-suicide/facts-and-stat

Minuchin, S. (1974) Families and Family Therapy, Harvard University Press, Cambridge, Massachusetts.

Moisey, S.D. (2004) 'Students with disabilities in distance education: Characteristics, course enrolment and completion, and support services', Journal of Distance Education, vol. 9, 73–91.

Monahan, J. & Steadman, H.J. (eds) Violence and Mental Disorder: Developments in Risk Assessment, University of Chicago Press, Chicago.

Monti, P. M. & O'Leary, T.A. (1999) 'Coping and social skills training for alcohol and cocaine dependence', Psychiatric Clinics of North America, 22(2) 447–470.

Moreau, M.J. 1977, 'A Structural Approach to Social Work', unpublished paper, Carleton University School of Social Work, Ontario.

— (1979) 'A Structural Approach to Social Work Practice', Canadian Journal of Social Work Education, vol. 5, no. 1, 78–94.

Morgan C. (1983) Beyond Method, Strategies for Social Research, Sage Publications, California.

Morton, J. & Buckingham, B. (1994) Service Options for Clients with Severe or Borderline Personality Disorders, Consultants' Report, Psychiatric Services Branch, Health and Community Services, Victoria.

Mueser, K. (1999) 'Co-Morbid Cannabis Use and Serious Mental health issues – Therapeutic Challenges', Inaugural International Cannabis and Psychosis Conference Final Papers, Melbourne.

Mueser, K. & Noordsy, D.L. (1996) 'Group Treatment for Dually Diagnosed Clients', in Drake, R.E. & Mueser, K.T. (eds) (1996).

Mueser, K., Bellack, A. & Blachard, J. (1992) 'Co-morbidity and Substance Abuse: Implications for Treatment', Journal of Consulting and Clinical Psychology, 60: 845–856.

Muir, K., Fisher, K.R., Dadich, A. & A'Bello, D. (2008) 'Challenging the exclusion of people with mental health issues: The mental health housing and accommodation support initiative', Australian Journal of Social Issues, 43(2) 479–497.

Mulaik, J. (1992) 'Non–compliance with Medication Regimens in Severely and Persistently Ill Schizophrenic Patients', Issues in Mental Health Nursing, vol. 13, 219–227.

Mullaly, B. (1997) Structural Social Work, Oxford University Press, Toronto. 322

Mullen, P., Martin, J. & Anderson, J. (1993) 'Childhood Sexual Abuse and Mental Health in Adult Life', British Journal of Psychiatry, 163:721–32.

Munby, J. & Johnston, D.W. (1980) 'Agoraphobia: long term follow up of behavioural treatment', British Journal of Psychiatry, 135, 418–27.

Murray Parkes, C. (1987) Bereavement, Studies of Grief in Adult Life, Penguin Books, Harmondsworth.

Murthy, R.K. (2008) Monitoring Sexual and Reproductive Health and Rights in the Context of Disasters in Asia, Gender Aspects of Disaster Recovery and Reconstruction,

World Bank Institute Distance Learning Natural Disaster Risk Management Program, Washington, DC.

Nathan, P.E., Gorman, J.M. (eds) (1998) *A guide to treatments that work*, Oxford University Press, New York.

National Clearinghouse for Alcohol and Drug Information (2005) Women and Substance Abuse Issues, at http://ncadi.samhsa.gov accessed 10/6/05.

National Clearinghouse for Alcohol and Drug Information (2005) If Someone Close…Has a Problem With Alcohol or Other Drugs, at www.health.org/gov/pubs accessed 10/6/05.

National Drug and Alcohol Research Centre (1977) *National Survey of Mental Health and Wellbeing*, NDARC Technical Report No. 63, Sydney.

National Mental Health Strategy (1995) *What is Stigma?* AGPS, Canberra.

— (2000a) *What Are Anxiety Disorders?* Mental Health Foundation, Richmond.

— (2000b) *What is Schizophrenia?* Mental Health Foundation, Richmond.

National Network of Adult and Adolescent Children who have a Mentally Ill Parentis (NNAAMI) (2000) home page at: http//www.home.vicnet.net.au-nnaami

National Survey of Mental Health and Well-Being (1997) at www.mydr.com.au

Negy, C., Woods, D. & Carlson, R., 'The Relationship Between Female Inmates, Coping and Adjustment in a Medium Security Prison', *Criminal Justice and Behaviour*, 24, 224–233.

Neisser, U. (1982) *Memory Observed: Remembering in Natural Contexts*, Freeman and Co., San Francisco.

New South Wales Parliament Legislative Council Standing Committee on Social Issues (1996) *Sexual Violence: Addressing the Crime*, Sydney.

New Zealand Mental Health Commission (1998) Blueprint for Mental Health Services in New Zealand, at www.info@mhc.govt.nz

— (2001) Housing Checklists for Health, Housing and Income Sectors, at www.info@mhc.govt.nz

— (2002a) Mental Health Recovery Competencies Teaching Resource Kit, p. 18, at www.info@mhc.govt.nz

— (2002b) Recovery Competencies for New Zealand Mental Health Workers, at www.info@mhc.govt.nz

Novaco, R.W. (1979) 'The cognitive regulation of anger and stress', in Kendall, P.C. & Hollon S.D. (eds) (1979).

Nueberger, J. (2004) *Dying Well: A Guide to Enabling a Good Death*, Radcliffe Publishing, London.

Nuechterlein K. (1987) 'Vulnerability Models for Schizophrenia: State of the Art', in Hafner, H. & Janzarik, W. (eds) (1987).

Oakley, A. & Bohan, M. (2003) 'We Know We Are Doing Our Share…', in *Carers Victoria Annual Report* (2003).

O'Hagan, M. (2004a) Keynote Address, VICSERV Conference, Recovery: Challenging the Paradigm, 29–30 April, The Heath Function Centre, Caulfield Racecourse, Melbourne.

— (2004b)'Recovery in New Zealand – Lessons for Australia?', *Ausinetter*, issue 20, no. 1.

Opolski, M., Marshall, C. & Howell, C. (2008) 'Management of Recurrent Depression', *Australian Family Physician*, 37(9):704–708.

Orme, J. (1998) 'Feminist Social Work', in Adams, R., Dominelli, L. & Payne (1998).

Ornstein, R. (ed.) *The Nature of Human Consciousness: A Book of Readings*, W.H. Freeman & Co., San Francisco. 323

Oxfam (2005) *The tsunami's impact on women*, Oxfam International, Mumbai.

Parsloe, P. (ed.) (2001) *Risk Assessment in Social Care and Social Work*, Jessica Kingsley Publishers, London.

Pathe, M. (1993) *The Cycle of Abuse in Women Prisoners; A Preliminary Report*, Rosanna Forensic Psychiatry Centre, Victoria.

Payne, M. (1997) *Modern Social Work Theory*, second edition, Macmillan Press, London.

Pease, B. (2004) 'Rethinking profeminist men's behaviour change programs,' *Women Against Violence* (16):3–40.

Pease, B. & Fook, J. (1999) *Transforming Social Work Practice*, Allen & Unwin, Sydney.

Pemberton, A. & Locke, R. (1975) 'Knowledge, Order and Power in Social Work and Social Welfare', in Throssell, H. (1975).

Pemberton, L. (2004) 'A Consumer Perspective on Best Practices in Mental Health', lecture presented in mental health course at RMIT University, Melbourne.

Phillips, J., Ray, M & Marshall, M. (2006) *Social Work with Older People*, fourth edition, Palgrave, Basingstroke.

Pietsch, J. & Cuff, R. (1995) *Hidden Children: Families Caught Between Two Systems*, Mental Health Research Institute, Melbourne.

Pilgrim, D. (2005) *Key concepts in mental health*, Sage Publications Ltd, London.

— (2011) 'The hegemony of cognitive-behaviour

therapy in modern mental health care', *Health Sociology Review*, 20, 2, 120–33

Pincha, C. (2008) *Indian Ocean Tsunami Through the Gender Lens*, Oxfam International, Mumbai.

Pincus, L. (1976) *Death and the Family*, Faber, London.

Porter, L. (2003) 'Sudden Death Dogs Ex-Prisoners', *The Age*, Melbourne.

Power, K. G., Simpson, R. J., Swanson, V., Wallace, L.A., Feistner, A. T. C., & Sharp, D. (1990) 'A controlled comparison of cognitive–behaviour therpay, diazepam, and placebo, alone and in combination, for the treatment of generalized anxiety', *Journal of Anxiety Disorders*, 4, 267–292.

Pridmore, S. (1984) *The Case of Joshua Kirk*, Schizophrenia Fellowship, Melbourne.

PubMedHealth (2010) Post–traumatic stress disorder, US National Library of Medicine, National Institute of Health, at http://www.ncbi.nlm.nih.gov/pubmedhealth/PMH0001923

Quadrelli, C. (1997) 'Women in Prison', *Themis*, 2(2) pp. 15–22, Queensland University of Technology, Faculty of Law, Justice Studies.

Raeside, C. (1995) 'Post Traumatic Stress Disorders in a Female Prison Population', Examination for Membership, Dissertation for Part 2, Royal Australian and New Zealand College of Psychiatrists.

Rao, A. & Kelleher, D. (2003) 'Institutions, organizations and gender equality in an era of globalization', *Gender and Development*, 11(1) 142–145.

— (2005) Is there life after gender mainstreaming?', *Gender and Development*, 13(2) 57–69.

Real, T. (1997) *I Don't Want to Talk About It, Overcoming the Secret Legacy of Male Depression*, Newleaf, New York.

Reidpath, D., Chan, K., Gifford, S. & Allotey, P. (2005) '"He hath the French pox": stigma, social value and social exclusion', *Sociology of Health and Illness*, vol. 27, no. 4, 468–489.

Reiger, D., Farmer, M., Rae, D., Locke, B, Keith, S., Judd, L. & Goodwin, F. (1990) 'Co-morbidity of Mental Disorders with Alcohol and other Drug Use: Results from the Epidemiological Catchment Area Study', *JAMA*, 264 (19) 2511–18.

Reuter, P. & MacCoun (1999) 'Weighing the Harms of Cannabis Use and Cannabis Protection', Inaugural International Cannabis and Psychosis Conference Final Papers, Melbourne.

Rice, S. (2002) 'Magic Happens: Revisiting the Spirituality and Social Work Debate', *Australian Social Work*, vol. 54, no. 3, 303–312.

Richardson, J. (2005) 'Priorities of health policy: Cost shifting or population health', *Australia and New Zealand Health Policy*, vol. 2, 1–19.

Ring, D., Brophy, L. & Gimlinger, A. (2001) 'Examining Community Treatment Orders in Victoria – A Preliminary Enquiry into their Efficacy', *Health Issues Magazine*, 66, 13–17.

Ring, I. & Brown, N. (2002) 'Indigenous Health: Chronically Inadequate Responses to Damning Statistics', *Medical Journal of Australia*, vol. 177, no. 11, 629–631 324.

Rock, P. (1979) *The Making of Symbolic Interactionism*, Macmillan Press, London.

Rolfe, T., McGorry, P., Cocks, J., Yuen, H., Longley, T. and Plowright, D. (1999) 'Cannabis Use in First Episode Psychosis, Incidence and Short-term Outcome', Inaugural International Cannabis and Psychosis Conference Final Papers, Melbourne.

Romans, S., Martin, J. & Mullen, P. (1997) 'Childhood Sexual Abuse and Later Psychological Problems: Neither Necessary, Sufficient Nor Acting Alone', *Criminal Behaviour and Mental Health*, 7:327–338.

Romme, M. & Escher, A. (1996) 'Empowering People Who Hear Voices', in Haddock, G. & Slade, P. (eds) (1996).

Rosen, A., Hadzi-Pavlovic, D., Parker, G. & Traur, T. (2006) *The Life Skills Profile*, Sydney, Royal North Dhore Hospital and Community Mental Health Services.

Rosenham, D. (1973) 'On Being Sane in Insane Places', *Science*, vol. 179.

Rothman, T. (ed.) (1970) *Changing Patterns in Psychiatric Care*, Rush Research Foundation, New York.

Royal Australian and New Zealand College of Psychiatrists (2004) 'Clinical Practice Guidelines Team for Depression. Australian and New Zealand clinical practice guidelines for the treatment of depression', *Australian and New Zealand Journal of Psychiatry* 38:389–407.

Rummery, F. (1996) Psychiatric definitions as sane as they seem, Balancing the Scales, National Conference on Sexual Assault Proceedings, Perth, 20–21 June, 3.

Rutherford, A. (1997) 'Women, Sentencing and Prisons', *New Law Journal*, 21 March, 424–5.

Sahler, O.J., Varni, J.W., Fairclough, D.L., Butler, R.W., Noll, R.B., Dolgin, M.J., Phipps, S., Copeland, D.R., Katz, Ernest R. & Mulhern, R.K. (2002) 'Problem–solving skills training for mothers of children with newly diagnosed cancer:

A randomized trial', *Journal of Developmental & Behavioral Pediatrics*, 23(2) 77–86.

Salthouse, S. & Frohmader, C. (2004) 'Real trouble in the home: the domestic violence reality for women with disabilities', *DVIRC Newsletter*, summer edition, Melbourne.

Saunders, P. (2007) 'The costs of disability and the incidence of poverty', *Australian Journal of Social Issues*, 42(4) 461–480.

SANE Australia (2003) Why Stigma Matters, at www.sane.org/stigmamatter.html

— (2005) People Need People, at http://www.sane.org

Sax, S. (1972) *Medical Care in the Melting Pot: An Australian Review*, Angus & Robertson, Sydney.

— (1973) *Report of Interim Committee*, National Hospitals and Health Services Commission, Canberra.

Saxon, R. & Emslie, A. (1998) *Women's Health Consultation: Final Report*, The Health Development Group, Melbourne.

Scheff, T.J. (1968) 'Negotiating Reality: Notes on Power in the Assessment of Responsibility', *Social Problems*, vol. 16, no. 1, 3–7.

Schwartz, M. (1994) Mental Status Examination, Participant Notes.

Schizophrenia Fellowship of New South Wales (2016) Schizophrenia Statistics.http://www.sfnsw.org.au/Mental-Illness/Schizophrenia/Schizophrenia-Statistics

Segal, Z., Williams J. & Teasdale J. (2003) *Mindfulness-based cognitive therapy for depression: A new approach to preventing relapse*, Guilford Press, New York.

Shankar, J., Martin, J. & McDonald, C. (2009) 'Emerging areas of practice for mental health social workers: Education and employment', *Australian Social Work*, vol. 62, no. 1, 28–45.

Sharpe, S. (1999) *The Bewitchment of Anne Gunter*, Routledge, New York.

Shedler, J. & Block (1990) 'Adolescent Drug Use and Psychological Health: A Longitudinal Inquiry', *American Psychologist*, 45, 612–630.

Sherl, D.J. & Macht, L.B. (1979) 'De-Instititionalisation in the Absence of Consensus', *Hospital and Community Psychiatry*, no. 30, 599–604.

Singer, J. (1966) *Daydreaming*, Random House, New York.

Singer, M., Bussey, J., Song, L. & Lunghofer, L. (1995) 'The Psychosocial Issues of Women Serving Time in Jail', *Social Work*, 40(1) 103–113.

Sisters Inside (2001) Age Does Matter, submission to the Juvenile Justice Amendment Bill 2001, Consultation Draft, at www.sistersinside.com.au/reports

— (2004) Submission, March 2003, Poverty in Australia Inquiry, Sisters Inside, Queensland, at www.sistersinside.com.au/reports

Skelton, R. (2012) 'Symbols of despair and a national disgrace', *The Saturday Age*, 11 February.

Skinner, B. (1961) *Cumulative Record*, USA, Appleton Century Crofts.

Southwell, J. (2004) *Support Groups for People Affected by Family Violence*, Domestic Violence Resource Centre, Melbourne.

Soyka, M., Kathman, N., Finelli, A., Hofstetter, S., Imler, B. & Sand, P. (1993) 'Prevalence of Drug and Alcohol Abuse in Schizophrenic In-patients', *European Archives Psychiatry Clinical Neuro-science*, 242, 362–372.

Spaniol, L., Gagne C. & Koehler M. (eds) (1997) *Psychological and social aspects of psychiatric disability*, Centre for Psychiatric Rehabilitation, Boston.

Stahl, S. (1996) *Essential Psychopharmacology*, Cambridge University Press, Cambridge.

State Government of Victoria (2010) Victorian Bushfire Support, Department of Health, at http://www.health.vic.gov.au

Steenkamp, M. & Harrison, J. (2000) *Suicide and Hospitalised Self-harm in Australia*, AIHW, Canberra.

Stein, L.I. & Test M.A. (1978) *Alternatives to Mental Hospital Treatment*, Plenum Press, New York.

— (1980) 'Alternatives to Mental Hospital Treatment: Social Cost', *Archives of General Psychiatry*, vol. 37, 409–12.

Steinhauer, P. & Rae-Grant, Q. (1983) *Psychological Problems of the Child in the Family*, Basic Books, New York.

Stephens, C., Porter, J., Nettleton, C. & Willis, R. (2006) 'Disappearing, Displaced and Undervalued: A Call to Action for Indigenous Health Worldwide', *Lancet*, 367(9527):2019–2028.

Substance Abuse and Mental Health Services Association (2003) National Household Survey on Drug Abuse, 2003, Children Living with Substance-Abusing or Substance-Dependent Parents, United States Department of Health and Human Services, at http://oas.samhsa.govaccessed 9/6/05.

Sullivan, W. (1997) 'A long and winding road: The process of recovery from severe mental health issues', in Spaniol, L., Gagne C. & Koehler M. (eds) (1997).

Swain, P. (2000) 'Admitted and Detained: Community Members and Mental Health Review Boards', *Journal of Psychiatry, Psychology and Law*, 7(1) 79–99.

— (ed.) (2009) *In the Shadow of the Law*, The Federation Press, NSW.

Szasz, T.S. (1961) *The Myth of Mental health issues*, Hoeber-Rowe, New York.

— (1963) *Law, Liberty and Psychiatry*, Macmillan, New York.

Tait, C. (ed.) (1969) *Altered States of Consciousness*, John Wiley & Sons, New York.

Tang, T, DeRubeis, R, Hollon, S. & Shelton, R. (2007) 'Sudden gains in cognitive therapy of depression and depression relapse/recurrence', *Journal of Consulting & Clinical Psychology*, 75:404–8.

Taylor, S. (1996) 'Meta-analysis of cognitive behavioural treatments for social phobia', *Journal of Behaviour Therapy and Experimental Psychiatry*, 27, 1–9.

Teasdale, J.D., Scott, J., Moore, R.G., Hayhurst, H., Pope, M. & Paykel, E.S. (2001) 'How does cognitive therapy prevent relapse in residual depression? Evidence from a controlled trial',. *Journal of Consulting & Clinical Psychology*, 69(3) 347–357.

Teplin, L., Abram, K. & McClelland, G. (1996) 'Prevalence of Psychiatric Disorders Among Incarcerated Women', *Archives of General Psychiatry*, 53, 505–19.

— 1997) 'Mentally Disordered Women in Jail: Who Receives Services?', *American Journal of Public Health*, 87, 604–9.

Thompson, N. (1998) *Promoting Equality: Challenging Discrimination and Oppression in the Human Services*, Macmillan, London.

Throssell, H. (1975) *Social Work: Radical Essays*, University of Queensland Press, St Lucia.

Tien, A. & Anthony, J. (1990) 'Epidemiological Analysis of Alcohol and Drug Use as Risk Factors for Psychotic Experiences', *Journal of Nervous and Mental Disease*, 178, 473–480.

Todd, F., Joyce, P. & Mulder, R. (1999) 'Cannabis is Associated with Increased Levels of Paranoia in Depressed Males', Inaugural International Cannabis and Psychosis Conference Final Papers, Melbourne.

Tschudin, V. (1997) *Counselling for Loss and Bereavement*, Bailliere Tindall, London.

Tsuang, M., Tohen, M. & Zahner, G. (eds) *Textbook in Psychiatric Epidemiology*, Wiley and Sons, New York.

Turner, F.J. (2002) *Diagnosis in Social Work: New Imperatives*, Hawthorn Press, New York.

Tutnjevic, T. (2003) Gender in Crisis Response: *A Guide to the Gender-Poverty-Employment Link: Infocus Programme on Crisis Response and Reconstruction*, International Labor Office, Geneva.

Uldall, K.K. & Palmer, N.B. (2004) 'Sexual Minorities and Mental Health: The Need for a Public Health Response', *Journal of Gay & Lesbian Psychotherapy*, 8: 3, 11– 24.

UNIMAS (2005) *Evaluation of Social Work Students on Field Placement*, Faculty of Social Science, University of Malaysia Sarawak, Kuching.

United Nations (2007) *Gender Perspective: Working Together for Disaster Risk Management: Good Practices and Lessons Learned*, International Strategy for Disaster Reduction, UN/ISDR Secretariat, Geneva.

United Nations Commissioner for Refugees and the Victorian Foundation for Survivors of Torture (2002) *Refugee Resettlement: An International Handbook to Guide Reception and Integration*, VFST, Melbourne.

United Nations Economic Commission for Latin America and the Caribbean (2003) *Handbook for Estimating the Socio–Economic and Environmental Effects of Disasters*, UNECLAC, Santiago, Chile.

United Nations /International Committee for Strategy for Disaster Recovery (2002) *Gender Mainstreaming in Disaster Recovery*, UN/ISDR Secretariat, Geneva.

United Nations (1991) *Principles for the Protection of Persons with Mental health issues and the Improvement of Mental Health Care*.

United States Department of Health and Human Services (2005) Ecstasy, Other Club Drugs and Other Hallucinogens, Substance Abuse and Mental Health Services Administration, at http://oas.samhsa.gov/ecstasy.htm accessed 9/6/05.

Van der Kolk, J., Perry, C. & Herman, J. (1991) 'Childhood Origins of Self-Destructive Behaviour', *American Journal of Psychiatry*, 148 (12):1665–71.

Van Dongen, C. (1996) 'Quality of Life and Self–Esteem in Working and Non–working persons with Mental health issues', *Community Mental Health Journal*, New York, vol. 32, issue 6, 535–549.

Victorian Bushfires Royal Commission (2009) Transcript of Proceedings, CRS Worldwave, Transcripts of proceedings, Day 1–Day 30, Melbourne.

Victorian Department of Health and Community Services (1994) *Victoria's Mental Health*

Services: Improved Access through Coordinated Client Care, Psychiatric Services Branch, 26.

— (1996) *Victoria's Mental Health Service: The Framework for Service Delivery*, Psychiatric Services Division.

— (1996) *General Adult Community Mental Health Services: Guidelines for Service Provision*, Psychiatric Services Branch, 50.

— (1997) *Victoria's Mental Health Services Tailoring Services to Meet the Needs of Women*, Aged, Community and Mental Health Division, 16–17.

— (2009) *Because mental health matters: Victorian Mental Health Reform Strategy 2009–2019*, DHS Mental Health and Drugs Division, Melbourne.

Victorian Department of Human Services (1996) *Victoria's Mental Health Services Working with Consumers: Guidelines for Consumer Participation in Mental Health Services*, Aged, Community and Mental Health Division.

Victorian Foundation for Survivors of Torture Inc. (1998) *Rebuilding Shattered Lives*, VFST, Melbourne.

Victorian Mental health issues Awareness Council (1996) *Lemon Tree Learning Project*, Bulletin No. 6, Melbourne.

Victorian Taskforce Report (1997) *Suicide Prevention*, Victorian Government, Melbourne.

Videka-Sherman, L. (1988) 'Meta-Analysis of Research on Social Work Practice in Mental Health', *Australian Social Work*, 325–8.

Watkins, J.(1998) Hearing Voices, Hill of Content, Melbourne.

Wearing, B. (1986) 'Feminist Theory in Social Work' in Marchant, H. & Wearing, B. (eds (1986).

Webster-Stratton, C., Reid J., & Hammond, M. (2001) 'Social skills and problem-solving training for children with early-onset conduct problems: who benefits?', *Journal of Child Psychology & Psychiatry & Allied Disciplines*, 42(7) 943–52.

Weissman, M.M., Prusoff, B.A., DiMascio, A., Neu, C., Goklaney, M., & Klerman, G.L. (1979) 'The efficacy of drugs and psychotherapy in the treatment of acute depressive episodes', *American Journal of Psychiatry*, 136(4B) 555–558

Willshire, D. & Newnham, L. (1995) Review Options for Behaviourally Disordered Prisoners at Fairlea, unpublished paper.

Wilson v Mental Health Review Board &Ors (2000) VSC404 (6 October 2000) at http://www.austlii.edu.au/cgi-bin/disp.pl/au/cases/vic/VSC/2000/404

Wilson I, Duszynski K. & Mant A. (2003) 'A 5-year follow-up of general practice patients experiencing depression', *Family Practice* 20:685–9.

Wilson, J., & Leasure, R. (1991) 'Cruel and Unusual Punishment: The Health Care of Women in Prison', Health Care Issues, 16(2) 32–38.

Wilson, T. (2002) *Strangers to Ourselves: Discovering the Adaptive Unconscious*, Harvard University Press, Cambridge, Massachusetts.

Wirth, H. & Harari, R. (2000) 'Deconstructing Depression: A Narrative Groupwork Approach', *Dulwich Centre Journal*, nos 1 & 2, 42–51.

Wolfensberger, W. (ed.) (1972) *Normalization: The Principles of Normalization in Human Services*, Canadian Association for the Mentally Retarded, Canada.

World Bank (2009) *Guidelines for Gender Sensitive Crises Response and Reconstruction Planning, Gender Aspects of Disaster Recovery and Reconstruction*, World Bank Institute Distance Learning Natural Disaster Risk Management Program, Washington DC.

World Health Organisation *The ICD–10 Classification of Mental and Behavioral Disorders: Clinical Descriptions and Diagnostic Guidelines*, World Health Organisation, Geneva.

World Health Organisation *International Classification of Diseases*, WHO, Washington.

— (2000) *Treatment Protocol Project for Management of Mental Disorders*, third edition, World Health Organisation Collaborating Centre for Mental Health and Substance Abuse, Sydney.

— (2009) What is mental health?, at http://www.who.int

Yarran v The Queen (2003) WASCA261 (5 November 2003) at http://www.austlii.edu.au/cgi–bin/disp.pl/au/cases/wa/WASCA/2003/261

Yonder, A., Akcar, S. & Gopolan, P. (2005) 'Women's Participation in Disaster Relief and Recovery', *Seeds*, No. 22, Population Council, New York.

Zastrow C. (1999) *The Practice of Social Work*, sixth edition, Brookes/Cole, New York.

Ziguras, S., Henley, K., Conron, K. & Catford, N. (1999) 'Social work in mental health services: A survey of the field', *Australian Social Work*, 52, 53–59.

Zubin & Spring (1977) 'Vulnerability – A New View of Schizophrenia', *Journal of Abnormal Psychology*, 86:103–126.

Notes

Introduction

1. Horwood, B. (1996).
2. Engel, G. (1977).
3. All identifying information has been changed.

Chapter 1

1. Kocher, P. (1972) p. 2.
2. Barry, P. (2002) pp. 191–2.
3. American Psychiatric Association (1994) p. 767.
4. Freud, S. (1966) p. 261.
5. Watkins, J. (1998) pp. 25–51.
6. Lavie, P. (1996) p. 70.
7. Farraday, A. (1975) p. 66.
8. Lavie, P. (1996) pp. 89–90.
9. Ibid., pp. 90–91.
10. Ibid., p. 92.
11. Grinstein, A. (1968) p. 460.
12. Lavie, P. (1996) p. 81.
13. Bleuler, E. (1950) p. 440.
14. Singer, J. (1966).
15. Farraday, A. (1975) p. 25
16. Steinhauer, P. & Rae-Grant, Q. (1983) p. 26.
17. See Pincus, L. (1976).
18. Nueberger, J. (2004).
19. Tschudin, V. (1997) p. 20.
20. Murray Parkes, C. (1987) p. 21.
21. Watkins, J. (1998) pp. 13–14.
22. See Joseph's account of the death of his wife Maria and her appearance after her death in Martin, J. (2003).
23. Ensink, B. (1992).
24. James, W. (1973) p. 9.
25. It has been estimated that rates of post–traumatic stress disorder for refugees vary between 39 per cent and 100 per cent compared with 1 per cent for the general population in United Nations Commissioner for Refugees and the Victorian Foundation for Survivors of Torture (2002) p. 233.
26. See Kevasham, M., David, A., Steingard, S. & Lisham, W. (1992).
27. Steinhauer, P. & Rae–Grant, Q. (1983).
28. See Chapter 12.
29. Luce, G. (1973).
30. The term 'psychedelic' means 'mind manifesting' and was first used by Humphrey Osmond (1957). He argued that terms such as

'hallucinatory' were misleading as they did not capture the range of effects of these drugs, with hallucinations not seen as a major characteristic in Tait, C. (1969) p. 321.
31. Feeney, E. (2004) p. 89.
32. Huxley, p. 151.
33. Huxley, p. 146.
34. Deikman, A. (1973).
35. Wilson, T. (2002) p. 95.
36. Deikman, A. (1973) p. 228.
37. Watkins, J. (1998) pp. 30–48.
38. James, W. (1973) p. 79.
39. Aaronson, B. (1969).
40. Freud, S. (1966).
41. Watkins, J. (1998) p. 68.
42. Ibid., p. 76.
43. Rosenham, D. (1973).
44. Watkins, J. (1998) p. 78.
45. Lehmann, J. (1975) p. 14.
46. Ibid.
47. Romme, M. & Escher, A. (1996).
48. American Psychiatric Association (1994).
49. Ibid.
50. Watkins, J. (1998) p. 96.

Chapter 2

1. See Mechanic, D. (1989).
2. Gallagher, B.J. (1987).
3. Rothman T. (ed.) (1970).
4. Gallagher B.J. (1987).
5. Sharpe (1999) p. 188.
6. Ibid., p. 58.
7. Mackay, J. (1999) p. 483.
8. Ibid., p. 472.
9. Gallagher, B.J. (1987).
10. The Museum of Victoria has a collection of restraints used in psychiatric hospitals, previously held at the Mental Health Museum in Parkville, available for private viewing by request.
11. Cunningham-Dax, E. (1961.
12. Gallagher, B.J. (1987).
13. Grobb G. (1966).
14. Ibid.; and Gallagher B.J.
15. Mechanic, D. (1989).
16. Cunningham-Dax, E. (1961).
17. Ibid., p. 20.
18. Caplan G. (1961); and Mechanic, D. (1989).

19. Wolfensberger, W. (ed.) (1972).
20. Goffman, E. (1961).
21. Szasz T.S. (1961); and Szasz T.S. (1963).
22. Laing, R.D. (1967). Also see Laing, R.D. (1965) and Laing, R.D. (1961) .
23. See Johnson, K. (1998) for a discussion of the deinstitutionalisation of women and the closure of an intellectual disability institution.
24. Ibid., p. 157.
25. Mechanic, D. (1989).
26. Sax, S. (1972); and Sax, S. (1973).
27. Henry, G. (1985).
28. Hoult, J. (1983).
29. Stein L.I. & Test M.A. (1978).
30. Hoult, J. (1983).
31. Sherl D.J. & Macht L.B. (1979).
32. Hoult, J. (1983).
33. See the annual reports of the Victorian Office of the Public Advocate, at http://www.opa.vic.gov.au

Chapter 3

1. Knapp, M., McDaid, D., Mossialos, E. & Thornicroft, G. (2007) pp. 1–14.
2. World Health Organisation (2009).
3. Mathers, C. & Loncar, D. (2006).
4. Mcgivern, D., Pellerito, S. & Mowbray, C. (2003); and McLean, P. & Andrews, J. 1999.
5. New Zealand Mental Health Commission (1998).
6. New Zealand Mental Health Commission (2002b). Also see New Zealand Mental Health Commission (2002a).
7. Mathers, C. & Loncar, D. (2006).
8. World Health Organisation (2009).
9. Leeder, S. (2003).
10. Braverman, P. & Gruskin, S. (2003) p. 539.
11. World Health Organisation (2009).
12 Ibid.
13. Reidpath, D., Chan, K., Gifford, S. & Allotey, P. (2005) p. 468.
14. Richardson, J. (2005).
15. Harding, C., Brooks, G., Asolaga, T. and Breier, A. (1987).
16. Sullivan, W. (1997).
17. Davidson, L., Stayner, D. Nickou, C., Styron, T. H., Rowe, M. & Chinman, M. (2004) p. 10.
18. Anthony, W. A. (1993).
19. O'Hagan, M. (2004b) p. 5.
20. Ibid.
21. New Zealand Mental Health Commission (2002) p. 6
22. Sullivan, W. (1997).
23. Deegan, P. (1996).
24. SANE Australia (2005).
25. Australian Bureau of Statistics (2002) p. 1.
26. National Survey of Mental Health and Well-Being (1997).
27. Martin J. (1990).
28. Davidson, L., Stayner, D. Nickou, C., Styron, T.H., Rowe, M. & Chinman, M. (2004) p. 11.
29. Ibid, p. 12.
30. O'Hagan, M. (2004) p.6.
31. SANE Australia (2006); and Granello, D. & Wheaton, J. (2001) p. 9.
32. Reidpath, D., Chan, K., Gifford, S. & Allotey, P. (2005) p. 485.
33. National Mental Health Strategy (1995) p. 1.
34. Jamison, K.R. (2006) pp. 533–34.
35. Uldall, K.K. & Palmer, N.B.(2004) p. 11.
36. Burdekin, B. (1993).
37. Granello, D. & Wheaton, J. (2001) pp. 9–17.
38. Corrigan, P., River, L., London, R. Wasowski, K., Campion, J. (2000) pp. 91–102.
39. Burris, S. (2006) p. 529.
40. Davidson, L., Stayner, D. Nickou, C., Styron, T. H., Rowe, M. & Chinman, M. (2004) p. 11.
41. Australian Bureau of Statistics (2002b) p. 1.
42. SANE Australia (2003); and Corrigan, P., River, L., London, R. Wasowski, K. & Campion, J. (2000) pp. 91–102; Lyons, M. & Ziviani, J. (1995) pp. 1002–1008; and Elliot, T. & Frank, R. (1990) pp. 135–47.
43. Martin, J. & Oswin, F. (2010) p. 45.
44. Pilgrim, D. (2005) p. 158.
45. *Mental Health (Compulsory Assessment and Treatment) Act 1992* (Reprint as at 17 November 2003).
46. Victorian Government Department of Human Services (1996) p. 30; and Victorian Government Department of Human Services (1996).
47. Gerrand, V. (1993) p. 69.
48. There are numerous texts and guidelines on how to work effectively with interpreters. See the best practice principles for working with interpreters by Loula Rodopoulos in 'Culture and Linguistic Entanglement' in Swain, P. (2002) pp. 25–6.
49. Hess, L. (1992).
50. Kreig, A. (2006) pp. 534–536; Ring, I. & Brown, N. (2002) pp. 629–631; and Hunter, E. & Harvey, D. (2002) pp. 14–23.
51. Cunningham, J., Cass, A. & Arnold, P. (2005) pp. 505–506; Elliot–Farrelly, T. (2004) pp. 1–8; Stephens, C., Porter, J., Nettleton, C. & Willis, R. (2006) pp. 2019–2028; and Brown, R. (2005) pp. 33–41. 331
52. King, R., Appleby, M. & Brown, C. (1995) pp. 1–4.

53. Kanowski, L., Kitchener, B. & Jorm, A. (eds) (2008).
54. Ibid, p. 4.
55. Victorian Government Department of Human Services (1996) p. 30.
56. Martin, J. (1999).
57. For a discussion of the psycho-social impact of torture and trauma and worker skills, see Victorian Foundation for Survivors of Torture Inc. (1998).
58. See Kenny, M. Fiske, L and Ife, J. (2002).
59. Acoca, L. (1998) p .63; and Wilson, J., and Leasure, R. (1991) p. 34.
60. Victorian Government Department of Human Services (1994, p. 36.
61. Victorian Government Department of Health and Community Services (1994) p. 36.
62. Cox, M. (1994)
63. New South Wales Parliament Legislative Council Standing Committee on Social Issues (1996).
64. Romans, S., Martin, J. & Mullen, P. (1997) pp. 327–338.
65. McClellan, D., Farabee, D. & Crouch, B. (1997) p. 470; and Mullen, P., Martin, J. & Anderson, J. (1993) pp. 721–32.
66. Victorian Government Department of Human Services (1997) p. 5.
67. Herrman, H., Mills, J., Doidge, G., McGorry, P. & Singh, B. (1994) pp. 63–8.
68. Alder, C. (1997) p. 52; McClellan, D., Farabee, D. & Crouch, B. (1997) p. 455; Singer, M., Bussey, J., Song, L. & Lunghofer, L. (1995) pp. 103–113; and Pathe, M. (1993).
69. Alder, C. (1997) pp. 43–59.
70. Gerrand, V. (1993) p. 3.
71. Victorian Government Department of Human Services (1997) p. 13; and Victorian Government Department of Human Services (1996) p. 27.
72. Carnaby, H. (1998) p. 77.
73. Shankar, J., Martin, J. & McDonald, C. (2009) pp. 28–45.
74. Collins, M. & Mowbray, C. (2005) pp. 80–315.
75. Cavallaro, T., Foley, P., Saunders, J. & Bowman, K. (2005); and Moisey, S.D. (2004) pp. 73–91.
76. Hassed, C., Sierpina, V. & Kreitzer, M. (2008) pp. 394–7.
77. Martin, J. & Oswin, F. (2010) pp. 44–66.
78. Conger, J. (1979) p. .
79. Davidson, L., Stayner, D. Nickou, C., Styron, T.H., Rowe, M. & Chinman, M. (2004) p. 10.
80. Shankar, J., Martin, J. & McDonald, C. (2009) pp. 28–45.
81. Keating, P. (2004).
82. D'Arcy, M. (1993).
83. Ibid, p. 10.
84. Fabian, E. (1989) pp. 39–49.
85. See Bryson, G., Lysaker, P. & Bell, M. (2002) pp. 249–258; Hachey, R., Boyer, G. & Mercier, C. (2001) pp. 112–121; and Van Dongen, C. (1996) pp. 535–549.
86. Van Dongen, C. (1996) p. 535.
87. Anthony, W. (1994) pp. 3–13.
88. Bryson, G., Lysaker, P. & Bell, M. (2002) p. 250.
89. Anthony, W. (1994) pp. 3–13.
90. Van Dongen, C. (1996) pp. 535–549.
91. See Mulaik, J. (1992) pp. 219–227; and Diamond, R. (1985) pp. 29–35.
92. Van Dongen, C. (1996) p. 40.
93. Hachey, R., Boyer, G. & Mercier, C. (2001) p. 112.

Chapter 4

1. See http://www.aasw for a copy of the Social Work Code of Ethics.
2. See http://www.health.gov.au/hsdd/mentalhe for details of the Commonwealth Standards of Practice in Mental Health.
3. See *Mental Health Act 2007* (NSW) Mental Health and Related Services Act (NT) *Mental Health Act 2000* (Qld) *Mental Health (Treatment and Care Act) 1994* (ACT) *Mental Health Act 2009* (SA) *Mental Health Act 1996* (Tas) *Mental Health Act 1986*, including amendments as at 24 August 2010 (Vic) *Mental Health Act 1996* (WA). Refer to http://www.austlii.edu.au for copies of these mental health Acts as well as copies of all other relevant legislation and decisions by the Mental Health Review Boards.
4. Lawrence, F. (2011).
5. See details of the *Children, Youth and Families Act (2005)* including amendments as at January 2011, at http://www.austlii.edu.au
6. Ibid.
7. See the United Nations Principles for the Care and Protection of Persons with Mental health issues at: www.un.org/esa/socdev/enable/disdevelopmental.htm
8. United Nations (1991) Principle 9.1.
9. See Healey, B. and Brophy, L. (2002); and Ring, D., Brophy, L. & Gimlinger, A. (2001).
10. Until the mid-1970s in Australia a person could be detained as an involuntary patient if he or she 'appeared to be mentally ill'. Involuntary admission did not also require danger to self or others.
11. See Department of Health and Community Services (1994).
12. See Wilson v Mental Health Review Board &

Ors (2000) VSC404 (6 October 2000) at http://www.austlii.edu.au/cgi–bin/disp.pl/au/ cases/vic/VSC/2000/404

13. See Gibbs, A.

14. See McIvor, R. (1998).

15. This ward was named after John Cade, who discovered lithium.

16. Reidpath, D., Chan, K., Gifford, S. & Allotey, P. (2005).

17. World Health Organisation (2009) para. 1.

18. Victorian Department of Human Services (2009); Hassed, C., Sierpina, V. & Kreitzer, M. (2008); and World Health Organisation (2009) para. 1.

19. Ziguras, S., Henley, K., Conron, K. & Catford, N. (1999).

20. Human Rights and Equal Opportunity Commission (1993).

21. National Survey of Mental Health and Well-Being (1997).

22. Pilgrim, D. (2005).

23. Department of Health & Ageing (DOHA). (2011c).

24. Mental Health Council of Australia & the Brain and Mind Research Institute (2005).

25. Australian Psychological Society (APS). (2007).

26. Australian Association of Social Workers (AASW) (2007).

27. Bland, R., Renouf, N. & Tullgren (2009).

28. Coalition of Australian Governments (2006).

29. Shankar, J., Martin, J. & McDonald, C. (2009). See Chapter 11.

30. Australian Association of Social Workers (AASW) (2010b); Australian Association of Social Workers (AASW) (2008).

31. Australian Association of Social Workers (AASW) (1999); Australian Association of Social Workers (AASW) (2008).

32. Bland, R., Renouf, N. & Tullgren (2009).

33. Australian Association of Social Workers (AASW) (2008).

34. Australian Association of Social Workers (AASW) (2011).

35. Ibid., p. 9.

36. AASW (2010).

37. See Australian Health Ministers (1992); and Australian Health Ministers (1991).

38. Commonwealth Department of Health and Family Services (1997).

39. Commonwealth Department of Health and Family Services (1997).

40. United Nations (1991).

41. See Chapter 12 for further discussion of information sharing with carers.

42. Victorian Department of Health and Community Services (1994) p. 26.

43. Swain, P. (ed.) (2009).

44. Australian Association of Social Workers (AASW) (2010).

45. Recommendation from National Suicide Taskforce, AGPS, Canberra.

46. Victorian Department of Human Services (1997) p. 15; and Victorian Government Department of Health and Community Services (1996) p. 29.

47. Victorian Department of Human Services (1997).

48. See Yarran v The Queen (2003) WASCA 261 (5 November 2003) at http://www.austlii.edu.au/cgi–bin/disp.pl/au/cases/wa/WASCA/2003/261

49. See Chapter 3 for discussion of the impact on daily living of not being believed.

50. See the United Nations Declaration of Human Rights at:www.un.org/en/documents/udhr/

51. Mental Health Legal Centre Inc (Vic) at http://www.vicnet.net.au/–mhlc

52. See Swain, P. (2000) pp. 79–99.

53. Victorian Government Department of Human Services (1997) p. 17; and Victorian Government Department of Human Services (1996) p. 50.

Chapter 5

1. Payne (1997).

2. Barry, P. (2002) p. 86.

3. Ibid., p. 87.

4. Ibid., p. 272.

5. Erikson, E.H. (1980); and Barry, P. (2002) pp. 99–103.

6. Ibid., p. 101.

7. Maslow, A. (1998).

8. Haley, J. (1971).

9. See Minuchin, S. (1974).

10. Scheff, T.J. (1968) pp. 3–7; Foucault, M. (1965); and Goffman, E. (1961.

11. Ife, J. (1996); Mullaly, B. (1997); Dalrymple, J. & Burke, B. (1995); and Fook, J. (1993).

12. Corrigan P. & Leonard, P. (1978); Throssell, H. (1975; and Pemberton, A. & Locke, R. (1975) pp. 27–46.

13. Bailey, R. & Brake, M. (eds) (1975); and Galper, J. (1975).

14. Galper, J. (1975) p. 23.

15. Moreau, M.J. (1979) p. 83.

16. Wearing, B. (1986) pp. 33–53.

17. Dominelli, L. & McLeod, E. (1989) p. 156.

18. Cox, M. (1994).

19. Bainbridge, L. (1999).

20. Gerrand, V. (1993) p. 23.

21. Victorian Government Department of Human Services (1997) p. 3.

22. Ibid., p.4.
23. Teplin, L., Abram, K. & McClelland, G. (1997) p. 604; and Gerrand, V. (1993) p. 24.
24. The mental health of women prisoners is discussed in more detail in Chapter 13.
25. Gerrand, V. (1993) p. 32.
26. Ibid, p. 3.
27. Saxon, R. & Emslie, A. (1998) pp. 27–31.
28. Gerrand, V. (1993) p. 33.
29. Ibid., p. 22.
30. Saxon, R. & Emslie, A. (1998) p. 46.
31. Alder, C. (1997) p. 55.
32. Gerrand, V. (1993) p. 33.
33. Fitzroy Legal Service (1988) p. 10.
34. Raeside, C. (1995); and Easteal, P. (1992).
35. Raeside, C. (1995) p. 65.
36. Gerrand, V. (1993) pp. 3 and 24.
37. Orme, J. (1998) p. 218.
38. Thompson, N. (1998). Also see the discussion of stigma in Chapter 3.
39. New Zealand Mental Health Commission (2001) p. 1; and Thompson, N. (1998) p. 221.
40. Dalrymple, J. & Burke, B. (1995).
41. Ibid, p. 165; and Dominelli, L. (1998) p. 19.
42. Foucault, M. (1972).
43. Lyotard, J.F. (1989).
44. Jameson, J. (1984) pp. 53–92.
45. Leonard, P. (1993).
46. See Frame, J. (1997; Jeffs, S. (1993); Deveson, A. (1991); and Pridmore, S. (1984).

Chapter 6

1. See Appendix for a mental health assessment interview schedule.
2. Maidment, J. & Egan, R. (2004).
3. See Zastrow C. (1999); and Geldard, D. & Geldard, K. (2005).
4. See Moreau, M.J. (1979) pp. 78–94; and Moreau, M.J. (1977).
5. Brammer, L. (2003).
6. It is important that workers follow protocols for the sharing of file information as well as being aware of freedom of information legislation governing access to personal files. If files are being shared it is generally useful to look at the files together so that the information can be translated if necessary and the person can share their responses to reading such personal and often distressing information.
7. Bainbridge, L. (1999).
8. Coppock, V. & Hopton, J.
9. See Chapter 12.
10. See Comptom, B. & Gallaway, B. (1999) for details on how to draw a genogram and also the genogram presented in Chapter 8.

11. See Lindsay, R. (2002); and Rice, S. (2002) pp. 303–312.
12. Schwartz, M. (1994) p. 5.
13. See Barry, P. (2002) pp.185–196 for a copy of the nursing mental status examination guide. This includes the terminology used by medical staff when conducting a mental status examination. It is useful for social workers to know this language so that they are able to communicate effectively with workers from other disciplines.
14. Barry, P. (2002) pp. 190–191.
15. Watkins, J. (1998).
16. Schwartz, M. (1994) p. 7.
17. Ibid., p. 7.
18. Ibid., p. 8.
19. Barry, P. (2002) p. 190.
20. Turner, F.J (2002).
21. Hughes, M. & Heycox (2010).
22. Phillips, J., Ray, M & Marshall, M. (2006).
23. The Mini Mental Status Examination, http://www.depression-guide.com/mini-mental-stateexamination. htm
24. Department of Health and Ageing (2011) adapted from http://www.gpcare.org/ outcome per cent20measures/SF–12 per cent20(Short per cent20 Form).html
25. Ibid., adapted from http://www.gpcare.org/ outcome per cent20measures/1K10 per cent20Test.html
26. Ibid., adapted from: http://www.gpcare.org/ outcome per cent20measures/HoNOS per cent20Score per cent20 Sheet.html
27. Rosen, A.

Chapter 7

1. World Health Organisation, *The ICD–10 Classification of Mental and Behavioral Disorders: Clinical Descriptions and Diagnostic Guidelines.*
2. American Psychiatric Association (1994).
3. Main interventions are listed for each diagnosis and these are discussed in Chapter 10 and Chapter 11.
4. Turner, F.J. (2002) p. 21.
5. Zastrow C. (1999) p. 59.
6. Turner, F.J. (2002) p. 30.
7. Ibid, .p. 33.
8. NZ Mental Health Commission (2002) p. 18
9. Pemberton, L. (2004).
10. Mental Health First Aid Australia (2012).
11. Watkins, J. (1998) p. 63.
12. Mental Health First Aid Australia (2007).
13. National Mental Health Strategy (2000) p. 1.
14. Torrey, E F. (1987) pp. 598–608.

15. Saha, S., Chant, D. Welham, J. & McGrath, J. (2005).
16. Schizophrenia Fellowship of New South Wales, 2016. Schizophrenia Statistics. http://www.sfnsw.org.au/Mental-Illness/Schizophrenia/Schizophrenia-Statistics.
17. National Mental Health Strategy (2000) p. 1.
18. Hambrecht, M. (1999) p. 115.
19. National Mental Health Strategy (2000) p. 1.
20. Hall, W. & Degenhardt, L. (1999) p. 99; and Gottesman, I. (1991).
21. Zubin & Spring (1977) pp. 103–126.
22. Nuechterlein K. (1987).
23. Bromet, E., Dew, A. & Eaton, W. (1995); and Gottesman, I. (1991).
24. Hambrecht, M. (1999) p. 113.
25. Bromet, E., Dew, A. & Eaton, W. (1995).
26. National Mental Health Strategy (2000) p. 4.
27. Barry, P. (2002) p. 264.
28. Real, T. (1997) p. 34.
29. Ibid., p. 34.
30. Ibid., p. 33.
31. Barry, P. (2002) p. 241.
32. Ibid., p. 23.
33. Watkins, J. (1998) p. 67; and Schatzberg, A. & Rothschild, A. (1992) pp. 149–56.
34. Watkins, J. (1998) p. 71.
35. National Mental Health Strategy (2000) p. 2.
36. Ibid., p. 3.
37. Department of Health and Ageing (2010a:1).
38. Real, T. (1997) p. 81.
39. Morton, J. & Buckingham, B. (1994).
40. Ibid.
41. American Psychiatric Association (1994).
42. Kulkarni, J., Kopolov, D. & Keks, N. (1991).
43. Hall, R., Popkin, M. & Faillace, L. (1978).
44. Barry, P. (2002) p. 241.

Chapter 9

1. Human Rights and Equal Opportunity Commission (1995).
2. Ibid.
3. Victorian Government Department of Human Services (1996) p. 4.
4. Victorian Government Department of Health and Community Services(1996) pp. 27–8.
5. Martin, J. (1999) p. 53.
6. O'Hagan, M. (2004).
7. Epstein, M. & Wadsworth, Y. (1996) p. 213.
8. The crisis of suicide is discussed in Chapter 11.
9. Conflict Resolution Network.
10. Victorian Mental health issues Awareness Council (1996) p. 2.
11. Scheff, T.J. (1968) pp. 3–7.
12. UNIMAS (2005).

13. McGuiness, M. & Wadsworth, Y. (1992) p. 76.
14. Carers Victoria (2011).
15. This figure includes all carers not just those caring for someone with a mental health issue in Gilmore, L. (2003) p. 3.
16. Ibid., p. 3.
17. Milburn, C. (2000).
18. Carers of the Mentally Ill (1996).
19. For a gender analysis of community care, see Fawcett, B. (1996).
20. Carers of the Mentally Ill (1996).
21. Refer to http://www.austlii.edu.au for copies of Mental Health Acts as well as copies of all other relevant legislation and decisions by the Mental Health Review Boards.
22. Carers of the Mentally Ill (1996).
23. Carers Victoria, *Annual Report 2002–2003*, p. 10.
24. Ibid.
25. Fawcett, B. (1996).
26. Australian Bureau of Statistics (2003) p. 4.
27. In Australia in 2001, it was estimated that lost earnings from people unable to work due to schizophrenia were $488 million with an additional $88 million in carer costs. Direct health system costs were $661 million. This represents six times the health care costs of the average Australian: Access Economics (2002).
28. Epstein, M. & Wadsworth, Y. (1996) p. 200.
335

Chapter 10

1. Martin, J. (2010b).
2. Denzin, N.K. (1983) pp. 129–146; Rock, P. (1979).
3. Boyd, M.A. (2001) p. 12.
4. Glicken, M. (2004) p. 176.
5. Seligman's work is referred to in Glicken, M. (2004) p. 174.
6. Maslow's hierarchy of needs is discussed in Chapter 5.
7. Gerrand, V. (1993) p. 39.
8. See Chapter 11.
9. Boyd, M.A. (2001) p. 8.
10. Real, T. (1997) p. 310.
11. Ibid., p. 323.
12. Access Economics (2002).
13. Martin, J. (1999) p. 59.
14. Ibid., p. 429.
15. Ibid., p. 75.
16. Barry, P. (2002) p. 420.
17. Victorian Department of Human Services (1997) p. 10.
18. Cid, quoted in Cusworth, F. (2003) p. 19.
19. Victorian Department of Health and Community Services (1994) p. 36.

20. Victorian Department of Human Services (1996) pp. 53–4.
21. Gerrand, V. (1993) p. 69.
22. Pietsch, J. & Cuff, R. (1995).
23. Gerrand, V. (1993) p. 69.
24. Victorian Department of Human Services (1997) p. 5.
25. Ibid, p. 5.
26. Elliot, B. (2000) p. 102.
27. Ibid., p. 16.
28. Ibid., p. 43.
29. Ibid., p. 44.
30. Payne, M. (1997).
31. Pease, B. (2004) pp. 33–34.
32. McLellan, B. (2004) p. 48
33. Herman, J., cited in Fergus, L. & Keel, M. (2005) p. 3.
34. McLellan, B. (2004) p. 52.
35. Fergus, L. & Keel, M. (2005) p. 3.
36. Mammen, G. (2006) p. 12.
37. Southwell, J. (2004).
38. Salthouse, S. & Frohmader, C. (2004) pp. 12–13.
39. Fergus, L. & Keel, M. (2005) p. 3.
40. Rummery, F. (1996) p.3.
41. Herman, H. 1992, cited in ibid, p. 9.
42. Henderson, C. & Bateman, J. (2006); Bateman, J. & Henderson, C. (2010).
43. Mental Health Coordinating Council and Adults Surviving Child Abuse (2013)
44. Payne (1997) p. 157.
45. McDermott, F. (2003) p. 353.
46. Wirth, H. & Harari, R. (2000) pp. 42–51.
47. SANE Australia (2005).
48. See the discussion of groups in Chapter 3.
49. Department of Human Services (July 1996) pp. 49–50; Department of Health and Community Services (1994) p. 37.
50. See Chapter 11 for discussion of the White Wreath Association led by the mother of a young man who suicided, and Chapter 13 for discussion of the consumer run organisation Sisters Inside.
51. Mullaly, R. (1993).
52. Dalrymple, J. & Burke, B. (1995).
53. Fook, J. (1999) p. 131.
54. See New Zealand Mental Health Commission (1998).
55. Geldard, D. & Geldard, K. (2005) p. 210.

Chapter 11

1. See Chapter 1 for details of the Medicare Better Access Program as well as other funded programs including ATAPS.
2. General Practice Mental Health Standards Collaboration, Focused Psychological Strategies 2010, at http://www.racgp.org.au
3. Department of Health and Ageing (2009).
4. Ibid.
5. Ibid.
6. Martin, J. (2010b).
7. See Definitions and implementation plans for FPS for GPs, at www.gpcare.org
8. Ethnic Heath Initiative (2011).
9. Craighead, W.E., Miklowitz, D.J., Vajk, D.J., & Frank, E. (1998; and Lampe, L. (1996) pp. 1561–1567.
10. Definitions and implementation plans for FPS for GPs: Psycho–education, at www.gpcare.org
11. Miller, W., Benefield, R., & Tonigan, S. (1993) pp. 4550–61.
12. See Prochaska and DiClemente's Stages of Change Model for Social Workers, at http://socialworkpodcast.blogspot.com/2009/10/prochaska-and-diclementes-stages-of.html
13. Emmons, K. M. & Rollnick, S. (2001) pp. 68–74.
14. Miller, W. R. & Rollnick, S. (1991).
15. Ibid., p. 99.
16. Nathan, P. E. & Gorman, J.M. (eds) (1998).
17. Andrews, G. (1993) pp. 447–51.
18. Fava, G.A., Bartolucci, G., Rafanelli, C. & Mangelli, L. (2001) pp. 556–9; and Ladouceur, R., Dugas, M. J., Freeston, M. H., Leger, E., Gagnon, E., & Thibodeau, N. (2000) pp. 957–964.
19. See Chapter 6 for a discussion of systems theory.
20. See Watkins, J. (1998) especially. pp. 207–212.
21. Munby, J. & Johnston, D.W. (1980) pp. 418–27; and Abramowitz, J.S. (1997) pp. 44–52.
22. Taylor, S. (1996) pp. 1–9.
23. Ladouceur, R., Dugas, M.J., Freeston, M.H., Leger, E., Gagnon, E., & Thibodeau, N. (2000) pp. 957–964.
24. Lewinsohn, P.M. & Gotlib, I.H. (1995) pp. 352–375.
25. Beck, A.T. (1976).
26. Hollon, S.D., Shelton, R.C., & Loosen, P.T. (1991) pp. 88–99; and Power, K.G., Simpson, R.J., Swanson, V., Wallace, L.A., Feistner, A.T.C., & Sharp, D. (1990) pp. 267–292.
27. Teasdale, J.D., Scott, J., Moore, R.G., Hayhurst, H., Pope, M. & Paykel, E.S. (2001) pp. 347–357.
28. Ellis, A., & Harper, R.A. (1975).
29. Definitions and implementation plans for FPS for GPs: Cognitive therapy, at www.gpcare. org
30. Adapted from Definitions and implementation

plans for FPS for GPs: Cognitive therapy, at www.gpcare.org

31. Reproduced from Definitions and implementation plans for FPS for GPs: Cognitive therapy, at www.gpcare.org

32. Adapted from Opolski, M., Marshall, C. & Howell, C. (2008) p. 706.

33. Wilson I, Duszynski K. & Mant A. (2003) pp. 685–9.

34. Andrews G. (2001) pp. 419–21.

35. Opolski, M., Marshall, C. & Howell, C. (2008) pp. 704–708.

36. Adapted from Opolski, M., Marshall, C. & Howell, C. (2008) p. 705.

37. Royal Australian and New Zealand College of Psychiatrists (2004) pp. 389–407.

38. Tang, T., DeRubeis R., Hollon S. & Shelton R. (2007) pp. 404–8.

39. Segal, Z., Williams J. & Teasdale J. (2003).

40. Adapted from Opolski, M., Marshall, C. & Howell, C. (2008) p. 707.

41. Barlow, D.H., Lawton Esler, J. & Vitali, A.E. (1998).

42. Martin, J. (2010).

43. See Chapter 4 for a discussion of the effects of meditation.

44. Centre for Clinical Interventions (2016)

45. Craighead, W. E., Miklowitz, D. J., Vajk, D. J., & Frank, E. (1998); Andrews, G., Crino, R., Hunt, C., Lampe, L. & Page, A. (1994); and Sahler, O.J., Varni, J.W., Fairclough, D.L., Butler, R.W., Noll, R.B., Dolgin, M.J., Phipps, S., Copeland, D.R., Katz, Ernest R. & Mulhern, R.K. (2002) pp. 77–86.

46. Beck, R. & Fernandez, E. (1998) pp. 63–4.

47. Novaco, R.W. (1979).

48. Ibid., p. 269.

49. See Barkley, R.A., Edwards, G., Laneri, M., Flatcher, K., & Metevia, L. (2001) pp. 926–941; Done, D.J. & Thomas, J.A. (2001) pp. 816–821; Monti, P.M. & O'Leary, T.A. (1999) pp. 447–470; and World Health Organisation (2000).

50. The Management of Mental Disorders, at www.gpcare.org.

51. Craighead, W.E., Miklowitz, D.J., Vajk, D.J., & Frank, E. (1998); Kopelowicz, A. & Liberman, R.P. (1998); Taylor, S. (1996) pp. 1–9; and Webster-Stratton, C., Reid J., & Hammond, M. (2001) pp. 943–52.

52. Bolton, R. (1998).

53. Martin, J. (2007).

54. Alberti, R. & Emmons, M. (1998); and Conflict Resolution Network (1993).

55. Definitions and implementation plans for FPS for GPs: Cognitive therapy, at www.gpcare.org

56. Ibid.

57. Definitions and implementation plans for FPS for GPs: Parenting skills training, at www.gpcare.org

58. Ibid.

59. Ibid.

60. Martin, J. (2007).

61. Weissman, M.M., Prusoff, B.A., DiMascio, A., Neu, C., Goklaney, M. & Klerman, G.L. (1979) pp. 555–558; and Elkin, I., Shea, M.T., Watkins, J.T., Imber, S.D., Sotsky, S.M., Collins, J.F, Glass, D.R., Pilkonis, P.A., Leber, W.R., Docherty, J.P., Fiester, S.J., & Parloff, M.B. (1989) pp. 971–982.

62. Klerman, G.L., Weissman, M.M., Rounsaville, B.J., & Chevron, E.S. (1984).

63. Gillies, L.A. (2001) pp. 309–331.

64. Alasuutati, P. (1995); and Denzin, N.K. (1997).

65. Elliot, B. (2000) p. 21.

66. Neisser, U. (1982).

67. Ibid., p. 22

Chapter 12

1. Australian Institute for Suicide Research and Prevention (2012); and Mindframe (2011).

2. Australian Bureau of Statistics (2011).

3. Mindframe (2016).

4. Harrison, J., Elnour, A. & Pointer, S. (2009).

5. Australian Bureau of Statistics (2002a) p. 1.

6. Ibid, p. 1.

7. Mindframe (2011) p. 1.

8. Australian Bureau of Statistics (2011).

9. Australian Bureau of Statistics (2016).

10. Australian Institute for Suicide Research and Prevention, Home Page, Griffith University, Queensland.

11. Mindframe (2011).

12. Skelton, R. (2012) p. 1.

13. Mindframe (2011).

14. Steenkamp, M. and Harrison, J. (2000).

15. Mindframe (2011).

16. National Drug and Alcohol Research Centre (1977) p. 3.

17. Mims (2003) pp. 1–2.

18. Mindframe (2011).

19. Australian Bureau of Statistics (2016).

20. Creative Spirits (2016)

21. Ibid.

22. Porter, L. (2003) p. 1.

23. Mindframe (2011).

24. Australian Institute for Suicide Research and Prevention (2012).

25. Mindframe (2011).

26. Mims (2003) p. 1.

27. Access Economics (2002).
28. Ibid, p. 2.
29. Ibid, p. 2.
30. SANE Australia (2005).
31. Appleby, M., King, R. and Johnson, B. (1996) pp. 6–7.
32. Ibid, p. 6.
33. Van der Kolk, J., Perry, C. and Herman, J. (1991).
34. Leibling, H., Chipcase, H. and Velangi, R. (1995).
35. Ibid; and Burstow, B. (1992).
36. Harris, E.C. and Barraclough, B. (1977).
37. Skelton, R. (2012) p. 4.
38. Access Economics (2002).
39. Harris, E.C. and Barraclough, B. (1977).
40. Ibid.
41. Appleby, M. King, R. and Johnson, B.(1996) p. 22.
42. Langan, J. (2001) p. 155.
43. Martin, J. (1990).
44. Ibid.
45. Campbell, P. and Lindow, V. (1997).
46. Gunnell, D.J. and Frankel, S. (1994) .
47. Appleby, M., King, R. and Johnson, B. (1996) p. 8.
48. Langan, J. (2001) p. 155.
49. Ibid, p. 173.
50. Ibid, p. 156.
51. Estroff S.E. and Zimmer C. (1994).
52. Langan, J. (2001) p. 161.
53. Hiday, V.A. (1995).
54. Appleby, M., King, R. and Johnson, B. (1996) p. 24.
55. SANE Australia (2005).
56. Martin, J., McKay, E. and Thomas, T. (2005).
57. Australian Bureau of Statistics (2002b) p. 4.
58. Ibid, p. 7.
59. Ibid, p. 5.
60. Appleby, M., King, R. and Johnson, B.(1996) p. 24.
61. Ibid, p. 30.
62. Barry, P. (2002) p. 279.
63. Appleby, M., King, R. and Johnson, B. (1996) p. 20.
64. Ibid, p. 12.
65. Health Services Division (2000) p. 8.
66. Appleby, M. King, R. and Johnson, B. (1996) p. 17.
67. National Network of Adult and Adolescent Children who have a Mentally Ill Parent/s (2000).
68. Milburn, C. (2000).
69. Access Economics (2002).
70. King, R., Appleby, M. and Brown, C. (1995) pp. 1–4.
71. See Victorian Taskforce Report (1997); and Department of Human Services (1996).
72. Australian Bureau of Statistics (2003) p. 1.
73. Ibid.
74. Ibid, p. 1.
75. Mindframe (2011) p. 1.

Chapter 13

1. Australian Government Department of Health and Ageing (2005) p. 1.
2. United States Department of Health and Human Services (2005).
3. Graham, H. & Maslin, J. (1999) p. 61.
4. Hall, W. & Degenhardt, L. (1999); and Hambrecht, M. & Hafner, H. (1996) pp. 1–9.
5. Mueser, K. (1999); and Mueser, K., Bellack, A. & Blachard, J. (1992) pp. 845–856.
6. Department of Human Services (1997) p. 1; and Alcohol and Other Drugs Council of Australia (2005).
7. Mueser, K. (1999) p. 155.
8. Alcohol and Other Drugs Council of Australia (2005) p. 1.
9. Alcohol and Other Drugs Council of Australia (2005).
10. National Clearinghouse for Alcohol and Drug Information (2005).
11. United States Department of Health and Human Services (2005) p. 1.
12. National Clearinghouse for Alcohol and Drug Information (2005) p. 1.
13. American Psychiatric Association (1994).
14. Ibid.
15. Real. T. (1997) p. 62.
16. National Clearinghouse for Alcohol and Drug Information (2005).
17. Substance Abuse and Mental Health Services Association (2003) p. 2.
18. Real. T. (1997) p. 61.
19. Hall, W. & Degenhardt, L. (1999) p. 102; Hambrecht, M. (1999, p. 111; Mueser, K. (1999); and Mueser, K., Bellack, A. & Blachard, J. (1992) pp 845–856.
20. Mueser, K. (1999) p. 158.
21. Kavanagh, D. (1999) p. 126.
22. Graham, H. & Maslin, J. (1999) p. 61; and Hambrecht, M. (1999).
23. Addington, J. (1999) p. 8; Curry, C., Phillips, L., Yuen, H.P., Adlard, S. & McGorry, P. (1999) p. 43; and Dixon, L., Haas, G., Weiden, P.J., Sweeney, J. & Frances, A.J. (1991) pp. 224–230.
24. Hall, W. & Degenhardt, L. (1999) p. 102; and Hambrecht, M. (1999).
25. Hambrecht, M. (1999) p. 111; and Mueser, K. (1999).

26. Hall, W. & Degenhardt, L. (1999). 27. Alcohol and Other Drugs Council of Australia (2003).

28. For research in the UK see Graham, H. & Maslin, J. (1999). For research in the USA see Lehman, A., Myers, C., Corty, E. & Thompson, J. (1994) pp. 106–112; and Reiger, D., Farmer, M., Rae, D., Locke, B, Keith, S., Judd, L. & Goodwin, F. (1990) pp. 2511–18. For research in Australia see Hall, W., Teeson, M., Lynskey, M. & Degenhardt, L. (1998). For research in Germany see Hambrecht, M. (1999); Krausz, M., Haasen, C., Mass, R., Wagner, H., Peter, H. & Freyberger, H. (1996) pp. 11–16; and Soyka, M., Kathman, N., Finelli, A., Hofstetter, S., Imler, B. & Sand, P. 1993) pp. 362–372.

29. Australian Bureau of Statistics (2003) p. 1.

30. Reuter, P. & MacCoun (1999) p. 186; and Shedler, J. and Block (1990) pp. 612–630.

31. Reuter, P. and MacCoun (1999) p. 191.

32. Hambrecht, M. & Hafner, H. (1996) pp. 1–9.

33. Addington, J. (1999) p. 9; Brewer, W., van Ammers, E., Francey, S., Velakoulis, D., Yung, A., McGorry, P., Copolov, D., Singh, B. & Pantelis, C. (1999). p. 18; and Copolov, D., Bradbury, R., Dong, P., Dean, B. & Lim, A., p. 35.

34. Brewer, W., van Ammers, E., Francey, S., Velakoulis, D., Yung, A., McGorry, P., Copolov, D., Singh, B. & Pantelis, C. (1999) p. 18.

35. Ibid.

36. Addington, J. (1999) p. 10; and Loebel, A. D., Lieberman, J.A. & Alvir, J.M. (1992) pp. 1183–88.

37. Mackie, K. & Sorom, A. (1999) p. 138.

38. Ibid.

39. Ibid.

40. Ibid., p. 147.

41. Curry, C., Phillips, L., Yuen, H. P., Adlard, S. & McGorry, P. (1999) p. 42; and Department of Human Services (1997) p. 1.

42. Adams, I. & Martin, B. (1996) pp. 1585–1614.

43. Stahl, S. (1996).

44. Brewer, W., van Ammers, E., Francey, S., Velakoulis, D., Yung, A., McGorry, P., Copolov, D., Singh, B. & Pantelis, C. (1999) p. 24.

45. Curry, C., Phillips, L., Yuen, H. P., Adlard, S. & McGorry, P. (1999) p. 43.

46. Donnelly, N. & Hall, W. (1994).

47. Hambrecht, M. (1999) p. 113.

48. Hall, W. & Degenhardt, L. (1999); and Curry, C., Phillips, L., Yuen, H. P., Adlard, S. & McGorry, P. (1999).

49. Brewer, W., van Ammers, E., Francey, S., Velakoulis, D., Yung, A., McGorry, P., Copolov, D., Singh, B. & Pantelis, C. (1999); and Rolfe, T., McGorry, P., Cocks, J., Yuen, H., Longley, T. & Plowright, D. (1999).

50. Todd, F., Joyce, P. & Mulder, R. (1999); and refer to discussion of depression in Chapter 5.

51. Graham, H. & Maslin, J. (1999) p. 62; Hall, W. & Degenhardt, L. (1999) p. 102; and Dixon, L., Haas, G., Weiden, P.J., Sweeney, J. & Frances, A.J. (1991) pp 224–230.

52. Todd, F., Joyce, P. & Mulder, R. (1999).

53. Graham, H. & Maslin, J. (1999) p. 65.

54. Hall, W. & Degenhardt, L. (1999) p. 88; Hambrecht, M. (1999); and Linszen, D., Dingemans, P. & Lenior, M. (1994) pp. 273–279.

55. Hambrecht, M. (1999) p. 116.

56. Hall, W. & Degenhardt, L. (1999) p. 98.

57. Ibid., p. 88.

58. Real. T. (1997) p.79.

59. Department of Human Services (1997) p. 3.

60. Tien, A. & Anthony, J. (1990) pp. 473–480.

61. Mueser, K. (1999) p. 159.

62. National Clearinghouse for Alcohol and Drug Information (2005) p. 1.

63. Reuter, P. & MacCoun (1999) p. 196.

64. Real. T. (1997).

65. Ibid.

66. Ibid., p. 79.

67. Ibid., p. 67.

68. Ibid., p. 79.

69. Mueser, K. (1999) p. 154.

70. Graham, H & Maslin, J. (1999) p. 64.

71. Kavanagh, D. (1999) p. 125.

72. Ibid.

73. Real. T. (1997) p.75.

74. Ibid., p. 81.

75. Langan, J. (2001) p. 161; and Greyner, B., Solowij, N. & Barlow, K. (1999). 340

76. National Clearinghouse for Alcohol and Drug Information (2005) p. 2.

77. Ibid.

78. Ibid., p. 4.

79. Mueser, K. (1999) p. 58; and Drake, R., Mercer-McFadden, C., Mueser, K., McHugo, G., & Bond, G. (1998) pp. 443–455.

80. Alcohol and Other Drugs Council of Australia (2005).

81. Curry, C., Phillips, L., Yuen, H. P., Adlard, S. & McGorry, P. (1999) p. 51.

82. Kavanagh, D. (1999) p. 127.

83. Mueser, K. (1999) p. 159.

84. See the discussion of behaviour modification in Chapter 9

85. Mueser, K. (1999) p. 160.
86. Ibid., p. 160.
87. Addington, J. (1999); McGorry, P., Edwards, J. & Mihalopoulos, C. (1996) pp. 305–326; and Falloon, I. (1992) pp. 4–15; Loebel, A.D., Lieberman, J.A. & Alvir, J.M.(1992) pp. 1183–88.

Chapter 14

1. Sisters Inside (2003) p. 21.
2. Armstrong, K., Chatrand, V. & Baldry, E. (2005) p. 17.
3. Ibid., pp. 15–16.
4. Ibid., p. 16.
5. This finding is supported in a number of studies including Teplin, L., Abram, K. & McClelland, G. (1996) pp. 505–19; and Raeside, C. (1995); Maden, T., Swinton, M. & Gunn, J. (1994) pp. 44–54; and Easteal, P. (1992).
6. Raeside, C. (1995); and Easteal, P. (1992).
7. Rutherford, A. (1997) p. 424.
8. Armstrong, K., Chatrand, V. & Baldry, E. (2005) p. 22.
9. Martin, J. (1999).
10. Sisters Inside (2004) p. 23.
11. Jordan, K., Schlenger, W., Fairbank, J. & Caddell, J. (1996) pp. 513–19; Teplin, L., Abram, K. & McClelland, G. (1996) pp. 505–19; and Raeside, C. (1995).
12. Maden, T., Swinton, M. & Gunn, J. (1994) pp. 44–54.
13. The NSW Department of Corrective Services cited in Armstrong, K., Chatrand, V. & Baldry, E. (2005) p. 17.
14. Armstrong, K., Chatrand, V. & Baldry, E. (2005) p. 15.
15. Gerrand, V. (1993).
16. Birecree, E., Bloom, J., Leverette, M. & Williams, M. (1994) pp. 217–230.
17. Teplin, L., Abram, K. and McClelland, G. (1996) pp. 505–19; Raeside, C. (1995), Birecree, E., Bloom, J., Leverette, M. & Williams, M. (1994) pp. 217–230; Herrman, H., Mills, J., Doidge, G., McGorry, P. & Singh, B. (1994) pp. 63–8; and Denton, B. (1993) pp. 173–77.
18. Denton, B. (1993) pp. 173–77.
19. Martin, J. (1999).
20. Morton J. & Buckingham, B. (1994); and Raeside, C. (1995).
21. Saxon, R. & Emslie, A. (1998) p. 31.
22. Jordan, K., Schlenger, W., Fairbank, J. & Caddell, J. (1996) pp. 513–19; Raeside, C. (1995); and Easteal, P. (1992).
23. Raeside, C. (1995); Easteal, P. (1992); and Fitzroy Legal Service (1988).
24. Denton, B. (1993) pp.173–77; Raeside, C. (1995); and Easteal, P. (1992).
25. Quadrelli, C. (1997) pp. 15–22.
26. Alder, C. (1997) pp. 43–59; and Hampton, B. (1993).
27. Quadrelli, C. (1997) pp. 15–22.
28. Easteal, P. (1992).
29. Sisters Inside (2004) p. 23.
30. Ibid.
31. Rutherford, A. (1997) pp. 424–5.
32. Sisters Inside (2004) p. 10.
33. Ibid.
34. Rutherford, A. (1997) pp. 424–5; and Singer, M., Bussey, J., Song, L. & Lunghofer, L. (1995) pp. 103–113.
35. See the discussion of developmental theory in Chapter 6.
36. Sisters Inside (2004) p. 10.
37. Martin, J. (1999).
38. Sisters Inside (2003) pp. 11–12; Carnaby, H. (1998) p.15.
39. Armstrong, K., Chatrand, V. & Baldry, E. (2005) p. 22.
40. Sisters Inside (2004) p. 21.
41. Easteal, P. (1992); and Wilson, J., & Leasure, R. (1991) pp. 32–38.
42. Armstrong, K., Chatrand, V. & Baldry, E. (2005) pp. 16 and 20.
43. Sisters Inside (2004) p. 14.
44. Armstrong, K., Chatrand, V. & Baldry, E. (2005) p. 20. For a discussion of human rights see Chapter 4; and for a copy of the United Nations Declaration of Human Rights see the United Nations Declaration of Human Rights at:www.un.org/en/documents/udhr/
45. Armstrong, K., Chatrand, V. & Baldry, E. (2005) p. 19.
46. Ibid., p. 18.
47. Sisters Inside (2004) p. 23, and see Sisters Inside (2001).
48. Martin, J. (1999).
49. Sisters Inside (2004) p. 19.
50. Acoca, L. (1998) pp. 49–69.
51. Belknap, J. (1996) p. 34.
52. Connor, H. (1997) pp. 45–53.
53. Sisters Inside (2004) p. 15.
54. Easteal, P. (1992).
55. Willshire, D. & Newnham, L. (1995); and Morton J. & Buckingham, B. (1994).
56. Ibid.
57. Derks, F., Blankstein, J. & Hendrickx, J. (1993) pp. 217–40.
58. Ibid., p. 229.
59. Negy, C., Woods, D. & Carlson, R., p. 224.
60. Martin, J. (1999).

61. Ibid.
62. Carnaby, H. (1998) p. 15.
63. Sisters Inside (2004) pp. 1–5. (1996) pp. 505–19.

Chapter 15

1. Allen-Kelly, K. 2009, p. 32.
2. Tutnjevic, T. 2003.
3. Oxfam 2005.
4. United Nations, 2007.
5. Saunders 2007; Healy and Hillman 2008.
6. Bradshaw 2004.
7. Baker & Tually, 2008.
8. Muir & Fisher et al. 2008; Healey & Hillman 2008.
9. Murthy, R. K. 2008.
10. Haynes, K. and Tibbits, B. 2008.
11. Brandes, I. 2003.
12. Department of Human Services, 2005.
13. World Bank, 2009; United Nations, 2007.
14. Pincha, C. 2008.
15. Delaney, P. & Schrader, E. 2000.
16. United Nations /International Committee for Strategy for Disaster Recovery, 2002.
17. World Bank, 2009.
18. United Nations /International Committee for Strategy for Disaster Recovery, 2002.
19. World Bank, 2009.
20. Rao, A. & Kelleher, 2003; 2005.
21. Delaney, P. & Schrader, E. 2000.
22. Adapted from World Bank 2009.
23. World Bank, 2009.
24. Murthy, R. K., 2008.
25. Oxfam, 2005.
26. United Nations Economic Commission for Latin America and the Caribbean, 2003; Yonder, A., Akcar, S. & Gopolan, P., 2005.
27. World Bank, 2009.
28. Delaney, P. & Schrader, E. 2000; World Bank, 2009; Murthy, R. K., 2008.
29. Emergency Management Australia, 20 I 0, para 11.
30. Karanci, N., Alkan, N., Aksit, B., Sucuoglu, H. & Balta, E. 1999.
31. Jang, L. & LaMendola, W., 2007.
32. Delaney, P. & Schrader, E., 2000.
33. Karanci, N., Alkan, N., Aksit, B., Sucuoglu, H. & Balta, E., 1999.
34. Ariyabandu, M., 2006, p.9.
35. Bradshaw, S., Linneker, B. & Zunniga, R, 2001.
36. Jang, L. & LaMendola, W. 2007, p.305.
37. World Bank, 2009.
38. Ibid
39. Delaney, P. & Schrader, E., 2000.
40. Ibid
41. Jang, L. & LaMendola, W., 2007.
42. Emergency Management Australia, 2010.
43. Ibid.
44. Commonwealth of Australia, 2005, p.22.
45. Haynes, K. & Tibbits, B. 2008.
46. VRBC Day 29, 24.6.09, p. 55.
47. VRBC Day 27, 19.6.09, p. 101.
48. VRBC Day 17 3.06.09, p. 47; VRBC, Day 30 25.6.09, p. 123.
49. VBRC Day 23 15.6.09, 95.
50. VBRC Day 28 23.6.09, 79.
51. VBRC Day 20 10.6.09, 79.
52. VBRC Day 17 3.6.09, 102.
53. VBRC Day 1I 26.5.09, 105.
54. VBRC Day 20 10.6.09, 85.
55. VBRC Day 17 3.6.09, 165.
56. Department of Human Services, 2009, p. l0.
57. Ibid.
58. Department of Human Services, 2010.
59. lbid.
60. Australian Centre for Posttraumatic Mental Health, 2009.
61. VBRC Day 14, 29.5.09, 78.
62. State Government of Victoria, 2010.

Index

www.ingramcontent.com/pod-product-compliance
Lightning Source LLC
Chambersburg PA
CBHW080618030426
42336CB00018B/3007